THE
HADES
MOON

THE
HADES MOON

PLUTO IN ASPECT TO THE MOON

JUDY HALL

SAMUEL WEISER, INC.

York Beach, Maine

First published in 1998 by
Samuel Weiser, Inc.
Box 612
York Beach, ME 03910-0612

Library of Congress Cataloging-in-Publication Data
Hall, Judy
    The Hades moon : Pluto in aspect to the moon / Judy Hall.
        p.   cm.
    Includes bibliographical references and index.
    ISBN 1–57863–039–8 (pbk. : alk. paper)
    1. Astrology.   2. Moon—Miscellanea.   3. Pluto (Planet)—
—Miscellanea.   I. Title.
    BF1723.H35   1998
    133.5'32—dc21   97–51638
                                                            CIP

EB

Typeset in Bembo

Cover art is a collage by Judy Hall
Cover design by Ray Rue

Printed in the United States of America

04   03   02   01   00   99   98
10   9   8   7   6   5   4   3   2   1

For Howard
in the hope that it was
worth more than half a chapter.

CONTENTS

FIGURES

CHARTS

ACKNOWLEDGMENTS

My Scorpionic partner Robert Jacobs has taught me much about the workings of Pluto and the Hades Moon over the years, for which I have learned to be grateful. He was also invaluable in finding just the right book and coming up with exactly the quote or story I needed by way of illustration. My love and thanks to you.

Sally Davis of the British Astrological Association's Data Service was invaluable in providing and checking data, as was David Fisher, her predecessor.

I would like to thank all my clients and friends who offered their stories for this book; and those who gave unstintingly of their time and assistance, in particular Bernie Andrews, who spent many hours at his computer searching data bases, Paul Newman for data, Jane Altounyan for her mythic suggestions, Janet Thompson, Jayn Ingrey, Colin and Elizabeth Stewart, Robert Christoforides for his meticulous scholarship and inspired poetry, Brian John Andrews for teaching me so much, and David Lawson because he told me when it was time to stop!

A special thanks to Maggie Colby for her beautiful calligraphy and wonderful soul.

And finally, to my agent Susan Mears. My love and thanks.

I have watched Pluto working in my clients' lives and have read about it in books, and heard other astrologers talk about it. All of this knowledge has been incorporated into my *knowing*. Where possible, I have attributed sources. I am also aware that there is a "pool of knowledge" into which we all dip in our dreams and intuitions. More than once I have been writing about my insights only to find someone else talking about them at the same time. At other times, the supporting evidence would come to light months or even years later. This material has been footnoted but no distinction has been made between primary and secondary sources. So, if anyone feels that the work is "theirs," I can only say that the collective energy works particularly strongly whenever Pluto is involved, and we can only channel this energy. We do not own it.

The following publisheres have generously given permissions to use quotations from copyrighted works. From *A History of England,* by Keith Feiling, copyright 1950, used by permission of Macmillan Ltd. From *Milestones of History,* Roger Morgan, editor, used by permission of Weidenfeld and Nicolson Publishers. From *The Spear of Destiny,* by Trevor Ravenscroft, copyright 1972; 1982, used by permission of Samuel Weiser, Inc.

INTRODUCTION: THE DARK MOON

The dark moon leads to the underworld, but it also makes transformation possible.
—Demetra George[1]

EVERY THREE DAYS or so, as it wends its way around the zodiac, the cyclical, receptive Moon makes a major contact with the planet Pluto, Lord of the Underworld: known in Greek myth as Hades, "The Invisible One." The celestial bodies make contact for only a few hours each time, but the effect is extremely powerful. This dark chthonic contact between Pluto and the Moon is the Hades Moon. The resulting subterranean convulsions, mirrored in our inner psyche, have been captured in myth and imagination since time began. It is a particularly graphic illustration of the hermetic principle "as above, so below: as within, so without." Our psyches resonate with the movements of the planets, our consciousness vibrates to the archetypal energies of the ancient gods with whom they are linked. Our inner and outer realities are tied to the tides that flow in deepest space, in the collective unconscious, and in the innermost particles of our being. We are the planets.

The Hades Moon story is an eternal saga of birth, death, and rebirth; abandonment and rejection; catharsis and crisis; hubris and nemesis; karma, transformation and new life. It is the eternal saga of suffocating, symbiotic and incestuous matriarchal patterns interwining down the generations to suck life from the blood-kin. This dark Moon underlies eternal mysteries and taboos. It drives the great dramas of life. No other planetary contact has such a depth of trauma, compulsion, and alienation. No other aspect has quite the same metamorphic and healing potential. Understanding Moon-Pluto contacts means opening to the possibility of renewal and regeneration, not just on a personal level—but for the planet and humankind as a whole.

Seven generations, half a century of personal initiation, and twenty years experience as a karmic astrologer lie behind this book. I have a tight square from Pluto to the Moon, intensified by the Scorpio placement of the Moon and accentuated by Pluto on the Ascendant. With a family history of Moon-Pluto aspects going back five generations and forward into the next two, and seemingly endless karma carried over from other lives, I was compelled into the Plutonian underworld of emotional trauma and covert power struggles. I had to connect the instinctual fears of a paranoid Moon with the alienated, deeply enigmatic Pluto energy, and somehow find the power to transform the archaic patterns held within its depths. To encompass the destructive patterns of other lives, with their toxic emotional residue, within the healing potential of this cathartic aspect. Healing in this context does not mean "curing" or "getting rid of," nor "making better." The healing lay in acceptance of this dark side of myself. I needed to recognize loss and endings as part of the cyclical experience of life. I had to plug into the positive, regenerative aspect of Pluto to activate my own creative lunar energies. It was a life or death struggle, and I made the journey to the purifying flames of Pluto's realm many times. But each time I emerged stronger, with new insights. Each time a small piece of my inner self was transmuted, and gradually I began to recognize the purpose behind the aspect. Pluto is, after all, the Bringer into Consciousness as well as Lord of the Dead.

Although I had been working with astrology for some time, my first real insight into the effect of the Hades Moon came almost twenty years ago when I had a consultation with Howard Sasportas. Looking back, and after having had the privilege of knowing Howard well for many years, it still amuses me to remember Howard pussy-footing around for twenty minutes while trying to hone in on this particular part of the chart. Anyone who knew Howard will know that, direct and to the point Aries that he was, he rarely ever skirted issues. But, as he said after the consultation: "For all I knew, here was some little housewife from Essex coming with no knowledge of all this power, and all this karma she had to take hold of." When he finally did point to that Pluto on the Ascendant with its square to the Moon and tentatively said: "This often indicates mothering karma and maybe death around childbirth," and I responded quite casually with: "Oh yes, I know I died in childbirth last time round," his face was comical to behold.

I told him that, at the birth of my daughter in this present life, I had had a near death experience in which I was somewhere on the ceiling watching myself as I struggled in the cold and clinical environment of a teaching hospital to give birth. I was also watching myself in a very different scene: a straw-filled pallet on a cold earth floor with an old crone trying to deliver the baby. Around me were several children. We were desperately poor and I just could not stand it, and opted out. Many years later, just before I met Howard in fact, someone said to me accusingly: "You were my mother but you died and left me." And he went on to relate exactly that same scene. In the near death experience, the guide who was with me said: "You opted out before, you are opting out now. You will have to come back yet again. So, you have a choice, to go or to stay and see it through." I stayed, reluctantly, not really knowing what I was taking on. Within six months my husband was dead and I had to bring up my daughter alone. In our consultation, Howard had touched on the issues of loss, rejection, and abandonment that so often accompany the Hades Moon.

When Howard spoke about the Pluto-Moon connection with the Devouring Mother, and the mothering karma that passed down the generations, a great deal clicked into place. Suddenly my childhood made sense. At the time I was not consciously aware that all my female relatives as far back as I could trace had strong, stressful Pluto-Moon contacts. But I knew it made sense of the family history. For some time after the consultation I consoled myself with the thought: "Well, what do you expect with a pattern like that." I went into therapy to deal with "my mother problem" and my poor mother was blamed for a great deal until one day I suddenly had the dreadful insight: I, too, was a Pluto-Moon mother, as my daughter would no doubt testify. It was one of those life-changing moments, a true albeit painful revelation. This was the point where I had to stop blaming my parents and take responsibility for my own life: a decision that brought tremendous changes. My Hades Moon did not go away, but the eruptions of my unconscious were channelled into constructive pathways rather than being left to blast the unfortunate person who happened to inadvertently trigger them. In time, I learned to know my dark places very well indeed.

Howard's first question when I told him about my own past life "seeing" was: "Can you read past lives for other people? Pluto Moon is usually naturally psychic," and I said yes, both from a psychic tuning in, and the fact that I always saw past life patterns in the chart. As a result, I found myself talking to one of Howard's groups about my chart and reincarnation experiences. I discovered that I had been practicing karmic astrology without knowing what it was! Soon, I was teaching with Howard on the subject and it was Howard who urged me to write my first book.[2] When he was facing his own rather more permanent transition into Pluto's realm, I told him I was gathering material for this present book. His response was to wonder whether I would have enough material. Even I have been surprised by just how much emerged from the Underworld. I have felt Pluto at work in the strange synchronicities and experiences that underlie so many of my Hades Moon contacts. Aware that nemesis so often follows hubris, that most ancient of offenses to the gods, I hesitate to say that I know *all* about it yet. One thing I have learned, there is always another layer to strip away with Pluto.

When Howard first talked to me in that first consultation about power and its connection with Pluto/Scorpio Christine Hartley, who had been my mentor and teacher for reincarnation work, was trying to get me to train with her in magical work but I had a great resistance to this. Howard threw up his hands and said: "You can't do this. Here's someone trying to give you all this power, and you are refusing." I could, and it was many more years before another pupil of Christine's, who did not want to do reincarnation but learned the Western Mystery Tradition and its magical working from her, came to see me. How we laughed when we realized how that cunning old lady had taught us both the same techniques, but called them different names (she did, after all, have Sun-Pluto conjunct the Midheaven in Gemini aspecting a Virgo Moon). Recognizing and taking hold of my power has been a major issue for me. It certainly frightened me in those days, and the intensity of Pluto on the Ascendant repelled many people before I felt at home with it. It has also generated many conflicts and "magical battles" in my life. But now, I use it in my work and feel comfortable with Pluto and my own inner darkness, from which I draw my creative and healing energy.

After such a visceral contact with the Hades Moon, I suppose it is not surprising that I should attract numerous clients with Moon-Pluto contacts. I have learned so much from them. All re-enact the same patterns and undergo the same descent into the Underworld. Some return transformed, others compulsively recreate the struggle to be born anew. Those making the journey have said: "Please write about this, we need to know." I have done so not with the object of in any way apportioning blame but in an effort to understand and integrate, and then move on. Nor am I suggesting that it is only the Hades Moon which lies behind these experiences, I am aware that other aspects are involved and I have taken only one small part of the chart. But it is in the Hades Moon that the essence is distilled, this is where we venture into the Underworld and confront these issues face to face. Other aspects support, or sabotage, the process.

I believe that we choose our charts, and that we are born with precisely the aspects we need for our soul's growth. I am aware that, from the perspective of earthly incarnation, we cannot always objectively understand just why we chose this life path. Incarnation often feels more like a punishment or a task way beyond our capabilities, especially where Pluto is concerned. But many years of regressing people to the "between life state" convinced me that we do take on not only our karmic inheritance but also the ancestral patterns that we need to complete our experience. So, my question is: Why did I need a Moon-Pluto connection? My concern: what can I—and others—learn from it? How can we incorporate that understanding into our lives? How can we heal our past and be truly whole?

I have found that, in writing, answers come. This book had been gestating for at least seventeen years and yet writing it was like completing a detective novel when you don't know who did it until the last page. In true Plutonian fashion, the book arrived in pieces. Half was written more than thirteen years ago. Case material and reminders emerged with timely but often mysterious synchronicity or source. My favorite gift from the cosmos was receiving the *Natural Death Handbook*, when I had ordered *Testament*, on the day I was to do a Pluto death ritual. Synchronicity happened all through the writing of this book. I began to feel that the Lord of the Underworld was all around me if only I could penetrate his helmet of invisibility.

And, of course, he is very close to me. With fifteen years of Pluto transits ahead, including Pluto now on my natal Sun and then conjuncting Mercury in opposition to Uranus, and transiting Uranus about to oppose natal Pluto, it seemed an appropriate moment to cast more light into a dark Hadean place. As I have come to value my own dark places, I wanted to sink down into the collective chasm of the Hades Moon, taking with me the inner light of understanding, but content for it to be the dark luminosity of insight and intuition rather than the blinding ray of the analytical mind. I wanted to explore the poetic spaces of my inner being, and the terrors and nightmares of my soul. In other words, to take advantage of the crack between two worlds, what Clarissa Pinkola Estes calls "the place where visitations, miracles, imaginations, inspirations, and healings of all natures occur."[3] I wanted to venture into Hades once again, and return enlightened.

Not surprisingly, I found myself living this out literally. A sudden, serious illness took me into the weekend of hell that was the stretched-to-breaking-point British National Health Service at its most pressured. The overworked medical staff were conspicuous by their absence. Like the invisible Pluto, they may have been aware of what was going on, but it certainly was not apparent to me. I felt abandoned, rejected, alienated. I was in Tartarus. My partner, a doctor, was himself ill and unable to visit me. There was no one to notice how rapidly my dis-ease was progressing. No one, except my daughter, to hear how ill I was. Patient's Charter notwithstanding, I was left unfed and untreated, and finally dumped on a surgical ward "to recuperate." Mustering the remnants of my power, and knowing that if I did not leave soon I would die, I discharged myself.

Transferring to a private hospital was like entering the Elysian Fields, but enormous amounts of fear surfaced in my body. It was not fear of death (that would have been a welcome release). It was far older and more atavistic than that. The experience had activated childhood and past life issues. Wave after wave of overwhelming emotions and physical panic swept through me. At a cellular level, I felt as though I was letting go of the terror of the ages. My rational mind was switched off. All I could do was go with those feelings into the center of my being, washing up eventually on the shore of acceptance. I was indeed in Pluto's realm—exactly where I was supposed to be. With the usual timeliness, I had found a publisher and was committed to delivering a manuscript. So, my way of healing was to finish writing this book. Inevitably, I suppose, this being Pluto we are dealing with, I came to a point where the book was getting deeper and deeper, longer and longer. I still had not touched on half the topics I had planned. Delivery was late. Birth was stalled. I was compulsively entrenched in the Underworld. Eventually, an astrologer friend said: "Face it Judy, with your chart you are spending your whole life exploring Plutonian issues. You cannot possibly cover them all in one book. It is time to stop and let go. Let what you have said be enough." I stopped. This book is the result.

I do not want this to be a theoretical book, so the story of the Hades Moon is told through people's experiences. These experiences are ubiquitous and universal, participated in by all those who have an intimate aquaintance with Hades. To gain the most from the book, you need to read with openness and empathy, putting aside your rational mind. This is not a subject to "make sense of" from an intellectual perspective. Immerse yourself, join me, my friends and clients, on a journey into the Underworld. Share this exploration of myth and inner space for it can lead to an intuitive knowing of what it is to have a Hades Moon.

CHAPTER 1

BY THE LIGHT OF THE SLIGHTLY TARNISHED MOON

Pluto in any aspect to a personal planet means that there is an increase of consciousness due, a re-birth of sorts, with respect to that part of oneself symbolized by the other planet.
—Stephen Arroyo[1]

AN ASTROLOGICAL CHART is a map of the solar system seen from the perspective of Earth. The luminaries appear to be rotating around the center of the chart, the unmarked and unnamed Earth and its Underworld; with enigmatic Pluto lurking in the depths of space, inner and outer. The macrocosm is seen through a finely focused lens, the microcosm of the individual whose chart is being considered. So, the natal chart is a map of individual consciousness manifesting out of the sea of the collective unconscious which surrounds it, a consciousness colored and shaped by the relationship of its disparate parts.

THREE LUMINARIES AND THE EARTH

From the Earth, the Sun and the Moon *seem* to be the same size. Both were a source of awe and numinous power for our ancestors, but the Moon was worshipped long before the Sun. Linked to fertility and death, the Moon was primarily seen as "feminine" and most of the deities connected with it are female, although ancient Egypt had its full complement of lunar gods—and solar goddesses. The Moon is a cyclic deity. Like the tides, she ebbs and flows. She has her new, young face, and her ancient, timeless form.

Time is different on the Moon. There the brightness of "day" and the darkness of "night" each last for fourteen days—half a Moon cycle. The Sun presents a ubiquitously bright face to Earth, but the rhythmic Moon shows a face which seemingly changes, waxing and waning mysteriously from dark to crescent to full, and then returning to the dark. This is because the Moon is actually presenting the same face to Earth all the time and its light is reflected from the Sun. As Earth from time to time intervenes between Moon and Sun, we see a changing face.

These two luminaries and Earth have a special relationship to each other. Although the Moon is rotating around Earth, its gravitational center is the Sun; so Earth and Moon are "twin souls" orbiting around a mutual attraction—the Sun. Similarly, the planet Pluto and its Moon, Charon, are twin bodies circulating around the Sun. Charon, like Earth's Moon, does not orbit Pluto's gravitational center directly. The two dance in a complex relationship around a mutual point of gravity, far removed from the self-conscious Sun.

Symbolically, Earth can be seen as representing physical incarnation and material life. Its deeper, instinctual energies are an archaic, ingrained, collective level of earthy consciousness (the Plutonian Underworld); while the Sun is the pull to Spirit and Self, a differentiation into individuality and separate awareness. It is the life-giver, a source of power and indicator of destiny. The receptive Moon acts as a bridge and mediator between the two. No one can look at the Sun directly without being blinded. So, the reflective Moon vitalizes and fertilizes Earth by stepping down the Sun's light. It then destroys and annihilates consciousness by shutting off that bright light so that the forces of the instinctual Underworld can rise up for a time and engulf the Earth. This rhythmic cycle holds the balance for the polarities embodied in the apparent duality of earthly existence: sex and gender; light and dark, day and night; god and goddess; life and death; left and right brain functions, etc.

Pluto's orbit is highly elliptical, bringing it in from the outer reaches of our solar system to pass within the orbit of Neptune. The unconscious breaks through, it penetrates the watery bounds of Neptunian illusion, as we shall see. Pluto, too, is a giver of light, a luminary. He lights up the deepest recesses of our being, a dark place which is Hades, his mythological underworld home. His ferryman, Charon, conveys us into the center of our Self, the place of initiation and pure truth. There is nowhere to hide, and no need for concealment. Pluto offers us the riches of truly knowing our whole Self.

THE LUNAR EFFECT

The Moon is said to govern the body. The lunar tides affect the fluid in our bodies. Men, just as much as women, experience surges and fluctuations in the flow of hormones, blood, and lymph. Our bodies are over 70 percent water so it is no wonder they respond so intimately to the pull of the Moon. They carry the messengers of the lunar emotional self, mediating between the physical and subtle bodies of earthly incarnation.

We could look on the Moon as the Neoplatonist Soul of the World, which mediated between the spiritual realm of the gods and the sensory, material realm of mortal beings. We could also look on it as Jung's collective unconscious in which dwell the psychological principles known as archetypes—the gods who interact with human existence. The collective unconscious is the respository for all past experience. It is the storehouse of racial memory and the ingrained patterns that motivate all human behavior. It is the genetic code of human evolution. These are lunar attributes. However, this identification with the collective unconscious may be more appropriate to Pluto, while the Moon is a more personal, and accessible, level of the unconscious (see figure 8, page 32).

THE NEW MOON HANGS PREGNANT WITH THE OLD

Our earliest ancestors had no clocks, but they did have a reliable marker of the passage of time—the Moon. They observed that the Moon was continually changing, and yet uniformly followed a rhythmic cycle of unfoldment and withdrawal. This is

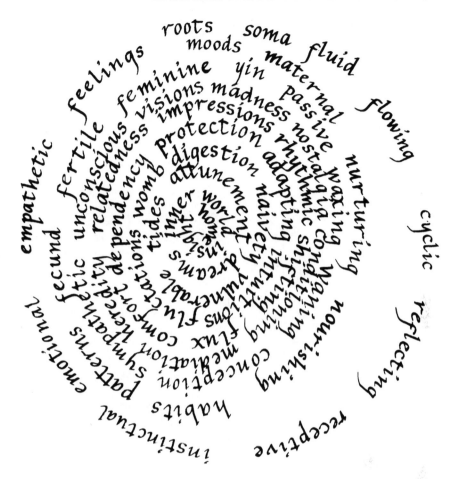

Figure 1. Moon words.

the great paradox of the Moon. It faithfully records the Great Round, and reflects the cycle of life from conception to death in its appearance and disappearance. The magical, otherworldly light that bleaches the color from the landscape signals the time to emerge from the Underworld. Its withdrawal into darkness is the moment of entry into the netherworld. It relentlessly signposts the passage of the seasons, and of procreation. Thirty-five thousand years ago, notches were cut into bone to mark the lunar phases: the calendar had come into being. Such calendars kept track of women's menstruation, indicating the fertile New Moon of ovulation and conception, and the "Full Moon moment" of birth. They ticked off the ten lunar months needed for gestation and parturition.

When the light of the Moon is potent and unimpeded, the menstrual cycle usually follows the flowering of the Moon—that female matrix out of which everything is born and to which everything must return as it dies. At each stage, all the other stages, both those that have gone before and those that are to come, are held in seed form, ready to unfold. At New Moon, if we look really hard, we can just make out the dark form of the germinal Full Moon. As the Moon waxes, it swells gravid with potential until the Full Moon is delivered and the Old Moon emerges. In her bright phase, the Moon gives life. In her dark phase, the Moon sheds blood and is the destructive power of nature and consequent death. Together, the two phases are the cycle of life.

In modern times we live in a light-polluted environment and, for most of us in the Western world, the full power of the Moon is experienced rarely. But go to a less populated place and you will immediately be aware of exactly where the Moon is in her cycle. At the three-day Dark of the Moon, nothing is visible, blackness prevails. The goddess has withdrawn her face from the world. In Greek mythology, Demeter is grieving for Persephone. In Egyptian understanding, Isis seeks Osiris. The world is plunged into mourning. This is the time of greatest mystery, the Hecate time for divination and prophecy, for magic and healing, for retiring to the menstrual hut to dream dreams. Then slowly, by degrees, the mystical light is once more seen in the heavens, growing organically as the waxing Moon gestates her own light. This crescent Moon is receptive, bowl-shaped, waiting to be fertilized, or ravished. This is virginal Persephone awaiting her initiation into womanhood.

The Full Moon shines down pitilessly, exposing everything that moves. It is the moment for the as yet unmanifested to come into consciousness. This Moon seems to hang pregnant with promise, or subtle threat, and indeed the ancients revered the Moon as a triple-faced, fecund deity who fertilized, and presided over, the passages of life. Demeter is but one of many Moon goddesses who have absolute power over life, death, and fertility. Then, with surprising suddenness, the Moon vanishes back into the darkness. When the Moon is coming up to Full there is a day or two of wondering: is it yet? Is it time? No such confusion accompanies the shadowy Waning Moon. Suddenly, a slice of light is gone. Quickly it shrinks to the crescent and then descends into full night, the realm of Hecate. Magic and mystery are once more abroad in the world and the Gates to Hades are open wide.

The mythologically expressed lunar cycle can also, therefore, be seen as loss, quest and resurrection; as gestation, fruition, and decay. The dark of the Moon is a time for introspection, moving into oneself and having visions, for purifying and releasing old patterns, for allowing the past to break down into fertile compost so that something new can emerge, the moment of transformation and renewal. The New Moon is the time to plan fresh projects, to prepare for bringing that vision out into the light, to conceive new patterns and receive fresh inspiration. The Full Moon is the creative time, the period when we can manifest and make known who we are, living out our renewal and resurrection. It is the moment of interacting with, and being energetic in, the world—birthing our creations. This is the time when we are outwardly most active and vital in who we are. Then fruition is reached and, with the decaying Waning Moon, we are are ready to eliminate, to cleanse and clear the detritus of our experience. This is the moment of letting go and starting anew, the time when we accompany the Sumerian goddess Innana into the underworld to meet her dark sister Ereshkigal. The cycle of introversion and extroversion, receptivity and activity, change and unfoldment begins again. The

Moon also signifies inheritance from the past. Looked at from the karmic perspective, the phase of the Moon at which we were born might also hold a clue as to how long we have been dealing with the karmic issues in our chart, notwithstanding that the aspects between inner and outer planets also show this clearly. Fixed squares, for example, are karmic issues that have been around for many lifetimes, whereas cardinal squares are "karma in the making." Trines are issues that we have more or less "got right" and are now being tested to see if we really have grasped the lesson. However, the New Moon might be embarking on the experience for the first time, or on a new way of dealing with it. The Full Moon could well be focusing on an issue, seeing it clearly for the first time, perhaps, although the issue itself had been around for some time. By the time we get to the last quarter, the issue is old and we are ready to let go. As Liz Greene says: "A balsamic Moon has begun to unload its parcel of experience, and there is a melancholy, sacrificial, almost weary quality to this lunar phase."[2]

LUNAR ENERGY

The Moon cannot be outgrown or transcended, but if its underlying needs are understood, it can be transformed. It describes our innate response to life and we will explore its manifestations in much greater detail through this book. The archetypal Moon is expressed through myriad goddesses and inner processes as befits an energy which is inherently present from conception to death (see chapter 2). It is our basic security needs, expressed from the first moment a baby reaches out for food and sustenance, and throughout the whole of life to the last dying breath. It is our neediness and our vulnerability, our roots and our continuity.

The Moon has always had close links with the womb. Both waxed and waned, swelled and then gave birth. But, to the ancient Greeks the womb also had an affinity with irrational emotion. It was believed that the womb went wandering, giving rise to hysteria and other disturbances. And, of course, through the ages the Full Moon has been indissolubly linked to madness and mayhem. The lunar energy carries this aspect of "out of control" emotion, irrational and feeling-dominated behavior. Most men tend to project this side of the planet onto women in general, although pre-menstrual women and those in mid-life have borne the brunt of the collective attitude to menarche and menopause. Another side of the Plutonian planetary energy which has been projected, and one which women suffered much persecution over, is the fey, intuitive, "witch" who was so feared by the medieval church and others, a fear that still lingers today.

Lunar energy is about fluctuation, feelings, mood, and emotion. It is an inarticulate energy and can rarely openly express what it needs, or the source of its emotions. It is an autonomous, organic life process, controlling the body, taking in nourishment, assimilating experience, and following ingrained patterns from the past. Our automatic reaction to a preprogramed response. It is our heredity, our family, and tribal awareness, and the emotional baggage we carry with us. However, the Moon is also where we need to adapt, not through struggle but by surrendering to the inevitable process of death, decay, and new life. This process is facilitated by an attunement to Pluto. Familiarity with his realm lends comfort to the destruction and re-creation process. Adaptation proceeds at a greater pace when spurred on by Plutonian necessity. If we view the Moon as Gatekeeper to the Unconscious, a doorway through which the transpersonal energies of the outer planets must pass, we can see that an attunement to Pluto would indeed compel one toward transformation, no matter how much the psyche might, at the individual level, resist. So, the Moon focuses the Plutonian urge to transform, its fickle light shows us the pathway into the unconscious.

PURVEYOR OF THE MOTHER ARCHETYPE

Above all else, the Moon carries the archetype of Mother, the primal matter from whom all emerges, on whom all life depends. This is not the personal mother, although she may reflect it. Nor does the actual mother need to have an identical Moon placement to reflect this archetype back to her child. It is what, at the deepest level of being, Mother signifies in all her aspects. It is how Mother is perceived, what is expected of a mother, and how the person (male or female) with a certain Moon placement will behave in a nurturing role. This is the Terrible Mother, who holds the power of life and death, the Nurturing Mother who succours the needy, and the Primordial Mother who is the source of life itself. So, the sign placement of the Moon, and its aspects, describes the archetypal image of Mother that the child carries; it describes what the person needs and anticipates from Mother.

The Great Mother shows her faces through Persephone, Demeter, Hecate, and the other, much older, goddesses whom we will encounter as we journey through the Underworld of the Hades Moon. She has awesome, numinous power and is worshipped for her death-dealing face just as much as for her life giving power. The human child is, of course, dependent on mother for an inordinately long time, and is aware that if she cuts off nurturing, death could well result. This death may be physical, but it may equally well be emotional or intellectual. Without love and care, children become apathetic and do not thrive. Left too long in this state, they shut down, functioning only through their autonomous lunar body processes.

It is this death-dealing aspect of the lunar energy, the devouring shadow, with which we all are, at some level, familiar. This is the stuff of nightmares, a shade which haunts the edges of our awareness. It is the blood-sucking vampirism of unsatisfied need, and the hopelessness of the unnurtured. The Moon is the untamed, savage face of instinct, an instinct that will kill to protect its young, or murder them to survive. So, an over-protective mother is just one side of the shadow-Moon. An irrational fear of annihilation and death that takes no prisoners and gives no quarter is another. "Mother Russia," the Berlin wall, American imperialism and its paranoid, fear-driven fight against communism stemmed directly from the Moon's overwhelming need to preserve at all costs the security of what is known and familiar.

Hitler's rise to power coincided with the discovery of Pluto. His collective-shadow 8th-house Gemini-Pluto oratory mesmerizing the inconjunct 3rd house Capricorn Moon into complicity, illustrates society's need, and also the individual's wish, to project all the rage and insecurity onto an enemy who is "out there," as the rise of a new bogeyman, Saddam Hussein, so soon after the fall of the Berlin Wall neatly confirmed. And, of course, the Gulf War was really about greed, power, and manipulation of the world's fuel sources but was masked by a spurious caring for the invaded and oppressed Kuwait—typical of the collective shadow-lunar energies at work—liberally seeded by Pluto in Scorpio sextiling the New Moon in Capricorn the day before the war. Just before midnight (GMT) on the eve of the war saw a solar eclipse in Capricorn. Authoritarian Capricorn is a sign that may demand a scapegoat for the collective "evil," and the Gulf War had much collective karma behind it. A solar eclipse is a time when the light of personal consciousness (the Sun) is blotted out and the unconscious and collective forces of the Moon are able to surface. In Capricorn, cosmic consciousness pours down upon Earth. This can be an explosive time, when repressed energies erupt, especially when fueled by Pluto.

The shadow-Moon is treacherous and deceitful, as witnessed by the treatment of the Kurds who were encouraged by the West to rise up against Saddam, only to be abandoned and left to their fate when their usefulness was over. It is the blotting out of a race, the Marsh Arabs who were exterminated by Saddam while the rest of the world closed their collective eyes. This is the Terrible Mother projected out into the world. However, it is in personal interaction that the shadow-Moon perhaps takes its greatest toll, as we shall see in chapters 3 and 4.

Unresolved parental and emotional issues are carried by the shadow-Moon, as are the frustrations and resentments that pass on down the generations. The shadow-Moon's heredity is dark and devious, embittered and emotionally voracious. This is the inwardly raging and claustrophobic mother who demands nurturing from her children, who looks to them to feed her lunar needs. This is the mother who is overly identified with her family, ruthless in destroying anything she perceives as a threat to her unique position of power; or the mother who emotionally annihilates a child who attempts to break away. "Emotional brutalization"[3] is practiced by such mothers under the guise of "concern" or "love." This is a side of the negative lunar energy that we will meet again and again. In such a family, the child may well become the "heroic redeemer" for the mother, who will live out all her unmet potential through the child. It may well end in a ritualized sacrifice of the child on the pyre of the mother's overwhelming ego.

When matriarchy rules, the child may well be idealized, becoming the center of the woman's world: a chosen child. "Nurturing" is all important, and the child remains locked in a narcissistic, omnipotent egocentricity. In such a case, the child is the Sun around which the Moon mother endlessly revolves, locked in a love duel that cries out for drastic intervention. Mythical Pluto must arise out of the Underworld to snatch innocent Persephone from her (or his) suffocating parent. We will explore many more facets of the devouring mother and her child as we penetrate the Hades Moon.

• • •

To which particular facet of the lunar energy (and the archetypes attached to that) we are attuned will depend on many factors. But clues can be gleaned from the placement of the Moon in the birthchart, its aspects, and the phase of the Moon in which we were born. Aspects, or the lack of them, are important indications of family and emotional interconnectedness. The phase of the Moon under which someone is born may indicate the child's place in the family. The New Moon could indicate the "baby of the family," no matter how the birth order may fall. This child may always remain a baby in the parents' eyes, and is given little autonomy, remaining at the innocent Persephone or eternal puer stage long after physical maturity. At the Full Moon motherhood is glorified—or idealized—and the Demeter mother's influence may well be lifelong and well-nigh impossible to break. On the other hand, mother and child may be "at arms length," united in an eternal dance of symbiotic antipathy. With the falling away of the Waning Moon, the child may well experience isolation and alienation. This is the child who does not fit into the family or who is rejected for some reason, the one who is on intimate terms with that guardian of the dark places, Hecate.

Someone with an unaspected Moon may be totally feeling-controlled, especially if the Moon is in a water sign, or cut off from all emotion, projecting it out onto another, particularly when the Moon is in an air sign. When the Moon is waxing from New toward Full, the maiden kore or Persephone archetype can easily surface (see chapter 2). Close to the Full Moon, the mature mother, Demeter, takes over, and as the Moon passes into Dark, the crone Hecate emerges from the Underworld. Whether it will be the positive or shadow side of the Moon that manifests may be determined by the aspects, although this is not always the case, and different facets may be stimulated by passing transits. The so-called easy, flowing aspects, such as trines or sextiles, can indicate a comfortable Moon, while the challenging squares, oppositions or inconjuncts and, in this case specifically, the conjunction, tend to hook into the shadowier side of the lunar archetypes. Aspects from Saturn usually indicate a great difficulty and inhibition around expressing the Moon. A Uranus contact is typically an unpredictable, erratic expression; a Neptune connection an elusive, idealized one. However, it is in the murky depths of the Hades Moon alliance that the most potent archetype, that of the devouring mother, emerges.

The Lunar Influence

The sign and house placement of the Moon shows us the area of life in which our instincts will function most strongly, an ingrained pattern of behavior that we have carried with us for many lifetimes. It is our personal unconscious. The Moon also indicates our response to emotion: whether we are totally overwhelmed by it, theoretically in control of it, motivated by it, or whether we tend to repress it and live "in our head." The Moon is also an indication of what will nourish us, the kind of experiences we need in order to feel "well fed," the emotional sustenance we will instinctively seek out.

Sometimes it feels like there is a strange otherworldly influence on us: this is the effect of the lunar light, and of the karmic residue we carry. The Moon brings in powerful influences from our past, whenever that might be. Our Moon sign is, in my experience, a much more ingrained energy than our Sun, which we are still developing. So, the Moon is where we retreat to when challenged; it is comfortable and known, whereas the Sun still has some mystery for us. However, if the Moon energy is used unconsciously, it can pull us into destructive patterns of behavior. On the other hand, conscious use of the Moon is life-enhancing and fertile.

If we consciously choose to descend into the instinctual darkness of our lunar self, we can reconnect to our ancient wisdom. Within this darkness the detritus of outgrown consciousness can make fertile compost for the growth of new awareness, provided that the cyclical light of the Moon is allowed to shine when appropriate. Compost without light and air becomes a stinking, crawling morass of decay. Regularly aerated, it becomes a rich and nourishing source of goodness. It is important to recognize when light is required and when it is inappropriate. Attunement to our inner cycles will indicate the time for inward reflection, the moment when the old has to die, the period of dormancy, and the springing into new life. The unconscious, unaware Moon energies manifest as a compulsive pull back into the past, the consciously expressed lunar energies nurture the growth of oneself and others.

As we have seen, the Moon placement, and its aspects, also describes how we are attuned to the Mother archetype; it illustrates the inner picture of "Mother" that we carry with us, whether it is the "good mother" or the "devouring mother" that is strongest within us. It tells us the kind of nurturing we need, the lunar food we crave; and what we expect to receive: the two may differ widely—especially when Pluto is in aspect to the Moon.

THE PLUTO EFFECT

> *At best the image of Pluto is of dark and mysterious fate; at worst he conjures up visions of sinister shadows and threatening distintegration.*
>
> —Karen Hilverson[4]

THE PLUTO CYCLE

Pluto's orbit is one of the most elliptical, and its eccentric journey penetrates within Neptune's sphere. Pluto spends widely differing lengths of time in each sign, taking roughly 31 years to travel through Taurus and yet only 12 years to move through Scorpio, its natural home (see figure 2, page 10). Metaphorically speaking, certain signs are much better able to process Pluto's effect and therefore offer less resistance to its passage. Entrenched Taurus resists at all costs the Plutonian disintegration, and consequent transformation. Scorpio positively revels in it. The Underworld is Scorpio's natural domain.

Pluto's sign placement in the natal chart is, of course, a generational one, something we share with everyone born during the same period. In Pluto's longer sojourns, it may also be a placement shared by parent and child. Pluto's house placement is more personal. It shows us where we are plugged into the collective energies, where we make contact with the unconscious. Liz Greene sees it as our fate. We can also view it as our karma: the credits and deficits of our past catching up with us. A lunar connection with Pluto emphasizes the compulsive pull to the past that is so often a part of the Hades Moon experience. But it also highlights the potential for transformation, its very intensity somehow propelling into the new way of being. The house in which Pluto resides points us to an area of life in which

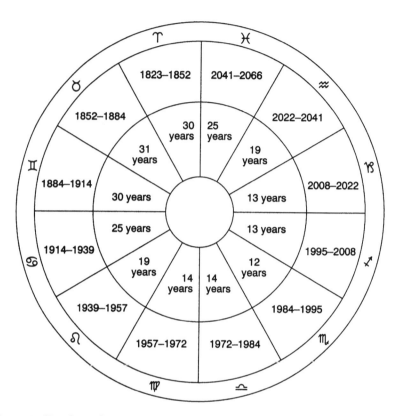

Figure 2. The Pluto Cycle. (Adapted from Haydn Paul's *Phoenix Rising*, Element Books, Shaftesbury, England, 1998, p. 130.)

the Hades Moon influence will strongly manifest. This is the place where we will meet our karma around Plutonian issues: power struggles and domination, alienation and isolation, birth and death, nurture and separation, corruption and pollution on all levels. But it is also where we find our inner riches, the treasure trove of our other lives. It pinpoints challenges but also signposts a crucial transformation to be made. (See figure 3, page 11.)

Pluto transits have both a personal and a collective effect. This is a subversive planet and its movement through the signs shows where it conflicts with the entrenched attitudes of a sign. It indicates where toxic energies must be eliminated and drives transformed. Pluto pinpoints our obsessions, and shows where we may well take ourselves too seriously, so can highlight our need to lighten up. Pluto also has the function of bringing the shadow side out into the light of conscious awareness. And, finally, Pluto is where we face loss and death.

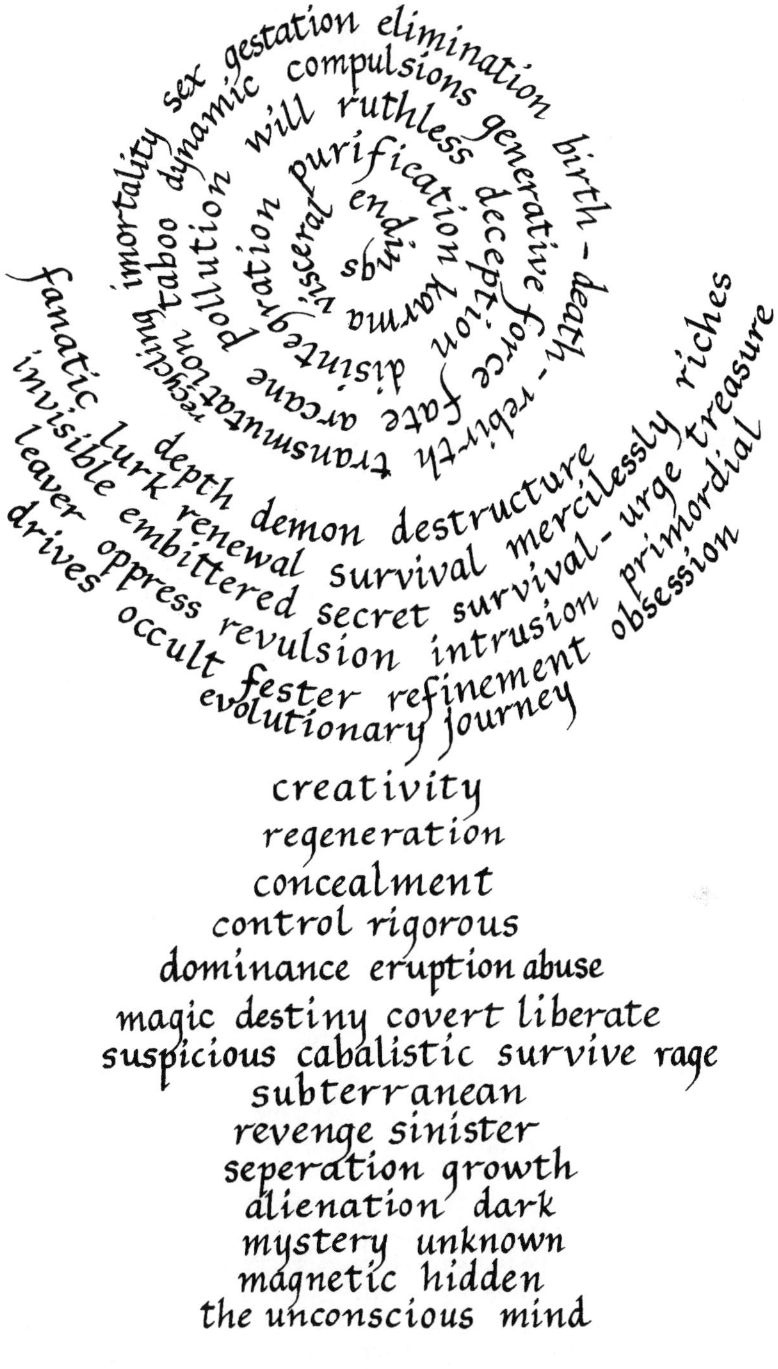

sex gestation elimination compulsions generative birth — death immortality taboo dynamic will ruthless deception generate deception — death — rebirth pollution purification karma ending visceral integration disintegration arcane fate force transmutation reducing depth demon destructure survival mercilessly riches lurk renewal survival — urge treasure fanatic invisible embittered secret survival intrusion primordial leaver oppress revulsion obsession drives occult fester refinement evolutionary journey

creativity
regeneration
concealment
control rigorous
dominance eruption abuse
magic destiny covert liberate
suspicious cabalistic survive rage
subterranean
revenge sinister
seperation growth
alienation dark
mystery unknown
magnetic hidden
the unconscious mind

Figure 3. Pluto words.

Pluto transits are periods of soul growth, although symbolic death and descent into the Underworld is often the first stage in moving "up" the evolutionary ladder. Pluto brings about profound change and regeneration from a cellular level up. By transit, during the average lifetime, Pluto will pass through between a third and a half of the chart, depending where it is in its cycle. Its effect when aspecting a natal planet is, therefore, long-lasting and profound. It can be felt for at least two years, and often more. During that two-year period Pluto may well pass over the aspected planet's natal position three times due to the, apparent, backward effect of retrogradation.

Pluto's position by sign (natal or transiting) shows how the sign energies will interact with Pluto and affect the collective energies of humankind, and how these will be expressed socially. It shows the particular Plutonian themes to which the individual will be attuned. It signifies a generational impulse toward manifesting the energies of that sign. If the manifestation is not conscious, and Pluto is, after all, a transpersonal planet so conscious recognition is rare, then the shadow side of the sign may well emerge. By house placement (natal or transiting), it shows how those collective energies will be personalized by the individual, and where the energies will be expressed through a particular area of life. It shows where we carry karma around the Plutonian energies as expressed through that house, and the reparation we may be called upon to make. It pinpoints the area of life in which critical transformation could occur, and often points to explosive endings or beginnings, especially in life phases. Pluto identifies crucial areas of challenge, areas in which the person appears to be driven toward disintegration of the old, or is subject to compulsive acting out of ingrained patterns. This is the point of greatest potential, the meeting place of the Underworld and the transformatory energies of the Lord of Enlightenment.

PLUTO AND ALCHEMY

Are you willing to be sponged out, erased, cancelled, made nothing?
Dipped into oblivion?
If not, you will never really change.

—D. H. Lawrence[5]

Experiencing Pluto in our life is an alchemical process. In alchemy, raw primal matter was concocted, putrefied, placed in a retort, heated, condensed and otherwise processed in an effort to find purified "gold." This process is symbolic of our search to find the Plutonian riches at the center of our most base experiences. If we transcend this process, rise up out of the *prima materia* of our lives, skate on the surface and refuse to journey into the alchemical retort which is Hades, then we lose this opportunity to create new energy in our lives.

For the alchemists, putrefaction was an essential preamble to the process. The base materials were faecal, malodorous, and Plutonic. In keeping with a Plutonian process, what went into the retort was more redolent of garbage than of gold. This is the stage of life where Ereshkigal has hung Inanna on the meat hook to become rotten meat (see page 23). The transits of Pluto show where our psychic garbage can become our *prima materia*, the basic ingredient of life. As Pluto moves around the heavens (and the natal chart), it brings into consciousness all that has festered, putrefied. It forces us to recognize where the psychic faecal matter has become stuck, blocking the flow of energy. This is the point where transformation can begin, a transformation that has to start at the cellular level and spread out from there. As Thomas Moore has pointed out, in the view of many alchemists (and psychotherapists) if you do not already have a mess, you are at a disadvantage and need to get one.[6] Pluto reminds us that we do all have "a mess." It brings out our *prima materia* from the shadows. It connects us to our "shit," the base material for psychotherapy and other such Plutonian processes.

As the alchemical process proceeds, our past experience becomes the breeding ground for insight and experience. At times the process has to wait, suspended, while secret fermentation takes place. The bubbles of forgotten memory rise into consciousness. Things get heated up: it is hot in Hades. Both passion and anger bring things to the boil. Our experience is condensed, solidified, intensified so that we can feel its essence. Often the cells of our body respond with symptoms of disease—viruses and other Plutonian conditions that normally lurk and fester in our hidden places make themselves known as our body detoxifies. The emotional blocks and stuck feelings we are carrying loosen, disintegrate, and the debris is carried into the retort. It is vaporized, blowing away our fantasies and illusions, and revealing the core. It discloses a space where something new can incubate. Slowly the purification proceeds until the nugget of gold is unveiled—the transformed self.

FROM INCARNATION TO INITIATION: PLUTO THROUGH CANCER TO CAPRICORN

In esoteric astrology, Cancer (mass consciousness) is seen as the point of incarnation into matter, the place of suffering. Suffering is the pain we, and all humankind feel, as a result of unresolved fear, guilt, and ignorance. This is ignorance of our "divine" roots, of our collective oneness. The suffering comes through our separation from our real selves and lack of knowledge of our integral wholeness. It also arises out of the collective karma generated in the past, karma for which no one person is responsible, but which nevertheless has an extremely powerful effect as we shall see. Suffering is the shadow side of the Capricorn scapegoat, Cancer's opposite sign. Incarnation is where we undergo the lessons necessary for our soul's growth, especially on the emotional level.

Emotion is a Cancerian concomitant. Cancer is ruled by the sentient Moon, and is the feminine energy of the goddess made manifest as the Great Mother. This is where matter is birthed, given form, and mothered. Here the nurturing of home and family are all important. Here the emotional lessons commence. In Cancer the consciousness of self is established and begins to move out to make a mark on the world. Cancer is also a social sign, and someone with a strong Cancer Moon will often act as social worker to the world and its troubles. It is in Cancer that the Plutonian energy can ground itself as social change, or may reveal itself through familial conflict, at the same time stirring up uncertainty about just how secure this change will be.

Cancer is still on the personal evolutionary cycle, although the collective level is stirring. The sign is nationalistic, and possessive, and we will look at its connections with World War I and II in chapter 5. Appropriately enough, Pluto was in Cancer when the planet was first discovered in 1930, although its existence was being postulated as early as 1905 (when Pluto was in Gemini) by Percival Lowell. Typically, Lowell died in 1916 without having proved that this secretive planet was anything more than an arcane supposition. It was left to his successor, Clyde Tombaugh, to make a clear sighting in 1930 and provide firm astronomical data.

Surrender, death, and a journey into the Underworld are crucial for Initiation to take place. In the signs following Cancer the descent is made, the unconscious is explored in all its manifestations as the urge for transformation unfolds. This reaches its nadir in Scorpio, Pluto's sign, the point where personal power must be mastered. Scorpio is a sign where occult understanding is reached; maybe because Scorpio is so at home in the depths, this is also the sign that can reach the heights of spiritual consciousness. In esoteric astrology, Scorpio is the sign of discipleship, the point where the decision is made to return to the spiritual "Father" (or Mother). According to Hadyn Paul, Scorpio can be seen a symbolic gate through which Avatars enter the Earth plane, avatars being "mouthpieces of collective wisdom and evolutionary agents."[7]

As Pluto travels through Sagittarius, which represents the path ahead, it opens up a vision of what might be when we connect to Pluto's highest energies, and when we can ground collective power productively. In far-sighted Sagittarius, the energies of higher consciousness must unite with the instinctual realm: the centaur has his feet in the mud and his arrow aimed at the sky. Matter must be infused with vision. The soul must recognize its divine roots. By the time it reaches Capricorn (cosmic consciousness), the impulse has been firmly grounded in convention. Indeed, it may well be time for a new impetus toward change to emerge, one that is based on what is needed for the good of society as a whole, rather than that of the individuals who control it. Capricorn is a lesson in collective power. So, Capricorn is the start of another evolutionary cycle.

In esoteric astrology, Capricorn is the sign of initiation, the polar opposite of the descent into matter (Cancer). It is on the Capricornian mountaintop that we can reach up and touch the higher energies. This is the ascent into spiritual consciousness, the point where we become the co-creator of our world, having broken free from the grip of attachment to material form. This is where humankind must once again take up their spiritual heritage; where Pluto can be metamorphosed and higher consciousness be incorporated into consciousness as a whole. However, Capricorn is also where we must avoid the scapegoating of others, no longer holding them responsible for energies we refuse to own in ourselves. Capricorn is where we, and society as a whole, are transformed. This is where the collective impulse must be toward the highest good for all. Pluto moved into Cancer, the Gate of Incarnation, in 1914. In looking at Pluto's journey around the zodiac (see chapter 10), I have taken Cancer as the starting point and ended with the Gate into Initiation, Capricorn, which takes us us to 2022. Many prophecies foretell the end of the world and the annihilation of mankind through a Plutonian war by this date. I am not so sure. I believe that there are many endings and new beginnings. This is Pluto we are dealing with, so there may well be some kind of mutation or metamorphosis. As the mystic monk Matthew Fox has pointed out, millions of years ago, a supernova exploded and died. But, as it died, the basic elements of life were created. There was a "resurrection experience." So, this was a Plutonian renewal process. In the midst of death, we are in life. Pluto in Sagittarius is an opportunity for a shift in consciousness, an elimination of outgrown patterns of being. Since Pluto's urge toward transformation and renewal is equally as strong as the drive toward elimination and disintegration, I can only hope the two balance themselves by leaving behind the old destructive attitudes and ushering in the rebirth of planetary consciousness. That Plutonian regeneration must start with the microcosm—the cellular level of our bodies—and move out into the macrocosm, encompassing all.

THE HADES MOON EFFECT

This person needs, more than anything else, a concentrated program of self-transformation based on re-programming his or her instinctive response patterns in order to be able to adjust to any life experience with more flexibility and objectivity.

—Stephen Arroyo[8]

When Pluto aspects the Moon, the Hades Moon, the personal unconscious merges into the collective unconscious. (See figure 8, page 32.) Images and experiences can rise through the Moon from the Plutonian depths. The Hades Moon unites not just the planetary energies but that of the signs in which the planets are placed. (When referring to the summaries in chapter 10, to fully understand the effect of the Hades Moon in a chart, it will be necessary to synthesize the Moon placement with that of Pluto.)

Aspects and Orbs

The Moon energy is strongly colored by Pluto in any aspect to the Moon, even the seemingly minor ones, and especially some of the more obscure ones, such as the novile or quintile. Any contact between the Moon and Pluto should be looked on as the Hades Moon. The energies manifest most strongly in the conjunction, square, opposition, and quincunx/inconjunct (150°) aspects. Orbs need to be wide; I have seen squares which are up to 12° apart manifest very powerfully. Indeed it sometimes seems that the wider the orb, the more clearly the issues make themselves felt. I use 8° for all the major aspects, except the sextile (6° orb), and including the inconjunct/quincunx (150°), but I expand this for Moon-Pluto contacts as experience tells me that wider orbs work. Even with the minor aspects, such as semi-sextiles, the orb can be expanded from the usual 2° to 3° or 4°. For transits, the effect can be felt for at least 4°, and often much more, each side of exact.

Effects

The Pluto-Moon combination brings in a greater level of awareness, and a deeper connection to the unconscious, instinctual forces than the Moon alone. This combination has a peculiar intensity about it. An urge, often compulsive, to explore the

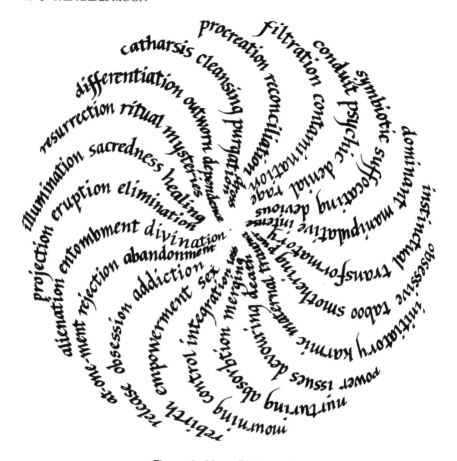

Figure 4. Moon-Pluto words.

taboo areas of life where others fear to tread. There is a "tinge of paranoia" attached to the Hades Moon (although this may be more obvious when the Moon is in a water sign). Paranoia is not necessarily a negative trait or a psychological ill. Thomas Moore[9] says that paranoia is "knowledge on the side . . . an unreflected, uncultivated dark suspicion that there is more going on in the world than we are aware of," and therefore it may point to knowledge we need to access. The positive side of this planetary combination is metanoia: a willingness to "turn around to face the darkness and reclaim our projections."[10] Certainly I always had a vague, uneasy feeling that something, or was it someone, was silently watching just out of sight. A feeling that, if I was too happy, if all went really well, then "they" would come for me, and I would be pulled back into the depths. I now recognize this mysterious "they" as characters from my own unconscious drama, but for years I would meet "them" in dreams and strange, unreal "otherworldly" experiences. Finally, in therapy, we met face to face. They do not hold the same terror now that they did in childhood. They have become familiar and known. In the same way, I recognize that my "enemies" are perfect mirrors for my disowned self. They point the way to the hidden riches that I need to reclaim in order to become whole. But, somewhere in the depths, there is still a vague haunting: the metanoia of "a parallel mind" with its unaccessed knowledge remains, pushing ever onward into the hadean void.

This particular combination of planets has powerful, unresolved emotional needs, and extremely deep fears about isolation, alienation, and rejection. It fears abandonment, usually arising out of past life experiences. Its needs are often unrecognized. When they are glimpsed, they are frequently deemed "unacceptable." So, they are projected "out there" onto another person. That other person may, for instance, be perceived as being rejecting, when in reality it is the Hades Moon who is unconsciously withdrawing because unexpressed needs are not being met. When these needs are lived out by the individual, it is in a compulsive, obsessive fashion. Relationship with the Hades Moon is intense, enigmatic, and highly charged. The lunar food required by this chthonic moon is somehow more compulsive, more obsessively sought after. Without it, the sense is I will die. So, if that food is sought from another, survival may be at stake. The thought comes: "Without them I will die." So, a desperate, possessive quality can underly even the lightest of relationships when the Moon contacts Pluto.

The Hades Moon mother archetype is somehow darker, more instinctual and destructive than the mother symbolized by an unfettered Moon. An archetypal force, this is the dominating family matriarch, the woman who rules—with a rod of iron—and who annihilates all opposition or dissent. These are the *materfamilias* who put duty and family above all else. Elizabeth II, Queen of England, and her own mother, Elizabeth the Queen Mother, have this combination. There is clearly no possibility of the Queen (Sun Taurus, Moon in Leo exactly semi-sextile Pluto in Cancer) abdicating in favor of her son, Charles. But, the real power behind the throne is the "Queen Mum." An indomitable woman, born in 1900, she has a Scorpio Moon quincunx Pluto in Gemini. There is considerable evidence that a very different person lurks behind the smiling facade. Born to rule, with a Leo Sun, it has always been said that she did not want her husband to become king as she knew it would affect his health. She failed in her attempts to control the abdication of his brother. Notwithstanding, during World War II she was the "Great Mother," remaining at Buckingham Palace with her daughters to give the nation heart. In old age, she became the adviser to the family, working behind the scenes in typical Hades Moon style, having a strong influence on the young royals and their consorts. She was the fairy godmother (or wicked witch?) who groomed Princess Diana for her fairytale role, all the while knowing that the Scorpionic prince had a mistress, and perhaps suspecting that he would metamorphose into Pluto: the archetypal "Prince of Darkness" who would take the young Diana deep into the Underworld to meet her own self.

Not surprisingly, Princess Diana had an Aquarian Moon (conjunct the South Node) very widely opposing Pluto, Mars, and the North Node. Here was the innocent Persephone watched over by Hecate as she kept her appointment with fate. She carried that archetype for the collective unconscious, a role which ultimately brought to the surface all that festered under the cool facade of the royal house of Windsor. Her life was a perfect expression of the Hades Moon. Her unhappy childhood, the bulimia and emotional angst she suffered, and the anguish of her marriage with its all too public betrayals, were all the negative face of the chthonic Moon. Her work with charitable organizations, AIDS awareness, and the campaign against the devastating effect of landmines were the positive side of this transformatory Moon. When Diana died, transiting Pluto had retrograded back to the cusp of her 12th house, the karmic house. It was in suspended motion, having just turned stationary direct. A potent moment. It formed a T-square to her natal Pluto-Mars-North Node opposition to the Moon-South Node. It was a time when a great deal of the past could be released and her soul's purpose realized. Transformation was awaiting her. Her companion, Dodi Fayed's natal Mars in Gemini completed a karmic Grand Cross (see figure 5, page 19). The transiting Moon was conjunct his natal Pluto. This was no accident. It was fate or destiny, a manifestation of cosmic forces acting on behalf of the collective. The transiting Moon was conjunct Diana's natal Uranus and would shortly move onto her North Node-Mars-Pluto conjunction. At that time (midnight of the day following her death) there would be a solar eclipse on that conjunction. The light of individual self-consciousness would be extinguished, the forces of myth would rise up to claim her. She would become an icon for the collective.

The founding doyen of the British royal family—alien outsiders who had to change their name when their adopted country went to war with their country of origin—was Queen Victoria. She had the Sun and Moon conjunct in Gemini widely aspecting Pluto in Pisces. Behind her public face, Victoria's journals reveal a passionate, sensual, angry woman who became totally dependent on her husband and, after his death, her gilly,* John Brown. Victoria ruled Britain with an expansionist rod of iron and yet she turned to her husband for every decision. This lady was not just a Queen, she was Empress, too: mother to half the world. But she displayed all the insecurities of the Hades Moon. After the death of her husband, she demanded that one of her daughters remain at home with her. Demeter-like, she simply would not let go.

The Hades Moon is the shadow mother that moves beneath the conscious life of her children. As we will see, she lives out her frustrations through her children and passes her dark secrets down through the generations that follow. But here again, transformation is possible for mother and child. It takes a certain willingness to let go, possibly to die. But, just as the seeds of destruction are contained within this mother archetype, so too are the seeds of soul growth. These seeds germinate by the hidden light of Pluto transits.

As we shall see, there are many other issues encompassed within the powerful embrace of the Lord of Darkness and the Light of the World. (For a wider understanding of how the Hades Moon operates in each sign and how Pluto behaves in the different signs and houses, with its generational effect, see chapter 10.)

---

*A "gilly" is Scots for a Highland Chief's attendant.

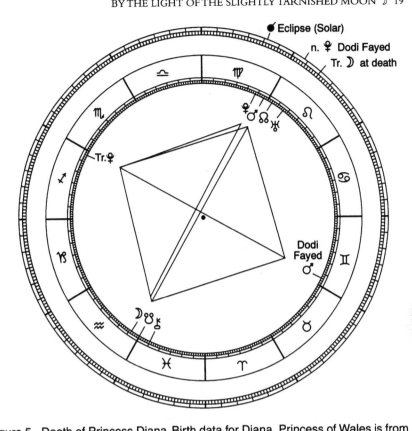

Figure 5. Death of Princess Diana. Birth data for Diana, Princess of Wales is from Data Plus, UK. July 1, 1961, 19.45 GDT, 52N50, 0E30. Source: from her mother, and from Diana to her astrologer Debbie Franks. The car accident took place between 12.24 and 12.27 A.M. MET, Paris, August 31, 1997. Life pronounced extinct 02:00 GMT, but she died sometime previous to this. Source: Data Plus. The ambulance arrived some twenty minutes later and found her "mortally wounded." They revived her at the scene and she was not taken to the hospital "for some time" (Source BBC TV news report). The doctors ceased working on her at 3.45 A.M., her official "death" (Source: Data Plus). Dodi Al Fayed was born April 15, 1955, 7.00, 31N12, 29E54. Time is not exact. Source: Data Plus quotes Diana as having given Taurus Rising to her astrologer Debbie Frank.

PLUTO TRANSITS AND THE HADES MOON

Pluto passing through the signs has a generational effect, and Pluto moving through the individual houses in a personal chart activates the issues of that house in a Plutonian way. But it is in the aspects that transiting Pluto makes to the natal Hades Moon that the potentially transforming energies most clearly make themselves felt.

GOING DOWN THE HOLE

Pluto transits take a long, long time to pass. Intimations can be picked up for anything up to two years before the transit is exact. This is where we enter Pluto's crucible. Putrefaction occurs. The alchemy begins. The transit itself will often take a year or so. We ferment. If we are willing to let go, our past experience vaporizes, making space for something other. Another two years are needed for the effects to work themselves through. If we have cooperated with the god, after purification comes transformation. If not, we may feel we have lost everything. So often the effect is a stripping away, a laying bare of the bones of the issue. Undealt with "stuff" emerges from the unconscious and demands to be recognized. Pluto transits show us the *prima materia* with which we are working and unlock its potential. We meet issues that we will confront again and again during this book. I well remember a graphic dream a client of mine reported:

> I was in a huge pit of shit, up to my neck in it. You were in there, shoveling with me.

Transiting Pluto was activating his natal T-square—Venus in opposition to the Moon square Pluto.

Little can be done at this stage. It is a question of being with the energies, of accepting that one must enter Hades, willingly or unwillingly, of sinking down into that primordial gloom—what an Aquarian friend of mine calls "going down the hole":

> In November '83 I went down the hole. Emotionally I was terrified all the time, but not of anything in particular. Every night for months and months and months I woke up in a sweat in the middle of the night. I didn't have any sense of humor and if someone had given me a million dollars I wouldn't have taken any notice, I was that rotten. There was one night when I half woke up and had an experience of going into a tunnel of light, the way people describe a near-death experience. I felt for a moment that that was it, I was dying. Ironically, I realized I had just paid my rent for the month but I didn't even find that funny.

Ronald (Chart 1, p. 21) has the Sun and Moon in early Aquarius widely inconjuncting Pluto (allowing an 8° orb for quincunxes). He has issues of isolation, alienation, not being in touch with his emotions, and a deep fear of chaos. He had been meditating for some years (Neptune) but had done no personal work on himself when, in November 1983, transiting Pluto entered Scorpio and began a long term square to natal Sun and Moon. Along with several other significant transits, he was also approaching his first Saturn return, that time of reassessment and reorientation. There was immense internal pressure from his so long ignored emotions. He was the Kore, or puer, skipping lightly over the earth. The time was ripe for a trip into Hades. An articulate Aquarian, he gives a graphic account of what it was like to be under that Pluto transit:

> I felt like I had really bad flu, no energy, not able to concentrate and feeling awful. This went on for three years. There was no particular worry, just being really tense and

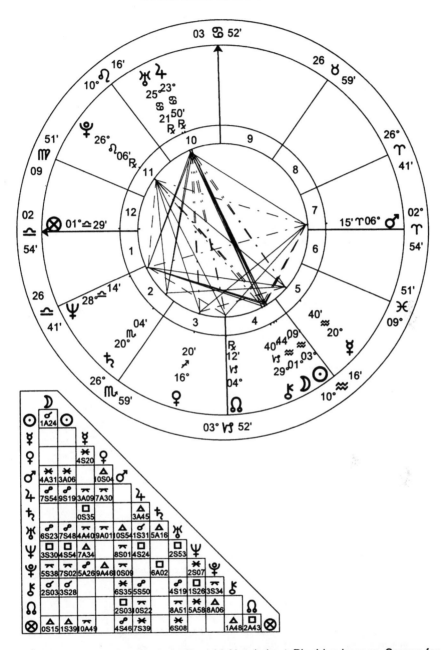

Chart 1. Going down the hole. Ronald. Natal chart. Placidus houses. Source for birth time: mother. Chart used by permission. Data withheld for confidentiality.

nervous and not being able to relax at all. The main thing was a permanent, unde-fined fear in everything and that was horrible. Not trusting and never feeling safe. I was alienated from everyone and everything. And yet there were many times when I had to be with people simply because I was so afraid and yet I couldn't connect with them. I felt totally isolated and not able to connect with anything. Nothing ever felt comfortable, it was always uncomfortable.

Mac was the only one who understood because he had been through it. He un-derstood but he had no sympathy at all. He'd go and get the Bach Flower remedies and say "That'll sort you out" and that was it. He would never listen but he did un-derstand about being down the hole because that was his expression. [Mac, whom we will meet later has an intimate acquaintance with the Hades Moon.] Most people did not really notice, which was quite strange.

That people "did not notice" is an interesting external manifestation of his Aquar-ian Moon detachedness and isolation. But finally, when he was coming out of the long-term effects he was able to get a more objective view through an understand-ing of astrology and myth:

Gradually it started to get better and it was toward the end of three or four years that I went to see Howard [Sasportas]. Before then I was too scared to go in case he said some-thing terrible was going on in my chart. He said it was the Sun-Moon square to tran-siting Pluto and told the story of the Hydra. When you cut its heads off it just grows more, so every time you cut one off it grows two in its place. That's not the way to deal with the Hydra. The way is to get in the swamp with it and to get down to its level and just to lift it, and its roots, so that it brings it out of the water. In that way you just be with the energy. You don't use the energy because that is like cutting its heads off and that is murderous energy. And you don't block and repress it because it will make you ill or kill you. It is just being there with it, being with the energy and knowing it. But, of course, at the time I didn't know all this and I didn't know it was transforming en-ergy. I just thought I was down the hole and that was it. I thought I would never come out again, because that is the feeling. It is all encompassing and all encasing.

Howard also spoke of Ereshkigal and the "balls of muck from under someone's finger nails." Whoever it was rolled into Ereshkigal's realm and saved her [sic]. That was going into the Plutonic hell but you couldn't walk in or you would not survive. In a way that's a bit similar to the Hydra one because it was like if you fight that energy, or direct it, then it would be destructive. It is a case of being aware of the energy, just being with it, which feels unnatural because when you are in that situation, you really want to do something about it and change it. Yet it is the situation itself that is doing the changing.

The Sumerian myth of Inanna and Ereshkigal[11] is the oldest written version of the descent into the Underworld, and one which shows the feminine, raging face of the Pluto energy. Inanna, the Queen of Heaven, decides to go into the Underworld: this is a voluntary descent. She visits her dark sister Ereshkigal, the Queen of the Great Below, whose husband is about to be buried. Ereshkigal insists that her sister follow the rite of entry into her realm. She is brought "naked and bowed low." At each of seven gates, Inanna is gradually stripped of her regalia. Her corpse is hung on a peg, where it rots. Her servant entreats help from Inanna's father, the Moon God, and also the Sky God. Both refuse to help. They know better than to interfere in the processes of the Underworld. Eventually Enki, the God of the Waters and Wisdom, fashions two small mourners from the dirt beneath his fingernails. They slip into the Underworld, carrying the water of life. They commiserate with Ereshkigal over her misery, and mourn with her. The mourners do nothing except reflect back to Ereshkigal the pain she is feeling. Comforted, Ereshkigal offers them a reward. They ask for the corpse of Inanna. Ereshkigal allows Inanna to return to the surface, on condition that a substitute is sent below. Inanna sends her husband, Dumuzi to the Underworld (the origin of the sacrifice, the "making sacred," of the male energy to impregnate the earth). When Inanna returns "above," to consciousness, she is revitalized with the waters of life. Angry and demonic she rages, all the instinctual energies are let loose. Then she calms into an acceptance of her new, initiated, self.

This image of Inanna hung on a peg to rot is both a powerful and ubiquitious one. An Aquarian teenage boy, who later became an innovative performance artist, painted a striking portrait of his beloved maternal grandmother—hung on a meathook and menaced by a fierce dog. At the time, his mother was divorcing his extremely eccentric father and his grandmother offered a place of refuge. However, the boy also blamed his conventional "suburban" grandmother for the marriage breakup. "She was always saying Dad was crazy and urged my mother to leave for our sake." Pluto can, as we shall see, stand for the grandmother just as much as for the mother. When he painted the portrait, transiting Pluto was conjunct his natal Libran Moon semi-sextile Pluto, neatly illustrating the duality and torn loyalties he found himself inhabiting.

I am always interested in how much of a myth is retained by someone who heard it sometime earlier, especially at a time of great internal distress. Ronald remembered the small beings who mourned, who shared the pain, which was exactly what he himself so needed and did not find until he had the consultation with Howard. His friend Mac, although knowing what it was like, did not listen and gave him remedies to kill the pain instead of helping him to be with it. Ronald also remembered it as the dark Ereshkigal who was saved, not the bright goddess of the upper world, Inanna. This was the part of his consciousness which he was recovering, the dark goddess and the instinctual energy symbolized by the Moon-Pluto connection.

His outer world was mirroring his inner psychic activity. In typical Aquarian fashion he had chosen a university doctorate that was way ahead of its time, and one that also reflected his overriding concern—Pluto. He channelled his intellectual energy into studying a subject pertinent to the experience he was undergoing—pollution control.

Ronald does, of course, have that natal T-square with Uranus-Jupiter, Sun-Moon and Neptune, and a finger of fate with Venus involved. This means that relationships have to be right on the physical, emotional, and mental levels or they would not be the special relationship he so desired. He said in 1994 that in all his relationships at least one of those levels was missing, so he still had not found the right partner. As transiting Uranus had conjuncted Venus during the period of the Pluto-Moon transit, I asked what happened to his relationships at that time:

> *Relationships were crap. Toward the end when I was coming out of the Pluto phase I went out with a rather whacky woman and that was OK because life was so bad that a bad relationship was quite good. Then in '86 I met Mary, who was expressive and impulsive. That was really good because it broke a lot of boundaries for me, a way of breaking out of being stuck. Previously I had been stuck and unable to move or make decisions because there was no life force there, I was drained.*

Acutely aware that the tendency of Aquarius is to severely repress any emotion, and especially painful ones, I also asked him what kind of Plutonian stuff had come up during the period of the transit:

> *My dad had been a really angry old bastard, not physically violent but a bad tempered, crotchety old crow [Pluto quincunx the 4th house Sun, Sun sextile Mars] and I used to say that our not getting on well was partly my fault [Neptune square Sun taking on the scapegoat role]. One day I was talking to my acupuncturist about my dad. She said: "Well if you think he was a fucking bastard, say so." I was quite shocked, I didn't expect her to speak like that. Two weeks later someone else said exactly the same and I realized I had been holding back all this anger [Natal Mars in Aries held in check by a "nice" Libra Ascendant, in addition to the festering rage of Moon-Pluto]. It was toward '85–'86 [when Pluto was quincunx natal Mars] that I started to do things to let go of anger. I could always get angry in certain situations but not others, so this was a time of realizing I was blocking anger. I started to let that out, which helped quite a lot. That was quite a big shift.*

Instead of remaining purely in his Aquarian head energy, he moved the energy into his body:

> *Pillow bashing helped, and running was excellent for getting energy physicalized and feeling it again because I think the whole thing about that time was that it was a time of nonfeeling, apart from feeling bloody miserable. Then I started playing football again and if I was angry I would play much better, because I would have much more energy. Doing the Mastery Workshop at the Actors Institute in '87 [when Pluto had retrograded back to within a degree of quincunxing Mars again] was good because we did some really good anger exercises and I was ready for that then. Ready for going ape-shit with anger and keeping it flowing. It's not just short bursts, you keep on doing it for a long time and that's a brilliant way of letting it go. But then if you do too much of that it can leave you feeling really raw and rough.*

I asked him what had come out of the transit:

> *The single biggest thing that I realized at the end of that was that I didn't need to repress emotions as much as I had done, and I probably still don't, and that was what came out of it. The whole thing felt like years of blocked emotion, every kind of emotion, just bursting to get out.*

And finally we came to the crux of that 4th house Moon inconjunct to Pluto:

It all related back to my mother dying of cancer when I was 14 and my brother committing suicide when I was 21, and then my father going mad and dying when I was about 25. I didn't express any emotion at the time in relation to any of these things except I cried once when my mother died. So none of that emotion had been dealt with—that was the intellectual connection I made. The emotion suddenly came out as these horrible feelings, eventually as anger. By recognizing that the anger was blocked energy, getting angry was easier for me to release than crying. The feeling at the time was that I would never be right again, that I would always be suffering from the fear and tension, and even thinking about it now feels horrible [he had had to put himself in a protective pink bubble to tell me about it].

Since then the biggest things have been a continuation of learning how to express and how to be with feelings, instead of fighting things off or fighting with them or whatever. Allowing is the best descriptive term I can find of how best to deal with blocked feelings. Allowing things to happen, allowing things to be, or move or whatever, rather than trying to control and hold. For a lot of that time back in '83–'84 I felt I was being held and gripped. I couldn't just feel and flow and relax, it was gripping and horrible.

The other thing, of course, is being able to understand other people's miseries much better once you have been through something like that yourself. A lot of the times people have problems or unpleasant feelings or are going through emotional traumas and nothing has actually happened, events are just attached to feelings rather than causing them. After three or four years of that, it makes it much easier to help other people.

Ronald then combined two extremely Plutonian occupations. He researched pollution control, and he became a therapist who took his clients into some very deep and dark places indeed. Knowing the territory intimately, he was not afraid of the underworld he encountered. In 1996 when Pluto sextiled the Sun-Moon conjunction and Uranus conjuncted it, Ronald renewed his relationship with Mary, a Scorpio who had been into Hades herself and survived. He suddenly packed in a highly stressful job and moved "Down Under," ending his Aquarian isolation by joining his old lover. After a year, they married, something he would never have believed possible in 1983. He became a highly successful full-time therapist, a much more positive use of his Plutonian energies.

There does not have to be a direct natal connection between Pluto and the Moon for Hades Moon issues to surface during Pluto transits. This is especially so if the natal Moon is in Scorpio (a Hadean Moon in itself). A young man found that his maternal grandfather, who had brought him up, died when transiting Pluto conjuncted his Scorpio Moon, precipitating yet another breakdown in his mentally unstable mother, and throwing him at age 15 onto his own inner and outer resources. However, transiting Pluto moved on and, at age 22, when transiting Pluto sextiled natal Pluto, his birth-father, whom he had not seen for twenty-one years, suddenly phoned to say his paternal grandmother was dying and wanted to see him. This precipitated contact with his absent father, opening the way for a healing and reconciliation of all the pain held within that Scorpio Moon and his difficult aspects to the Sun.

A HARD GIFT

In a more direct connection, transiting Pluto conjuncting natal Chiron brought out all the underlying hadean woundedness in an Aquarian Moon opposite Pluto and square the Sun configuration, which sat across the Ascendant, Descendant, MC of a chart (see figure 6, below). The full depth of the pain, and an opportunity for healing, suddenly became apparent:

> *I began to slide into a kind of depression. The explosion that then occurred took me for three months into the darkest and most terrifying states I have ever experienced: dismemberment, disempowerment, primal rage, humiliation, inner and outer abandonment, helplessness and terror, past-life recall, infant memories and visions of the archetypal realms. My healing began when I paid attention to what my energy system was saying and I made a separation which felt like a great disappointment and loss. I know I must now embrace my independence and self-sufficiency, but it was a hard gift indeed. My life has been completely shattered. These discharges are now nearly complete and I am aware I am at another level of experience and a new beginning.*

Up until the transit, in accordance with the Aquarian Moon on the Ascendant, all the pain had been reflected "out there" onto therapy clients (Sun on the MC and Chiron in the 10th house of career). With the transit, the inner pain could no longer be ignored and she was thrown in on herself to deal with it. She was initiated into the underworld that was her natural home. When I sent her this piece for approval, she wrote back "Oh, how I longed for those little beings to come and be with me, to keep me company while I too hung on Inanna's peg and suffered with

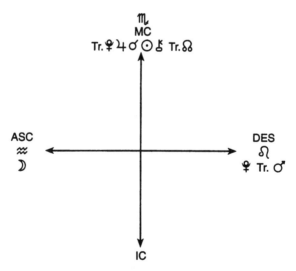

Figure 6. A hard gift. Transiting Pluto activating a Fixed Grand Cross.

Persephone in that Underworld." The experience did, however, herald a breakthrough at all levels of her life.

TRUSTING THE PROCESS

Not all Pluto transits are as extended, or as traumatic. For those who are at home with Pluto, the intensity of the transit remains, but the effect can be extremely creative and transformative, although some emotional angst almost always surfaces. Louise, whom we will meet later (see p. 252), is a Sun Scorpio with Pluto square Venus and trine the Moon. There is, however, no direct aspect between Venus and the Moon: Pluto provides the link. Her transit experiences were very different, and yet were equally Plutonian. When transiting Pluto neared her natal Sun, she went into an intense "shit or bust" relationship. Just days after the transit became exact for the third time (owing to retrograde action) she went into an equally intense, three-week period of grieving and emotional trauma as the relationship broke up. But she found this a positive experience. She "observed what was going on, stayed with the feelings, took time off from work and stayed with it; knew that this was Pluto and it must involve the depths of being." As a Scorpio, and an astrologer, she was familiar with the territory.

When she came to see me, just as the relationship was disintegrating, the most helpful thing I was able to do for her was to say: "Yes, this is how it is when you have this transit." I acted as the little creatures from under Enki's fingernails did for Ereshkigal, reflecting back how Plutonian she was feeling without trying to do any therapy or healing with her. I knew, and she knew, she needed to be there with it. She later said that it was this *knowing* that enabled her to move through it, that and the fact that someone else recognized how she was feeling. She now hopes to apply the insights she gained to a new relationship, and she already utilizes them in her astrological counselling work. When transiting Pluto opposed her Moon some time earlier, it was "one of the most creative experiences of my life. I got my physics degree, and came off drugs." She was literally reborn. When Pluto transited her Venus again recently, and indirectly triggered her Hades Moon, her mother was found to have terminal cancer. We will look at how Louise dealt with this in a later chapter.

Another example of a positive experience with Pluto transits came from Malcolm. Natally, he has the Sun unaspected in early Scorpio, and Mercury conjunct the Ascendant toward the end of Scorpio. He also has a Finger of Fate with Pluto inconjunct the Moon in Pisces, Saturn and Neptune inconjunct the Moon, and an outlet point formed from the Midheaven which opposes the Moon conjunct the IC. Malcolm, an old client, wrote to me following the breakup of a relationship, outlining what had been happening to him as transiting Pluto and Jupiter went over his Ascendant-Mercury, squared natal Pluto and trined his Moon (figure 7, page 28). At the same time, transiting Chiron was conjuncting his Midheaven, the outlet point for the Finger of Fate:

> *There is so much happening in my life, on an interior and exterior level, that I feel as if I were on a bus traveling very fast. Until I get some sense of arrival, some clearer*

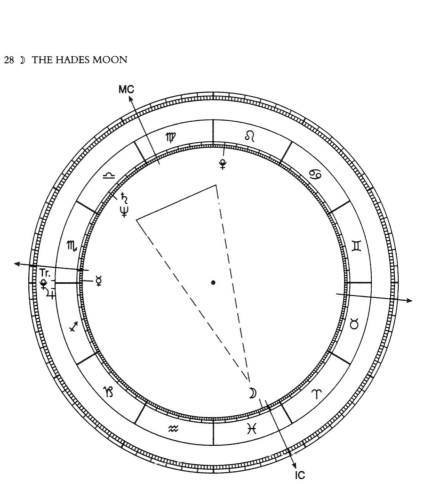

Figure 7. Trusting the process. The Finger of Fate and the transits of Jupiter and Pluto. Data used by permission.

sense of who I actually am, there doesn't seem to be much point in trying to renegotiate the relationship [which had broken up]. I think I have shut large segments of myself out of consciousness and consequently out of the two major relationships in my life so far. These are coming out forcefully now, demanding to be recognized and integrated. I have been getting very clear, and helpful, dreams. An image that recurred in my writing was of the twin who was killed or committed suicide. I suppose that stands for the suppressed part of me that is now waking up. All in all it feels like an incredibly positive period although there is a tremendous amount of fear and anxiety around which shades into excitement. I'm regaining lots of space inside and outside myself.

My relationship had been frustrating on a sexual level and I just don't want to put up with that any longer. Sexual needs of a different kind, which I have never been prepared to act on before, are demanding that I acknowledge them and seek satisfaction. Part of my feeling positive is that I seem to have a much better idea of what a relationship is, about the mutual fulfilling of needs, leaving space, and acknowledging that you can't be everything to each other. My suppressed dark side means that I have spent a lot of time in relationships denying myself and trying to shield the other from *the possible damage I might do them. Now I want to put all of me into a relationship and I know how much I need (and deserve!) love, physical contact, sexual nurturing, and attention and satisfaction. Another good feeling is that now the dark twin is out of the bag, my next relationship will be much more sensual, more exciting, and connected to myself as a creative person.*

I'm also learning to TRUST THE PROCESS and LIVE THE QUESTIONS. So I know it would be quite unhelpful for you to tell me what is going to happen. But can you help me to live it all more consciously and richly and to honor but not be frozen by my fears?"

We will meet the issues raised in these transits as we dig deeper into the Hades Moon. As the "devouring aspect" is the one that we must face at birth, and sometimes in utero, we will start with the mothering issues. But first it will be helpful to delve into mythology for a little more light on Hades and the gods and goddesses who inhabit its realms.

CHAPTER 2

THE MYTHIC MOON

The two worlds, the divine and the human . . . are actually one. The realm of the gods is a forgotten dimension of the world we know.

—Joseph Campbell[1]

MYTH IS A DIRECT ROUTE into the Plutonian Underworld. Present day depth psychologists and mythographers are rediscovering the link between myth and our inner psychic reality. Regression therapists, another part of my work, meet it all the time. Myth is a guide to the contents of consciousness at all levels, particularly the layers that lie outside everyday awareness—what we now term the unconscious mind. It is yet another example of "As above, so below; as within, so without." The archetypal psychologist James Hillman has said that: "The underworld has gone into the unconscious, even become the unconscious,"[2] but the Underworld always has been the unconscious. The archaic myths are "maps of the unconscious" just as the natal chart maps our inner psychic reality. Both myth and astrology offer us ways to truly know ourselves, in all our hadean depth.

To name this place the subconscious or unconscious mind, or even the collective unconsciousness, does not mean that it, and therefore we, do not *know*. Unconscious is not unaware or non-sentient. The Underworld has awareness and a consciousness of its own. We do not recognize this unless we take the time to listen and learn its language—dreams, myth, metaphor, and astrology.

Indeed, the language of both myth and the collective unconscious is symbol and imagery. It should not be taken literally. The meaning must be teased out through our intuitive perception, by unspoken glimpses of another reality. This other reality is our psychic heritage, the place where the personal unconscious of the Moon and the collective unconscious of Pluto unite. This is the place of myth and the home of the gods: the point where the astrological and the mythological meet. Mythographer Robert Calasso has said that these myths are still "out there," waiting to be seen by us so that they can awaken us."[3] I would argue that the myths are still all around us and "in here," within our own selves. For our ancestors there was no separation between Underworld and unconscious; they were one and the same, and so it is for us.

Greek myth, to which astrologers have turned for illumination, and the philosophical system which emerged from it, owed much to Egypt. The Greek pantheon incorporated many aspects of Egyptian deities. The *Book of what is in the Duat*, one of the Egyptian so-called *Books of the Dead* has been translated *The Book of what is in the Underworld*. It can equally be seen as a guide to the archetypes and gods who inhabit (un)consciousness, and to our experiences as we journey through the dark places of our own minds. It is only an increasing intellectualization that has created the apparent split. To our forefathers—and mothers—it was one and the same. It is through myth that the contents of the unconscious are brought back into our consciousness.

In ancient times the myths were re-enacted as temple rituals and later in the theaters as sacred psychological dramas in which the initiates/audience were totally involved in a participation mystique of shared experience and intuitive recognition. Myth is the dramatization of the contents of consciousness in all its forms. Over the centuries the myths were subtly altered, reflecting new perceptions and concerns. But the basic truths remained. "Mythical figures live many lives, die many deaths. . . . But in each of these lives and deaths all the others are present and we can hear their echo. Only when we become aware of a sudden consistency between incompatibles can we say we have crossed the threshold of myth."[4] To see Oedipus kill his father and lie with his mother is to recreate the psychic truth of that part of the Moon-Pluto astrological aspect that must break free from ancestral patterns and re-unite with the inner feminine. To journey with Persephone to meet Pluto is to make the inner separation from the mother and reach individuation. To meet the Erinnyes as they exact vengenace is to reconnect to a different face of the Hades Moon, and of the psyche. So, through exploring myth and our own psyches we can learn much about the archetypal and astrological energies that we recognize as Moon and Pluto.

A MODEL OF CONSCIOUSNESS

Figure 8 (page 32) shows a model of consciousness which incorporates all the discrete parts within the whole. When drawn, the model has to be flat, but it is in reality multidimensional. Higher consciousness surrounds and touches every part, rather like the skull enclosing the brain. We experience these different facets of consciousness through our psyche, an integrating force related to personality, ego, and conscious mind, but which has its roots in the inner Self. Unifying all is the eternal, spiritual Self which encompasses, but is not limited by, the transdimensional levels of consciousness.

Like "mind," consciousness does not have a physical location in the body. But, I find it useful to connect it to certain physical points so that I ground it in the body. In this book, when I speak of "higher" or "lower" energies, this is not a judgmental term. Words get in the way when contemplating symbols and any view of consciousness can only be symbolic. So, to put into words what is really beyond words, I visualize consciousness in terms of frequencies. The spiritual frequency is vibrating much faster; it is literally a higher vibration; and the unconscious energies vibrate at a lower vibration; with everyday awareness somewhere in the middle of the scale. Like a musical scale, these vibrations resonate with each other. The apparently disparate parts seem subject to dissonance simply because they have not been tuned to each other.

In this model, everyday awareness consists of two totally dissimilar ways of perceiving the world, each controlled by a different part of the brain. The left brain is

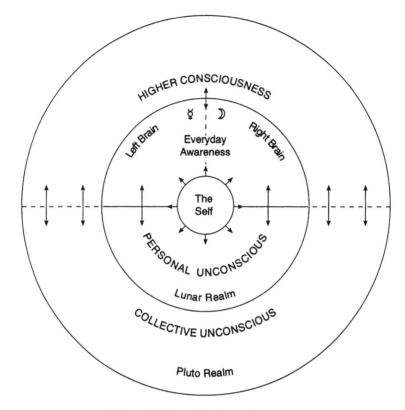

Figure 8. A model of consciousness.

linear, language oriented. It is essentially mercurial—logical, analytic, and rational. It is concerned with reasoning, intellect, sequences, abstraction, and categories. It is time-oriented, and plans and judges within clearly defined parameters. I see this as the "masculine" side of the brain. The right brain is "feminine." It is essential lunar—non-verbal, dealing in images, metaphors, and feelings. This is the place where myth resides. It is the seat of the intuition, dreams, and ideas. It is holistic and synthesizing. It is outside time, and, although it has spatial perception, it has no rigid boundaries. The personal unconscious, the lunar level of Hades, lies "below" everyday awareness: that is, it resonates at a deeper frequency. If we want to locate the unconscious physically, we could say it was in the brain stem, that ancient, primitive part of the brain buried deep within the cerebral cortex. This is the seat of instinctual behavior and survival mechanisms. Deeper still in terms of vibration lies the collective unconscious; the Plutonian level of Hades, home of myth and archetype. But, just because we call it the unconscious, we should not look at this realm as a seething mass of nescient instincts and incoherent primordial drives. Jung emphasized the wisdom of the unconscious. It is this realm which hides within it the blueprint not only for our behavioral patterns, but also for our spiritual evolution.

"Higher" consciousness, which is resonating at a faster frequency, not only surrounds everyday awareness but also meets and encompasses the collective unconscious. If we want a location to focus on, we can look to the crown chakra at the top of the head, although of course this is an energy center, not a physical body. That the higher consciousness merges with the unconscious is very clear to anyone who has ever meditated or utilized creative visualization. Symbols and archetypes arise from the unconscious, making themselves known during this work. Clearly there is a viable pathway between the two. The personal unconscious, too, is linked to spiritual consciousness. Beginners in meditation usually experience old emotions "erupting" out of the personal unconscious. So, consciousness interpenetrates itself.

THE PLACE WHERE ASTROLOGY AND MYTH UNITE

Each planet and sign is not only literally connected with an Olympian god or deity, but with an archetypal psychodynamic force. They are part of the world, of the universe, and must be part of us.

—Richard Idemon[5]

Astrologically, much has been written on the Moon, less on Pluto as befits one of the newer and least understood of the planets. This is as it should be. In mythology, Pluto was concealed by his helmet of invisibility whenever he ventured above ground. His most (in)famous act, the abduction of Persephone, was typically Plutonian—treacherous, earth-shattering and deeply transformative. It invoked the great mysteries of life. It is a metaphor for the dark and devious energies that lie far below our conscious awareness, and which suddenly break into the light of consciousness with cataclysmic effect. It is where we are forced to relinquish control. There is a certain quirkiness to Pluto which is apparent in how the planet got its name. Having originally been named for the man who found it, it was then called Pluto, not after the mythological figure but, apparently, after the Walt Disney dog of that name!

That Pluto's discovery was so soon followed by the development of atomic power, unleashing the potential for nuclear holocaust, is also extremely relevant to our experience of the astrological Pluto. Cathartic Pluto transits take us down into our own depths and bring us face to face with all that is taboo and alien in ourselves, all that we have repressed. The taboo we face here is not the "off-limits" of Saturn, but rather all that is sacred and set aside within us, all that lies beyond the boundaries of the known. It is a place of danger where all manner of terrors wait to be unleashed, the home of demons which, with childish omnipotence, we fear might just destroy the world. It is also a place of terrifying potential, the enormity of which may overwhelm us at any moment as it did with Persephone. Pluto is where we plunge into the void to seek our lost innocence. Innocence is not a state of unawareness; it is our primal knowing, pure and complete, encompassing everything. And, as Charles Carter has pointed out, Pluto transits are a "resurrection of things past and half forgotten." Pluto transits pinpoint our moments of soul growth, point us to an initiation that begins with our symbolic or metaphoric death and are completed by our resurrection to new life. Hades is where the toxic boil of our past experience is lanced. It is where we are purified and healed in the fires of our experience. Anarchic Pluto is the planet of psychological enlightenment, and of the collective unconscious. Pluto's discovery also coincided with the development of depth psychology and mass genocide. Pluto's placement in the chart shows where we are linked into the greater whole and how we will express the collective energies in our life. The collective is the breeding ground for myth, and myth reflects the universal truths that are part of our collective experience. To understand myth is to understand what it is to be fully human.

THE PLUTO-HADES MYTH

The Pluto-Persephone-Demeter myth embodies many of the central themes of the Hades Moon: birth, death and rebirth; the devouring mother and the need to relinquish control; betrayal and abandonment, grief and devastation, treasure and transformation, the rapist and the descent into the Underworld, to name but a few. Persephone's abduction was also her initiation into womanhood. And, despite, in the best tradition of Moon-Pluto mothers, Demeter's manipulative and possessive efforts to keep the psychic umbilical cord tied tight, Persephone was at home in the Underworld. In subequent tales, none of the Greek heroes who went to call on her ever found a sign saying: "Gone home to mother." Indeed, in the earliest matriarchal versions of the myth, it is Persephone who voluntarily descends into the Underworld to initiate the dead into their new world because they have no one to care for them. This is the period before there were patriarchal gods and there is no mention of Pluto in this myth. Persephone is Queen of the Underworld in her own right, as an aspect of the Great Mother Goddess. She takes with her poppies, pomegranate seeds, and bread. As she greets each soul and annoints them with the juice, she says:

> You have waxed into the fullness of life
> And waned into darkness
> May you be renewed in tranquility and wisdom.

In this version of the myth, Demeter, the Grain-Mother, still mourns and leaves the earth barren through the winter period. But in the Spring, Persephone returns of her own volition. The corn sprouts and mother and daughter are reunited. This was an age when the separate functions of consciousness were far less differentiated. The intuitive matriarchal religion was naturally in touch with both the inner and outer reality, and initiates of the mystery religions also voluntarily entered the Underworld. The rape of Persephone, and the introduction of Pluto into the myth, came about with the change from a matriarchal to patriarchal religion. The patriarchy was much less comfortable with the notion of an Underworld, a lunar realm. So a stern and pitiless god was put in charge to watch over this fearsome place. Boundaries were placed around the unconscious.

   If we want to know how Pluto functions, we, too, must go down into Hades; the Underworld of Greek myth and the burning-ground of all our illusions. The

Underworld was a shadowy place, but one which could be communicated with, indeed visited and, occasionally, returned from. This journey was made by all the great heroes. They did not go because they had died, but rather because they sought the transformative gifts to be found there. Gifts for which Persephone, as consort and Queen of the Underworld, performed the acts of mediation and way-shower.

The word Pluto comes from the latin word *pluton* meaning riches. Although linked to buried treasure, Pluto's wealth was much more than this. From his abode under the ground he was believed to not only rule the dead but also to influence the fertility of the earth and the crops which grew upon it. Pluto was therefore intimately bound up in the whole procreation cycle—birth, death and rebirth. He can be seen as the god of creativity, and indeed his mother was Rhea, an earth goddess, herself daughter of the Great Mother, Gaia "the deep-breasted earth." As Haydn Paul has pointed out, the earliest goddess images "emphasized a self-fertilizing deity, a phallic Mother who receded deeper into her own depths and dark mysteries, leaving her phallic potency to be invested in her God-son."[6] Pluto was in direct line of descent.

THE UNDERWORLD

Pluto was Lord of the Underworld, the abode of the dead. In Greek myth, he is Hades, also the name of his realm. In part it is a mournful, sunless region where the souls of the dead take refuge while awaiting rebirth. In another aspect, it is a blessed place where souls find benediction. In the great epic poems it is seen as a kind of limbo, lying beyond the edge of the earth, which was encircled by a great river. Later it came to be viewed as somewhere in the center of the earth, accessible through caves, fissures, volcanoes, and other fearsome, Plutonian places. Few things grew in this desolate land beyond some black poplars and a few willows, although this was also modified as time went on. The favorite food of the dead, Asphodel, a funeral plant of ruins and cemeteries whose name means *scepter*, was reputed to grow there. Interestingly, the medicinal properties of this herb are "acrid, heating and diuretic,"[7] and it is said to be useful in menstrual obstruction and as an antispasmodic: all conditions closely linked to the eliminative and procreative attributes of the astrological Pluto and the nature of his realm.

Access to Hades was also possible through its rivers. These rivers are the powerful instinctual forces of the unconscious mind, and signify that which we must leave behind, or transmute, as we enter Pluto's realm. The Acheron, derived from "affliction," is the river of sadness flowing into the Coctuys, the wailing river of lamentation. This is where the traveler faces endings, separation, and loss, with its consequent grief and mourning process. The Styx, or river of poison, is where we face our bitterness, resentment, rage, and desire for revenge. The Phlegethon is where we burn in the addictive fires of our unsatisfied and insatiable desires; and the Aornis, or "birdless" river, is where we must face our hopelessness and leave behind our earth-bound nature. Lost souls were mercifully dipped into the Lethe, or river of forgetfulness, before being reborn. As Gandhi said: "It is nature's kindness that we do not remember past births. . . . Life would be a burden if we carried such a tremendous load of memories. A wise man deliberately forgets many things."[8]

However, in order to rediscover our true wisdom, we may later need to reconnect to the lost memories of Pluto's realm.

To reach the Underworld, souls of the dead traversed one or more of these rivers. But their tribulations were not yet over. At some point in their journey they met Charon, the ferryman, a difficult man to deal with. If the dead, or the living, did not have the fare ready, they would be condemned to wander as "shades" throughout eternity. Before reaching the Kingdom of Hades, the traveler had to cross the Grove of Persephone. Here the goddess would meet supplicants who came to beg her aid in their heroic undertakings. Here, too, they would meet their last obstacle before being received by "He who receives so many." Cerberus, a monstrous watchdog, dripped venom from his several heads, but fortunately had a penchant for honey cakes. Cerberus was eventually overcome by Hercules, who lifted him up into the light, symbolizing the vanquishment of our fears by the light of consciousness. This slaying of the guardian opened the way for the process of inner transformation to begin. It created a space where previously there had been something monstrous and unspeakable. "The slaying of monsters . . . leaves an evocative vacuum where before there was a clutter, thick with heads and tentacles, a scaly arabesque."[9]

Having reached Hades, the soul was judged by Pluto and his assessors in a ritual which owed much to ancient Eqypt and the Lord of the Dead, Osiris. Those who were fortunate and who had lived "good" lives, were sent to the Elysian Fields or the Isles of the Blessed—the part of the consciousness that is accessible and "light." Those not so fortunate, and particularly those who had angered the gods in some way, were sent to Tartarus, a doomful realm with imaginative tortures— that part of consciousness which forms the human shadow. We also have to face our shadow qualities when we enter Hades. Our shadow qualities are all those unacceptable facets of ourselves that we have rejected and relegated out of conscious awareness into our own personal underworld; together with our unlived potential, all the opportunities for growth that we have not taken.

In Hades we must also face all that has been collectively relegated to the nether regions over aeons of time. This is the old meaning and function of purgatory, and hell.

Appropriately, Tartarus was surrounded by the Burning River of Desire, the Phlegethon. The damned were eternally tormented by their insatiable desires, a psychological state not unfamiliar today. They went through a process of purification which would, ultimately, lead to their rebirth. And, of course, everyone who lived in the Underworld had faced, and transcended, the boundaries of their mortality. Pluto's gift, or curse, depending on your point of view and how far you have traveled through Hades, is immortality and knowledge of one's own indestructability.

Other denizens of the Underworld included Thanatos, the god of death, and his brother Hypnos, the god of sleep. In esoteric understanding, we are sleeping until we awaken to our "higher" nature; that is, until we become fully conscious of all the parts of ourself. Hypnos' son was Morpheus, the god of dreams, one of the ways in which the unconscious communicates with us. Although Thanatos was occasionally portrayed in his sinister aspect, he was more usually represented as a winged spirit, the kindly face of death. Thanatos was rarely directly involved in bringing death. Once the Fates had decreed the hour of a man's demise, the Keres, otherwise known as the dogs of Hades because of their liking for fresh blood, would "seize the unhappy mortal, deliver the decisive blow, and carry him down to the land of shadows."[10] The equally fearsome Erinnyes had a special mission. They punished parricides (father-killers) and oath-breakers. As Howard Sasportas once pointed out,[11] when the outer-world parents have been vanquished through psychological process and the inner-world archetypal parents have been integrated into the whole person, "fate" often seems to bring vengeance rather than reward for this heroic act. However, as Orestes found out, when approached with respect, and due reverence, the Erinnyes finally transformed into the Eumenides, the Benevolent Ones—or "Kindly Ladies" as they were named by Athene, the goddess of wisdom, when she honored them in her land in return for Orestes' life.

A frequent visitor to Hades was Hermes, or Mercury, who acted as psychopomp, conductor of souls to the land of the dead. He could freely travel between the different realms. Mercury is, of course, connected to the mind and the intellect and is the messenger of the gods. The waning-moon goddess Hecate was also a "dweller on the threshold," who was to be found in caves and crossroads. She is another ancient goddess who was incorporated into the Greek hierarchy and she has a part to play in the Hades Moon saga as we shall see later.

THE LORD OF THE UNDERWORLD

Pluto/Hades had a very troubled childhood. In fact, he could be said to come from the archetypal disfunctional family. One of the six children of the incestuous marriage of Rhea and Cronus (Saturn), he was swallowed at birth. His father had been told by an oracle that he would be supplanted by one of his children. This was a family pattern as his father, Uranus, had been castrated and reduced to impotence by his son, leaving that son, Cronus/Saturn, to reign. The Greek myth of how chaos and anarchy (Uranus) is vanquished by order and time (Saturn) is an ancient one, echoing the earlier Egyptian creation story and all Egyptian temple ritual was concerned with keeping chaos "in its proper place." Chaos and order are inherent and indivisible; the whole of life is a cycle of rising and falling, birth and death, beginning and ending. This is a physical and physiological truth, as well as a psychological one, and the whole Hades saga is an allegory for our inner process and that of the earth on which we live.

The earth mother, Rhea had had three girls, Demeter (who will shortly make her appearance in the story), Hestia, and Hera; and two boys, Hades and Poseidon (Neptune), all of whom had been swallowed. When she became pregnant again she begged her parents, Uranus and Gaia, to help her save the child. Having birthed the baby deep in a cavern in Crete, she entrusted him to Gaia. Rhea handed her husband an enormous stone wrapped in swaddling clothes, which he duly swallowed. The new child, Zeus or Jupiter, was brought up by his grandparents. He was wet-nursed by the goat Amaltheia, from whom came the Jupitarian horn of plenty, or cornucopia, a symbol later to be associated with Hades as well as Zeus. Zeus was a lineage-breaker, a dismemberer of family patterns. As soon as he was grown to manhood, Zeus forced Cronus/Saturn to regurgitate his children. According to

Homer, Cronus was driven from the sky and chained in the region beneath the earth. His realm was divided up. Zeus/Jupiter took Mount Olympus, the abode of the gods, and also the earth. Poseidon/Neptune inherited the watery realm. Hades/Pluto became absolute ruler of everything under the earth. It would appear that Hades, therefore, had control over his father, who was repressed and enchained somewhere in the depths of Hades. This new pattern may well have contributed to Pluto's myth. He was a loner, seldom visiting above-ground and, as we shall see, seemingly had little of the social skills which enabled him to find a mate. In two other myths, his intended mates elude him. In the end, he resorted to abduction and rape to gain his queen, Persephone.

However, Robert Calasso has uncovered a fascinating Pluto myth in the *Callimacheus Hymns*, which reveals a different side to the god and his sexual experiences. It concerns his relationship with the Sun god, Apollo, who was twin brother to Artemis, a Moon goddess. They were the product of another disfunctional family in that Zeus/Jupiter had seduced their mother. She was then pursued by his wife Hera seeking vengeance (although in the most ancient versions, Zeus was married to their mother at the time of their conception but abandoned her for Hera, a most Plutonian experience). Apollo's relationship with Zeus was always problematic and Zeus had particular reason to fear Apollo. Prometheus, he who had stolen fire from the gods and therefore given humankind self-sufficiency, had prophesied that a son of Zeus would one day usurp his father. Zeus, of course, came from a deeply imbedded family pattern of parricide. Apollo was a very bright god indeed. He was the "solar light" rather than the Sun itself, which was represented by Helios who, in yet another Egyptian reflection, drove the chariot of the Sun across the sky each day. Helios sheds light on everyone and everything, and can be seen as universal consciousness and the creative fire of life itself. Apollo is much more personal, the individual Self of the astrological Sun. He is where the creative energy is made manifest, where self-consciousness begins. Apollo can also be seen in the puer archetype, the eternally youthful golden child. But, as we shall see, even the puer has to venture into Hades at some time, and the spur is usually love.

The god Apollo was prone to fatal love affairs with young men, and to problems with his father. Apollo also has an old feud with death. His son, Asclepius, a healer, brought a man back from the dead but, for reasons we need not to go into here, it is Apollo who is punished. Zeus was going to hurl him into Tartarus but relented and sent him to be a servant to Admetus, "King of Pherea in Thessaly." Thessaly's presiding deity was Hecate, "the night roaming goddess who rends the darkness with her torches," the dark phase of the Moon, and who has a role in the great Persephone mystery. Apollo had to stay with Admetus a "Great Year," until the stars returned to their original positions. This was identified by Robert Calasso as "a nine year period" but it may well have had another, more symbolic meaning. It may have corresponded to the Platonic or astrological "Great Year" of one revolution through the constellations, which takes 25,920 years. Certainly, it could be connected with yet another representation of the Sun "dying" and being absent for a ritual period. But it may also be mythologizing a great psychological truth.

Admetus was handsome, famous for his herds of cattle, loved sumptuous feasts and was famed for his hospitality. Apollo, who served him as a simple herdsman, became "inflamed by love for young Admetus" and foresook his lyre to play on a simple reed pipe. Seemingly, Admetus returned his love and "granted him favors." Admetus also, apparently paid the Sun God for his services. Apollo is thus the first "rent boy" in Greek myth. In the Hymns and certain of the Greek plays, Apollo persuades Admetus' wife to take her husband's place when it is his time to die. In so doing, Apollo saves the Lord of the Dead from death itself. Robert Calasso identifies Admetus and his "lovely wife" as no less than Hades and Persephone. Here we see a different face of Hades, one who is warmly attractive, hospitable and able to attract great love, even to the point of his wife being ready to sacrifice herself on his behalf. As Robert Calasso says, this is where we learn what the *kore* (Persephone) failed to tell us, that the "god of the invisible" is a lover as well as an abductor.[12] Here we see just how seductive the shadow qualities can be, especially when they are projected out onto a "lover" in the exterior world. If Robert Calasso is right, we also see here the light of personal consciousness, the puer-like Sun God Apollo, himself going down into Hades, the unconscious, and prostituting himself to its ruler, Death. As we shall see, in addiction and other Hades Moon situations, personal consciousness can become infatuated with the Bringer of Enlightenment. But, the creative core is transformed through relationship with the unconscious.

To return to the main Pluto myth, in some versions it is suggested that Aphrodite (Venus), the goddess of love, decided that cold-hearted Pluto needed warming up and secretly struck him with passion for Persephone, the daughter of his sister Demeter. Demeter had, in keeping with the machinations and complexity of the Greek gods, been seduced by her brother Zeus in his favorite guise of a bull. In some early myths Demeter was married to Zeus before he wed Hera. In others, he took the form of a giant serpent to couple with Demeter in a re-creation of the primal creation myth. A myth which is in itself a barely remembered glimpse of life in the womb. Persephone was a product of their union. Demeter was the goddess of earth in the sense of fertile and cultivated soil and of its fruits, such as grain. She is actually a much older fertility goddess who had, as with so many others, been incorporated into the Greek pantheon. Persephone, or Kore, is her "underworld," seed self, and it is probable that the two goddesses were once one. However, as part of the development of separate self-consciousness, Demeter had to meet her own projection: Kore, a young innocent girl. Consciousness could observe itself in the act of differentiation. In her own rape and abduction, Demeter had stayed "above ground." Now, in the guise of Kore, she must venture below. She returns as the mature, initiated Persephone ("she who must be feared"). The cycle is complete. Other versions of the abduction of Persephone story, including the Homeric Hymns, claim that Pluto and her father Zeus connived together to ensure that Pluto could snatch the virginal Persephone (whose name also means "she who destroys the light") from her mother's overzealous care: an archetypal act of betrayal by the all-powerful male which rebounded into the Kore taking up her own personal power.

MOTHER AND MAIDEN

The Demeter-Persephone story is the myth of the maiden, mother, and crone: the triple aspects of generation, preservation and destruction: the cycle of life. It is also a story of the "empty nest syndrome," of letting go and of reconciliation, the archetypal mother and daughter tale which has much significance for the Hades Moon.

When we meet Demeter, she is Mother (the Full Moon) and her maiden aspect (the New Moon) is personified by her daughter, Kore (meaning girl) or Persephone. Demeter is one of the fertility goddesses who gives birth to the son who becomes her consort. However, she is perhaps best known as the archetypal "one parent family" in the role of mother to Persephone and it is this aspect on which the myth centers. Persephone is, naturally enough, a beautiful maiden who is desired by Pluto and he plots her abduction with her father, Zeus. One moment she is innocently picking flowers with her companions. The next, as she puts out her hand to a particularly beautiful flower, the earth opens beneath her feet and Pluto emerges in his chariot, snatches her up, and takes her to his kingdom.

This is one of the few times that Pluto appears without the helmet which renders him invisible. For once, the conscious self can see what it is that emerges from the Underworld of the unconscious. Here is the unexpected trauma, the drama that suddenly pulls us down into the depths of our own being. Here is the rapist, translated in the 20th century world into the therapist, who accompanies the journey down into Hades, the unconscious. If we do not go willingly, rape or abuse, physical or psychological, may well be the trigger for our own descent. Interestingly enough, Persephone's abduction is witnessed by two deities: Helios, the Sun God, symbolic of the universal Self and the impersonal light of the collective consciousness; and the crone Hecate, the mature face of the Moon Goddess, the instinctual part of ourselves. These two planets, the luminaries, are, of course, in astrology those nearest to consciousness and most aware of what is going on within the psyche.

Demeter, who had heard Persephone's despairing cry, searches frantically for nine days for her lost daughter. Her grief is so great that she does not eat, sleep or bathe. A scenario typical of the depression and "empty nest syndrome" that can hit mothers when their children leave home. On the tenth day she meets the third face of woman, the Waning Moon goddess Hecate, whom Homer describes as "the luminous one." Hecate takes her to Helios. He tells Demeter of the plot to kidnap her daughter, and points out her brother-husband Zeus' part in the matter. Helios suggests that she should accept the situation as Pluto is "not unworthy as a son-in-law among the gods." Demeter, however, refuses to accept the betrayal of her child by her own father. Deep in depression, she retires from Olympus and, disguised as an old woman, wanders the countryside until she is given a job as a nursemaid. Here, in parallel with the Isis myth (the consort of Osiris, the Egyptian Lord of the Underworld), she begins to make the child divine. Each night she holds him in a fire to make him immortal. Unfortunately, the child's mother intervenes, and Demeter reveals her true identity and says to Metanira, his mother:

> You don't even know
> when fate
> is bringing you something good
> or something bad

. . .

I would have made
your dear child
deathless
ageless
forever.[13]

This vignette of the child who is to be made divine may well have been lifted wholesale from the earlier Egyptian tale of death and resurrection, the Isis and Osiris myth, as the tale is virtually identical. It is an allegory for the psychological dissolution that splits off the inner child within every man and woman, which must be purged and purified by fire (Pluto) in order to reveal the divine within. Most mothers are afraid for the child (whether their own inner child or that of their body) and refuse to let it go through the ordeal which will bring immortal life. Demeter, like her Egyptian moon-goddess sister Isis, can facilitate this process of dissolution, purification and re-unification with the divine.

Thwarted in her plans, Demeter then causes a temple to be built, in which she sits and grieves for her child. And her grief is terrible indeed. This is a serious matter as, without Demeter, goddess of fertility, nothing will grow. There is a famine and the land is desolate. Finally, Zeus sends messengers imploring her to return. But, furious still, Demeter refuses until her daughter is returned to her.

Hermes, Mercurial messenger of the gods, is sent to Hades where he, according to the later myths, finds a depressed and weepy Persephone only too eager to return to her mother. Pluto agrees to return her, but first gives her sweet pomegranate seeds to eat. The pomegranate is symbol of fecundity and rebirth. Its seeds are used to make a soothing medicine, so Pluto may not necessarily have been quite as cunning as history has painted him. The pomegranate's symbolic significance arises from its shape and internal structure, representing "the reconciliation of the multiple and diverse within apparent unity,"[14] a Plutonian attribute. As a goddess, Persephone's natural food is ambrosia, the nectar of the gods. Pomegranate is a food of Earth, of incarnation into matter and, therefore, of death. United with her mother, the first question Persephone is asked is whether she has eaten in the Underworld. Had she not accepted the seeds, Persephone could have returned to life above ground permanently. As it is, she has tasted the fruit of knowledge and she must spend one-third of the year below ground with Pluto as Queen of the Underworld. Having once been awoken by Pluto, one cannot return to the state of unconsciousness.

After Persephone's return, Demeter gave the Greeks the Eleusinian Mysteries in celebration. The initiates, who numbered thousands, swore never to reveal their experiences. Although some of the famous writers who partook of the mysteries have left us hints, in two thousand years no one broke that vow. We know that the central theme was death of the old, renewal and rebirth, culminating in the showing of a single ear of grain. It is believed that sacred marriage was part of the rites, together with the birth of the divine child. We know also that "the Sun shone at midnight," a hint maybe of the part the Sun God played in the proceedings. But the rest remains in the collective imagination and can only be accessed through attunement to the gods and the collective unconscious, or a reading of the Akashic record of past history.

THE ARCHETYPES

The Demeter-Persephone story is a fertility myth allegorizing the "dead" seed being planted in the ground, remaining invisible for a while and then, with the coming of Spring, sprouting into new life. It is also the three faces of the Moon—New, Full and Waning, or Dark. It is the eternal, archetypal tale of birth, death, and rebirth, and the Eleusinian Mysteries offered the initiate a chance to transcend the fear of death. But it is much much more than this. It is the story of our psychological growth, a growth which, particularly if we have the Hades Moon, must inevitably involve a descent into the stygian darkness of Pluto's realm—our own unconscious. We must descend to find understanding, to break the ingrained patterns from the past that bind us, and to integrate all the split off parts of ourself, liberating our potential.

In our own unconscious, and in the collective unconscious to which it is linked, we find all the great archetypes of human experience. Archetypes are universal symbols arising out of the collective unconscious, portrayed through myth and inner experience. Archetypes, like planets, have two sides: positive and negative, clear manifestation and shadow. The Greek gods and goddesses whose story we have been following are archetypes. The gods are amoral and impersonal, because the archetypal energy they portray does not make ethical or moral judgments. It acts on instinct not intellect. It simply is. Unlike some other religions, there was little that was divine and perfect on Olympus. The pragmatic Greeks saw their gods as an externalized part of their own inner process, acting out all the foibles and unpleasant character traits we meet in ourselves each day. We each of us, male or female, take on all the roles in the abduction of Persephone, particularly during Pluto transits. This is an inner drama being re-enacted time after time.

People or events in the outer world may play out roles in the drama—an exteriorization of our inner world. If we are not consciously owning the archetypal energies within us, then Pluto will appear from beneath the earth, to ravish us or to carry off those we love most. If we are not cooperating with the process of becoming more conscious, or with that of separating from our parents, we take on the Persephone victim role. If we are not letting go of our parental role, we fall into the deep grief of Demeter and become the devouring mother, making all around her barren. If we are not dealing with our endings and renewal, we meet Pluto in the guise of the rapist. If we are consciously involved, this may be through therapy or our own death processes—of which there are many before physical death.

THE MAIDEN: THE PERSEPHONE ARCHETYPE

Persephone has two faces. Her "young" face is the maiden, the Kore, who is an integral part of the fertility trinity and the Moon cycle. She is the New Moon aspect. Here she is undifferentiated consciousness, naive and unformed. Living happily on the surface of her life, she is content to wander the earth with her mother until Pluto intervenes. This is the New Moon phase which signifies repetition of old patterns but holds the seed of new beginnings, unmanifested innocence taking form. Her much more ancient face is the mature goddess, the Queen of the Underworld who rules over the dead souls and who can guide the living who wish to journey there. This is the, often unacknowledged, face of the New Moon that is "pregnant with the old." It forms the bridge between the inner journey of the Dark of the Moon and the bright, outerworld of consciousness and doing seen at the Full Moon.

Despite the myth that allows her to spend two-thirds of the year above ground with her mother, as Jean Bolen points out,[15] none of the Greek heroes who visited Hades found Persephone absent. Nor is she an innocent, totally faithful to her husband. In at least one myth, she fights with Aphrodite (Venus) over the beautiful Adonis who, ironically, has been sent to her for safe-keeping. This myth is an allegory involving the consort who dies and rises again. While in Persephone's keeping, he is dead; but returned to Aphrodite, the goddess of love, he is life itself and the return of fertility. However, Adonis needs the fertilizing touch of the Queen of Death for life to quicken and spark. In a woman, Adonis is her masculine self, or animus. An energy that needs to be reawakened and integrated if a woman is to be creative on a non-biological level.

If a woman is attuned to the Kore archetype, she is ever-youthful, sexually unaware and uncommitted. Often totally dependent on her mother, she acts out the part of "anima-woman" for men—seemingly all things to all men because, pliable and unformed, she reflects what they wish to see, she who delights in pleasing. If a man is attuned to the Kore archetype, whether it be in his inner feminine anima or in the outerworld, he is the eternally youthful *puer*, whom we will meet again, as it forms an important part of the Hades Moon archetype.

Clearly this youthful Kore can also form part of the Persephone shadow. A singular naivety and insularness can lie at the heart of the apparently lustful woman, or man, whose unacknowledged and unawakened sexuality, and consequent lack of commitment, is reflected back through partners. They, seemingly, reject the desire for closeness and union. Such a man or woman may, actually or metaphorically, find him or herself living the abduction and rape of Persephone when Pluto bursts through from the Underworld. This is potentially a crisis which activates and moves him or her into the mature Persephone role, although it may also be a repetitive Moon-Pluto pattern playing itself out. This "unawakened" Persephone, powerless and passive is, in psychotherapist Roger Woolger's opinion,[16] the eternal, sacrificial victim projecting all his or her power "out there" onto mother, matriarch, or man. She, or he, eternally recreates the conditions which led to her, or his, downfall. Such a "maiden" desperately needs to be handed over to the dark powers of Pluto for a journey down into her, or his, own unconscious. She, or he, can then be made sacred and incorporated into her, or his, being through an initiation into the mature spirit. She, or he, is then the reconciliation of the opposites of dark and light; the integration of the powerful, unconscious forces of the psyche with the brightness of consciousness.

Men who are unconsciously attuned to Persephone are endlessly fascinated with fey,* psychic women, but terrified of their power. When the mature, receptive, Persephone archetype is activated, this is the guide to the Underworld, the

*The fey woman is mysterious and otherworldly. She is fateful, ethereal, but earthy—like Morgan le Fey in Arthurian legend.

man or woman who is at home in the realm of the intuition and unconscious, and who has the capacity for deeply-moving spiritual and sexual experiences which take him or her beyond individuality into unity with the cosmos. She, or he, is psychic and perceptive, attuned to forces beyond the comprehension of most people, and this is the potential midwife for birthing the sacred nature in everyone.

The mature Persephone archetype can be helpful for anyone who has undergone any kind of Plutonian abuse. Mature Persephone has regained her power, has overcome her abduction and violation, and has found healing in the darkness. The positive Persephone-woman, or man, is at home within the depths of the psyche, Pluto's realm, and can act as a guide for others journeying into their own unconscious. She, or he, is attuned to the birth-death-rebirth cycle and may find her or himself instinctively drawn to work with the dying, aiding them not only in their transition to another life, but also showing them how to live fully until they die.

THE MOTHER: THE DEMETER ARCHETYPE

Demeter is the archetypal mother and nurturer. She is the maternal instinct personified and we will meet her time and time again as we explore the Hades Moon. She is the mature, Full Moon aspect of the matriarchal, lunar cycle. Her nourishment is not only to her children, however; Demeter provides physical, psychological, and spiritual nurturing for everyone—particularly through the "helping professions." Nevertheless, Demeter also encompasses the opposite principle. When the goddess' child is taken away, she rages and cuts off support for mankind, becoming the devouring mother and "Great No-Sayer." The earth is made barren.

In men who are attuned to the Demeter archetype, Mother rules. They will be attracted to, and yet repelled by, women who embody the powerfully maternal and devouring side of Demeter. Being afraid of "bull-mothers," as one Pluto-Moon attuned man calls them, they are nevertheless drawn to women who embody this archetype. Such a man may also have a powerful anima figure to deal with, ceaselessly running from confrontation with the power that such a figure holds, and, of course, being endlessly attracted to women who embody just that quality. Relationships become a battlefield or, like Pluto, the man resorts to ravishment and deception to obtain what he wants. The reaction may be to stay as child (the puer archetype) or to enter into addiction and depression as a way of rebelling against, and potentially finally breaking free from, such total control. The Demeter-attuned man goes down into Hades many times before he finds his own, positively nurturing, inner mother.

Powerfully attuned but repressed Demeter women may act out one of Demeter's other aspects—the Goddess who mates with her son/lover as a renewal of self. Such a mother "devours" her son, using him as a substitute husband to feed her emotional needs. Emotional incest is common, but physical incest may also take place, especially when acted out through a surrogate son-lover. Demeter-attuned women all too often turn the lover into their child, or their child into the lover (surrogate or otherwise). This mother psychologically rapes her child. She binds her son (or daughter) to her and the child-in-the-man dare not love another woman. The child is sacrificed to the mother's overwhelming need for emotional security which, in this archetype, is rarely to be found with her adult partner. He may be absent, emotionally or physically, and will usually fail to meet her needs. Frustrated, she turns to the son (or daughter, this is not purely a mother-son phenomenon). As a result, the "child" expresses only the feelings that mother finds reassuring and acceptable. Such a "child" is then cut off from genuine feeling and this carries over into adulthood. This archetype may also have a powerful hold over men who project their feeling-needs onto a Demeter-figure and who, all too willingly, sacrifice themselves onto the Great Mother's altar.

Demeter may be a crucial part of the mid-life experience for the Moon-Pluto attuned woman or man. It is the Demeter archetype who suffers from the "empty nest syndrome" simply because her instinct to have children is so strong and her grief at the loss of her fertility so overwhelming. When the Demeter-woman's "child" leaves home, she may well fall into deep depression and see this as "the end," no matter what other responsibilities she may have. Her response to loss, or threat of confrontation, is to withhold nurturing, to refuse to meet the needs of others and of herself. In an effort to retain control, the Demeter-woman's reaction to mid-life may well be to withdraw, to be unavailable. Demeter-women often see themselves as victims. They give until literally they have nothing left to give and yet deeply resent the calls made on their exhausted energies. For instance, her children, who have made lives for themselves, may find that they are approved of only if that life fits into what mother "knows is right" for them. Her husband may find that he has lost his wife while she struggles to let go of (or retain her hold on) her children, or of her desire to have children—one of the major Moon-Pluto lessons is that creativity is not necessarily biological.

The Demeter shadow is possessiveness allied to fear of loss, purposelessness and depression. It is "passive-aggression," hostility that is hidden and fearful, based on unspoken resentment and unacknowledged feelings. It "forgets to do" rather than saying a clear no. The Demeter shadow is afraid of the Underworld (i.e., the unconscious), and refuses to allow her offspring, and her own inner child, to go through the psychological integration that exploring the depths of the psyche can bring. The Demeter shadow, therefore, may prefer "helping" someone, and thereby keeping them dependent. This mother shadow does not allow a child, or herself, to explore the shadow and become whole once more. It may also use "helping someone else" as an excuse for avoiding change and personal growth. It can also be an exploitive shadow, manipulating and maneuvering to get its own way. It is the "little-girl" who refuses to grow up, the woman who calls her husband "daddy," and especially the woman who refuses to make the transition to the "crone" aspect of life. This shadow is the mother who has to be nurtured by her children, who must be placated and wooed for fear she turns into the devouring mother. Her threat is loss of love. Her legacy is blighted, barren life.

The positive Demeter-woman, on the other hand, has faced loss and come through with increased wisdom so that she can accompany others on their journey. She has learned how to mother herself, to be her own child, with love and generosity of spirit, but also with a protective awareness that allows her to know when enough is enough (both for herself and others). She has an attunement to the cycles of nature; she understands the need for death, how to be in the dark place where new seeds sprout without constantly poking around to be sure they have germinated. She is content to wait for everything to mature in its season, knowing that the harvest will come.

THE CRONE: THE HECATE ARCHETYPE

The figure of Hecate plays a seemingly minor and yet crucial role in the Demeter story. It is the dark face of the Moon goddess, and therefore an instinctual part of the self; she witnessed the abduction of Persephone and was able to act as mediator when Demeter tried to negotiate with Zeus to rescue her daughter. Thus, she has the function of bringing together lost parts of the self. Hecate is also a goddess of purification and illumination. Indeed, Hecate can be seen as presiding over Persephone's initiation and descent into her unconscious, accompanying her return and spiritual integration. In Hecate we have the completion of the trinity: the Crone is united with Maiden and Mother, the three faces of the Moon come together.

Hecate is an ancient goddess of the crossroads, the all-seeing eye who looks to past, present, and future, ruling heaven, earth and underworld. She is the shamaness who stands at the point where the four directions meet. She is an intuitive divinity associated with magic and prophecy, attributes of the Hades Moon. Hecate is believed to have evolved from the Egyptian midwife goddess Hekat, a wise-woman who was in command of the "Mother's words of power." As the sacred midwife, Hekat birthed the Sun each morning. According to some sources, Hekat (and Hecate) also steered the Moon-Boat by night, and guided it through the otherworld by day.

In Greece a divinity of the Underworld, Hecate was originally a goddess reflecting the phases of the Moon, who symbolized the three ages of woman. Later, she was incorporated as a child of Hera and Zeus. In this particular myth, she incurred the wrath of her mother by stealing Hera's rouge, and hid in the bed of a woman who was giving birth. The contact with the puerperal blood rendered Hecate impure and she was plunged into the Acheron (one of the rivers leading to Hades) to cleanse her, but she was carried away by the river (a Plutonian event). Her stealing Hera's "rouge" is most probably a metaphor for the cessation of Hera's menstrual bleeding leading to menopause, and the onset of Hecate's own menses which was seen as stealing her mother's blood. Hera is a goddess of power, but a great deal of her power is invested in being Zeus' wife. Hera is not a goddess to willingly surrender her dominance, nor to become a woman in her own right. Like many dominant women, she fears the change of menopause. So, Hecate is blamed for the event. In the ancient myths, blood is life—and spirit. In hiding in childbed, Hecate is breaching a taboo that made puerperal blood set aside and holy. Although she becomes "impure," it is the start of her own initiation—not only into womanhood, but also into her own self.

As a result, she became a goddess of the Underworld and lived in a cave at the entrance to Hades. The goddess of enchantment and magic, she haunted tombs. Victims of murder were often buried at crossroads, hence her link with crossroads. The symbolism is deeper than this, however. Hecate is linked to choices and to "The Way." She is at her most powerful when the Moon wanes, the instinctual time for journeying into the Underworld through dreams and visions. She rules the great crossroads of life, such as puberty, marriage, birth, and menopause, when feminine power is closest to the surface. These are times of initiation, of going into the self for both men and women, but women tend to be more conscious of the process. Hecate has a torch to light the darkness, and thus performs the function of taking one deep into oneself, and of linking the conscious with the unconscious. She is, therefore, an excellent guide for inner work.

The Hecate-woman is the link between the different levels of consciousness, and can move between them with confidence. This is the sorceress woman. She understands the magical dimension of life. Not afraid to face death and old age, she is unlikely to withhold her power for fear of men—over whom she may well hold a dark enchantment. She is Kali, Lilith, the Morgan le Fey of the Arthurian legends, a woman who fascinates men with her aura of mystique and magic, and the threat of her destructive power.

The Hecate shadow may well be linked to this fascination, and to dark powers used to unconsciously manipulate and coerce those around her. Her link to the depths is great, but the shadow's awareness is shallow, and therefore everything dark and mysterious is projected onto "another," as is the case with Hecate-attuned men. Thus, in the outer world, the Hecate shadow will constantly encounter that which he or she avoids owning in him or herself—power. When the Hecate man or woman does not consciously own power, and thereby does not use it wisely, he or she may well take others down into the darkness, but deny responsibility, ensuring their disintegration.

The positive Hecate-archetype is extremely helpful for those making rites of passage or indeed any transition. She guides dreamers and travelers through the spirit world, and initiates them into a different dimension of consciousness. As a goddess of the Underworld, Hecate is waiting whenever we meet an end or face loss. Like Pluto, she reaches up and draws us down into the darkness. She accompanies our transitions and our transformation. As with Persephone, she is there to offer good counsel. She teaches us how to let go of the past. As Crone, Hecate lights the way and shares her sacred wisdom. Hecate is the third age of woman. When the Hecate-woman (or man) consciously integrates the shadow and owns power, then she, or he, can act as a light for those who are penetrating their own darkness and can bring together the lost parts of the self. Instinctual Hecate is also a link to the archetypes who dwell deep in the collective unconscious. "On an inner level, Hekate is a guardian figure of the mysterious depths of our unconscious that access the collective memory of the primal void and whirling forces at the onset of creation."[17] So, Hecate can be seen as the female face of Pluto, the great integrator.

THE PLUTO-HADES ARCHETYPE

Pluto is the archetypal destroyer, rapist, demon lover, dictator, tyrannical father (or mother—Pluto also has a feminine face) and masterful husband. But he is also creator, healer, therapist, initiator, and enlightener. In his links with Osiris he is Lord of Resurrection and karmic justice. As with Persephone, there are two faces to Hades. One is the personal archetype of the god, and the other the transpersonal, archetypal realm of human, and indeed divine, darkness, which has always been a fearsome place. Even on Mount Olympus, the realm of Zeus, Hades was feared. As God of the Underworld, he held ultimate sway over everything that lived—and died. Zeus had to bow to his commands. But, the gods and goddesses of ancient Greece preferred to be identified with the light and airy realm on top of the mountain, much as most people do today. So, the Underworld was seen as a place of monsters and demons, to be avoided at all costs until a residence permit became mandatory. Hades is, therefore, within ourselves. It is the realm where we meet our own inner demons, face our fears, and confront our own dark spaces. Nevertheless, it is also the archetypal sphere of healing, integration, and resurrection. Today, most people find themselves in Hades through depression, grief, or loss. Only the very courageous—or foolhardy—voluntarily descend into the depths to find Pluto's riches.

Pluto as a god is the dark man who haunts our dreams. He kills or he loves us and both are the same. When Pluto was retrograding back over my Sun, I dreamed of a dark man chasing me. He was slashing at me with a Scorpionic scalpel. I awoke terrified and sick with fear, and yet saying to myself: "At least you are feeling, you haven't shut down." Going back into the dream, I tried two approaches. In the first I turned to face him, and found myself armed with a machete with which I, without thought, cleaved him in two. Immediately I felt a deep grief, as though something priceless had been lost. Rerunning the dream again, I allowed him to catch me. He split me from neck to crotch, but then reached in and brought out a child, which he handed to me. The dream propelled me back into writing this book, which had been "on hold" while other books came to birth.

This is the archetype of the rapist, the initiator into the mysteries of the unconscious. Psychotherapist can also be written Psycho-the-rapist: the person who ravishes the soul and brings it into the light of day. This is the archetype that connects to our inner darkness—our compulsions and obsessions, our dominating and ingrained patterns, our desire to control, to manipulate and disrupt. This archetype collides with our deepest conditioning, our most treasured illusions and rampant paranoia. This is the death archetype, the destructive face of man and his unattained dreams. This is where will and power run amok, the point where we contact the collective shadow, and project it out to the world. But, this is also where we find the challenge of "unfleshed-out potentials awaiting birth,"[18] the place of creation. It is where we meet all the abuses and misuses of powerful figures unrecognized, and thereby unowned, as "ours." As such, Pluto is rarely welcomed by those on whom he comes to call, much less accepted as a valued part of the psyche. For most people, the Pluto archetype is repressed way down below the conscious level where it forms part of the individual, and the collective, shadow.

However, the archetype also has a richness and depth which can only be contacted through the subjectivity and interiority of the solitary, inward path. In this expression of the archetype, solitude and seclusion produce inner strength and breadth of purpose. This is the creative archetype, the one that recognizes the many deaths that go into renewal and rebirth. Here is the artist, the counsellor, the therapist, and the surgeon. One of the major strengths of the positive Pluto archetype is that, familiar with the dreams and images of the inner world that link to the collective unconscious, it rarely fears the transition known as death. Indeed, the Pluto archetype positively welcomes any kind of death or ending as a chance to grow into something new or deeper. This is Pluto as destroyer, just as Shiva with his endless dance to keep chaos at bay, is also destroyer and creator at one and the same time. This "god" is the creation-preservation-destruction cycle of life itself.

Pluto-attuned men may well live out different faces of the archetype depending on how consciously they are connected to it. This archetype is the introvert, the intuitive perceiver, the inhibited, repressed loner, the aggressive go-getter, or, at the outer edge, the clandestine rapist or murderer (and there are many ways of killing, we are not necessarily looking at physical death here). In some men whose Pluto energies lie far below the surface, there can be little to see: socially inept they are literally invisible to the outerworld. In other men in whom Pluto is strong but unrecognized, their subjective impressions will hold sway. The "paranoid-schizoid" who is fearful of everything and everyone, and who sees persecution everywhere, is one extreme. As is the addict (man or woman) who deliberately tries to inhabit Pluto's realm and who compulsively acts out his or her own destruction. Equally Plutonian is the man or woman who deliberately risks everything, pits himself against danger or exposes himself to hazard "simply because it is there." Or, the person who has a terminal illness and who uses it to explore life and death in all its richness. Pluto's energy is ruthless and cathartic. So, a single-minded business wo/man who goes all out for success is expressing the archetype, as is the man or woman who has a "breakdown," or who lives in severe depression. The surgeon (whether professionally employed or not) who can cut away all that is diseased and unhealthy is Pluto attuned, as is the therapist, who has explored the depths as opposed to intellectualizing about them.

Here we can take time out to look at those pioneers of depth psychology, Sigmund Freud and C. G. Jung who, in the fullness of time had to break away from his mentor and pursue his own pathway (a Hades Moon theme). Both men had a powerful connection to the Hades Moon that led them into the Underworld. Freud had a novile (40°) aspect between Pluto at 4′27 Taurus and the Moon at 14′31 Gemini, in the waxing first quarter of the Moon. Jeff Green has identified the novile as "the point where personal and individual meaning is gained through identification and gestation of the evolutionary purpose."[19] Jung had a wide Moon-Pluto conjunction in Taurus in the waning third quarter of the Moon.

Freud's theories developed out of observing patients who had psychological problems, that is from a study of "abnormal" psychology, and not from his own personal experience (although it is clear that Freud's own childhood, with its dark family secrets, would have been fertile ground had he been able to explore it). That Freud observed rather than participated is typical of the intellectual Gemini Moon. That he then contrived a theory which he applied to the whole can be linked to his 6th house Pluto and 8th house Moon. He believed the patient's difficulties stemmed from how instinctual energy (the Moon) was channelled. He saw the patient as having little control over that process because behavior was motivated by unconscious elements of the personality. He, therefore, recognized a personal unconscious. He identified two impulses at work in the psyche. *Eros* was for self-preservation and preservation of the species (which is, of course, related to the

Moon). The other, *thanatos*, was an urge toward destruction including that of the self (an aspect of Pluto). Freud also identified childhood (the Moon once again) as the time when personality was formed through interaction with the family and also through modification of the prime sexual instinct (a Plutonian factor).

Jung was a contemporary of Freud and carried on a lively correspondence with him in which they debated Jung's differing views on how the personality developed. However, Jung eventually had to break with Freud as their theories had diverged so widely. This was at the end of 1913, when Pluto briefly entered Cancer before retrograding back into Gemini. At the time, Jung's progressed Moon was quincunx the natal Moon-Pluto conjunction and Uranus was on the Ascendant signifying a time to break from the past. However, the Pluto connection also made a trip into Hades necessary. Jung had an intensely introspective four years, almost a mental breakdown, in which he journeyed into his own unconscious, and explored myth and religion. His descent into the Underworld became the *prima materia* out of which his psychological and spiritual understanding was born.

That Jung was strongly attuned to Pluto was graphically brought home in one of his most famous dreams. He faced something monumental, of which he was terrified. It turned out to be an enormous turd which fell from under God's golden throne onto the sparkling new roof of a cathedral. The roof shattered and the walls of the cathedral were torn asunder.[20] Faecal matter is an attribute of Pluto, and is an essential ingredient in alchemical transformation. At the time of the dream, Jung, then 12, had feared that he was in danger of commiting an unpardonable sin and incurring eternal damnation. The dream brought him a sense of divine grace falling on him, an "unutterable bliss."

Jung made two highly Plutonian statements: "This was the primal stuff which compelled me to work . . . ," and, "My life has been permeated and held together by one idea and one goal: to penetrate into the secret of the personality."[21] His practical, one-pointed Taurean Moon needed the concrete experience of another world to hone his craft. These Plutonian experiences brought about a spiritual psychology and an identification not only of the personal unconscious but of the collective unconscious and the archetypes that inhabited it. Jung's psychology has to do with finding, and integrating, the Self and one's own personal center, as befits the Moon in Taurus, which must make the creative energy manifest and bring it into form. One of his most important discoveries was that an awareness of the contents of the unconscious vastly speeded up the process of transformation of the psyche, and his therapy was therefore based on that exploration. Jung was born, most appropriately, in the waning quarter of the Moon as it moved toward dark. He first saw the light of day as the last rays of the setting sun shone in the room. Consciousness was sinking, the lunar forces were rising. So, he had a natural affinity with night and the forces of the Underworld. He was the first modern psychologist to fully recognize the importance of the Shadow in the human psyche.

Jung had a fairly wide conjunction from the Moon at 15′30 Taurus to Pluto at 23′26 in the 3rd house of communication. Jeff Green identifies this applying conjunction of the Moon to Pluto as an evolutionary cycle having "been completed in the personal journey. . . . A totally new evolutionary cycle is about to begin. Planets forming this type of conjunction to Pluto become the potential vehicles through which the universal, the timeless, or the Source, can be consciously experienced or sensed. Conversely, they can serve as the vehicles through which the individual experiences confusion, disassociation, alienation, and discontentment in order to learn about the nature of personal delusions, dreams and illusions."[22]

THE DARK LOVER

> *A savage place! as holy and enchanted*
> *As e'er beneath a waning moon was haunted*
> *By woman wailing for her demon-lover!*
> *And from this chasm, with ceaseless turmoil seething*
> *As if this earth in fast thick pants were breathing,*
> *A mighty fountain momently was forced.*
>
> —Coleridge[23]

Jung's animus and anima figures, our inner figure of the opposite gender, carry both light and dark sides. In men and women, it can emerge as the Dark Lover. But it may also emerge as another Plutonian figure—a creative daimon or muse who drives the psyche inexorably toward inspiration and empowerment. The daimon or muse may well, however, wear the guise of the dark lover, especially when he or she first appears. This daimon may not necessarily be an archetype or inner figure emerging. It may well be part of the god—an independent spirit who seeks us out—yet another aspect of Pluto. The dark lover is particularly associated with the Hades Moon. Loretta Proctor[24] has pointed out how many male writers who have explored the theme of the dark lover have had a powerful Moon-Pluto aspect, particularly the conjunction. However, in women, too, the dark lover emerges with Pluto and can be traced in both fiction and real life.

In a woman, Pluto is often concealed or projected out onto the men with whom she comes into contact. When Pluto is visible, the energy is intense and vehement. Often it is compulsive and obsessive. Controlling rather than directed, the Pluto energy pulls down into the depths time and time again, or erupts in violent emotion and outerworld experiences, as we shall see. So often, Pluto forms part of the inner shadow or animus. This is heightened (or rather deepened) when the Moon is also involved. A Pluto-attuned animus may well present as the psychic or actual "demon" lover. Demon lovers tend to be devastatingly handsome, plausible, totally devious, and prone to leaving abruptly. Women who meet this personification of Pluto are pulled irrevocably down into the depths to meet their own inner reserves. Many Moon-Pluto-attuned women have described to me dreams or psychic visitations by the Demon Lover, and countless others have recounted all too earthy and physical confrontations. Nevertheless, these figures can be constructive as well as destructive. It all depends how they are used.

Mr. Rochester in *Jane Eyre* is a Pluto-animus figure who depicts the kind of Plutonian tragedy required to take a woman down into her depths to find her own strength. Before Jane meets her employer, she is told that his visits are "rare, sudden and unexpected." When she encounters him on the road, but still does not know him, she describes him as of "dark face, stern features and a heavy brow." He falls from his horse, just the kind of Plutonian "accident" we should be looking for by now. Jane says later: "The incident had occurred and gone for me: it was an incident of no moment, no romance, no interest in a sense; yet it marked with change one single hour of a monotonous life. . . . The new face was like a new picture introduced to the gallery of memory; it was dissimilar to all the others hanging there: first because it was masculine, and secondly because it was dark, strong and stern."[25]

The whole book is full of Plutonian phrases and lunar imagery. The wedding is dramatically halted by the revelation that Mr. Rochester already has a "lunatic" for a wife; she is the mad, desperate creature who is incarcerated in his attic. She is a creature who tries on several occasions to burn him alive, a woman whom he calls "a demon," a denizen of hell. But she is nevertheless his wife. Jane insists she will leave the house, despite her strong feelings for Rochester. He (or is it Pluto) responds by accusing: ". . . you would snatch love and innocence from me." But Jane is adamant, she has to go. Mary Ann Evans (the writer George Eliot) commented on Jane's resistance: "All self-sacrifice is good—but one would like it to be in a somewhat nobler cause than that of a diabolical law which chains a man soul and body to a putrefying carcase."[26] Here we have the much older underworld myth of Inanna and Ereshkigal played out. For both Jane and Mr. Rochester, everything is stripped away. They, together with his "lunatic" wife, are hung on the meathook to rot. They are in Pluto's realm.

But, the Persephone archetype in the guise of Jane narrowly avoids the clutches of Pluto. She may have been temporarily seduced by passion, but her mind and her soul remained her own. Demeter (or was it the mysterious watcher Hecate?) may have had a hand in this as Jane, when tempted to stay, has a vision:

> The gleam was such as the moon imparts to vapours she is about to sever. I watched her come—watched with the strangest anticipation, as though some word of doom were to be written on her disk. She broke forth as never moon yet burst from cloud: a hand first penetrated the sable folds and waved them away; then, not a moon, but a white human form shone in the azure, inclining a glorious brow earthwards. It gazed and gazed on me. It spoke to my spirit: immeasureably distant was the tone, yet so near, it whispered in my heart—my daughter, flee temptation![27]

And Jane, of course, as a dutiful daughter of Demeter, flees into an experience that brings her to the very brink of death. One cannot escape Pluto that easily! Eventually, however, Jane returns to her dark lover, all but destroyed by his own Plutonian experiences. With infinite compassion, she embraces his (and her own) darkness. She is now attuned to the mature Persephone archetype. There is deep healing within the Hades Moon for those who have the courage to confront the secrets of the past, and to let them go.

Another side of the Pluto archetype and the dark lover is seen in *Wuthering Heights*, a novel that explores "the collective shadow."[28] Here we have a powerful, obsessive love at work. Heathcliff, a brooding, passionate, moody, intense man loves the turbulent Catherine Earnshaw from childhood. They are "soul companions" with an almost mystical understanding of each other that transcends physical passion:

My love for Heathcliff resembles the eternal rocks beneath, a source of little visible delight but necessary. . . . I am Heathcliff. He's always, always in my mind, not as a pleasure . . . but as my own being.[29]

Catherine Earnshaw refuses marriage, however, betraying their love because of Heathcliff's social inferiority (his origins are unknown). He then marries a woman who is his social superior, but this woman finds it hard to come to terms with his savagery. Wayward Catherine weds a "cold fish" who finds no joy in her wild abandon. But each still yearns for the other. Pregnant, Catherine dies. Willing himself to death, "taking even that great finale in his own hands, like a god,"[30] Healthcliff joins her and the two lovers haunt the moors together, united at last.

Charlotte Bronte, author of *Jane Eyre*, is a singularly Moon-Pluto attuned person, as are her sisters Emily (who wrote *Wuthering Heights*) and Anne (who penned *The Tenant of Wildfell Hall*). They clearly resonate with the archetypal realm of Pluto, as do all the Brontes—through whom strong Pluto-Mars contacts also entwine. Mr. Rochester, the dark animus, had his roots in the childhood stories Charlotte wrote with her brother, Branwell. Branwell (Scorpio Moon trine Pluto) was the Dark Moon god around whom the whole family revolved and on whom all creative hopes were centered. Great sacrifices were made to educate him in a manner befitting a young god. Together Charolotte and Branwell created a fantasy world, Angria. Branwell's contribution was of war and battles. His male characters were heroes, albeit unscrupulous and devious—typically Plutonian. As one Bronte biographer put it: "Branwell was always raining destruction upon his creations—he was that kind of god."[31] Branwell would later live out all the self-destructiveness of the Pluto shadow. Charlotte added love interest in the shape of darkly handsome, masterful men to whom the women were in thrall; another side of the Plutonian archetype.

It was Branwell who, in the early years, carried the dark animus for Charlotte. He was the "dream-partner"[32] with whom she shared a creative bond that excluded their siblings. Charlotte later took back that projection and eventually made it her own in the shape of Mr. Rochester. Once she had left home to become a teacher, her diary records more than one erotic daydream (clearly deliberately invoked) in which a swarthy lover awaits her—hardly the stuff of acceptable Victorian fantasy, especially for a young woman who was at the time responsible for the moral rectitude of the girls in her care. But it shows what an imagination lurked under the conventional parsonage-bred facade. And, it clearly illustrates the unstoppable passion of Charlotte's Venus in Aries breaking through into consciousness.

Emily, on the other hand, seems to have contained her own dark animus within her soul and to have met her daimon, whom she called her "radiant angel" early on in life:

When weary with the long day's care
And earthly change from pain to pain,
And lost and ready to despair,
Thy kind voice calls me back again—

O my true friend, I am not alone,
While thou canst speak with such a tone!

But thou art ever there to bring
The hovering visions back and breathe
New glories o'er the blighted spring
And call a lovelier life from death,
And whisper with a voice divine
Of real worlds as bright as thine.

I trust not to thy phantom bliss,
Yet still in evenings quiet hour
With never-failing thankfulness
I welcome thee, benignant power,
Sure solace of human cares,
And brighter hope when hope despairs.[33]

Gondal, the fantasy world Emily wrote about with her sister Anne was icy, cold, and remote, but nonetheless passionate and emotionally charged. It featured hadean dungeons, vaults and cells.[34] Emily was much more mystically inclined than Charlotte, with a strong spiritual leaning. She, more than any other Bronte, explored the interior life. She yearned to live in the metaphysical world and it is clear from her poetry that she had out-of-body experiences:

I did not dream; remembrance still
Clasped round my heart its fetters chill;
But I am sure the soul is free
To leave its clay a little while . . .
Yet if the soul can thus return
I need not and I will not mourn.[35]

On the moors, she was one with nature. Repudiating conventional religion, she felt a Neptunian oneness with creation:

What have these lonely mountains worth revealing?
More glory and more grief than I can tell:
The earth that wakes one human heart to feeling
Can centre both the worlds of Heaven and Hell.[36]

This is where she found her sustenance and her strength. When her death came, she eagerly embraced it. Indeed, she seems to have willed it. Catching cold at her brother Branwell's funeral, she refused all medical treatment. She withdrew into herself and died of an "inflammation of the lungs" three months later. Her time of death is recorded. Perhaps not surprisingly, the Moon was in Libra opposing Pluto in the 12th house that day. The transiting Moon inconjuncted her natal Pluto.

For Emily, the full flowering of her womanhood could take place in the spiritual dimensions that succeeded death. "Wholeness had an absolute existence beyond this world."[37] Her novel, much more shocking to readers of the time than Charlotte's, follows the "degradation of a soul," Heathcliff, as he plots Plutonian revenge and falls into addiction and self-destruction. Emily had watched her own brother fall into the same pit. But, unlike Charlotte, Emily was full of compassion for Branwell's tormented soul, which is perhaps why Heathcliff, his alter ego, is such a compelling figure. He is primal rage personified, an aspect as we shall see of the Hades Moon. But Heathcliff is reunited in death with his great love and this may have been what Emily sought—union with that dark lover who haunted her visions, visions which she had lost in the months preceding her death. Was that dark lover her hadean brother, or another? Did Pluto await his willing bride?

Branwell Bronte (Chart 2, page 56) is the only family member for whom there is a recorded time of birth, and he has that double Hades Moon. His Moon, as well as aspecting Pluto, is placed in Scorpio. A resonance with the Hades Moon can, however, be picked up in all the family charts. All could, at some time during the day of birth, have had Pluto-Moon aspects. I have, therefore, worked with surmised times of birth, not confirmed times. This is clearly not ideal but I am happy to do so as the whole family reeks of a shared familiarity with the Hades Moon. Indeed, it could be argued that this family thread enables us to establish probable birth times. (In my experience, surmised times of birth based on Pluto-Moon contacts have inevitably been confirmed whenever a birthtime later came to light.)

One of Charlotte's biographers describes the family as living "lonely and tragic lives full of emotional intensity." And yet, most charts for Emily and Charlotte Bronte show no connection between the Moon and Pluto. In Emily's chart (Chart 3, page 57) the Cancer Moon opposes Jupiter and may have a semi-sextile to the Sun. Nothing which would point to the turbulence and passion of *Wuthering Heights* and her powerfully emotional poetry. Charlotte (Chart 4, page 58) has an imaginative, romantic sextile with Neptune and a chilly, and far from intense, Moon-Saturn conjunction in Aquarius. While this conjunction clearly indicates the separation from her mother, and the steely emotional resolve that turned down three suitors because they could not truly *know* her, it does little to explain how a parsonage-reared spinster could write with such repressed passion and emotional intensity. (Loretta Proctor puts it down to Mars-Pluto and others have put it down to Venus in Aries. This placement, while exceedingly passionate, lacks the tenacious intensity Charlotte displays.) Nor does the accepted chart describe why her whole life reeked of the Hades Moon.

Hades Moon emotions are like a dormant volcano, apparently quiescent on the surface, but underneath they seethe and heave. Then, one day, without warning, they erupt. An emotional explosion (or implosion) out of all proportion to the trigger occurs. With the Brontes, this force was channelled into their fictional lives, but had its roots in their own unconscious mind. As with Emily, Charlotte's chart only makes sense if she has the emotionally intense Hades Moon. I would argue that Charlotte Bronte's most likely time of birth is close to 9:10 A.M., and Emily's sometime before dawn.

A Cancer Ascendant, given by the conjectured time of birth, would explain Charlotte's fierce protection of "the family," and the pains she took to hide her real identity behind a male pseudonym. She maintained this pretense long after her real

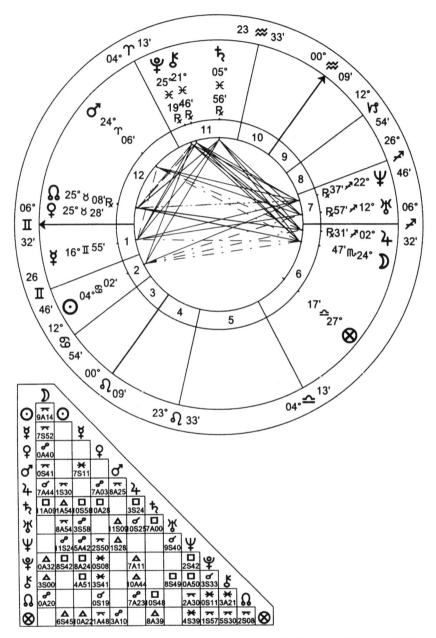

Chart 2. Branwell Bronte. Born June 26, 1817, GMT 2.01, 53N44, 001W45.
Placidus houses. Data from Loretta Proctor and Bronte Society. Source: diary.

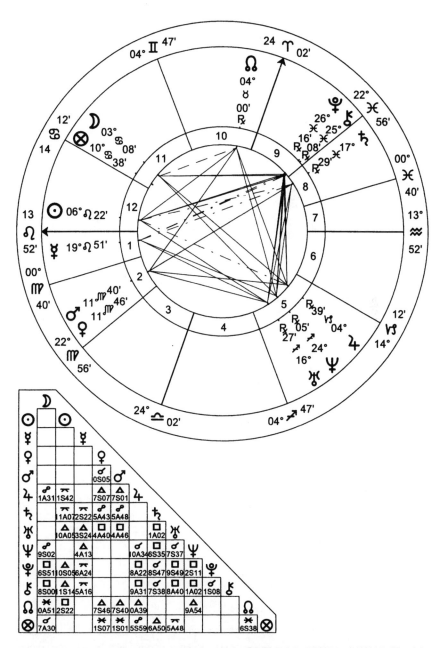

Chart 3. Emily Bronte. Born July 30, 1818, GMT 5.00, 53N44, 01W45. Placidus houses. Data from Loretta Proctor and Bronte Society. Source: Time used was dowsed, for no time of birth was recorded.

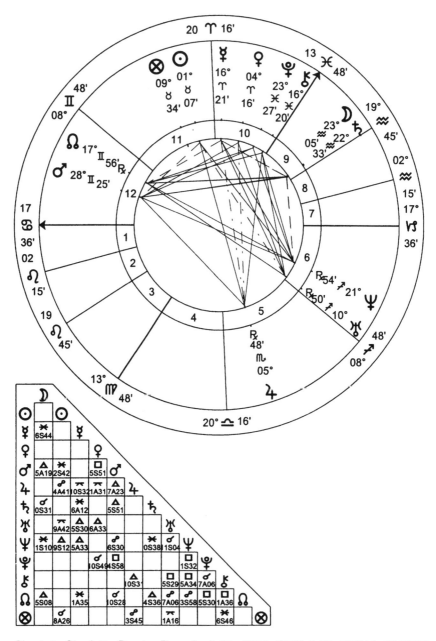

Chart 4. Charlotte Bronte. Born April 21, 1816, GMT 9.10, 53N44, 001W45. Placidus houses. Data from Loretta Proctor and Bronte Society. Source: Time was dowsed, for no time of birth was recorded.

identity had become known. Charlotte rarely ventured out into the public world of the literary figure; she did not wish to be recognized, she only wanted to observe others. Her ultimate surrender to domesticity and marriage, after which she published no more and died within a year, suggests, as Loretta Proctor has pointed out, that "her soul was convinced that she did not deserve to be happy, or that birth and death were literally one," a sentiment which could only come out of a Hades Moon.

The 9:10 A.M. chart not only shows the natal Moon-Saturn conjunction and sextile to Neptune, but also has the Moon semi-sextile Pluto and quintile Uranus. The semi-sextile aspect often indicates someone who lives out the qualities of the planets involved through projection onto others—in this case, the characters in her books, and her family, especially Branwell. It is probable that her sister Anne (Chart 5, page 60), whose mother died within a year of her birth, also shared this aspect.

Emily, an emotionally intense but isolated and reclusive young woman, was born at the dark of a watery Cancerian Moon. It was Emily who most resisted leaving home, and who found her greatest solace in the loneliness of the vast, uninhabited Yorkshire moors. Like Hecate, she was unafraid of the dark places, and made her own choices. She was the hidden onlooker who missed nothing and who could freely move between the different levels of consciousness. Emily was uniquely aware of the characters in her own inner drama:

> Three gods, within this little frame,
> Are warring night and day.
> Heaven could not hold them all, and yet
> They are all held in me;
> And must be mine till I forget
> My present entity![38]

And there is no doubt she knew Pluto, even if it was under another name, as these lines from "*The Philosopher*" show:

> I saw a spirit, standing, Man,
> Where thou dost stand—an hour ago,
> And round his feet three rivers ran,
> Of equal depth, and equal flow—
> A golden stream—and one like blood;
> And one like sapphire seemed to be;
> But where they joined their triple flood
> It tumbled in an inky sea.
>
> The spirit bent his dazzling gaze
> Down through that ocean's gloomy Night,
> Then kindling all, with sudden blaze,
> The glad deep sparkled wide and bright—
> White as the sun, far, far more fair
> Than its divided sources were!

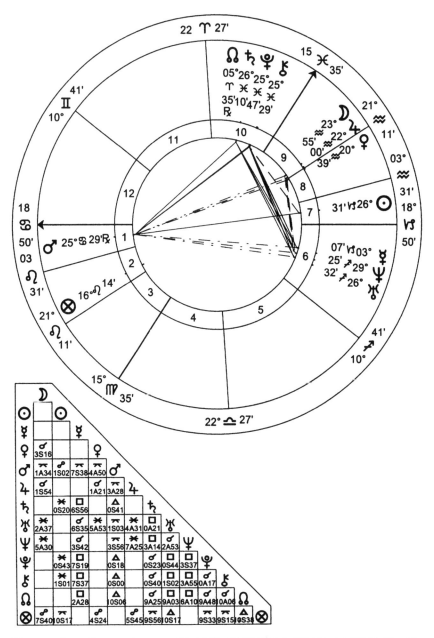

Chart 5. Anne Bronte. January 17, 1820, GMT 15.30, 53N44, 001W45. Placidus houses. Data from Loretta Proctor and Bronte Society. Source: Time was dowsed, for no time of birth was recorded.

And even for that Spirit, Seer,
I've watched and sought my life-time long;
Sought him in Heaven, Hell, Earth and Air—
An endless search, and always wrong! . . .³⁹

If Emily ever harbored romantic notions about a flesh and blood man, it was her deepest secret. Unlike Charlotte, who shared her romantic dreams and obsessive infatuations with her diary and two friends, in the diary fragments that remain (many were destroyed by Charlotte after Emily's death) Emily never mentions even the most tenuous of contact with a man. Her Cancer Moon camouflaged her depth of feeling and turbulent emotions. Her book was written under a male pseudonym and even when the secret was out, few believed that a woman could have written such a story which the critics panned as "gloomy," "dismal," and "disagreeable." After Emily's death, Charlotte tried to pretend that her sister had no personal knowledge of the experiences or emotions she portrayed so graphically.

The mother, Maria (Chart 6, page 62), most likely was born at a time which would give her a Libra Moon trine Pluto rather than a Virgo Moon unaspected by the Lord of Death. If born early in the morning, the father Patrick (Chart 7, page 63) would have Moon in Cancer quincunx Pluto. The only brother, Branwell, has that double dose of the Hades Moon. His was, without doubt, a tormented Plutonian soul. He lived out the shadow Pluto archetype. His abode was Hades, undergoing periods of madness as a result of his addiction to alcohol and opium. Shortly before his death he said, "I have lain during nine long weeks utterly shattered in body and broken down in mind."⁴⁰ He, too, had hung on Ereshkigal's meathook. But his resurrection and transformation was to come through death. Branwell never did manage to live out his artistic potential.

Charlotte, Anne, and Emily's lives, and the novels that came out of them, pick up themes with which we will become increasingly familiar. They were part of a symbiotic family unit, none of which could function alone, a family which carried more than its share of deep dark secrets. They were passionate and intensely creative, almost from birth, and yet concealed this from the outside world. They were psychic: Charlotte's diary records "conjuring up the shades of those who had gone before" and Emily had visions and "visitations." Charlotte and Emily wrote novels that featured "ghostly presences" and visions. They had an intimate acquaintance with death and abandonment. Their mother died of stomach cancer when Charlotte was 5, Emily 2 and Anne only 1—a particularly painful form of "abandonment." The eldest Bronte sister became surrogate mother, but died also. Indeed, two siblings died of neglected childhood TB brought on by the appalling conditions at a charity school, a school at which Charlotte and Emily experienced abuse and isolation, under the direction of a bigoted man who misused his considerable power over those in his care. He believed that physical deprivation was good for the soul. Charlotte later used him, and the death of her "so-good" sister, in *Jane Eyre*.

The family was brought up out of duty by an aunt who had no sympathy for the motherless children in her care. The brother Branwell (Scorpio Moon trine Pluto) willingly succumbed to addiction and died "alternatively blaspheming and repenting." Charlotte herself died following exhausting sickness in pregnancy. The

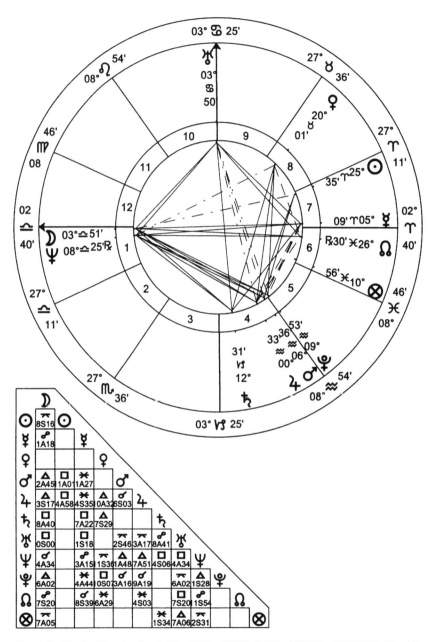

Chart 6. Maria Bronte. April 15, 1783, GMT 17.00, 50N00, 005W00. Placidus houses. Data from Loretta Proctor and Bronte Society, and biographers. Source: Time was dowsed, for no time of birth was recorded.

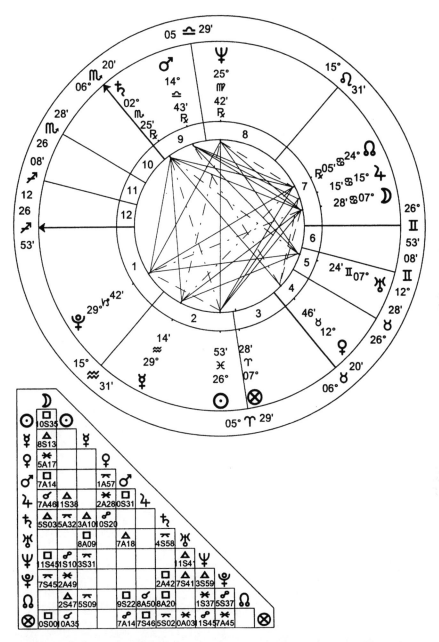

Chart 7. Patrick Bronte. March 17, 1777, GMT 3.00, 54N30, 006W00. Placidus houses. Data from Loretta Proctor and Bronte Society. Source: Time was dowsed, for no time of birth was recorded.

one ongoing nurturing female presence was a family servant. She, ironically, appears to have infected Charlotte with the stomach bug (possibly typhoid) that would end both their lives.

In her mid-20s, Charlotte conceived a compulsive "love" for a married man she met when studying abroad with Emily. He taught them language and literature and there is no doubt he had a tremendous emotional impact on Charlotte, and on her writing, which matured under his tutelage. He appears to have had far less influence on Emily who remained aloof from his charms. Charlotte felt deeply rejected when he terminated the relationship—which had been carried on mainly by passionate correspondence on her part after her return from Belgium. It was the time of her Saturn return. Her (fantasy?) lover had, she believed, encouraged her passion and then, at the instigation of his wife, who was troubled by such an intense association with one of his pupils, ignored her. Charlotte plunged into deep, Plutonian gloom. This relationship was the *prima materia* of Charlotte's tightly contained but deeply emotional writing. A thinly disguised Monsieur Heger appears in her first, unpublished, novel (*The Professor*) and in her last novel (*Villette*). We can hear Plutonian echoes in two of the poems she wrote after he terminated the relationship:

What fate, what influence lit the flame
  I still feel inly, deeply burn?

. . . . Even now the fire
  Though smothered, slackened, repelled, is burning
At my life's source.[41]

Behind a quiet exterior, Charlotte was a powerful matriarch, rigidly controlling the creation fantasies arising from the peculiarly fertile *prima materia* that lurked under the facade of a highly conventional parsonage. Her father told strange tales of his moorland parishioners, people who inhabited a world far removed from conventional life. These stories, and those of Tabby the parsonage servant, were the inspiration for *Wuthering Heights* and *The Tenant of Wildfell Hall*. Charlotte and her sisters had the gift of turning their observations and their own experiences into literature, literally tapping into the collective, archetypal forces that underlie human experience. They ventured into the taboo places where other less Plutonian souls feared to tread—loss, abuse, misuse of power, erotic and forbidden love—and explored what lay beneath the outwardly repressed and conventional lives of women at that time.

There was a peculiarly symbiotic quality to Charlotte's relationship with her siblings and there is a hint of Plutonian mystery and deviousness in that recently she has been accused of destroying the sequel to *Wuthering Heights* after the death of the author, Emily.[42] Charlotte allegedly believed that it was a brutal, coarse, and vulgar work—exactly what she thought of *Wuthering Heights* and *The Tenant of Wildfell Hall*. She had opposed publication by her sister Anne on the grounds that it would ruin the family reputation. Anne's second book opened up to public scrutiny the, then unacknowledged, life of the battered wife. *Wildfell Hall* is a powerfully Plutonian tale of rejection and isolation, alcoholism and debauchery, family violence and lingering death, with a strongly protective and manipulative mother thrown in for good measure. It is the story of a mysterious, talented woman who comes to live in an isolated farmhouse on the moor. She has a young child but no husband, and clearly harbors many secrets. Eventually she returns home to nurse the dissolute, abusive husband from whom she fled (whose invisible Plutonian presence can be felt throughout the book). When he dies, she goes back to yet another "dark lover," a man who has fallen obsessively in love with her and who compels her to reveal her secrets.

The Bronte women's literary characters were clear—but most likely unconscious—expressions of the Hades-Moon archetype in the Bronte family. Both Anne and Emily clearly drew on their experiences with Branwell, the dark Plutonian canker at the heart of the family. It would seem probable that they were, through the pages of their books, each bringing their own Plutonian animus to life. However, in Charlotte this was more overt, projected onto the men in her life (of which there were several). Emily's covert relationship with her animus was explored through her personal poems (never intended for publication) and only publicly surfaced when Heathcliff burst into being, after which she willingly surrendered her life. She was the most self-sufficient of the sisters and did not appear to need an outer partner. She carried the independent, instinctual Hecate archetype for the family.

Charlotte lived out the ancestral family pattern, what Freud called an "archaic inheritance." Her mother Maria, an Aries and a deeply frustrated woman who appears to have married somewhat beneath her station and suffered social isolation as a result, died at age 44 (although Emily's biographer says she was only 38). Charlotte in turn married, in her view, slightly beneath herself, at age 38. (Demeter thought Pluto was not good enough for her daughter. Pluto Moon mothers rarely do. Are we seeing here the shadowy presence of Maria and her mother's mother before her?) Maria never regained her strength after giving birth to Anne, her last child. She quickly succumbed to stomach cancer. She had produced six children in seven years and was no doubt exhausted by the overwhelming process of continuous pregnancy, birth, and motherhood. Demeter-like, her last thought was for her "poor children." Charlotte, in an unconscious echo of her mother, died while pregnant.

Charlotte's father, with tenaciously-clinging-to-the-past Cancer Moon (possibly inconjunct Pluto), never did accept his wife's death. After the mother's demise, death became a "dark secret." Having denied and blocked the mourning process, the whole family was caught up in it at an unconscious level. Time stood still for the next thirty years. He virtually ignored his daughters, sending most of the girls away to the school that was a living hell. When he did speak to them, as children, they had to wear masks, as Patrick Bronte believed they could express more of themselves that way. The children were raised for the most part in Plutonian isolation, their only social contact was with their siblings and through occasional, and often unwelcome, forays out into the world. Their tyrannical father, with more than a touch of paranoia, referred to the world outside the parsonage as "delusive and ensnaring." It was known to the Bronte children as "Babylon."

This suffocating, symbiotic childhood carried over into adult life. Whenever any member of the family went away from home they sickened and had to return.

Wherever possible, two of the family worked or traveled together, but even this was not enough to forestall devastating homesickness and encroaching depression, especially for Emily. Eventually, they remained at home. Charlotte admitted to a friend that she was "buried alive," but it was a burial that created space to work. The sisters bounced ideas off each other, sharing the creative process during long dark walks around the parlour. During this period Charlotte wrote *Jane Eyre*; her sister Anne completed *Agnes Grey* and produced *The Tenant of Wildfell Hall*; Emily brought *Wuthering Heights* to life, and Charlotte began work on *Shirley*. Then, Branwell, Emily, and Anne died within nine months of each other (around their first Saturn Return). It was as though they were psychically joined and could not survive without each other. After their deaths, Charlotte describes herself as "stripped and bereaved." Committed to remaining at home to look after her invalid father, she worked frantically on her novel. All her mourning and deep emotions were sublimated into her work.

After Emily's death (on a Moon-Pluto opposition, see Chart 8, page 67), Charlotte edited *Wuthering Heights* for a new publisher, prefacing it with an *apologia* in which she distanced Emily as far as possible from the disgust with which the public would greet its Plutonian contents. She assured readers that Emily herself had never known such feelings nor been involved in such outrageous events which "came out of the moors" (this despite Branwell's slide into oblivion).

One more novel followed, and two possible relationships failed—courtships again conducted mainly by correspondence. *Villette* was the most autobiographical of Charlotte's novels. Following the failure of a romance, due to an indomitable mother's opposition (a typical Hades Moon response), she suddenly switched the ending. The hero had been based on her publisher. When it became clear that their relationship was ending, the heroine turned her attention back to a Belgian professor—Monsieur Heger was resurrected. Her publisher was not pleased with this ending, nor were the critics. After the double blow, Charlotte imploded into a deep depression. In her emotional frustration, she tried to write, but never completed, her final novel, *Emma*. In a deleted passage in the manuscript, Pluto finally catches up with Persephone. The hero, a man of mature years, abducts the young heroine to his bed.

In February 1854, Charlotte's publisher married. In March Charlotte became engaged to Arthur Bell Nicholls. He had wooed her for seven long years and was adamant that only Charlotte would do as his wife. Not surprisingly this double Capricorn (Sun and Moon) had Venus conjunct Neptune square Pluto. All the obsessive qualities of Pluto went into his pursuit of Charlotte. When she refused, he threatened to kill himself. He left her alone, probably the best move he could make in the circumstances for the courtship then proceeded via the letters that so enamored Charlotte. The marriage was implacably opposed by her father. Arthur Bell Nicholls was his curate and, therefore, both Charlotte and her father looked down on him. What finally persuaded Charlotte and her father to agree was Nicholls' promise to look after Mr. Bronte for the rest of his life.

Nicholls was not a literary man, and Charlotte expressed many doubts in the months leading up to the marriage. The Victorian ideal of marriage was far removed from the peculiar freedom Charlotte had known. A wife was a man's chat-

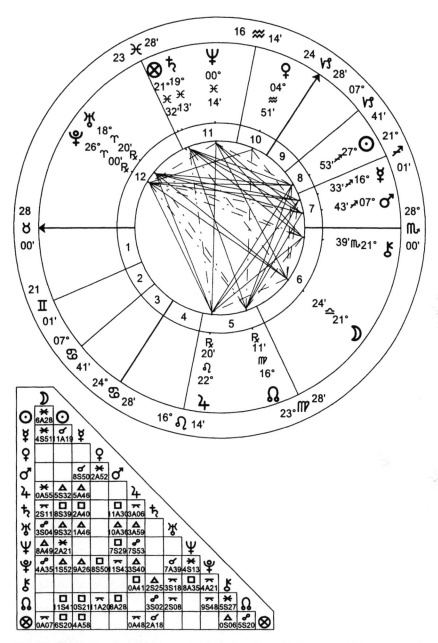

Chart 8. Emily Bronte's death. December 19, 1848, GMT 14.00, 53N59, 001W55. Placidus houses. Data from Loretta Proctor and Bronte Society. Source: Early afternoon is recorded in a family diary.

tel, his to command. Could Nicholls understand her interior life and the compulsion to write? Could he give her the space she so desperately needed. It seemed not. So, why did she marry? Well, apart from the obvious security for a spinster of limited means, her biographer Lyndall Gordon believes that Nicholls, like Pluto, could free her from invisibility. For the first time in her life, a man loved her more than she needed him. He knew her and accepted her, for the most part, as she was. He also seems to have released the passion in Charlotte. The marriage was surprisingly happy. There may be another reason, too. When he later edited *Emma*, it was Nicholls who restored the abduction scene Charlotte had deleted. Was he Pluto in disguise? Had she found yet another aspect of her inner animus, that dark lover she so craved? Certainly he was possessive and jealous enough (Pluto-Venus) to demand his wife's total attention. But did he go beyond this? Charlotte was, for once in her life, reticent about this side of her marriage, so we can only surmise. However, having fallen into Pluto's clutches once more, Charlotte lived out that dark family secret. Nine months into the marriage and pregnant, age 38, she, too, was dead. Of all the Brontes, she was the only one who expressed love and regret at her death. Her last words were of love and appreciation to her husband. Transiting Pluto had just passed over her natal Sun. Her death followed closely upon that of her surrogate mother-figure, the childhood nursemaid. Her father outlived her by six years. True to his promise, Nicholls looked after him to the end.

I like synchronicity; to me it shows that Plutonian forces are operating to bring things into right relationship. It has an air of "fateful encounter" about it. So, when I was working on this chapter, I was delighted to see an article by Loretta Proctor[43] on the Bronte family, and to find so many of my own ideas echoed there. When I contacted Loretta, she, too, felt that, although she had been writing about Pluto-Mars aspects, Charlotte must have had a Moon-Pluto connection. "Her life reeked of it as did all the family." She has also made a study of the Brontes and feels that the mother, Maria, was a deeply frustrated woman who never had a chance to express her own creativity, and that the unmanifested creativity lived on through her children (so typical of Hades Moon psychic inheritance). On the day of Maria's birth the Moon moved from Virgo to Libra and into aspect with Pluto. We can either see her as a mother who died in the service of her family (Virgo) or a woman who sacrificed herself to the demands of her relationship (Libra): contrasting aspects of the Demeter archetype.

Branwell Bronte was the most openly Plutonic of the family. He had an obsession with death, which he graphically portrayed "hanging over him" while he lay in bed. He, perhaps more than any other, lived out the shadow Hades Moon, and it may be that his sisters were inspired reflectors of his Plutonian self. As Loretta Proctor points out, "In Branwell Bronte's chart, the Moon in Scorpio trines Pluto, which with his Cancerian Sun, makes the mother image especially powerful. As we know, the Moon is considered the feminine, anima or soul image in a man's chart, his relationship with the Great Mother in all her aspects. Pluto colors the mother image with a sense of the dark, destructive and yet transformative mother. She is the Dark Moon that shows no light and appears for a brief while invisible in the night sky; she is woman in her menstrual black-blood time of the month, dark and barren as opposed to fruitful and fair. Rather than being her usual pleasant, outgoing self, she shows a rageful, depressed and deeper side of her nature. And so this unlived shadow side of Maria Branwell Bronte lived on in her children's psyches."[44] And indeed, Branwell was set on a course of self-destruction from which he seemed unable to break free. While Emily and Anne, having published and been damned, could only flee into death. Charlotte, too, seemed unable to live a "normal" domestic life. The Dark Moon archetype was too strong.

• • •

Men who are strongly attuned to the unconscious Pluto archetype may have an immature Persephone anima who manifests as a "fantasy lover." In Branwell Bronte's case, this was an older woman, the wife of his employer. In the wake of the scandal that followed, Branwell fled into addiction. This "fantasy lover" may be founded on a woman, glimpsed but once, who then "grows" within the psyche into a fully fledged inner-world figure with whom a subjective relationship is formed, as with Dante's Beatrice.[45] When the Hades Moon is involved, the inner figure is, unknowingly, founded on Mother, beside whom all other women pale into insignificance. Should the man find an anima-reflector in the outer-world, the resulting relationship is intense, cathartic, and, often traumatic, as he is pulled down to meet the source of his projections. It can also be deeply healing if he recognizes the source of his illusions and reconnects to his own feminine energies.

The negative Pluto archetype, or shadow, emerges most strongly in abusive "power-over" issues. The man, or woman, who is held hostage to this archetype uses, misuses and abuses power, subtly coercing, or beguiling, those around him; or is enthralled by the power of another. The Pluto shadow contains all the energies that humankind prefer to reject as "not mine." So, cruelty, authoritarianism, destruction, domination, and obsession are relegated to the shadow of the collective unconscious. These energies are then externalized. Plutonian figures, such as Hitler or Saddam Hussein, carry the archetype for the collective, and war is manifested. Rape and plunder, abuse and misuse are reflected in genocide, environmental pollution, and economic degradation. The creator becomes the devourer, a theme shared with the Demeter archetype.

When we are consciously attuned to the Pluto archetype, we go willingly through the fires of transformation and emerge reborn into our greatest potential. We find our power and use it wisely and well. We are, like the Eleusinian initiate, no longer afraid of death, and we embrace all our transitions, interacting with others in a transformed way. We have been into the Underworld, and survived.

• • •

As we explore the manifestations of the Hades Moon and its astrological working in real life, we will encounter the gods and goddesses again and again as they underpin all our life experiences, but most especially the deeper and darker facets of ourselves that inhabit the Underworld. For Jung, the human psyche did not merely exist within the body: "In so far as the psyche has a non-spatial aspect, there may be a psyche 'outside the body,' a region so utterly different from 'my' psychic sphere that one has to get out of oneself . . . to get there."[46] This would seem to be a Plutonian part of the unconscious, something which is "in here" and yet "beyond." Patrick Harpur wrote in *Chalice* magazine that "It might be a whole world, present in this one but invisible until we are initiated (or 'abducted') into it by its denizens. . . . It is as if, were we to penetrate deeply enough into ourselves, to the limits of the collective unconscious, the latter turns inside out." Once again, the unconscious and the Underworld are one, we have returned to Hades and its mythological inhabitants. This is the dramatization of the contents of consciousness. This is where the Dark Moon dwells.

CHAPTER 3

THE DEVOURING MOON

When a mother . . . abuses her child, she is devouring his soul, his core self. . . . One of his great journeys in life is to retrieve his soul from the depths of the Goddess's belly.
—Michael Gurian[1]

A S WE SAW IN CHAPTER 1, the natal Moon is the significator of Mother and of the mothering patterns that have been handed down through generations. Aspects to the Moon show the particular archetype, or archetypes, and the style of mothering to which we are attuned. The Moon indicates what we will meet when we incarnate. An evocation of childhood, it reflects our expectations around conception, gestation, and birth. It is our experience and, when aspected by Pluto, our dread, of being mothered and being a mother, of being nurtured. The Hades Moon can be an abusive Moon, an abuse that is subtle and covert. Abuse here is the denial of the basic selfhood of another person. Such a denial allows parents to do what they will with "their" child. When we have a Moon-Pluto connection, we have a primal fear of being devoured. As one woman put it: "Why is she [my mother] consuming my juices" (mother: Pluto conjunct Moon in Gemini; daughter: Moon in Aries square Pluto conjunct South Node and Mercury in Cancer). For the daughter, this was an old pattern. Much will depend on the other planetary aspects in the chart, particularly to the Moon; some aspects may neutralize the Hades Moon effect, others may exacerbate it beyond bearing.

ARCHETYPAL EXPECTATIONS

The Hades Moon effect is greatly intensified when both mother and child have Pluto in aspect to the Moon, or when there are cross Hades Moon aspects between the charts. But this Moon can also represent the father, particularly for girl-children. It is whichever parent, or person, is seen as the primary nurturing source. As Richard Idemon explains: "The Moon is a nurturing kind of planet, and it could feel violated by Pluto when Pluto aspects it in synastry. So the erotic side of Pluto might feel threatening or invasive to the inner mother or the inner child of the Moon person. Moon-Pluto interaspects are especially difficult in the charts of a parent and child, because there is something potentially incestuous that happens when these two planets get together. It's as if nurturing becomes contaminated with eros, with sex and power, with the desire to seduce and overcome."[2] However,

I have found that it makes little difference whose planet does the actual aspecting, the violation and incestuousness pass both ways along a Hades Moon interaspect whatever the relationship. Having so much the power over the child, it is usually the parent who is experienced as "Plutonian," but Pluto is reflected through the Moon and projected onto the parent whatever the actual dynamics of the contact. As Richard Idemon goes on to say:

> If your mother's or father's Pluto hits your Moon by synastry, you could feel erotic or incestuous messages coming from them, or you might experience them as power trippers. In other words, it's not just milk that comes in your bottle, but something Plutonian is being transmitted as well. The problem is enhanced if your mother, for instance, is not getting her erotic needs met by your father, and therefore turns to you (the child) for that kind of fulfillment. Or if your father is not getting his erotic needs met by your mother, and he then looks to you for that kind of involvement. Normally, it tends to go cross-sexually—mother to son, and father to daughter. In any case, it indicates that the person who is meant to nurture you is also giving you messages of a sexual or erotic nature. As a child, you will find this very confusing, because of the incest taboo. Your adult relationships could be complicated by this issue, because you'll feel uneasy about sex with anyone you are close to.[3]

Much of our experience operates at an unconscious level. We are not necessarily looking here at the actual mother. It is rather our Hades Moon influenced perception of mother, and the archetypal mother we carry. It is what we notice at an unconscious, barely verbal, level. Our experience is filtered through the lens of our perception and expectations, expectations which may well go back into other lives. Nevertheless, Hades Moon children do seem to have an uncanny knack of attracting a Moon-Pluto mother who embodies these archetypal qualities.

The negative Hades Moon archetypal mother is dominating, demanding, invasive, manipulative, all powerful. She rules by approval, or lack of it; she is overprotective and subtly persuasive, but this, especially when acted out by the actual mother, may be hidden behind a facade of apparent weakness or "love." So often the face shown to the family is different from that presented to the outside world. And all too frequently, the true maternal nature lurks beneath a facade of apparent kindliness and concern for her children. This mother "only does what is best" for her family, but is adept at emotional blackmail.

It may well be that the mother herself has no desire to be devouring. Indeed, she may be fighting for her freedom. In extreme cases, she may be experiencing her child as a parasitic force leaching her energy, and she may have an overwhelming need to cut the ties that bind the child to her. But her child demands continued support, drawing strength from the mother. Such mothers have often had to be particularly strong within *even though they may not feel that way*. One Sagittarian friend of mine had a Hades Moon daughter. To anyone looking on, and to herself, the mother did not appear to be dominating, but her daughter perceived her as so. An army wife, the mother had been in sole charge of the family for months at a time. Eventually, her husband left her to bring up three teenage children alone. Her daughter said: "You were always so good at everything, so competent, so much in control. I felt inadequate and unable to do anything for myself, so I relied on you." It came as a great surprise to the daughter to find that her mother had always felt herself to be an incompetent mother who did not do enough for her children. These feelings had eventually propelled the mother into therapy and she then trained as a psychotherapist. But it was some years before she addressed the issue of her daughter and was able to speak to her about the parasitic pull she was still experiencing from her.

Not surprisingly, as a young adult the daughter still relied on her mother to meet all her needs. When she became a mother herself, overwhelmed by the task of caring for her child, she took the child home to mother so that she herself could be nurtured and supported. Her mother, while offering support, gently tried to return her to her own home, but the daughter felt totally rejected. It took several months before the mother was able to convince the daughter that the relationship had to become that of an adult mother and daughter. And it was quite a few months before the daughter was ready to take this step. On the way, she had to confront many of her own dark places and insecurities. Her mother was there for her, not in a devouring, dominating way, but offering her the opportunity to grow from within and find her own strength. In doing so, she showed her the way forward in being a mother herself.

The positive Hades Moon Mother is empowering and cathartic. She is not afraid of the deep dark emotions that she and her child may need to experience. She understands, and is not afraid of, the obsessive emotional dynamics of Hades. Attuned to the transforming power of Pluto, she is able to be a guide into the wilderness within. As the challenge of Moon-Pluto aspects is to overcome the compulsiveness of the old emotional patterns, she is able to help the child break through into emotional self-reliance. But, the way she offers this lesson may well appear to be negative or destructive at first glance. She may teach through rejection and alienation, or by manipulating and engulfing the child to such an extent that there is no choice but to separate.

A family permeated with Moon-Pluto contacts may appear to be a family united against the world, but that unity may hide some very abusive, deep dark family secrets (always remembering that abuse is not necessarily a physical factor: Plutonian abuse occurs on the emotional, mental, and spiritual levels). The tendency is for Hades Moon matriarchs to "divide and rule," subtly setting one family member off against another, so that what is presented as a united front is actually mother's perception of how a family should be and is based on unhealthy, symbiotic dependence rather than on valuing each member for his or her own intrinsic individuality.

Gestation and birth is our initial experience of mothering. So often with the Hades Moon it is an act of death rather than life. Somehow the incarnating soul has to face extinction in order to live. Birth is life-threatening, and when birth has been successfully negotiated, the child may be met with rejection. As we shall see in chapter 4, the Hades Moon shows up strongly where children are adopted or brought up by surrogate parents. Ludwig van Beethoven, a solitary man, had the Moon at 18° Sagittarius semi-sextile Pluto at 17° Capricorn (an inconjunct aspect).

In a fictionalized biography,[4] author Leslie Kenton tells of Beethoven recounting the story of his birth, of how his mother had already had a stillborn child whom she had wished dead during the difficult birth. Her fear is that the child will "kill to live, tear the life from her in order to survive." He tells how she, in the midst of another agonizing protracted labor decides it cannot go on, and, by sheer force of will, delays the labor still further until the child is torn from her by the midwife. On seeing the infant Ludwig, she rejects him, sends him to live with a wet nurse, and adamantly refuses to tend him when he is returned by the nurse as too demanding, withholding mothering as he grows. This action has profound consequences throughout his life. Fact or fiction, this is the perfect reflection of an openly rejecting Hades Moon at work. Other Hades Moon children are denied nurturing in much more subtle ways.

A woman with the Moon conjunct Pluto in Cancer close to the midheaven asked me to do a karmic reading with her adopted son, who had the Moon in Pisces opposite Pluto in Virgo. His Moon was closely inconjunct her Pluto; it was clearly an old contact. She said she had experienced "no blending with him" and had had a vivid dream in which he was a Roman soldier who was whipping her. From the other synastry between the charts, they were clearly working out old, personal, issues of duty and an unrealistic expectation of "mothering." What struck me most forcefully from the photograph of her 29-year-old son was that this man, who had incarnated expecting rejection and had found it through being given up for adoption, was dressed in a diaper and was sucking on an empty baby's feeding bottle. As Richard Idemon says, it was not milk that was coming through his bottle. It was Pluto. He was clearly showing his unconscious lunar need for nurturing, a need which his adopted mother, who had taken on Pluto's role, had, somehow, never been able to fulfill.

In its worst manifestation, the Hades Moon is the uncut psychic umbilical cord that strangles our individuality and demands total loyalty to "She who must be obeyed." The archetypal Hades Moon mother is the "Great No Sayer," that terrible, devouring figure on whom we depend for our very life but who, on a whim or in anger, could snuff that life out like a candle. It is Demeter laying waste to the land in her apocalyptic grief. This Moon is attuned to all the dark mother archetypes, and meets them "out there" in the world and "in here" in the deeper recesses of the psyche. It is the stuff of nightmares and traumatic daylight hours:

Clutched within your cold-shadow embrace,
I have felt you, slow and brutal,
strip the colours from my life.

Now two remain. Pure.

One is black. It is my mind.
Stay away from my mind.
Sunwracked scorpions lurk by the door.
They will tear your blistering mouth to shreds.

The other is red. It is my heart.
Stay away from my heart.
It is swollen and thick with stitches ill-thread.
One cut, and the air will be blood.[5]

Mother's approval or disapproval becomes all consuming—and life threatening. Her love, or lack of it, is a weapon that can create or destroy at will. This is the devouring mother archetype to whom we were introduced in chapter 2. We will explore her precise effect on her children as we penetrate further into the Hades Moon. It is, however, a picture with which many Hades Moon children can identify. Some never break free, others go to hell and back to do so, but all know the fundamental fear of the devouring Moon.

Nevertheless, I have many clients, who on first hearing that the Hades Moon can indicate mother problems, say: "Oh no, I had/have a wonderful relationship with my mother." In cases where the actual mother was far removed from the archetype, some people have had the healing experience of "good mothering" (usually cases where the aspects were easy ones and the actual mother did not herself carry the Hades Moon). But, having explored the relationship further, and sometimes after years of therapy, other people will suddenly realize that the relationship appeared to be wonderful because it was so close that it became parasitic, so subjective that it allowed no separation between mother and child. Some people did not dare see it any other way than "blissful." It was how they had been programmed to view the experience rather than the actuality of it. Tony, whom we will meet later in the chapter, told me that he had had a wonderul childhood almost in the same sentence that he told me his mother had suffered from severe post natal depression when his younger brother was born and his father had been dying of cancer for eight years. Later he recognized how traumatized he had been, not only during that period, but prior to it as well. Indeed, his "happy childhood" had spanned the first two years only. But it took him until middle age to admit that fact. Viewed more objectively, as with so many Hades Moon children, it was symbiotic, claustrophic, and suffocating.

There is no privacy in the Hades Moon. Mother has to be involved in everything. Several people, men and women, have given the example of being bathed by their mothers way past puberty. Friends are vetted, activities approved—or they do not happen at all. It is Demeter and Persephone before the abduction. Explored more deeply, the devouring dynamics of that "wonderful relationship" become apparent. We can recognize why the virginal Persephone had to be taken down into the depths of her unconscious in order to find a mature identity.

With such a symbiotic relationship, the Hades Moon child learns to be wary, to respond to the subtle undercurrents in a home. Even when that home is apparently loving and happy, the psychic umbilical cord conveys to the child every moment of mother's unvoiced unhappiness, disappointment, frustration, and displeasure. This child has an antenna that picks up the hidden vibrations of maternal rage, and internalizes that rage as "my badness" rather than "her problem." This is the wounded child with an extremely thin skin and sensors that are acutely aware of pain, particularly emotional pain, transmitted by others but received as "mine." This is the child who, when questioned, will say: "Yes, I had a happy childhood," because any other answer would bring down the wrath of the archetype. But it is also the child who may have been so traumatized that the truth is hidden below layers of lies and evasions. So much depends on keeping mother sweet that no acknowledgment of her danger can be made. After all, without mother there would be nothing: "Hasn't she told me so a million times?" We cannot face her unforgiving rage. At some deep part of the adult psyche, that fear of being devoured or abandoned remains, but cannot be acknowledged until something happens to change the dynamics.

THE UNSAFE WOMB

This "danger from the mother" might well start pre-birth. It has long been known that the developing fetus manipulates the mother's physiology for its own ends. It is the fetus who, for instance, controls the amount of sugar in the mother's blood, and her blood pressure, etc., not the mother. One Hades Moon mother-to-be was so hyperaware of this process that she referred to the baby as "The Vampire."

Hormones are sent out by the fetus during the whole pregnancy. These hormones also trigger the birth process. However, quite apart from the karmic possibilities explored later, new theories about conception and gestation indicate that, far from being a blissful experience of harmonious union, life in the womb is a continuous battle for survival. Dr. David Haig[6] describes it as "a struggle for control between the mother and the fetus." In order to gain food from the mother's blood, the fetus, through the parasitic placenta, actually destroys the walls of the blood vessels in the uterus. The mother's body then tries to stop the placenta from invading too strongly through "killer cells" which ward off over-invasion by the "alien" cells. Dr. Charles Loke[7] says: "It [the placenta] is almost like a cancer eating into her [the mother's uterus]." Over 50 percent of pregnancies are miscarried, often because the mother's body rejects the "alien" at a very early stage. "Mother nature" appears to have her own way of limiting the population. A normal pregnancy depends on a viable equilibrium being maintained. When mother and baby fail to match strategies, problems begin. Over-invasion will rupture the uterus and the mother will die. Too much rejection on the part of the mother results in reduced blood supply to the fetus, who will expire.

Dr. Phil Bennett[8] has pointed out that it is genes which are desperate to survive, not fetuses who are merely carriers for the genes. Genes are intertwined strands of inherited urges toward control, toward things being a certain way. Warring inherited patterns are passed on through the parents' genes. The father's genes are directed toward a large baby which survives at all costs. The mother's genes oppose this. For her survival, the baby cannot grow too large in the womb. So, the "devouring mother" is both a physical and psychic reality. An inheritance passed down through the genes, the battle with the devouring mother starts pre-birth. She is much more than a mythological archetype. The Plutonian experience of rejection also begins in utero.

It may well be that Pluto-Moon attuned fetuses are the ones who resonate most strongly with this battle for survival. Certainly, in all the pre-birth work I have carried out with clients, it was those with the Hades Moon who were most tuned in to the possibility of destruction, and to the mother's fear of annihilation and loss of control that accompanied the pregnancy. And it is most often those women with the Hades Moon who find it difficult to be pregnant and suffer from what now seem to be inherited patterns of prenatal disease such as pre-eclampsia and other toxic states, states that are a by-product of this struggle for survival.

The Hades Moon, and the devouring mother, is reflected too in life-threatening childhood events: difficult birth, traumatic separations, alienation and rejection. It is the mother who becomes caretaker to the family, and then cannot let go and so devours her adult children. The mother whose powerful unmet lunar needs are projected onto her children, who must then sustain and fulfill them or be annihilated. It is the surrogate mother-mentor who, turned to for help in achieving independence, facilitates not life-enhancing separateness but rather engulfs the "child" into her own egotistical Demeter-like powerful overself. It is the Hades Moon person who must, above all others, learn that creativity is not necessarily biological. It is the fight to give birth to one's own Self.

With a natal Moon-Pluto connection, the maternal matrix, the "cosmic soup" out of which we are born and in which we must live, or die, is permeated with the darkness of Pluto. I had one client (Moon in Aquarius opposite Pluto conjunct Venus in Leo) who was convinced that his mother was trying to kill him. He thought it must have been a past life connection. When he began to explore his childhood, he found that she had tried to abort him but it had not worked (an event later confirmed by his father). He still carried the psychic imprint of that event. We had to go back in regression to before his birth and heal that trauma before he could feel safe with her as his mother. Needless to say, the interaction stretched way back in time and had never been easy.

The Hades Moon is what we expect, what we attract, what we manifest in our life. If it does not accompany our birth, and much of that will depend on the placement of Pluto in the chart and other aspects to the Moon, we will meet it sooner or later, in someone or other, if only to ensure that we really have broken free of the archtype's hold.

THE MATERNAL MATRIX

One moment I was out in wide, all-encompassing space. The next I was compressed to the size of a pin-head and nailed into place. I tried to expand, to move, but I was held inexorably. I had been conceived.

"Let me out," I cried, "Let me go, I don't want to be here. It was all a mistake." But I was told that, had I left, my spirit would not have returned, I had to see it through. And there I stayed for the next ten months, feeling suffocated and poisoned by the emanations of my mother's fear and rage. The whole time I wanted to leave, to go "home." I was hot, uncomfortable, confined, unable to breathe. I wanted "away,"

not "out." Between my Moon-Pluto fear of incarnation and my Hades Moon mother's desire to hold onto her child at all costs, getting born became a life and death struggle. One which I eventually "won" but took no pleasure in for many years.

This was my experience, under hypnosis, of conception and intrauterine life.

At a workshop, I was asked if I came from a big bang or damp squib? It took a moment to sink in that the question was about conception. John Christian, the workshop facilitator, felt that a life arising from a moment of huge mutual pleasure would clearly stamp a different imprint to one arising from duty or coercion. With my Hades Moon background, and the work I had done to explore my conception, I could only reply that I came from a very damp squib indeed. The sexual act had been to retain control over an errant husband, not for shared pleasure. For Hades Moon people, sexual activity can be a way of controlling and possessing the partner. It comes from "ownership" and domination rather than real love and intimacy. There is no sharing, just emotional consumption and engulfment. This is why so many people feel subtly frustrated and unhappy in their marriage. As a result conception, and subsequent life, are claustrophobic and manipulative, mirroring the parental ambience.

It is no wonder then that whenever Howard Sasportas, and others, waxed lyrical about the blissful oneness of life in the womb, I would be silently screaming "It isn't like that." Coming from a long line of Moon-Pluto women, and with Pluto on the Ascendant square the 4th house Moon in Scorpio, my maternal matrix was threatening, claustrophobic, and pathogenic. No Neptunian bliss here. Eventually, Howard modified his views to "five star wombs and no-star wombs" to encompass my, and my co-Hades Mooners' Plutonian experiences.

For me, as with so many Hades Moon connections, the womb was a tomb, a most unsafe place to be. It was wartime Britain; my father was flying with Bomber Command and his life expectancy was just six weeks. My mother was terrified and angry. Her body reflected that in "fight or flight" chemical secretions and the placenta was no defense against such pollution. She and her closest friend had decided to have babies so they would have something to remember their husbands by: "a part of him would remain with me." The friend had her baby first; he was stillborn. My mother, frightened of a similar loss, and unable to face her friend with a live baby, went way over time. The womb became a prison, but one from which I was loathe to escape.

I have spontaneously re-lived that intrauterine sojourn and my Plutonian birth many times. Each time another piece of the puzzle clicks into place, another facet is made more clear. For a long time the experience was silent, except for the thudding drumming of my mother's heart. But, on a trip to Rhodos, I went through an 860m long "rebirthing channel." Up to my thighs in water and in utter blackness, I had made the trip ten years previously. Then it was a silent, mystical, magical experience. This last time it was different. Behind me, a group of Germans were creating a fearsome noise. No words could be made out, just this jangling cacophany of sound that struck to my very core. A few meters into the tunnel, too late to go back, the blackness and the noise took over. I felt threatened, a nameless dread. I was walking through treacle, every step an effort. Enormous fear welled up in me. It was only by "standing in my hoop," the calm center of myself, and accepting the fear, that I was able to go forward toward the blessed light of the green lake at the end of the tunnel. I recognized that my journey down the birth canal, so reminiscent of the death tunnel, had been accompanied by this same enormous fear and the incoherent sounds of rage. Now, in Rhodos, once again Pluto was on the rise. The transiting Moon was sextile my natal Moon, and conjunct natal Chiron. The birth trauma was making itself felt once again. It was time for more healing.

The opportunity came shortly afterward at an all night Pluto Ritual that I joined when the initial writing of this book was well underway. It seemed too synchronous to miss. The participants, a fateful thirteen until someone else was dug up at the last minute to make even numbers, were told nothing except that we would be journeying across the river Styx and into Hades. To accompany the journey, transiting Pluto, the Sun, and Jupiter were conjunct at the end of Scorpio. The eclipsed Full Moon in Taurus had opposed Pluto the day before the ritual. Earlier in the month, the eclipsed Sun had been on my Scorpio Moon. During the ritual, the transiting Moon in Gemini (opposing my natal Mercury) was communicating the previously hidden knowledge that had been released into consciousness by those eclipses. It was also the period of my Chiron Return. Time to heal my karmic wound and all the pain of being in incarnation. On my first Chiron square—the focusing of the wound—at age 5½, I had almost died of pneumonia: I could not breathe. Incarnation was suffocating me. On my Chiron opposition, I gave birth to my daughter and underwent a near-death experience during the delivery. On the following square, I had a car crash "which should have been fatal" to quote the paramedic who attended. Physically, I was unhurt but I was in deep depression for months after that. I realized I had subsconsciously wanted it to be fatal. That double Hades Moon has a particularly strong death wish! With the Chiron Return, I was determined to heal the wound before Pluto moved onto my Sun and fifteen more years of Pluto transits began. But, it was not to be. As I found out, I needed my time in Hades.

During the ritual, the facilitators first read the myths of Ereshkigal and Persephone with which I was so familiar. Then it was announced that we were to make our death masks. My Plutonian partner for the evening had natal Moon conjunct Pluto in Cancer in the 8th house, which was then being opposed by the transiting Uranus Neptune conjunction, with transiting Pluto right on his Scorpio Ascendant. He was as familiar with Hades as I was.

He covered my hairline and eyebrows with petroleum jelly and started laying the wet plaster bandages on my face. He was well into the task when he suddenly realized he should have covered my whole face with the petroleum jelly. Off came the mask. Death number one had been aborted—or was it the first birth? On went the mask again. Only to find that this time, when it dried, the mask was stuck. With the aid of a pair of scissors, I was given a caesarian death, or birth, whichever way you want to look at it. However, I was so busy with my inner world at this time that the external factors made little impact. As the first bandages went on, a piece was read about dark and difficult descents and narrow places, the entrance to the Underworld. I found myself living my death from the spirit world into the womb-tomb, a death which I seemed to repeat twice because the first time I spontaneously aborted. Hence, the second time, instead of the spirit being loosely attached to the developing embryo, as I had envisaged, I was pinned there. My granddaughter (Aries Moon inconjunct Pluto on a Scorpio Ascendant), who had been stillborn the first time she tried to incarnate (Virgo Moon septile Pluto), once asked indignantly, age 4: "Do you know what that God did? He put me in a trap and sent me down to Earth, but I managed to escape. And you know what? He put me in another trap and sent me back again." Even though I do believe that we choose to come back, I know just how she felt!

During the mask-making, however, I re-lived many rituals and initiatory deaths. I joined my teacher, Christine Hartley, in the sarcophagus where she awakened to find herself entombed.[9] Having been given drugs to simulate death, she awoke before the priests had her safely in the temple. For Christine, that led to lives-long claustrophobia, but for me as I accompanied her, it was yet another rebirth, and a merging with her wisdom and power. No wonder my mask did not want to come off, I was only a fraction of the way through my initiatory journey when the time came to wriggle our faces to release the mask. Mine sprang free from my eyes and mouth (a great relief) but remained attached at hairline and, significantly, above my throat exactly as my face had been imprisoned at birth (I had presented face rather than crown up). Even now, I dislike a bright overhead light as it brings back the horrible shock of being thrust into incarnation only to find myself trapped at the last moment. My natal Pluto on the Ascendant needed a midwife to release. In his "delivery," my transiting-Pluto-on-the-Ascendant companion tore his mask off before I could help. Appropriately for transiting Pluto just entering his 1st house, and natal 8th-house Pluto, he gave birth to himself.

Although we were then supposed to dream, no further work was possible for me. I remained with one foot lodged in Hades. Indeed, as I was packing up to go, I knelt down and my left knee "popped" out. It was all I could do to hobble to my car and find my way home. I literally crawled into bed and lay in agony, relieved only by a good laugh at Patric Walker's newspaper horoscope for Sagittarius that day telling me that this was the time to stand firmly on my own two feet!

I then did a session with a shamanistic healer to release the negative Moon-Pluto pattern in my family. We intended to heal seven generations back so that the future generations could be freed. The Moon was in maternal Cancer, my 12th house, trining my natal Moon. It seemed an appropriate time to work both on the ancestral patterns and on regaining myself. It became just like a labor, with my birth sister empathetically urging me to "breathe," to get out of my head and into my belly to "push it out." As I squatted there, I traveled back through my birth and conception, letting out all the howls of rage from deep within my womb. Then the note changed, became a pure sonic vibration, a different note. With one last triumphant push, I expelled myself out through my throat. I felt reconnected to my creative energies.

Working with Pluto is rather like peeling an onion, however. There is layer upon layer, and I was aware that I needed to heal even more of my birth trauma. Almost a year later, I went to a workshop to celebrate Pluto and Jupiter moving into Sagittarius (and, incidentally, moving toward my Sun). It was my birthday and we had been promised a trip out through our death and into the between-life state and then back into incarnation. The workshop felt wrong from the start. I stuck it out in the hope of the rebirth to come—it was in any case beautifully mirroring the uterine hell I had once inhabited.

We lay down for the journey through death and out of the body. No problem here! I was gone. But then, as we were gradually and blissfully being reborn and I was on the verge of a creative and positive birth experience, music crashed in so loudly that I was jolted back into my body. It was so painful that I felt physically ill. I did not bother to go back for day two! Instead I performed an "Opening of the Mouth" ceremony on the death mask I had made in that other Pluto workshop. It triggered a creative birth beyond my expectations. Two books were written and published in three months, and a project I had been totally blocked on suddenly found a publisher and came back to life. *The Hades Moon* had to be put on the back burner until Pluto reached my Sun for the third time and I took another trip to Hades.

My experiences are typical of the Pluto-Moon "mothering" experience. Conception, gestation, and birth are frequently traumatic, life-threatening, and exceedingly painful, as are childhood and childbirth. So many Moon-Pluto children are born with the umbilical cord wrapped around their necks, or they have forceps or caesarian births, that I now automatically ask the question: "Did you almost die at birth?" The creative force often stagnates or turns sour. Creations on all levels are aborted or stillborn. For other Hades Moon people, however, there is joy and bliss in the desire to incarnate. "But, somehow," as one person put it, "When I was born, I found myself in a lunatic asylum and switched off." Or, they are so much wanted that they find themselves suffocating under the smothering maternal love that overwhelms them. The Hades Moon is, after all, a mirror and what is reflected in that mirror is Pluto.

For everyone, no matter what aspects their Moon may have, the birth experience is a brush with death. As Stanislav Grof puts it, "We actually all taste death somehow in the process of being born."[10] He points out that every uterine contraction cuts off the blood supply to the child; no nourishment or oxygen flows down the cord at that moment. For those few seconds, the child "dies." And, of course, this transition is a death, just as conception is a death from the world of the spirit into the world of the body. Now the journey is from the dependency of the womb into the hostile external environment of separation from Mother, a move that is fraught with danger as the baby, having sent out the hormonal signals that start labor, meets the intractable power of the cervix that only reluctantly dilates to allow passage.

Initially, birth is the Plutonian experience of an irresistible force meeting an immovable object. When the portal does finally open, and initiation into life begins, then the journey down the birth canal is an alternation of contraction and repulsion, as the child is expelled from the uterine waters into the harsh reality of the outside world. We are moving from the interconnectedness of the lunar unconscious into the separateness of the Sun, dying through Pluto so that we may be born again. In Grof's opinion, this automatically leads to spiritual openings in the psyche. No wonder part of the Egyptian Osirian initiation and the Greek Eleusinian Mysteries of Demeter and Persephone included a "death" passage through a narrow tunnel which led to spiritual rebirth.

This is why so many people, when reliving their birth, experience a sense of being trapped, confined with no way out; and find themselves choking as they try to take a breath before they have reached the air. That paradoxical sense of being squeezed and sucked back, expelled and yet held onto is an insidious metaphor for the struggle between life and death, oneness and individuality. Birth is the fight to die to oneness, to become differentiated. For the Hades Moon, however, the battle seems to be that much more intense, whether it is with death or with life. We will explore (chapter 4) just how many Hades Moons are met with rejection, abandonment, and alienation, or with a smothering, devouring maternal instinct that allows for no separation or individual development of self. While the physical umbilical cord might be cut at birth, the Hades Moon mother keeps the psychic umbilical cord strangulatingly tight, even when a vast distance intervenes, or when there is no biological birth-connection. Adoptive or surrogate mothers can be just as suffocating. We will look in chapter 9 at how birth trauma can be healed, and at positive approaches to birth that allow the spiritual dimension to unfold.

Fortunately for those with such a difficult experience of mother, Moon-Pluto aspects can also indicate a grandmother or other surrogate mother figure who is close but not overwhelming, someone who can be turned to for supportive nurturing, for a little bit of space and room to draw breath, for encouragement to develop a sense of self apart from Mother. Depending on the aspects involved, this may be a figure from a past life or part of our soul group who has incarnated with us specifically to support us while we go through our traumatic mothering and separation process (see chapters 4 and 6).

For other Hades Moon people, the (surrogate) mother turns out to actually be the birth grandmother. They are brought up as though they are the child of the grandmother and brother or sister to her children, sometimes with formal adoption but more usually without. In several cases, it has been because the mother gave birth at a very early age and, to avoid "shaming the family," her mother then took on the childrearing. This can cause great confusion when the child later learns the truth, especially if the birth mother suddenly decides to take her child back. One such child was passed backward and forward for years as the mother tried, but failed, to make a success of the mothering role. Fortunately for that child, the grandmother was always there to step in and give her a home when necessary. In another case, the grandmother (Moon square Pluto) desperately wanted "her child" (Moon opposite Pluto) and fought a court case to reobtain possession, but the court ruled against her and the child had to be returned to her mother (Moon trine Pluto). There have been many bitter battles fought between mother and daughter over whose "daughter" a child actually was.

Thomas Hamilton (Chart 9, page 83) who ran amok with a gun in a primary school classroom in Dunblane, Scotland, killing sixteen young children and himself, was brought up by his grandmother as though she was his mother. The woman who was really his mother had the illegitimate child but he was brought up to believe she was his sister. His Scorpio Moon, in the 5th house of children, squared Pluto conjunct the South Node. An isolated loner, he felt extremely alienated from

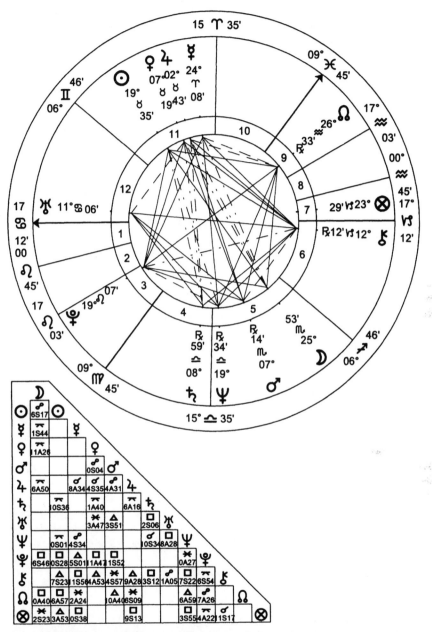

Chart 9. Thomas Hamilton. Born May 10, 1952, GMT 07.50, 55N53, 004W15. Placidus houses. Data from Jean Ridder-Patrick, and confirmed by Astrological Association Databank. There are two charts circulating for Hamilton; this is the correct one. Source: birth certificate.

society. He had been accused of being a pedophile, but protested his innocence. His doubly hadean Moon held long repressed resentments which erupted in violent action. His enormous frustration and the sense of being rejected by the world literally blew: transiting Mars was inconjunct his natal Pluto and trine natal Moon, bringing out all the inherent violence of the Hades Moon (see chapter 5).

The immediate reaction was extremely interesting. A stunned British parliament debated motions on increasing school security (there had been several such incidents, although this was the one with the highest death toll) and on banning handguns. All other business was put aside. Hamilton had been in the habit of contacting members of Parliament and had even written to the Queen to air his grievances (symbolically appealing to the Great Mother to take care of him). Just before the massacre, Pluto had turned retrograde. Shortly afterward, there was a lunar eclipse conjunct transiting Chiron in Libra, virtually conjuncting Thomas Hamilton's natal Neptune and then a solar eclipse in Aries 4° off his natal Mercury. Remember, eclipses have their strongest effect *before* they happen. Was there something left from the Pluto transit of Scorpio that needed to be drawn to the surface? Was Hamilton acting as a hadean "agent for the collective"? British astrologer Dennis Elwell has suggested that a cosmic process was at work in the collective psyche here (the world saw a tremendous upsurge of violence and terrorist activity at that time). He feels that by bringing together Plutonian key words, we can see regeneration arising from elimination, offering a heightened awareness. He felt that, terrible though they are, external events like Dunblane could well be a healing catharsis for the planet as a whole.

THE ABSENT FATHER

Many people with a strong Moon-Pluto mother experience a "disengaged father." To be absent, father does not need to be physically away from the home. This phenomenon can manifest in various ways according to the other aspects in the child's chart. He may be emotionally withdrawn, perhaps a puer who is unable to offer emotional bonding. He can be so busy attending to his wife's needs, that he has no energy left for his child. He may be a remote and austere figure who takes no part in nurturing. He may well have no idea who his child really is. On the other hand, he may appear to be a wonderful father. It is just that, when his support is needed, he is somehow *not there*. Or, as is often the case, he has an overwhelming addiction that holds all his attention (not necessarily drink or drugs; Hades Moon fathers have sexual addictions, are workaholics, or have outside interests that consume them). Nevertheless, as we shall see, Moon-Pluto fathers do have a habit of disappearing, of losing touch, or never being known at all.

MATERNAL BONDAGE

> *Separating from our mothers is a primordial door we must walk through if we are to learn about huge and deep parts of ourselves that our mothers have not been able to show us.*
> —Michael Gurian[11]

For psychological and emotional health in adulthood, the bonds that hold mother and child together have to be cut at an appropriate age, not too early, not too late.

As we have seen, Moon-Pluto mothers tend to keep the psychic umbilical cord suf-focatingly tight—and Moon-Pluto children are adept at sneaking around to retie the apron strings that hold them to mother. Or, as we shall explore later, the child may be met with abandonment and rejection, and the bond is cut far too early (al-though subtle psychic connections may continue even when the child has been adopted or when the parent has died). The Moon-Pluto child's equivalent attitude is to leave home, to go as far away as possible, to reject the parent. This may hap-pen on a psychic level long before it is physically possible to leave. Resentment then festers into hatred. But hatred does not help separation. Hatred consumes our thoughts and our energy and ties us to the object of our hatred ever more firmly.

In a healthy family with both parents present, a boy entering puberty will at first identify with and then confront his father. This weans him from the primal de-pendency on the mother and enables him to develop a sense of self. If a father, or suitable father figure, is not there, or if the father is weak, as is so often the case when mother is all-powerful, then adolescence renews the bond between mother and son. He is reluctant to leave home, becoming the uncommitted puer. His adult relationships with women will revolve around punishing them for his mother's "abuses, sins and crimes." He inhabits an internal dichotomy of desperate need for love and the impulse to push his partner away so that he can find the freedom from mother that he craves.

In girls, the release from bondage may only be achieved through marriage. All too often, she unconsciously chooses a mate who reflects her father's qualities. Moon-Pluto daughters inevitably have unfulfilled fathering needs, in which case, she will quickly find that her husband's unresolved issues intermesh with her own. She becomes the all-powerful one within the relationship and they play out mother and son and father and daughter issues that do not really belong to that relation-ship at all. The projections may well destroy the marriage. Or, the symbiotic rela-tionship with her mother will continue and intervene in the marital relationship. In this scenario, a daughter has no sense of her own identity. Both mother and daugh-ter need to let go so that they can move into an appropriate adult interaction.

In both men and women, difficulty in freeing from the mother results in fear of feminine power and of the depth of the feminine nature. But women may find that they have a complusion to explore those depths, while men fear it so deeply that they eventually attract exactly what they most dread and become sucked down into the depths. For both sexes, the healing comes in willingly surrendering to this process. By venturing into the depths and finding themselves reflected in the deep dark places that frame inner identity, Hades becomes the abode of the self, the place where we nurture ourselves, the site of our separation and individuality. Only there can true freedom from the mother be found, freedom that can be brought up into the outerworld.

GENDER DIFFERENCES

There is no doubt that, even though the basic resonances are the same, males and females experience different manifestations of the Pluto-Moon energy and re-spond accordingly. A Hades Moon mother may well be overprotective and smother all her children. But she treats them in a subtly different way. A daughter

has to be protected at all costs. What may be appropriate for a young girl is carried on into adulthood. A son, on the other hand, may be encouraged to become
a surrogate husband to mother at a very young age. Especially if, as is so often the
case, the husband/father has left home. There is also enormous confusion between
the archetypal mother image carried by the son, and the actual mother. Mother,
and women in general, are perceived through the lens of the devouring mother archetype. As Loren Pedersen says, "What is probably most confusing to a man in his
attempts to understand his relationships to his mother as well as to other women is
the role the archetypal mother continues to unconsciously play. This powerful image exerts its effect on his psyche in a way that tremendously exaggerates the way
his mother or other women appear to him. . . . Even after the personal mother has
been left behind, and even if she had died, the archetypal mother remains a potent
goddess image."[12]

In contrast, all the mother's unlived life is projected onto her daughter. She is
expected to actualize what mother has been unable to live out. So, careers are
geared to what mother would have wanted. Or suitable marriage partners are thrust
upon an inexperienced girl. As the mother is so often frustrated and disappointed
within her own marriage, she wants to be sure that her daughter will have a different experience. But the unconscious dynamics pull in a partner who repeats the
pattern.

Notwithstanding, many Hades Moon mothers want their daughter to remain
single. The ulterior motive is having a dutiful carer for their old age. In such cases,
daughters are warned about men, who are presented through the warped eyes of
mother love. Sex is a taboo even when the daughter is fully mature; moral disapproval may cover an innate abhorrence. An unspoken, but clearly emanated, disgust
permeates any possibility of relationship. But so often the disapproval is an unconscious ploy for Demeter to protect her daughter from the inner knowledge that
contact with Pluto could bring. She wants to keep the daughter tied tight, which
she equates with safety, and with love. Such "programing" may be blatant, open coercion to mother's point of view. But it may also be so subtle that a woman does
not perceive its existence in the depths of her being. But she is all too aware of the
traumatic and painful relationships it engenders as she matures.

The problem for both men and women with living out the parent's unfulfilled
life is that, if they succeed, then the shadow rises up. The shadow is jealousy and resentment. The parent feels, "Why could I not have that?" As the child is programmed to take care of the needs of the mother, to make sure she is happy, he or
she is caught in a terrible dilemma. To fulfill the enormous potential of the Hades
Moon is to become one's self, but to keep mother placated means hiding oneself.
So, all too often, the child is subtly set up to fail, to make the parent feel, "Well, it's
okay, she (or he) couldn't do it either."

SONS AND MOTHERS

Men have a different emotional experience with their mothers. There is an incestuousness between Hades Moon men and their mothers that is, usually, lacking in
women's experience. The boy is encouraged to bond to Mother—for life—and to

remain exactly that—a boy, the puer. What follows is one man's experience of this type of mothering, but it is a story that is repeated again and again.

An eternal puer, Lincoln is a Sun-Capricorn with Aries Rising. The Moon is in Taurus square Pluto in Leo and Venus in Aquarius. (The fixed signs show up frequently in men and women who have particularly difficult and entrenched Hades Moon experiences.) As a teenager he was captivated by his mother, and wrote poems about it. It was his way of transforming his experience of the unbearable dichotomy of being compulsively loved and devoured at one and the same time, and of loving beyond measure the woman who was eating him alive. The poem on page 74 is one of his, written when he had to return to the parental home after being away at university. We will look at more of his story when we explore addiction, but this is his retrospective look back, age 35, at what the paranoid over-protectiveness of a smothering Hades Moon mother meant to him:

My mother told me to always be careful—life was a threat, it was waiting just to hurt me. I couldn't understand what she meant, and I didn't want to know . . . now I know; she never let life touch her, and so she was always waiting, trapped inside years of fear and wanting, and dying every day because she was too scared to let life in, and too lonely to know that the world didn't care about her dreams. She warned me to be careful, she never went far enough to find out that being careful makes no difference—once you step outside anything is possible, and everything goes on. She taught me to be cautious and so now I look at those who smile and I wonder what they want. I check the sky every night, count the stars, and when I find the Moon is exactly where it should be, I look down into the world. I watch for someone, anyone who might hurt me—and I find the world is just the same; it doesn't care if I'm there or not; it's too busy spinning; and me I'm checking every sound, every shadow, and every sign, and everything is so easy to fit into my broken-jigsaw-nightmare-dream, and it always falls to bits, trying to find the missing piece, and refusing each and every picture that does- n't show the face of fear, the proof of all my childhood warnings; and life is left abused, yes, life is the only victim—it's twisted round and upside down and inside out, and it's raped and torn apart to fit a picture that my mother gave me, a picture that framed the world, made every moment a threat, every movement a warning—yes, I was nour- ished on the milk of human blindness. . . . I learned to live in a world I could not trust, I learned to look for danger in every footstep, every drop of rain. . . . I was guarded from the start, armed against the whole wide world, a world not to be trusted, a world that had no heart.

And my mother still believes her fears—she's never stepped outside her world, so full of threats and the bogey-man waiting round the corner. She's happy enough in- side her private little lie—nothing and no one can upset it, nothing can get close and no one can get inside.

Me, I'm still walking around with one eye looking ahead and one eye locked in- side, blinded by a picture that has nothing to do with the world all around me, and it's a lie, it's still-life, it's something I can see through, and for so long it had me blind. It's my mother's story, it's in black and white, it's her revenge for the life she denied, it's her way of forgetting that she couldn't, wouldn't, didn't open up and let the real world in, she refused to take a chance and betrayed the world, made it shrink and fade and stop turning—it fits her life, and her life is fit—for nothing—she showed it to me. She made sure I knew every single crack, every unfinished color, every stroke, it was no joke—she was doing her best, but she gave me a world I could never live in, too scared to breathe or even dream. I'm glad she was wrong but I wonder how much longer I can go on without a picture to believe in . . . she gave me her world, a world that had no Sun, no Moon, nothing living, no one laughing, and I know she was wrong, and what the hell—she gave birth to me and wrapped me uptight with the rags of her dreams and fears and the lies she told herself because she couldn't see that right in front of her— maybe she could . . . she passed her lousy excuse for not living to me, but she never told me it was a lifeless lying, dying, crying betrayal—a picture that no one would ever want to see because there's nothing to see, and I can see everything now, and my mother's colors are so lifeless, the frame so false, the hook too tight, and when will I see it go?

His mother held him in thrall for thirty-five years. (In his case, the archetypal expectation of mother coincided with the nature of the physical mother.) But, in the end he broke free and, over the next twelve years, his life changed dramatically. This extract from the letter Lincoln wrote when he, then aged 42, first consulted me conveys the suffocating environment he grew up in, and its destructive consequences:

I always felt very smothered, over-protected . . . she never let me go out with girls . . . I wasn't allowed out on my own for the evening until I was 17, and then because I was a few minutes late she told me I had her worried sick and I felt it was all my fault. I really resented her then . . . I remember the day I graduated from University: my parents came along to the ceremony, and I had refused to have my shoulder-length hair cut. Apparently as I walked across the stage to receive my degree, my mother had tears in her eyes: not tears of pride but of shame—she hated my long hair, and I was a reflection of her. . . . It's strange, I needed my parents' love and approval, but the only way I could get it was by hiding who I really was. . . . Years ago my father said he would probably die before my mother, and would I go home and look after her. I was horrified. I packed in social work and spent the next thirteen years destroying myself with alcohol and drugs. . . . In 1985 I had a serious car accident and ended up staying at my parents' house. My father told me that my mother had become twenty years younger: I was her helpless child again!

On the other hand, my parents were prepared to do anything they could to help me. At the time of my accident, I was wanted by the police—not for a major crime, but in my parents' eyes, any crime was a major crime. However, my parents nursed me back to health, even though they must have realized that in allowing me to be in their home, they were breaking the law—by harboring a criminal! That was not the only time they went out of their way for me during my years of alcoholism and addiction. More than once, my father bailed me out. More than once, he came looking for me, and he and my mother were willing to do anything they could to help me. From that point of view, I owe them a great deal. Their devotion may have been unhealthy, but it was also plain to see. They have never shut the door on me.

My mother has never had a life of her own: she has no outside interests, no friends apart from my father, and I sense that she's a very frustrated, unhappy woman, her children are her whole life. . . . Even when they phone I can feel her smothering me, and I want to push her away.

A counsellor suggested that I'd been brought up never to get married [the classic puer], though I still have trouble coming to terms with that one. . . . I know they have done the best they could. I will never get the love I need from them, the affirmation that it is good to be ME. I know now that I have to re-parent myself, to become an adult, to stop playing the game with my parents where I am the wayward child. I have never seen my parents hold hands. I never remember my mother being happy. There's nothing I can do about that. I have to live my own life, to do what is right for me, and stop seeking their approval (it's amazing, they are part of me, inside me).

As Michael Gurian says: "A son whose father gets killed off in the family system will suffer Hamlet's fate [loss, confusion, death], or find a dysfunction that will allow him psychological survival."[13] It took Lincoln a few years to put his insights into place. But he is now happily married and living his own life. He finally freed himself from the bonds of his devouring mother.

• • •

So many men have told me that they fell deeply in love with their Hades Moon mother, especially in their teens but often on into adulthood. This is a love that is erotic and highly charged. In most cases it is emotionally incestuous, in a few cases physically so. The son becomes a rival to the father, if the father is still around. No woman, except mother, can match up to this all-consuming "love." So men meet the unacceptable face of mother in their woman, and return home to mother, metaphorically or actually, when relationships break down.

Lincoln said that, as an adult, whenever he went home, he felt that his father was pushed aside and all his mother's attention was turned on him. That was how it had always been. His father accepted this. Indeed, the reason he gave for asking Lincoln to promise to return home and look after his mother in her old age was that this was what his mother would want. Lincoln said: "I feel I'm being asked to take his place. I had flashes of the 'Psycho' film, and thought, 'I don't want to screw my mother. Aargh!' " Nevertheless, he said that when he, in his 30s, looked back at the photographs of his mother, he "still fancied her": "God, she was stunning!" He told me in consultation that she had flirted with him when he was a teenager. She would not let him go out with girls: "There would be time for all that after university." Above all, she warned him: "Women are only out for one thing: a ring on their finger." It is no wonder that all his throbbing hormones were directed at the one woman it was safe to "love"—mother. And, although he sought a strong partner, what he met were unsafe woman who reflected his mother's overwhelming demands and sucked him in. Eventually, when he had done the necessary work in the dark spaces of his own self, Lincoln was able to find his mate. He married a powerful woman, a woman of deep insights and wisdom. He found his mature Persephone, or his Hecate. He shed his puer image and became the senex, the wise man who is the mature face of Capricorn.

For some men with Moon-Pluto, at a deep psychic level their desire is to unite with mother, to merge back into the womb that bore them. The challenge, however, is to unite with their own inner feminine, to break the bonds that hold them in thrall to mother and turn fearlessly within, to confront there the archetypal force that is Mother, to separate this mother from the personal mother, to reconnect to the great Goddess Mother who is the source of creative life. When the two are confused, a man finds himself stuck in Hades.

"MY MUMMY'S DEAD"

In an article in *The Mountain Astrologer*, Dana Gerbardt described her enduring memory of John Lennon "on stage in Madison Square Garden alone with a piano howling with infantile rage 'Mama I loved you, but you didn't love me,' ending with a painfilled chorus of 'Mama don't go, Daddy come home!' "[14]

John Lennon (Chart 10, page 91) is a classic example of a Hades Moon childhood deeply affecting the man. He had an almost exact opposition from Pluto in Leo to an isolated Moon in Aquarius. In an Equal House chart, it is across the 4th–10th house axis; in Placidus, the 5th–11th house. As if to emphasize the pain it symbolized, and the inventive matrix it created, Pluto was conjunct Chiron at his birth. Mercury squares that opposition and provides a release. Even as a young child, John used words like weapons. The feelings they expressed were raw, rageful, and darkly intense.

Lennon was born during a bombing raid on Liverpool. His mother was in labor for over thirty hours—a feature of Moon-Pluto births. As the air raid sirens wailed, his Aunt Mimi, who became his surrogate mother, picked her way through the war torn gloom to the hospital where her sister, Julia [Virgo Moon square Pluto in the last degree of Gemini], had just given birth. She was gazing adoringly at her nephew when he was unceremoniously removed from her arms and placed under the bed for safety. She was ordered to the cellar. Bombs were dropping all around.

Mimi said later that the moment she set eyes on John she knew he would be something special. He was the first boy to be born in the family for a long time. It was a family that had seen its share of tragedy, and which had its strong matriarchs.

John's mother had married a merchant sailor—a man who had been brought up in an orphanage and had no experience of family life. His being away at war did not stop Julia from enjoying life. (She clearly carried the immature Persephone archetype, being one of those mothers who appears to give everything but withholds real nurturing.) Albert Goldman[15] (one of Lennon's more controversial biographers) relates how Julia would leave the young child alone and go off to the local pub. John's first experience of abandonment came when he awoke night after night to find himself alone in the house. With a highly developed imagination even at that young age, he would see a ghost or goblin next to the bed and his screams of terror would bring the neighbors in. This, not unnaturally, resulted in a lifelong fear of sleeping in the dark. Julia's Pluto quincunxed John's Aquarian Moon and formed a Finger of Fate with his Moon-Venus inconjunct, Pluto-Chiron being the outlet point (see figure 9, p. 92). This Finger of Fate would be recreated by the transiting Moon at Julia's death. From other interaspects, karmically this could not have been their first life together as mother and son. It looks as though they incarnated together to work out abandonment and separation issues as well as an idealized, sym-

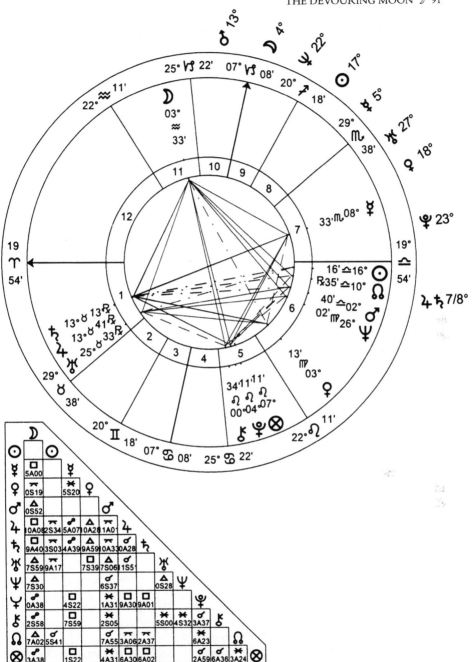

Chart 10. John Lennon. Born October 9, 1940, GMT 17.30, 53N25, 002W55. Placidus houses. Data from Pauline Stone and AA Database. Source: from John Lennon's Aunt Mimi. Outer ring is John Lennon's death, December 8, 1980, 10:50 EST, New York, NY. Mother's death July 15, 1958 (Moon 5°♋, Sun 20°♋, and Pluto 0♏♀).

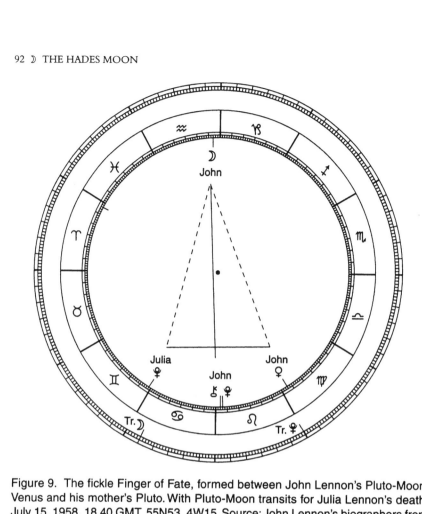

Figure 9. The fickle Finger of Fate, formed between John Lennon's Pluto-Moon-Venus and his mother's Pluto. With Pluto-Moon transits for Julia Lennon's death, July 15, 1958, 18.40 GMT, 55N53, 4W15. Source: John Lennon's biographers from his Aunt Mimi.

biotic "love" bond, so Julia could have been offering John a service through her apparent abandonment of him.

When his father returned from sea, the family moved back into Julia's parental home. Her mother died soon after John was born and her sister, Mimi, had married and left home. Julia's father went to live with his sister. As soon as Freddie Lennon returned to sea, Julia's social life continued. Lennon senior jumped ship in New York but was ordered onto another ship. He became involved in a wonderfully Plutonian activity—black market smuggling. He was arrested and spent a few days in a North African military prison. He then became involved with the local underground movement. He eventually returned home eighteen months later, during which time his pay had been stopped and Julia had had difficulty in surviving. Typically, this was a covered-up family secret. When Mimi had to explain to the young John why his parents marriage broke down, he was told that his father had jumped ship and abandoned his family.

In fact, in Freddie's absence, Julia met another man. She became pregnant. Her new lover would have taken her and the baby. But he did not want John, now age 5. Julia refused to abandon her son, and the lovers parted company. Julia's father insisted that either she must leave his house, or she must give up the baby. Mimi made arrangements for the child (a girl) to go to an orphanage called Strawberry Field [later to be immortalized in "Strawberry Fields Forever," a song that has been described as "a stoned descent into the maelstrom of the unconscious mind"[16]]. Freddie arrived home and offered to give the child his name, but Julia refused. The child was taken by the Salvation Army and given up for adoption. She has never been traced.

By now the marriage was in serious trouble. Julia had another lover, who lived in. John, displaying typical Hades Moon jealousy, was extremely angry and resentful, and expressed this through hostile behavior (a tendency he was to follow all his life). He was expelled from kindergarten, age 5½. This coincided with John's father returning home and punching the lover—an event witnessed by John. Julia left. John ran to his Aunt Mimi's house. Two week's later his father, whom Mimi had contacted, arrived and took John off on holiday. It was apparently his intention to take the boy to New Zealand with him. But, after six weeks Julia and her new man arrived. John, a Libra, was faced with the decision of whether to stay with his father or leave with his mother. At first he opted for his father. But true to his Libran nature, no sooner had his mother left than he was running down the road after her. John did not see his father again until he had become an adult and was famous. The breach between them never healed. (With Sun quincunx Saturn, this separation was exactly what John expected from a father. He had no doubt experienced this kind of loss and emotional distance in other lives.)

In yet another abandonment, instead of taking John home, Julia took John to his Aunt Mimi and left him there. Mimi became his foster mother and he rarely saw his own mother, or the two half sisters she bore. On several occasions when he did see his mother, it was because her new partner became violent when drunk and beat his mother. More matron than mother, Mimi was a classic Great No Sayer. The product of an unhappy childhood herself, it appears that she understood little about how to bring up a child, especially one who had been so emotionally tortured at such a young age, or one who suffered from such difficulties as dyslexia, myopia, and astigmatism, with more than a touch of megalomania thrown in. While seeing him as a special child, Mimi was determined to rigidly control John and "better him." She was a powerful, manipulative matriarch, exactly what Lennon's Pluto-Moon opposition expected in a mother, but totally at odds with his insouciant, fun-loving but emotionally unavailable, biological mother (indicated by his Aquarian Moon trine Neptune). However, the Hades Moon archetype was split. Julia, with Moon square Pluto, had played the rejecting part of the archetype for John. Mimi, on the other hand, played out the engulfing mother role. When John entered his middle teens and took up rock and roll, it was Julia to whom he turned. She had great sympathy with youth culture, something that was utterly alien to Mimi, with whom he still lived. His fledgling group often rehearsed in Julia's toilet, to her fervent applause. Apparently the acoustics were good. But it was a most Plutonian place to be!

Just when mother and son were becoming close, Julia was killed. She had gone to see Mimi following a fight with her drunken partner. As she was crossing the road, a car hit her. John, who was waiting at his mother's home, was devastated. At the time of his mother's death, the transiting Moon was at 5° Cancer (having conjuncted her natal Pluto earlier that day) and transiting Pluto was coming up to 1° Virgo, conjuncting John's natal Venus. The transit formed a Finger of Fate with his Moon, the outlet for which was his natal Chiron Pluto conjunction (see figure 9, p. 92). To John it felt like the hand of fate, a fate against which he raged but was powerless. Unable to openly express his grief, John was propelled even further into the alienation and isolation of his natal Aquarian Hades Moon and began to drink heavily. When drunk, he became violent.

Lennon never got over the loss of his mother—both as a child and again as a teenager.[17] He lacked a strong male role model to help him make the transition into manhood. His own father was absent, his surrogate father (Mimi's husband) had died sometime previously, and Julia's partner, with whom John got on well, was a charming but weak and violent alcoholic. It is no wonder that the bonds with his mothers remained suffocatingly tight and, in the end, he rebelled viciously against Mimi's controlling hold. Ten years after Julia's death, John and the Plastic Ono Band were bewailing "Mother, I wanted you, you didn't want me." All the anguish of his childhood years was poured into his music. The final song on the album lamented "My Mummy's Dead."

John's relationships with women were typical of a man with such rage: abusive, violent and, on the whole, short lived. Although he married Cynthia when she was pregnant, he still behaved like a bachelor and his relationship with the child, Julian (Moon at 9° Libra exactly semi-sextile Pluto at 9° Virgo), was always difficult.

John's ambivalence and dependence were eventually transferred to Yoko Ono, whom John always called "Mother." Here was a perfect hook for all his projections. They both believed that they had been together in previous lives.[18] In the relationship chart for the two of them (based on a midpoint in time), a chart which describes how the relationship will function, the Moon in the last degree of Sagittarius closely quincunxes Pluto in Cancer in the 12th house. "Mothering" is both inevitable and a source of immense conflict. The powerful, each-way Sun-Uranus interaspects indicate an old freedom-commitment dilemma and the Sun-Pluto repeating aspects describe an ancient struggle to become free of symbiotic dependence. But, with each-way Saturn-Venus contacts, it must have felt like fate when they met. John's Venus was conjunct Yoko's South Node, and her Venus trines his North Node. With this, and so many Neptune to the personal planet interaspects, it is no wonder they felt like soulmates. With her Pluto in the 10th house falling in John's 4th house, and John's Moon falling in her 4th house close to her Saturn, Yoko was the powerfully controlling Mother figure he craved, and yet dreaded. Their Moons form a septile aspect (52°), one of the aspects for karmic intent. Yoko's Moon trines John's Pluto, clearly describing her role as the "power behind the throne" as well as surrogate mother.

The two had a symbiotic and highly karmic relationship. John, in typical Libran fashion, believed that Yoko was quite literally his other half: the part of his soul that Plato describes having been forcibly separated by the gods.[19] Biographers have suggested that Yoko encouraged her husband in an infantile or even fetal dependence, a view which is supported by personal friends. At one stage, the two went into primal therapy together as a way of releasing John's emotional angst. Primal Scream, a cathartic Plutonian therapy, was based on the idea that if someone could go back into infanthood and howl out the pain of unmet needs, a rebirth could take place. Although in therapy for a comparatively short time, Lennon channelled the insights he gained into songs that expressed his pain. As Albert Goldman says: "Lennon's muse had always been a muse of fire, a howling devil that dwelt in a pit of molten lava at the bottom of his soul."[20] But, seemingly at Yoko's instigation, the therapy was aborted and Lennon was left to cope with the demons that had been unleashed.

Immediately afterward, John, on his 30th birthday, had his first adult face-to-face meeting with his biological father. He had been financially supporting him for sometime. The transiting Moon was conjunct the natal Moon, activating the Moon-Pluto-Chiron opposition. Transiting Uranus was conjunct his natal North Node. The meeting was not a success. All Lennon's primal rage toward his father was released. He did not speak to his father again until his father was on his deathbed. But, as Goldman puts it, his demonic spirit having been released, out roared the voice of inspiration. The "Primal Scream Album" was the result. It is an album of fear and rage—basic Hades Moon emotions. The first track re-enacted his abandonment by his mother, the last finally acknowledged that she was dead. The Lennons moved to New York and Lennon slowly disintegrated. He was in Pluto's pit. With Pluto conjuncting natal Neptune, his rebirth was on hold. Eventually, even Yoko rejected him. The couple separated for eighteen months at her instigation, supposedly so that he could "learn what he had to learn."

When they were reconciled, John told May Pang, with whom he had been living: "Mother has allowed me to come home." Shortly afterward, Yoko became pregnant. She had already had several miscarriages but threatened to have an abortion. Lennon did not want this, and so she told him that the baby would be his responsibility. The baby was born by caesarian section on John's birthday—a month premature to fit in with Yoko's belief that the child would inherit his father's soul on his death if they shared a birthday. Albert Goldman alleges that Yoko was suffering from heroin withdrawal at the time. She saw the birth as her "brush with death." Not surprisingly, when Sean Lennon was born, Pluto in Libra sextiled the Moon conjunct Neptune in Sagittarius. Transiting Moon-Neptune conjoined Yoko's natal Moon. Transiting Pluto conjuncted John Lennon's North Node. There was something deeply karmic about this child's contact with his parents. Sean's birth started Lennon's sojourn as an isolated "house husband" during which he neither wrote nor recorded any songs. He became increasingly dependent on Yoko, who ran their business affairs. His life was literally in the hands of Mother. For five years he suffered an intractable creative block. This eventually lifted when Yoko sent him to Bermuda for six months. Lennon went into a creative frenzy, returning with the songs that would form his last album.

In a photograph taken the day before his death, John is curled in a fetal position around Yoko. He is pressing a passionate kiss to her unresponsive cheek. When he died, the transiting Moon was exactly inconjunct his Chiron-Pluto conjunction. It had taken death to break Lennon free from his second surrogate mother, an act which must have seemed like the hand of fate reaching down once again. But it left a new generation, the rejected Julian and the engulfed Sean Lennon, to deal with the aftermath of the Hades Moon.

Lennon's death was not entirely unexpected. He had a number of premonitions of his death and knew he would die violently. The night before the assassination, he discussed this with Jack Douglas, who said that he seemed to be completely resigned to dying and was boasting that he would become even more famous than Elvis afterward. Douglas had heard Lennon speak of his death before, but this conversation had a sense of immediacy that was missing from previous incidents. From this and other experiences throughout his life, Lennon clearly inherited all the psychic abilities of Moon-Pluto as well as the death-wishing compulsion toward Hades that lay behind some of his more obsessive acts.

But, out of the pain of his early life and the continuing trauma of adulthood, John Lennon created his most memorable songs. His anguish was the *prima materia* that both propelled his imaginative life and fueled his self-destructive anger into recreating himself time and time again. Mercury squaring the Moon-Pluto-Chiron opposition allowed him to channel his intense emotions into his music.

MIND GAMES

There is a Plutonian postscript to the John Lennon story. A year or two after his death, an Englishwoman (Pluto square the Moon in 8th house Taurus, Sun-Neptune-Mercury-South Node conjunction on the Ascendant) had a series of strange dreams and visitations. It began with a graphic nightmare, gunshots and blood gushing uncontrollably. She ran into another room. Then a couple appeared. The man was very distinct. He had a grayish-white face and was very, very gaunt, with prominent cheekbones and hair that came halfway down his neck. He was wearing dark glasses and dark clothes. With him was a small, much more shadowy, female with a rounded face and dark hair. In the dream, the woman asked why they were frightening her. He told her they were just playing games and it would be their secret. With this, the fear went and she was enveloped in what she described as great warmth. He felt familiar to her but she could not place them. She awoke with music ringing in her head.

It was only sometime later, after he had made numerous appearances to her as a most unghostlike figure, that she recognized him as John Lennon, and the woman, who did not appear again, as Yoko Ono. She became obsessed with Lennon—not surprisingly when we look at the synastry between the charts. His Sun conjuncts her Neptune and Ascendant. His Moon-Pluto opposition makes a Grand Cross with her Moon-North Node conjunction and her South Node stellium, which is conjuncted by his Mercury. Her North Node-Moon conjunction is adjacent to his Jupiter-Saturn conjunction. His North Node conjuncts her Sun and Neptune, his Venus her Saturn. She said she felt like she had known him forever and was convinced they had a past life connection. For her, the boundary between the worlds was rather thin. As a child, John Lennon could "see through

walls" and as he grew up he practiced several occult techniques as well as undergoing many drug-induced experiences which pushed his psyche out of his body.
With those astrological connections, it would be easy for him to interpenetrate her
reality.

After several years she became convinced that he was trapped in the afterlife.
Unknown to her, Lennon himself had a belief that if you died a violent death you
would be condemned to wander lost in eternity. He gave her a great deal of information about his life and especially his death, most of which she did not know, and
much of which was unpublished at the time in any case. It was only when I researched her story in depth many years later that I was able to verify what she said,
and also to validate her experiences in the light of metaphysical truths that were unknown to her.

Eventually, she went to a psychic for help in releasing him. They prayed together and she could see him standing on the edge of a chasm. On the other side
was a bright light and, coming out of the light was his mother, Julia. She called to
him and he jumped over the chasm and into her arms. Sometime later, he appeared
to the woman again to say he was fine now and happy to be reunited with his
mother. Later, when she was battling with a tranquilizer dependency (partly as a result of her experiences), he appeared to her again and gave her support, saying it
was to thank her for her help.

Whether or not we believe that John Lennon would appear to a woman he
had never met and who had little interest in him when he was alive, her experience
was exceedingly real and had a powerful Moon-Pluto dimension to it, a dimension that encompassed Lennon's need to be reunited with his mother.

ENMESHED FAMILY PATTERNS

*Challenging Moon aspects indicate that the ghosts of the past, family traditions, and
established patterns, are unduly powerful and are preventing change.*
—Haydn Paul[21]

The Hades Moon legacy shows itself in ancient and convoluted patterns that entwine down through the generations. Typically, Moon-Pluto mothers divide and
rule their family, they make alliances and set one family member against another.
But, to the outside world, they present a united face. The dysfunctional family that
results remains enmeshed across generations. Siblings rarely unite to confront these
devastating unions. Partners who try to do so usually end up leaving rather than
succeeding in breaking their hold.

The Kennedy family seemed to me to be one of the great enmeshed families
of this century. When I began researching them for *The Karmic Journey*, I was fascinated to see how Pluto-Moon aspects showed up strongly in the women's charts. I
recognized that many Hades Moon issues were reflected in Kennedy lives, and in
those who were drawn into their circle. At the time I was looking at the astrological
foundations for Christine Hartley's theory that they were a reincarnation of the
powerful Borgia family who had ruled in Italy during the Renaissance. Like the
Kennedy's, many of the Borgias had met untimely ends, but they were distinguished

by their immensely strong family ties. Nepotism was rife in the Vatican under the direction of the Borgia Pope. As I moved deeper into *The Hades Moon*, I delved further into the origins of the Kennedy family and the place women had played in its evolution.

This was a family of strong matriarchs. Rose Kennedy, the doyen of them all, who lived to be well over 100, was preceded by Bridget Murphy, founder of the American dynasty. Bridget was a tough, independent, single-minded Irishwoman who emigrated alone to America in 1849 (her exact date of birth is unclear but she was born in 1821 and so was deemed past marriage age in her own country). She married a man she met on the ship, Patrick Kennedy. Unbeknown to them, he was suffering from tuberculosis. Ten years after they had arrived in America, Patrick died leaving Bridget with a young family. If she could not support them, they would be taken away from her and sent to a foundling home. She immediately went out to work, eventually buying a small shop and establishing herself as a businesswoman at a time when most women were either in the home or in service of some kind. Her fierce determination to protect her family at all costs passed on down through the generations.

When the Demeter-like Rose Fitzgerald (Libra Moon trine Pluto in Gemini) married Bridget's grandson Joseph, she inherited this legacy, a legacy that had passed down through Joe's mother, Mary Augusta. Joe Kennedy was an only son. According to Lawrence Leamer, Mary Augusta (Moon in late Leo trine Pluto in early Taurus) was a proud, imperious, controlling, and determined woman who molded her son from the day of his birth. Her ambition was to found a dynasty that meant he would achieve invincible wealth, status, and privilege. To this end, his mother was the "power behind the throne," manipulating Joe in a way that was impossible with his much more rough and ready, but politically astute father. P. J. Kennedy played the typical absent father to the Devouring Mother. He was much happier out with his cronies, or on the endless trips that his wife arranged for him. Mary Augusta preferred to stay at her power base—her home.

In true Libra Moon style, Rose sacrificed herself for her husband and his overwhelming political ambition. But, whereas she had seen herself as taking her rightful place beside him in his professional life, in reality she remained at home with the children while her husband enjoyed an almost bachelor existence of drink and women. For several years they maintained separate houses while he was away on political business. Rose, like so many Hades Moon women, was deeply disappointed and frustrated in her marriage. But at home she was the linchpin around whom the extended family revolved. She demanded that the entire family spend time during holidays in Hyannis Port, and no one dared to refuse. She was the arbiter of family life. Whenever there was an election to be fought, the family were there. If Rose disapproved, projects or people would be dropped. She spent her whole married life protecting the honor of the family and its reputation. It was she who decided what would, and more importantly, what would not be known about "The Family." Marriages might be on the rocks, grandchildren may be addicts or drop-outs, but Rose demanded that these things be kept secret and a united face presented to the world. Whenever a scandal threatened, the family closed ranks.

Right down through the generations, the powerful Kennedy clan had their share of hadean secrets. There was disgrace and dishonor, political intrigue, manipulation and maneuvers for power (within the family as well as in the outer world). Almost all the women experienced losing children at or near birth. The men had affairs and addictions. More than one of them were implicated in suspicious deaths. Several of the Kennedy children died young, and two were assassinated in middle age. Rose was survived by few of her large brood of children. Alcoholism, drug, and other addictions entwined down through the generations. As Rose Kennedy lay dying, the family concern, especially for the women gathered at her bedside, was not that she was passing on, but that the world should be protected from knowing that her grandson David (the son of Robert Kennedy) was a drug addict. The outcast David did die of an overdose in a hotel room, but the family machine swung into action to minimalize publicity. Keeping secrets was what this family did best.

Perhaps the darkest secret was that Rose's eldest daughter, Rosemary, was born brain damaged. The midwives deliberately held back the birth until a doctor could be present. The child lacked vitality and was extremely slow in her development. She had been starved of oxygen at a crucial moment. In her early 20s, Rosemary was charming but could never be intellectually mature. She was a young Virgoan Persephone, eternally innocent and naive. But she was a Persephone with a natural sex drive. This was an era when mental retardation was seen as a condition to be ashamed of, indicating something wrong with the family. Rosemary was regarded with embarrassment by her father, who was then a United States ambassador. When she vented her frustration on those looking after her, he had a brutal lobotomy performed on her. Shunned by the family, she was kept hidden away for much of her life. However, Rosemary's plight caused her sister Eunice (Virgo Moon, Jupiter, and Saturn conjunct Rosemary's Sun) to take up the cause of mental retardation and to start the Special Olympics. Her niece Caroline (Moon in Aquarius inconjunct Pluto), daughter of John F. and Jacqueline Kennedy, also had a special affinity with her aunt.

Rose's eldest son, John, who became a United States President, did not have a Hades Moon, but his enigmatic wife did. Jacqueline Kennedy's whispery little girl voice had shades of the young Persephone, but concealed a very different personality. She had the Moon in Aries square Pluto. Jackie was the child of divorced Catholic parents, something which had made her an outsider during her formative years and which taught her to keep her emotions firmly hidden. This training stood her in good stead when she had to face the fact that her husband was a compulsive womanizer, with dubious connections and several potential scandals waiting to emerge from the Underworld. She also endured a late miscarriage, the birth of a son who died three days after he was born, and the untimely demise of her husband. It has been suggested by several commentators that she married Jack Kennedy not for love but for power and position. She was attracted to him because his devilment and handsome demeanor reminded of her own father, "Black Jack" Bouvier, to whom she was exceedingly close. Black Jack, too, was a hard-drinking philanderer who had betrayed her mother time after time, a pattern Jackie was to find repeated in her own marriages.

After Jack Kennedy's death she married a particularly Plutonian character with his own share of dark secrets—and was branded a betrayer of the nation as a result. The playboy tycoon Aristotle Onassis also had the Moon square Pluto. His mother died when he was 12. His wife Tina (Moon square Pluto and Venus conjunct Pluto) died of a suspected barbiturate overdose twenty months after their son Alexander was killed in an air crash. His longterm mistress Maria Callas died of a heart attack—it has been suggested that she died of a broken heart. His daughter Christina (Moon opposite Pluto) suffered from weight problems and related drug addiction, and died when her daughter Athina was 4. Marriage to the immensely rich Onassis fueled Jackie's compulsive spending—addictions come in many forms.

After Onassis' death, Jacqueline Kennedy carved out a career for herself as a literary editor, stepping into her power. She lived with Maurice Tempelsman, a man who has been described as Machiavellian, ruthless, and obsessed with secrecy. He dealt in Pluto's wealth—diamonds, which are compressed deep underground into a gem people will kill for. A Jew whose family had fled from the Nazi invasion of Belgium, he narrowly missed the Holocaust. Tempelsman remained married to his wife, although he eventually moved out of the marital home and into Jackie's apartment. But, for the most part, the relationship was conducted in clandestine secrecy. Until her illness, few people knew that the two were lovers. Tempelsman was with Jackie when she died from Hodgkin's disease, a form of lymphatic cancer. Her daughter Caroline was also present at her death, as was her son John (Pisces Moon opposite Pluto). They would carry the Hades Moon forward into the next generation. The challenge of being a lineage-breaker passed to them.

Many people have wondered what Jackie saw in Maurice Tempelsman. If we look at Christine Hartley's belief that Jackie was the reincarnation of Lucrezia Borgia, and take a comment made by a fellow diamond broker that he was "a Renaissance Man" into account, perhaps we are looking here at the continuation of a karmic relationship from Renaissance Italy. The Borgias were major patrons of the arts and one of the great delights of Jacqueline and Maurice Tempelsman was to attend the opera or other artistic functions. Were they part of a family group which had reincarnated into the 20th century to work on the power issues such an enmeshed family carries from generation to generation, and from life to life?

LOVE OR ENMESHMENT?

Dr. Patricia Love[22] has identified the differences between enmeshed and healthy families. One of the major factors is that of a clear separation between the generations. A very loose boundary exists in enmeshed families (if a boundary exists at all) through which the child may have to meet the needs of the parent(s). In healthy families, love and affection can travel both ways through a permeable boundary, but it is the parent who meets the need of the child, not the child who meets the needs of the parent. We have already seen that one of the most common traits of a Moon-Pluto mother is that she allows no boundaries at all. So from this, we can deduce that Hades Moon families are likely to be enmeshed (unless the mother has come to an understanding of the dynamics and worked on the issues involved).

Pluto-Moon contacts tend to indicate unhealthy, symbiotic or conflicting family interaction. These dynamics are often hidden behind the facade of "a normal, happy family." This is devious Pluto we are dealing with after all. Apparent normalcy can conceal a great deal of latent abuse and festering foulness. Mirroring the behavior of the generation that has gone before, and unable to find a new way to be, the patterns replicate endlessly. Some family members go to great lengths to break away and leave home. But most carry the unresolved patterns and family secrets with them into new relationships. Others seem unable to break free. With Pluto on the Ascendant, square to a Scorpio Moon in the 4th house, my personal issues have been obvious from the start. But it took sustained digging, and the cooperation of my maternal grandmother and other doyens of the family to reveal just how far back the patterns went.

On my maternal side, I have traced back five generations of matriarchal women with strong Pluto-Moon connections. Not surprisingly their stories are so similar as to be almost indistinguishable. Prior to my grandmother, they married, often late in life, had large families and then their husbands died. Invariably they had their aged mother living with them while they struggled to bring up their young families alone. In true Pluto-Moon style, there were children who seemed unable, or unfitted, to leave home. To some extent my grandmother reversed this trend, or tried to. She eloped as a young woman. However, the marriage did not work out and she left him. She returned home to look after her daughter, her dominating but by then rather frail elderly mother, and one or two brothers who had somehow never got around to leaving home. Her youngest sister emigrated to the Canadian wilderness in an effort to leave "home," but she still lived out the destructive Pluto-Moon pattern in her marriage. Her son died under rather mysterious circumstances. Later, when my grandmother tried to trace her own husband, she found he had completely disappeared. No one was ever able to find out what happened to him. My mother married and her husband stayed around physically, but emotionally I experienced him as absent. Eventually he left physically as well. Having survived World War II against the odds, he was unprepared for the reality of family life. Although her mother did not live with her, my mother found herself looking after her elderly parent for many years.

I followed the family pattern in that I married young, had a daughter, and then my husband died. At that point, my father left my mother with me and went off to live with a ladyfriend, somehow omitting to tell my mother he was leaving for good (a typically Plutonian move). In an effort to escape, not having made any hadean insights by then, I married again. It was an unmitigated disaster (transiting Neptune was, after all, conjuncting my Moon), but when I left I vowed to live independently. I moved to the other end of the country, went into therapy and began the long transformation into the person I am today. When I saw Howard Sasportas all those years ago, he told me I had to be the one to break the family pattern, to find a more constructive way to deal with it so that future generations would be free. It remains to be seen what my Hades Moon granddaughters will do with the family pattern.

My family had a repeating pattern of difficult childbirth, which also goes with the Hades Moon. Pregnancy was often accompanied by grief. Death, of a mother or grandmother, just before the birth of a daughter happened too often to be ignored. It seems as though what passed down through the generations was an expectancy that birth was life-threatening. As far as I can ascertain, no births on the female line were easy and there were several stillborn children. By the time my Saturn-Moon daughter came to have her children, the family pattern manifested physically as a cervix which refused to dilate. Her Hades Moon children had to be born by caesarian section. There is a great lesson here about creativity, which has been traditionally linked to childbirth, but which is so much more. Many women with Moon-Pluto contacts delay having children either out of fear, consciously or unconsciously, or because of a certainty that they are meant to do something other with their lives.

Other Hades Moon families have repeating patterns of illness, addiction, or emotional disease. Family secrets, such as alcoholism, are enacted through succeeding generations. When the devouring mother archetype of the Hades Moon locks into the enmeshed family karma of a 4th, 10th, 8th or 12th house Pluto, death and destruction within the family inevitably precedes the richness of the transformation experience embodied at its heart. This seems to be especially so for Hades Moon men with Pluto-Moon mothers. Their matriarchal matrix is particularly poisonous and tenacious. These mothers do not give up their children easily, especially their sons. This is a story I have seen acted out so many times, with slight variations of sign, aspect, and house position, that I have come to look on it as one of the modern myths for our time. One of my favorite accounts comes from a forensic psychiatrist. On their return from their honeymoon, she and her new husband (10th house Aries Moon square Pluto in Cancer in the 12th) were regaling his parents with the delights of visiting Florence. Suddenly, apropos of nothing, his mother leaned forward and said: "Never mind dear, if it doesn't work out you can always come home to mother." Forty years later, mother, now in her 80s, is still waiting. She is still trying to reel in that psychic umbilical cord. When my friend was telling me the story, her husband suddenly leaned forward and said: "Do you know, for years I thought 'doing your duty' meant sitting on a pot of shit, that's how mother toilet trained me." It seemed an apt description for his Moon-Pluto upbringing.

When we look at the astrological interaction between family members, inevitably there will be both personal Moon-Pluto aspects and synastric aspects involving these two planets. These indicate a long history of karma around Moon-Pluto issues and the symbiotic family contacts it represents. Whether or not it is personal to the people concerned is indicated by repeating "each way" contacts. That is, if the Moon in one chart aspects Pluto in the other, and the Moon in that chart aspects Pluto in the first chart, then the interaction has been between those two particular people. The effect is exacerbated if both partners have natal Moon-Pluto aspects. If there is only a one way contact, that is to say if the Moon in one chart aspects Pluto in the other, but there is no contact from the Moon in the second chart back to Pluto in the first, then the two people concerned are simply working on the same issues—or the issues will arise in that specific relationship. There may be no past history between those two people; it depends on other "each-way-aspects" being present across the charts. In many respects the second type of interaction is easier because it is not so intensely personal and a little more objectivity may be brought to bear. But any Moon-Pluto contact is difficult. The potential for symbiosis and suffocation always lies beneath the surface of the Hades Moon.

This modern myth usually masquerades under the title of "a very close family." But, as Thomas Moore says, "When we idealize the family, we demonize it."[23]

A VERY CLOSE FAMILY

Tony was 14 when his father died: "You'll have to take your father's place now," his Hades Moon mother said at the funeral. Tony has a natal opposition of 12th-house Pluto to the Moon in Aquarius in the 6th. With his progressed Moon then conjuncting his mother's Pluto, he became her surrogate husband and carrier of the family karma. When his father died, Tony was not allowed home to say goodbye. Neither was he permitted to join the family to grieve in the days leading up to the funeral, and he had to return to boarding school immediately afterward. There was enormous unresolved grief.

He was told of the death by an unsympathetic housemaster, and kept it to himself. His isolated Aquarian Moon opposite Pluto in the secretive 12th house locked all his grief inside. By the time he was 17, he had experienced his first breakdown, which surfaced around the anniversary of his father's death (transiting Pluto inconjunct natal Moon stirring up all the unresolved grief). He became a doctor "to find a cure for cancer" [and so save his, already dead, father]. When Tony first consulted me, transiting Pluto was just moving up to his Scorpio Sun. He was still living with his possessive and tightly controlling mother, who treated him just like a small boy; and who, not surprisingly, has a Leo Moon semi-sextile Pluto in Cancer. He was locked into a cycle of depression and alcoholic breakdown from which he could see no way out (unknowingly repeating his father's pattern). We worked together intermittently over a period of ten years as he battled with his Hades Moon manifestations. His story shows just how entrenched the Hades Moon can be, and how the healing is unfolded through the appropriate transits and cannot be hurried.

When I looked at his chart, my first question was, "What was your parent's marriage like?" "Blissfully happy," he replied. "My mother nursed my father for years and was devoted to him." His father had throat cancer, provoking the question: what was going on that he could not swallow? I asked whether his father drank: "Oh no," Tony said in absolute horror: "Mother did not approve." Instinct and experience told me that here was an idealized picture that was far from the truth. Quite apart from the Pluto-Moon opposition across the 12th-6th-house axis, he had Chiron in the 4th house, which usually signifies a painful, wounding childhood, or a wounded parent. The 4th-house Chiron may well indicate a child who becomes the family scapegoat.

Pluto-Moon contacts can also indicate a deeply frustrated mother who is disappointed in her marriage, and there were other indications of parental discord. Further probing revealed that, apart from being extremely unhappy when sent away to boarding school (which, with typical Hades Moon introjection, he experienced as rejection and abandonment), Tony saw himself as having a happy childhood. But, as he shared his early memories, things just did not add up. Although his memory appeared to be seamless, there were clearly huge gaps and inconsistencies. A major factor seemed to be little memory of being at home. He attended several different schools in various parts of the country, despite his parents not having moved. His mother had (in her mid-30s) three children in less than five years and had "got a bit of post natal depression and had to go into hospital after the last birth." But the memory gaps clearly spanned several years.

As the Sun-Pluto transit worked its way through, and Tony's progressed Moon conjuncted that 12th-house Pluto, bringing the underlying issues to light, a series of coincidences brought hidden knowledge to the surface. Fate appeared to be at work. He entered a stable partnership, although many of his mothering issues were projected out onto his partner. His partner, however, had some insight into what was going on and turned the issues back to him to deal with. His partner "happened to meet" the daughter of the family with whom he had spent so much of his childhood. Within minutes, and without asking, she was told that his mother, far from having "the baby blues" actually suffered from protracted post-natal psychosis and spent years in and out of psychiatric hospitals. His father (Moon conjunct Pluto in Cancer) was a womanizing alcoholic, unable to care for the children, so they had been farmed out. Eventually, the situation became so bad that Social Services were about to take the children. Then his father was found to be suffering from cancer. His mother by a tremendous act of will (Mars conjunct Jupiter, quintile Saturn, and square Uranus) said she would pull herself together "for the sake of the family." And she did for the next thirty years and more; she became the caretaker parent who cannot let go of her children. Tony's partner was unsure whether to share this knowledge with him. His mother had often said that she did not know why Tony drank as "no one in our family ever did." Told in AA that there was always a family history of this illness, Tony had been greatly puzzled as he was not (consciously) aware of any family drinking problems. Tony was also clearly unaware of the nature, and extent, of his mother's illness. However, Tony had a series of dreams by which his lunar subconscious gently pushed the knowledge back into awareness. So, his partner told him what she had learned. He had clearly shut off, although the effect had been apparent. His Scorpionic death wish, the unconscious 12th-house Pluto emulation of his father, and the underground defiance against his possessive and domineering mother that his drinking represented, led to alcohol addiction and associated self-destructive behavior. The only way he could escape from her control was through his drinking. Conversely, she believed that she was the only person who could control his drinking and "make him better." However, she also had a great deal invested in him staying sick. That way she would not have to face her own hadean shadows, nor would she have to face the dark secret that entwined down through the families on both sides.

The revelations continued. His elderly, paternal, aunts (who "tippled" quietly but continuously) arrived unexpectedly for lunch and, having asked after his mother, said: "Of course, that marriage would never have lasted if your father hadn't got the cancer. When your brother was born [the youngest of the children], your mother had to send her brother to fetch your father back from the woman he'd moved in with. Then she went into hospital and all the problems began." Interestingly, and in accordance with his 12th-house Pluto position, his aunts did not mention his father's drinking, simply attributing the marriage difficulties to another woman and compressing a period of nine years into a few sentences.

It is clear that with such a close conjunction in Cancer, Tony's father had powerful Moon-Pluto issues of his own. Wife and mother no doubt became intertwined. Still enmeshed in the mothering issues, he sought his separation from the wife who carried the archetype for him. She could not let him go, and fought for repossession. At the same time, she genuinely believed that marriage was "for better or worse, in sickness and in health" and was prepared to stand by him despite her frustration and disappointment. The marriage was, however, happy in its last years when her husband was helpless and nursed devotedly, as one would a child (reflecting his Cancer Moon need for a surrogate mother).

Many Pluto-Moon women find themselves acting as mother to their lover. They are also the, usually self-appointed, guardians of the family and keep tight control over what is, and what is not, "known." One of the reasons that Tony was unaware of his father's alcoholism was that he never drank at home. He was "working late in the city," according to the over-protective mother. The children never saw their father drunk.

Tony had, nevertheless, as a young adult, found a newspaper cutting reporting his father's conviction for driving under the influence of drink and prescribed psychotropic medication (indicating treatment for depression). He had never dared to confront his mother about this, nor did he challenge the "no one in the family drinks" myth. It may be that in keeping this cutting, his mother was unconsciously (some might say deviously) opening the way for the intolerable burden of the secret to be lifted from her "by accident," but Tony felt unable to do this. Alcoholism no doubt went back far into the family. In one session with me, Tony had said that his paternal grandmother's apparent senility had improved spectacularly when the doctor told the family to lock up the gin, but he still had not been able to make the connection. When researching her family tree, his mother found a relative, a well-known scientist, had committed suicide by cutting his throat in his laboratory. With his mother's 12th house Pluto, one can only wonder what other secrets her teetotal family were keeping hidden.

There is evidence that the propensity to alcoholism is genetically transmitted. It would appear that Tony, in keeping with the 12th house Pluto and 6th house Moon, inherited this condition not only at the physical level but also at the psychic—as did one of his, adopted, Hades Moon cousins who also became an alcoholic. He, like Tony, absorbed the deep, dark family secret and manifested it in his own life. Tony's alcoholism was later to be diagnosed by a psychiatrist as self-medication for an underlying depressive illness that had been with him all his life. When his father died, and he "took his father's place," he became the person who carried all the family darkness and the depressive illness inherited from both sides. His mother had clearly not confronted her own unresolved issues, although she kept them firmly repressed for over thirty years.

His sister (Moon in Libra semi-square Pluto) had escaped the conflict by moving to another continent and then moving to a remote island miles out to sea from the coast of that continent. She did not experience her mother as suffocating, "just a little possessive and manipulating," although her mother frequently arranged interviews for her in "third world" countries to do the kind of nursing work her mother would like to have done. She, in effect, lived out her mother's unlived life. When she was in longterm relationships, she was afraid to tell her mother because of the power of disapproval at a distance. "We are such a close knit family" his mother said.

John Bradshaw has pointed out[24] that whereas the first born child lives out the family secret, the second born child is often the one who recognizes it. Tony's sister had "guessed" about her father's drinking years earlier, but never shared that knowledge with her brothers. A family confrontation might have held out a possibility for healing the problem. It felt safer for the whole family that Tony should remain the "identified patient" who carried all the family pain. Tony's younger brother (12th house Moon conjunct the Ascendant, square Saturn, but no Pluto aspect), whose unplanned arrival had been "the last straw" in the parental marriage was apparently, at this time, untouched. It would be some years yet before this younger brother was let into the family secret.

Tony made sporadic efforts to break away from "Mother," but seemed unable to carry it through. At one stage, he and his partner enrolled for a "Cutting the Ties that Bind" weekend workshop. But, late on the afternoon it was due to begin, he rang his partner to say that he could not go. During counselling, I carried out several tie cutting sessions with him as I had found these useful in similar cases. Each time, the suffocating ties had grown back again stronger than ever and it was a real struggle for him. It did not seem that the time was right (transiting Pluto had not yet come up to square his Moon). Also, I was acutely aware of his ambivalence. When we worked, he went along with the cutting, but seemed to be "going through the motions" rather than really wanting to break free at the deep level needed. He was reluctant to explore why this should be and I knew it could not be forced on him. After the transit of Pluto squaring natal Moon, Tony found it much easier to do this cutting.

As Tony's realizations about the family history increased, so did his drinking. His progressed Moon was again conjuncting his mother's Pluto. Her darkest secrets were being brought out into the light of consciousness. The part of him that was still locked in the "small boy fear" that he would die without his suffocating mother could not face knowing that which she had kept hidden for so long. At a gut level he knew he had to confront his mother if he was to survive, but the terror of the Hades Moon was too powerful, so he retreated more and more into his father's medicine—drink.

Tony said he had never really wanted to be a doctor, but his mother had been a nurse and doctors were "god." So, by becoming a doctor, he was inviting her approval. And there was the promise he had made to himself, age 9, that he would one day be a doctor and find the cure for cancer to save his father. One always has to remember that nemesis lurks close to Pluto, who has a dark, sardonic sense of humor. Each Christmas Tony would find himself working long hours in an Ear, Nose and Throat Department. He would also find himself caring for a terminally ill patient with throat cancer. Christmas was, of course, the last happy time he had spent with his father, although he had known his father was dying. Had he been able to recognize his father in his patients, he could perhaps have let go the futility of that promise to "save his father." At the same time, he could have embraced the opportunity to redeem the past by helping someone else make their Plutonian transition in their own time. Instead, in keeping with standard medical practice, he tried to keep them alive at all costs.

He drank on duty, unconsciously trying to get struck off the medical register so he could tell his mother it wasn't his fault, "they" wouldn't let him be a doctor anymore. Eventually, one Christmas too many, following a continuous 76-hour shift, he was suspended from duty and reported to the General Medical Council. Ironically, his assessors were split, reflecting his own ambivalence. One felt he should be struck off the medical register. The other assessor thought that he should be given the opportunity to overcome his problems. He was placed on probation.

I suggested a more constructive course of action based on his chart. Accept he could no longer save his father, then look to see whether healing really was his chosen profession. A 12th-house Pluto often has a compulsion to heal as a continuation of past life work, so I felt he may well have an unrecognized vocation beneath all the family overlay. He had trained as an acupuncturist, which he decided to pursue. When his progressed Moon conjuncted his own Pluto, he sent his mother a postcard from a remote Greek island announcing his intention to quit the National Health Service. A typically Scorpionic approach, but a start nevertheless. He went into treatment for his alcoholism, successfully.

To his surprise, the next time he visited his mother, she told him about his father, and even admitted to her own psychiatric illness, although the extent and duration were played down. She did not mention the problems in the marriage. It is doubtful whether her Leo-Moon pride would ever allow her to tell the full story. She was furious when she found out Tony already knew. She had shielded him from the truth so that he would "continue to look up to his father." However, when she realized that, at some deep level, Tony had known all along, and that having to shut off this knowledge had contributed to Tony's drinking, she began to question whether she had been right to shield the family.

At this point, Tony was no longer carrying all the family disease. He had a year or two free from a Pluto transit. Changing one person in the family alters the whole interaction. Often the family will put considerable pressure on the "identified patient" to become sick again so the family can retain the illusion of "health." My prediction was that his mother, who had held all three children in tight thrall, would panic at losing control and that all her unresolved issues would surface as an illness through which she would pull the family back to her.

It may be useful here to look at the family synastry and Moon-Pluto aspects (figure 10, p. 108). The inner ring shows the relevant family placements and the outer ring is the transists for the father's death. I take the same wide orb for synastry as for natal charts, especially when looking at Pluto-Moon contacts—which I will concentrate on here for simplicity, although all the synastry for the family reeked of ancient karmas. The mother has a Hades Moon inconjunct, but this is the semi-sextile which is often lived out through someone else. Her Moon opposes her second son's Moon in Aquarius, and her Pluto widely quincunxes it. As his Moon is conjunct the Ascendant, life for him is focused through the lens of Mother, and he projects his difficulties with her "out there" onto other women rather than dealing with

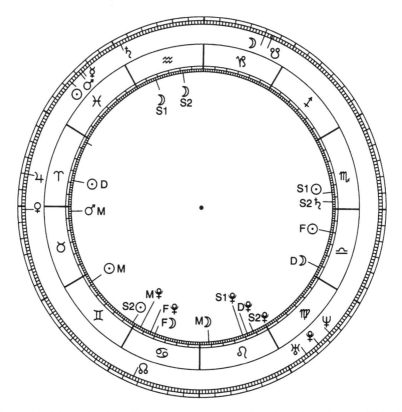

Figure 10. Enmeshed family patterns, an extraction from five charts within the same family. S1 = Tony; S2 = the second son (Tony's brother); D = the daughter (Tony's sister); M = Tony's mother; F = Tony's father. The transits of father's death (in outer ring) are relevant because they affect the entire family.

them at the source. His Saturn squares both his own and his mother's Moon and opposes his mother's Mars, forming a fixed Grand Cross between the charts. Fixed squares are indicative of very old, and deeply entrenched, karma.

The father's Moon-Pluto conjunction also quincunxes the second son's Moon. The daughter and second son both have Pluto opposing the oldest son's Moon. The daughter, with natal Moon semi-square Pluto, has her Moon squared by both parents' Pluto and her father's Moon, and her Moon sextiles her mother's Moon. It is an enmeshed, complex, and symbiotic interaction, revealing a great deal of "mothering karma" from previous incarnations among all the family, as well as the inherited patterns of 12th house placements and a powerful, but disguised, power struggle among them all. It was noticeable that none of the siblings ever backed each other when dealing with the mother. This was a fundamentally divided family, despite the enmeshment, and probably a dysfunction that spanned many lives.

The transits for the day of the father's death are significant. The transiting North Node was on his natal Moon-Pluto conjunction and the transiting Moon and South Node opposed it. He was living out his karmic purpose through his death, and cancer can sometimes been seen as "a passive form of suicide." The Moon-Node combination squared the daughter's Moon, opposed the mother's Pluto and inconjuncted her Moon. It was semi-sextile the second son's Moon, septile Tony's Moon and opposed Tony's natal Uranus, which is exactly conjunct his mother's Pluto. As Tony said: "It certainly released thirty years of chaos into my life." This, and transiting Uranus conjuncting his Mars, painfully described the battle he would have to break free of his possessive mother's suffocating hold. The family remained locked at that moment of death for thirty years.

There are equally strong Pluto-Sun contacts between the charts. This was a battle between a powerful father figure and a devouring mother with a matriarchal vengeance. She exactly fits the archetype of the devouring mother. Such a mother image is, as we have seen, all-powerful, nurturing her children with one hand while destroying them with the other. Her threat was withdrawal of love; their fear, that they would die without her. She brought the children up to be terrified of her disapproval and deeply resented any friendships they had that excluded her, especially when they became, technically if not emotionally, adult. Mother inculcated in them "a duty to look after her in her old age." Having pulled herself together "for the sake of the children," she had a great deal invested in keeping them "children," and could not acknowledge their adult independence. She had to rule their lives for the sake of her own sanity. The relationship was so symbiotic that it posed a death threat to all her offspring. It was not that she did not care about them; she did—all-consumingly. The psychic umbilical cords were tied tight. She could not let go. Her psychic health depended on it. Once, when Tony went into breakdown, she kept him at home and took him for long walks for two years "to make him better." "At the time I did not realize I was ill, I just thought I was bad," Tony said, reflecting just how well he had absorbed the family darkness.

It was with Tony that the greatest problems over relationships arose. When she told her son he had to take his father's place, she meant emotionally as well as "head of the household." Ironically, she could not see just how well he had carried out this command. In true Hades Moon style, he was her emotional partner and was creating exactly the same conditions in the home as her husband had, raising the family ghost. To her, Tony having a sexual relationship with someone else was her husband's adultery. When Tony moved in with his only longterm partner, the mother wrote to her saying: "You've stolen my son away from me. Send him back." It was the letter an abandoned wife would write to her rival. The unacknowledged incestuousness of the mother-son relationship was powerful. Neither of them were prepared to confront it, or let it go—a factor which contributed to Tony's drinking. Every time he went to bed with his partner, he was unconsciously facing his unfaithfulness to his mother.

Neither he nor his partner wanted to marry, a choice his mother was unable to accept. She used her "strict moral principles" as an excuse for disapproving, but could not have faced her surrogate husband's marriage either. She "just wanted her son back." Typical of her Leo Moon, her strict moral principles were pulled out whenever anyone did anything she could not control. She had not spoken to her two brothers for years because they divorced their wives. As Tony once said, "She wanted to condemn everyone else to the misery she inflicted on herself." This was an area of his life, and chart, that Tony was not confronting. But Pluto was inexorably moving toward squaring his Aquarius-Moon-to-Leo-Pluto opposition, and Pluto demands that we attend to our unfinished business. An invitation was being extended to dig for the treasure at the heart of Pluto's realm. A way was being opened to heal the whole family.

The mother developed high blood pressure, an interesting psychosomatic expression of all that was bursting to get out. Tony, with Pluto now forming a T-square to the natal Moon-Pluto opposition, visited regularly to give her acupuncture, but still could not talk to her about the issues involved. His great fear was that she would have a stroke. Hers was that she would lose all control. The second son, who by now knew the family secret, and the daughter, talked to her and helped her to see that the unresolved issues from their early childhood were surfacing. But somehow all three children could not come together to discuss the "family secret" which still had a hold, just as they had never united to support each other in challenging the mother's position of infinite power. The mother learned to meditate. Her blood pressure returned to normal.

Without the personal engulfment of the Pluto-Moon archetype, the second son was able to talk to his mother from a more adult standpoint. Although he was the last to be let into the family secret, perhaps because of his 12th-house Moon conjunct the Ascendant reflecting a little light into the Plutonian pit, he was the most able to discuss with his mother how it was affecting her health. He also refused to allow her to rule his life totally, although his Saturnian emotional isolation clearly arose out of his enmeshed contact with her. He was locked into an Aquarian rebellion against the powerful archetypal force that was "Mother." But the rebellion tied him to mother as closely as the Hades Moon would have done. Indeed, the Pluto-Moon synastry between their charts was the most powerful in the family. The Aquarian picture he carried of an unpredictable, "unstable" mother had been manifested in his mother's psychiatric condition; and the Saturn-Moon expectation of "bad" mothering was clear in the long separations he had endured—but of which he had no memory.

Once again, however, mother lost control of the family. This time the Plutonian disease manifested most appropriately as symptoms of continuous vomiting and diarrhea. She could no longer "keep anything down," nor "hold anything in." Nor could she assimilate the changes in the family matrix. As Pluto transited the last few degrees of Scorpio and a solar eclipse hit Tony's Sun, Tony and his sister became convinced their mother had cancer. Self-consciousness, and rationality, were eclipsed and the devouring mother archetype rose at full strength. Tony and his sister were sure she was dying, but were unable to discuss this with her or to confront their own fear of her death and where it would leave them. The second son asked his mother directly if she thought she was dying. "I don't think so," she said, although she revealed later that she, too, believed she had cancer. Her instinct was still to shield her adult children from the unthinkable act of her death.

I had felt sure that the mother did not have cancer: the timing seemed to be all wrong even though there was a lunar eclipse square the children's Pluto, forming a T-square to Tony's Moon-Pluto opposition at the time she was having her tests. The lunar eclipse seemed to have more to do with the controlling mother archetype than with the death of the actual mother. The Moon rules the pancreas and it ceasing to function seemed to indicate that her body was doing what her psyche could not. Nevertheless, my comment to Tony was that, whatever the diagnosis, I felt his mother was suffering from the terminal malignancy of bitterness, resentment, and Plutonian control. There was no sweetness in her life, and so her pancreas, which manufactures insulin and digestive enzymes, had nothing to feed on. As I saw it, only acceptance, forgiveness, and reconciliation could heal her Plutonian disease. Synchronistically, I "happened to see" a pancreas on television. My first thought, before I knew what it was, was that it was a particularly messy umbilical cord. I felt that it was symbolic of the internal cords she had been unable to cut with her children.

However, under the benign influence of Pluto retrograding in trine aspect to her Moon and Pluto, Tony's mother made a breakthrough with regard to rejected parts of her family. Having not spoken to two of her brothers for many years, she wrote to them in an effort to heal the gap. Her close brush with Pluto's realm, during which a beloved brother had also died, had brought with it a realization of her self-imposed isolation—and of the necessity for reconciliation. She took up painting, for she had shown great promise as a child; she had written poetry all her life and, at the age of 80, some of her poems were published. At long last she began living out her own unlived life.

Tony continued to heal his disease, especially following on from the effect of the eclipses. Part of that process was to separate from his mother on a psychic and cellular level. On a day when the Moon was conjunct his mother's Pluto, Tony did some deep body work to "clear his mother out of his cells." That night [by which time transiting Moon was inconjunct natal Moon], he dreamed that his gynecology notes had been lost, or stolen, in an antique market. "I thought it was very relevant and fairly self-explanatory. The dream meant that female domination from the past, and what I had been taught about their function in my life, had been removed," Tony said. The dream appeared to be saying that the Hades Moon had, in part at least, been healed.

When Tony's mother had her 80th birthday, all the family were summoned to her holiday home. Tony went alone, without asking whether his partner was invited too. This provoked an explosion by his partner, which let out an enormous stream of underlying resentment and anger for both her and Tony. She then practiced forgiving and letting go. The dynamics changed dramatically. The following week Tony and his partner went down to the holiday cottage. To their amazement, his mother offered them a room together. She had finally, after twelve years, accepted Tony's relationship and his partner. They spent a very pleasant weekend together. When his sister, who had returned home for the birthday, then went to stay with Tony, his mother made no protest (the year before she had forbidden her daughter to go and, dutiful daughter that she was, she had obeyed). Things had certainly changed. Tony moved on. His enmeshment with the family loosened; it was left to his Geminian brother to play puer to She Who Must be Obeyed.

THE FOUNTAIN OF ETERNAL YOUTH?

Despite his small-boy need of mothering, Tony matured. But his brother, with a Gemini Sun, carried that sign's abiding youthfulness. He was the uncommitted puer. The puer is an eternally youthful boy (although we must bear in mind that there is a feminine counterpart, the puella) who somehow cannot quite mature. Mercurial in nature, the puer has close links with the messenger of the gods, the planet Mercury, and with Gemini, but his roots can lie in the fertile compost of the Hades Moon. At a fundamental level, the puer is still tied to Mother. More often than not, he is the son of a disengaged or absent father. He is the man who is stuck in what has been described as "the eternal adolescence of the provisional life." Undifferentiated from mother, when he enters an adult relationship he acts out his dilemma, importuning his partner to "nurture me" and then pulling away to demand "let me go."

James Hillman describes the puer's characteristics as narcissistic, capricious, inquisitive, inventive, persuasive, tricky, and opportunist. He is prone to leaving for some other place, or person, full of nostalgia and longing, but is unfulfilled no matter where he goes. Uncommitted and irresponsible, he is loved by women he refuses and pursues the unattainable. He is "forever in danger of drowning."[25] Charming and libidinous, he has the insouciant appeal of a youth, not the mature man. Women want to mother him on sight. There is something androgenous about a puer, as though he hasn't totally settled on his gender, or his sexuality. As his identity is so bound up with that of Mother, he carries many feminine traits. He may be effeminate, but he may equally well be acting out the role of "macho-man" to cover his own confusion. Many Moon-Pluto attuned men live out the archetype of the puer in their everyday life. But beyond this, there is something other enticing them on, urging them to become something more than a psychological truism. That urge is toward spiritual truth.

The puer impulse is seen by James Hillman as a "call to the spirit," a link to the divine child within, or to the spirit above, rather than to the biological mother without. Hillman points out that it is problems with the mother, who looms in the foreground, obscuring the archetype behind the image that creates the difficulties the puer undergoes—or perhaps it would be more accurate to say the difficulties other people experience when in relationship with the puer. Hillman feels that, archetypally, the Great Mother is in love with the son-and-lover puer as a carrier of spirit. She is fertilized by him, but her incest with him brings about ecstatic excess and destruction (something we will explore further in chapter 8). When the archetype is distorted through an actual mother, then the puer is crippled and the spirit cannot fly as it is meant to. But when the puer reconnects to spirit, and thereby releases the negative mother, he becomes free to pursue his intuition and his knowingness.

THE WITHERING WOMB

As we have seen, the devouring mother eats her child alive. Incur her wrath and one look is enough. It withers the soul. But what happens when the mother is at last outgrown? When Pluto lights the fire that burns the ties that bind? When the child begins to fight for survival? To regain the soul that has been lost? To recognize the core self that makes him, or her a unique individual?

Well, initially, mother applies pressure, and manipulative inducement. She might try bargaining, or threatening. It depends on how overt an expression of the archetype she represents, on how strongly attuned to the Hades Moon she is, or on how much her own identity is tied up with being a mother. If she is typically Plutonian, then more pressure will follow. As expressions of the individual self tend to coincide with a transit, the nature of the response will vary according to the planetary principle that is being activated. It also depends on the mother's Sun sign. Illness, as with Tony's mother is a common ploy, but the mother may also withdraw into injured silence. She may play the martyr: "After all I've done for you," or she may bluster: "You'll be sorry, you can't live without me." The ultimate withdrawal is, of course, death, as John Lennon found. Some Hades Moon mothers resort to this when they realize they will no longer be in control, but there are many ways to die. The child may then have to deal with guilt as well as grief, especially if the new sense of self has not had time to flower.

Mother may switch her attention to another member of the family. Such mothers have even been known to find another child-partner outside the family. When one Hades Moon woman finally made her bid for freedom, age 52, she headed for Australia, for although she felt strong, she also felt she had a better chance of separating on the other side of the world. Her 86-year-old mother found a man. Unfortunately, but perhaps not surprisingly when we recognize the part Moon-Pluto aspects play in addiction and codependence, he had a history of alcoholism. The mother's Sun and the daughter's Moon were conjunct in Pisces, the escapist sign that plays the savior-victim-martyr role so well. Pisces is prone to live out its addictions through someone else. At the time, both luminaries were being heavily activated by transit of Saturn in Pisces opposite Chiron in Virgo (her Chiron return). It was time to heal the daughter's pain around lack of nurturing—to nurture her self—and to establish some boundaries. At first the mother told her daughter: "That's right, go off and leave me. I'll be all right. He needs me. I can keep him sober." But then there were calls in the middle of the night: "He is violent, he is abusing me."

If the child has developed sufficient sense of self, has regained enough soul, then this pressure can be resisted. The daughter told her mother to phone Al-Anon, the organization for the partners of alcoholics. She refused to return home. Her mother got on a plane. The daughter invited her to stay for a "short holiday," and then put her back on the plane. By the time mother returned home, she was ready to try the savior role again. The saga repeated itself, but the woman remained steadfast. She was now in a happy relationship and was enjoying exploring her new sense of self. The mother became ill—a heart problem. Her daughter flew home, assured herself that all was well and that her mother was being cared for properly, and went back to her adopted home. The next time she returned home it was for the funeral. But, as she said, she had done all she could. "It was her or me. Either I survived or she did. She would not, could not let me go. In the end that killed her, not me." She was able to forgive her mother for the years of tyranny that had held her in thrall, recognizing that this was out of a warped sense of "love."

Some mothers graphically live out the withering womb. Another woman (Moon conjunct Pluto in Cancer) found that, when she finally decided to leave home under the insistent urging of transiting Pluto in Scorpio trining the natal conjunction, her mother started hemorrhaging and had to have a hysterectomy. "Even the womb that bore you has been torn from me," said the despairing Demeter.

The "empty nest syndrome" is a peculiarly Plutonian experience. It attacks many women in mid-life, not necessarily those who have always found their identity in being Mother. Career women, too, can be devastated when their fledglings leave the nest. Menopause can indicate to any woman that her biological fertility is over. If she does not have another outlet for her creativity, then she will feel barren. These life events may well occur at the first Pluto square or trine to natal Pluto, which, with a Hades Moon, will of course mean that the Moon is also aspected. The outward life events are reflections of an inner experience. If the mother has prepared for this new phase of her life and established her own sense of identity, then she can let go. If the child and the mother are able to come to terms with the separation and move into a new phase of maturity, all goes well. But if the bonds have not been appropriately released and a new relationship established, then devastating grief takes over. This grief often surfaces as a deep depression in both mother and child. Mothers may also lose their own mother at this time, compounding their hadean experience.

As a general rule, depression is not honored. A person who suffers from depression is urged to "pull yourself together," and at best is plied with antidepressants, at worst is suspended on tranquillizers, and the last thing she is urged to do is explore her pain. If the mother (or the child) is able to enter her own inner psychic states and explore the basis for this depression, she will find hidden parts of her self. Like Ereshkigal, she needs mourners to commiserate with her and validate her pain. If she can sit with Demeter grieving, then her child may well be returned to her. But not in the old form—a resurrection must take place, a new relationship conceived. With Pluto involved, there has to be transformation. The outgrown patterns must fall away to reveal the new growth. This may well necessitate time spent "down the hole." We must always remember that Pluto keeps his treasure deep underground, and this transition phase can lead to untold riches of the soul.

CHAPTER 4

THE REJECTING MOON

The challenge at the Pluto point is to let go of our panic at the possibility of loss, and to allow the force of change to sweep over us. To abandon the defense mechanisms that have kept us safe and to accept necessary change even to the extent that we may seem to be annihilated by it.

—Stan Riddle[1]

AS WE SAW IN John's Lennon story, the abandonment of a child by the mother has lifelong (or liveslong) repercussions. Such abandonments occur in many ways. Death is one, parental remarriage is another, and adoption takes us deeper into the trauma of maternal dispossession. The mother does not have to leave home to abandon her child. Emotional rejection is as painful as physical loss. But all too often the child (or the adult) with the Hades Moon finds itself in a situation that brings all the issues of abandonment and rejection to the surface. This Moon is programed to resonate to rejection and loss, however it occurs. The karmic purpose behind it is to propel the person with the Hades Moon into a place where he or she can let go of the need for external mothering and learn to mother the individual self. It is a theme which travels down through the family tree. In a television program "Strange But True," Kevin Taylor told the story of his search for his roots. He had been adopted at birth; when he traced his mother, she too had been adopted; but, even more strange, so had her mother before her. He could not trace the family any further back. Kevin Taylor has the Moon conjunct Pluto in Virgo.

REJECTION, ABANDONMENT . . . AND ALIENATION

At a very deep level the Pluto-Moon combination feels alien, *somehow different.* There is a powerful fear of being pushed away for not belonging—in reaction to which the person with a Hades Moon will often refuse intimacy in case it elicits rejection. I had a client who, as a child, found herself in a hospital room screaming in pain and looking beseechingly toward her mother who had just arrived. Her mother said: "I can't bear this," and ran from the room. For the two weeks the child was in the hospital, the mother stayed away. For many years the woman-child thought it was her fault, she should not have given her mother that shock. As a result, she never let other people get close to her. But, deep down inside, she always held a feeling of rejection and never dared to show pain, or feelings, again. When she eventually discussed it with her mother, her mother said she had been torn apart by her child's pain and could not handle it.

I have also worked with people, themselves sometimes adopted but sometimes not, who have had an adopted sibling and who felt totally rejected by their parents having chosen to bring an "outsider" into the family. In one case it affected the woman so deeply that she cursed her mother and wished her dead. She nursed her mother when cancer literally ate her up, but she never forgave her. When she was a young teenager, her mother had brought another child home. There was no explanation of where she came from. Just the words, "She's staying with us now." The deeply distressed child was introduced into the woman's bed, as she put it, and wet it. The teenager was blamed for not realizing that the child wanted the toilet. This was the start of a five-year battle on the woman's part to oust this interloper. It was a battle she did not win. The resentment ate up not only her mother, but herself as well, and over forty years later she was still embittered and unreconciled to her past. When we explored it, the scenario went way back into the past. But, as she was not willing to work on it, it was impossible to change the dynamics, and no doubt it will continue in a future life.

Singer Michael Jackson has a sensitive Pisces Moon (the mother) in opposition to a powerful, picky Pluto-Sun (the father) conjunction in Virgo, which in turn conjuncts a child-like Mercury in playful, proud Leo. From all accounts, Michael's childhood, and that of his brothers and sisters, was pretty abusive. He was molded by his father into a stereotypical image and became part of the family group, who lived on the road most of the time. Perhaps not unnaturally, Michael lost sight of himself and has struggled to find his true image, endlessly recreating himself ever since. There is no resemblance at all between the small, smiling, typical black child who would toddle on stage to join his brothers, and the freakish, feminized man who performs with such calculating eroticism today. It appears that this is an outsider who does not fit either into his culture, his family, his body, or even his sexual gender, and who yearns to be something *other* and who resorts to cosmetic treatment to obtain his ideal. Much has been made of his alleged penchant for young boys. His own sister, La Toya, called a midnight press conference to say she could "no longer be a silent collaborator of his crimes against small boys."

In one perceptive article, the writer felt that what Jackson was doing in his "public face" was trying to recreate a dream childhood which had never existed, one in which he could have the happiness that eluded him.[2] At Neverland, his Californian ranch, he had all the "toys" a lost child could desire. The child, or children, he chose as companion would then be the fantasy image with which he could identify. All he needed was a "Wendy-figure" to mother him and the other lost boys. As the writer, Joan Smith, pointed out, this is the modern fairy tale, a reworking of the Peter Pan, or puer, myth. It is a portrayal of an asexual fantasy figure, who never grows up, something which she felt was far from the real truth. The public are avid consumers of such revelations, but Smith feels that behind this lies a much darker, more Plutonian story of sexual compulsion and immaturity. Michael Jackson's story is typical of the Piscean Hades Moon: he has admitted an addiction to painkillers, he has resorted to a surrogate mother, Elizabeth Taylor (8th-house Pluto trine 12th-house Moon in Scorpio) herself no stranger to addiction, adoption, and the dark face of the Hades Moon. His marriage to another deeply wounded "child," Lisa Presley, failed spectacularly. But it all fitted in perfectly with the current vogue for "revealing all" while concealing the real truth of that Hades Moon.

The past life scenarios associated with the Hades Moon alignment inevitably include experiences of being the outsider and of abandonment. Mac, whom we met in chapter 1, and will meet again in chapter 6, has Pluto opposite the Moon in Capricorn. In past life exploration, he regressed to being a small child sitting alone in the snow. His tribe had been traveling when a blizzard set in, and his mother, separated from her companions, had been unable to carry him to safety and so left the child sitting in the snow, as he saw it, to save herself. It was probable that she intended to go for help, but as his mother slowly faded into the distance, hypothermia set in and he died crying out for her in vain. In another life script, he was deliberately turned out into the cold weather by his peers. He had not fitted into the society, being something of a psychic and healer and therefore feared as a "witch." When an exceptionally cold winter set in and food was hard to find, his tribe turned on him, blaming him for the "curse" that had come upon them.

In his present life, his mother had died of cancer when he was young. However, his feeling of abandonment was earlier than this. When his younger brother was born, he was not told his mother was expecting a child. He had always wanted a parrot, and when his father came to tell him there was a surprise for him, he asked if it was a parrot. "Yes," said his father, "Your very own parrot. Aren't you a lucky boy." When he entered the bedroom, he was devastated to find his mother holding not a parrot but a baby. Sobbing, he ran from the room. No one went after him. He was never reassured that he was loved. Indeed, speaking of it years later, he said he felt he had never ever been loved. He was a disappointment to his parents, especially to his father, who treated him very coldly after his mother died. He never had a stable, longterm relationship. He felt rejected by society, and deliberately chose a lifestyle which reflected this. Having "accidently" burned his own house down, he then lived in a series of squats in semi-derelict houses. He kept very much to himself, unless he was drunk, when he would become gregarious—exuberantly so. The police were called several times.

Eventually he met a woman whom he was sure was his "soul sister." But he was also sure that she had been that mother who left him in the snow. They tried to work out the issues between them. But the pattern of rejection was too strong. She left to live with another man, and became pregnant almost immediately, "so that there was no chance of being pulled back." The lesson seemed to be to let go. But he retreated even further into himself and shut out the world. One day, when he was drunk, he saw his father standing in front of him. He lashed out with a brick—and found that he had smashed a plate glass window. "His father" was actually a reflection of himself. After that, he worked hard on forgiveness, but it took many years before he could feel that he meant it, and he never got over his feeling of alienation.

The German novelist Herman Hesse (Pisces Moon sextile Pluto in Taurus) wrote *Demian*, examining a boy's relationship with his mother. The troubled adolescent struggles to find self-realization. The book ends: "How could anyone die who never had a mother?" Alienation and self-realization are themes that run through Hesse's work, as are the Jungian concepts of introversion and extroversion, the collective unconscious and symbolism; indeed, many of his books may have been taken too literally. Symbol and metaphor are, as we have seen, the language of the Hades Moon. Hesse gave up his birth country, Germany, and became a Swiss citizen. He was a "man without a home" and spent much of his adult life in psychoanalysis. His semi-autobiographical novel, *Steppenwolf*, chronicles the humanization of an outsider, through relationship and what appears to be drug-induced experiences. On his 40th birthday, the day he has resolved to commit suicide, Steppenwolf is given "cigarettes" to smoke by a group of liberated women whom he meets while having a drink to pluck up courage to end it all. He enters the "Anarchist Magic Theater; Price of admission: your mind." In exploring his unconscious, he recognizes his innate humanity and reconciles his dilemmas.

Hans Christian Anderson (who has the same placements) also features alienation and abandonment in his fairy stories, as in *The Little Mermaid* and *The Ugly Duckling*.[4] They show how these experiences can be turned around, one of the functions of myth and fairy tales. *The Ugly Duckling*, for example, is a wonderful analogy of the misfit in the family, the outsider who is recognized and valued only by those who perceive the true nature of the swan who has emerged from the misidentified and rejected ugly duckling. Once he finds himself, he blossoms into beauty and is admired by everyone. The Little Mermaid gives up her natural home, and her ability to speak, in order to be with the man she loves. But she is rejected. In letting go, in returning back to the waters of the unconscious, she is rewarded with transformation to a different level of being. These are archetypal themes which we meet time and time again in literature and myth, and in the Hades Moon.

THE HADES MOON AND ADOPTION

The Hades Moon has powerful links with adoption from both sides. As already mentioned, so many people who had been adopted who came to me had strong Hades Moon contacts that I began to look on it as an "adoption indicator." But I also noticed that women who had to give up their children for adoption also had the Hades Moon. This is not surprising when we look on it as mothering karma and painful experiences around children. However, in many cases, the women who adopted children because they could not have them themselves, also had Pluto-Moon aspects. In some cases they could not have children because their partner was infertile, but in most cases it was because they themselves had gynecological blockages to conception or were unable to carry a child full-term. Considerable pain and misery could lie behind the decision to adopt as well as to give up a child for adoption. The Hades Moon can indicate a need to move beyond biological creativity into some other area of self-expression. But it can also point to a biological imperative to mother which is all-powerful. Actress Mia Farrow, who has the Moon in Capricorn inconjunct Pluto in Leo, has adopted children from all over the world. With her Capricorn Moon also opposing Saturn, this may well have been a way of working out issues from her own past. Notwithstanding, one of her children caused her considerable anguish through her sexual relationship with her adopted father,

Woody Allen, an experience which must have felt like a rejection of all that Mia Farrow had offered as both wife and mother.

No matter how much wanted by the adopting parents, a child who is adopted has inevitably been given up by its birth mother and so has had an early experience of abandonment. For many, this is overcome by the nurturing they then receive. But for others, it leaves a fundamental sense of *otherness*. As mentioned earlier, all the charts for adopted children that I have worked with have had some contact between Pluto and the Moon (orphaned children often have Saturn-Moon contacts as well as, or instead of, the Hades Moon). One of the rare exceptions to the Pluto-Moon theme comes in Arthur Bell Nicholls, Charlotte Bronte's husband. He was adopted at the age of 7 by a well-to-do uncle and, by all accounts, had a very happy life. Other people who were adopted as children, rather than babies, or who are adopted by a parent and a new partner do not always have the Hades Moon in their chart. Sometimes the Moon becomes connected to Pluto by transit or progression at the time of the adoption, but this is not necessarily so. It depends on the issues being worked through.

While some mothers willingly give up their children for adoption—one Hades Moon woman I counselled was a twin and had been given to her aunt in the delivery room because her mother could not face two children—many women are torn apart by the experience. In Britain particularly, the history of illegitimate children is strewn with inhumanity. Right up until the 1930s, women who gave birth to children outside wedlock were liable to find themselves locked up in a lunatic asylum. This was not a punishment; it was to safeguard society. Promiscuity (or behavior perceived as such) was looked upon as a mental illness. As the women were often distraught at being separated from their children, their emotional distress was looked upon as further evidence of mental disturbance. Some found themselves forcibly separated from their babies and hospitalized for life; many were not released until the massive closure of psychiatric hospitals in the 1980s and '90s. When they went out into the world again, it was almost impossible to readjust to "life outside." It was as though they had been imprisoned for all that time. Once World War II ended, this attitude softened slightly, but women were still placed under enormous pressure to have their babies adopted rather than bring them up as single mothers.

This was not the only reason children were adopted. Many other children were born as the result of affairs outside of marriage. While some were brought up as children of the marriage (and may have been subtly discriminated against by the "father"), others were given up for adoption "to save the marriage." Some children were brought up by someone else simply because their parents, or parent, could not cope. When marriages break down, it can be impossible for either parent to continue to nurture the child. Relatives may step in, or foster homes are found. Temporary care may be needed and the child finds him- or herself in a children's home. This experience is not necessarily bad. I worked with one man who had spent the greater part of his childhood in the extended family of an orphanage. He loved it. But he did not have the Hades Moon.

All adoptions seem to lead to the same intangible inner sense of "not totally belonging." Somehow the children, no matter how much loved and wanted they are by the adopting mother, or how young they are at the time, carry that unconscious memory of another mother, of belonging elsewhere, of an original maternal bond, which is not surprising considering that babies are programmed to imprint on their birth mother, and do so at a very early stage, as we shall see. They have, of course, been carried for ten lunar months in intimate contact with their mother, although as we have seen not all wombs are warm and welcoming.

Babies are also programmed to respond to maternal love. In a now famous study, baby apes were taken from their mothers and given the choice of surrogate mothers in the form of a soft, cuddly but non-food-supplying dummy or a harsh, wire dummy who nevertheless had the food. The babies chose the comforting "mother" over the one from whom they could obtain food. The "cuddly mum" came closest to the mother on whom they had imprinted at birth. But mothers do not always have a choice about giving up their children. They may be compelled to hand them over to someone else to nurture.

ADOPTION: A NATURAL MOTHER'S STORY

As we have already seen, family secrets tend to entwine down through generations. That someone had a child outside marriage, or even within it, often becomes a "dark secret" so that when a woman is confronted with the child she had to have adopted, it reverberates down through her "new" family. It can be a painful and difficult adjustment for a child to find he or she has an unknown brother or sister. Even when the reunion is sought by both sides, it can be a deeply emotional event, bringing to the surface feelings that have long been hidden. It is not only parents who seek out their adopted children, siblings do so, too. Equally, people find that the family they thought they had is not quite what it seems. A new generation can easily repeat the ancestral pattern without knowing it exists. This is particularly so with families, and partnerships, where adoption runs back through the family, as Lynn's story shows. Lynn has a Finger of Fate with a Moon-Neptune conjunction in Libra in the 12th house sextile Pluto in Leo in the 9th house close to the MC, inconjunct her Sun and Mercury in Pisces on the 4th-5th house cusp (Placidus houses). There was no planet at the outlet point close to the cusp of the 10th-11th houses, so she had to make her own release. Clearly she was dealing with powerful karmic issues with both her mother and father, issues that went way back into the family history (12th house Moon). It would seem that Lynn is a lineage-breaker who incarnated to heal the family tree.

Lynn's mother's time of birth is unknown, but if we use a sunrise chart, which shows karmic intention, her Moon in Aries is square Pluto in Cancer and stays in orb throughout the day. In the synastry of her chart with Lynn's, her Moon trines Lynn's Pluto, Lynn's Moon squares her Pluto. There are old mothering and abandonment issues here. When she died, Lynn's progressed Moon was midway between her natal Saturn (the Lord of Karma) and North Node (Karmic purpose), and semi-sextile natal and progressed Pluto. By transit, there was a Chiron-Mars-Saturn in Pisces opposite Pluto-Uranus in Virgo, forming a wide outlet point for that Finger of Fate:

> *Mum's death was very sudden and unexpected. She died of a heart attack while at a dinner dance with my father. The shock was tremendous because our relationship had*

been fairly stormy, certainly from my early teens, if not before that. As a young child I tried to please and live up to her expectations, which were quite high, and I seemed to be a constant disappointment to her. Because I couldn't meet her expectations, I went into "Well I can't win with this; I'm not going to be able to be what she wants." I began to rebel and throw tantrums and make life hard for everyone concerned. I actually felt she was very controlling, which really brought out the rebellious side of me. The arguments were heated and strong and after an argument she would sulk, as I did, so we ended up not speaking for days at a time.

We had just started to get on a little better, although I never actually felt I knew her [Lynn's natal Moon conjunct Neptune does not see the mother clearly]. So that when she died I was left with a tremendous amount of guilt and anger, and a sense of loss which came later, that I had never really known her as a person only as a parent. I never really felt a part of that family, I felt as though I was an alien, not belonging. A lot of the problems probably stem from my mother's own insecurities and issues, one of which was that she had very hard skin on the palms of her hands and soles of her feet, which I know she was self-conscious of, and which nothing could ever be done about. My brother has it and two of his children. It was through this I discovered my mother's background. I commented to my mother's cousin that it was strange that mother was the first born and had this skin on her hands and feet, and yet my brother and his children who have it were the second or third child.

She came out with, "Didn't you know your mother and I were sisters? Your mother was the younger, the second born." So that's how I found out that the people I thought were my grandparents weren't in fact. My mother was the second illegitimate child of someone I had always thought of as my great aunt. That revelation happened when I was 38 and transiting Pluto was buzzing around my Ascendant at the time. It was the last conjunction, the third contact, when all this came to light, giving a whole new understanding of the family background [Pluto bringing the secrets out of the 12th-house Moon cupboard]. My mother was obviously so screwed up about being illegitimate that neither my brother nor I were to be told and even after she died, my father never mentioned it to us.

My mother's own childhood must have been very fraught because she grew up in the village where her natural father was—he was already married and had five children of his own, and then my "great-aunt"/grandmother had two of his children, and I believe someone else had one of his children. So he was a mystery figure in the background and Mum never had any contact when she was growing up. She was brought up by an uncle and his wife as their own child. So it was a very secretive background, and as a child I was maybe picking up on the family secrets that were around [she is a very sensitive and psychic Pisces].

After Mum died, I couldn't stand being around the guy I had been going out with and who I was with when Mum died. I jacked it in. As a way of escaping my own feelings that I couldn't cope with at the time, I went into another relationship which I still don't understand the attraction of. I think a lot of the feelings around it were that he actually made me feel quite special at a time when there wasn't anybody around—Dad had retreated into his own space, he was finding it very difficult to cope and just going through the motions of living [his Moon in Capricorn would find it hard to deal with the emotions of loss]. So I escaped emotionally into this new relationship and later on that same year became pregnant. By that time my dad had started to take more interest in life and was actually taking someone out, so he'd perked up a bit.

When I found out I was pregnant, I didn't want to believe it, and put off telling anyone or doing anything about it for some time. I didn't know what I was going to do. That Christmas was difficult because Dad wanted my brother and myself to have a meal with the woman who later became my stepmother. I certainly wasn't having anything to do with that. I didn't even want to think about anyone else coming into the family. Dad had said they would be getting married before long, which brought up a lot of anger and grief around my mother's death less than twelve months earlier.

It must have been shortly after Christmas that I really couldn't leave it any longer to tell him I was pregnant. I remember the night I told him. He was upset but said that whatever my decision was about the child, whether to keep him or to have him adopted, he would support me—not financially—but that it was okay with him. The following day, by which time he'd discussed it with my stepmother-to-be [Aquarian Moon sesquiquadrate Pluto: showing evolutionary adjustments are called for], it was a different matter. [Lynn has a natal Sun trine Saturn. Her father's Sun squares her Saturn, his Saturn opposes her Sun. There was a sense of karmic obligation. At some deep level she expected him not to support her, but, with that trine aspect, hoped against hope that it would be different this time around. Her stepmother's Moon opposes her Pluto. This was a control-power issue which was not personal between the two of them, but which was familiar to each of them.]

It was put to me that if I kept my child, they wouldn't be getting married. And if they didn't get married, how could I take the child home, as there would be no one to help me look after him. I felt I was being emotionally blackmailed as well as being insecure and lonely, which was something I had felt all through my childhood, I didn't feel as though I had any real choice other than to have my child adopted. Being pregnant was a very bittersweet experience because I felt extremely well and glowed, but around that all the time was the knowledge that I would not have this child for very long. It was a very strange time.

My father got married when I was five months pregnant, and of course my stepmother coming to live with us was another traumatic experience, my brother and I certainly didn't want her around. Dad was very much focused on her and it felt as though we were no longer of any importance. Anyone with any common sense would have moved out there and then, but at the time it wasn't that easy. My feelings around this time were very mixed—a lot of anger, resentment, and sadness.

Michael was actually three weeks late being born [typical of the Hades Moon mother and child]. I was perhaps trying to hang onto him a little longer. I remember asking Dad when I was in the hospital if I could bring the baby home, and he was sad himself but said no, it wasn't possible. [Her son Michael has Pluto square the Moon in Gemini.]

So when I came out of the hospital, Michael went to foster parents and I went to see him most days, although I didn't tell anyone. He should have gone to meet his adoptive parents about a month after he was born, but was taken into the hospital for an emergency operation as the valve at the base of his stomach wasn't functioning, and he was throwing up all the time [Pluto-Uranus conjunction in Virgo]. I spent a lot of time with him in the hospital, and perhaps the bond was stronger than it might have been had he been adopted straight away. He was 2½ months old when he was adopted. My father and stepmother actually took us to the adoption society and I handed him over to his adoptive parents, although I couldn't face meeting them.

After that I was living in a black hole with a lot of strong deep emotions that I didn't know how to handle. Looking back, I had my son adopted in typical Piscean fashion. I felt as if I was making a sacrifice, very much the victim of it in order that my dad could get married. I was then expected to put it all behind me and get on with my life; it was finished, done with, never to be spoken of, and so a lot of the emotion was stuffed deep down inside.

In typical Pisces fashion, I got involved in another relationship to avoid feeling the things I didn't know how to handle. I felt as though I was madly in love. It was quite an obsessive relationship and we married a few months later. During this period, transiting Pluto was quincunx my natal Venus. This marriage was actually facing me with all the emotions I had stuffed down inside myself. It was a very erratic, tumultuous relationship. Neither of us were particularly mature. He was extremely jealous and possessive, and when he had been drinking, he was violent, so we would fight both verbally and physically. I was being faced with the stuff I had tried to avoid feeling although at the time I didn't realize that. My marriage was a very Plutonian experience, full of power struggles, manipulation, emotional blackmail, very degrading.

It was an extremely traumatic two years and it sapped me of any confidence I had left. I knew it was a mistake within a couple of weeks of being married, but it took me two years to leave that relationship. I felt I'd lived up to my mother's negative expectations of me and made a mess of everything. I felt inadequate and low in self-esteem. I was full of guilt and grief from having Michael adopted, as well as the grief and loss around my mother. My whole identity seemed to have been totally flattened.

In the period leading up to when I first met Michael again, I was in the early stages of the Huber Astrology Course and was also taking a counseling course. Transiting Pluto was in Scorpio trining my North Node, and transiting Jupiter was conjunct natal Pluto. During this period, the backlog of emotion came up to the surface. I was getting in touch with the grief and anger that I had pushed away and could not cope with earlier in life. This process led me to put my name on the Adoption Contact Register at the end of 1991, and in August 1992 I had a letter from them to say that they had forwarded my name and address to my son, which came as a shock, because while it was something I wanted, it brought up feelings of fear as well as excitement around it. I went through a whole variety of emotions and expectations, from the worst possible scenario, to him being the most perfect being that ever could be, but it wasn't until March 1993 that we actually met.

The first meeting with Michael was full of excitment and fear. I was very nervous, and when I first saw him I could hardly stand up, I had to hold onto a nearby table for support as my whole body shook from head to foot. I have never felt quite like that before or since. We got on amazingly well and he seemed very much in touch with his own feelings around being adopted and seemed to have worked through a lot of stuff. We talked about the reasons for his adoption and a bit about how I had felt afterward. He told me about his childhood, and how he had first thought of contacting me when he was 17, and going through a rebellious stage at home, and how his expectations of me then would have been far different from what they are now. So we also talked about our expectations of one another and the very strong bond between us, which is also loose, as no demands are made either way. It is never going to be what is considered a mother-son relationship, but we are special friends.

Over the last three years we have met a number of times, not frequently because he lives some distance away and has a busy life. We write occasionally and we speak to one another on the phone. When he and his wife came to stay, I was thrilled and suprised at how relaxed we were together. We had time for the two of us to talk. One thing he needed to clarify was that his relationship with his adoptive parents won't change because he's in touch with me—which I wouldn't want or expect. He said something to the effect that a parent is someone who brings a child up, and I think his intention was to clarify that I can't expect what he presumably sees as obligations/responsibilities to parents, which actually felt a relief to me—it leaves less clutter.

It is interesting that, although Lynn feels that she abandoned her son, he does not feel this. He received good parenting from his adoptive parents and that is sufficient for him. So, it looks as though Lynn may have suceeded in breaking the family pattern and begun a new interaction with her son.

When Lynn told her father that she had finally met her son again, he retreated into senility and eventually died without understanding what it meant to her. He simply could not handle it. But she has worked hard on healing the relationship with her stepmother and has forgiven her. Lynn, as with other successful reunions, did not seek her son in order to resume the role of mother. Janet, whom we will meet later, wanted to meet the person rather than the baby. She became "great pals" with her two boys. Lynn and Michael are "special friends." It works because neither demands what could not be. One of the reasons these reunions went so well was that both Janet and Lynn had done a great deal of work on getting to know themselves first.

ADOPTION: A SON'S TALE

Reunions do not always work out so well, and many parents and children do not want to be found. While I was in the middle of writing this piece, I switched on my car radio to hear: "It's not fair, why should we live in terror of a knock at the door. Adopted children ought to have some rights in this matter. We should be protected from these people who suddenly want to see the child they abandoned all those years ago." The speaker had called into a discussion program on whether or not birth mothers should have automatic access to information regarding the adoption of their child. Apparently some mothers were circumventing the process whereby prospective reunions were logged on the Adoption Contact Register. They were using dubious, and illegal, means to ferret out the details and then contacting the child direct. The caller was adamant that he did not want to be found by his birth mother. He was happy never to know his birth mother.

Edward's story, which follows, covers many of the themes with which we are becoming increasingly familiar as we explore Hades Moon families. It also shows how the issues carry over into the adopting family. Indeed, I have seen several cases where the natural mother did not have the Pluto-Moon aspect, but the adopting mother did. Mothers do not have to be birth-mothers to carry the Moon-Pluto archetype for their sons, nor do they have to have a Hades Moon to do so. If they do, then the effect is intensified and may well, when the synastric aspects are considered, point to a past life interaction. When I met Edward, his progressed Moon was in his Cancerian 12th house, inconjunct his Moon-Pluto opposition and transiting Pluto was square natal Pluto. It was time to throw some light into his past.

Edward came to a demonstration in which my *Zodiac Pack* image cards were used to place his visual chart on the floor.[5] An astrologer who specialized in viewing the chart as a map of childhood walked him around his visual chart, introducing him to the planets and signs as they went. The images on the cards graphically portray their meaning and facilitate an intuitive connection with the energies of the chart, so they bring up material from the subconscious mind as well as teaching astrological meaning. The journey began with his birth and early childhood (from the Ascendant through the 1st house). The first planet they met was leonine Pluto, which as can be seen from his chart (Chart 11, page 126), opposes Edward's Aquarian Moon (figure 11, page 127). Sitting holding the visual image of Pluto, Edward said that he had been adopted and could identify with the volcanic crater in the center of the card. This was how he had always felt inside himself. He also recognized the regal stance of the queenly lion as pertaining both to his adopted mother and to his own, somewhat elevated, view of himself that she had imparted.

As the journey around his chart progressed, and he reached the area of relationships, he sat with his solitary Hades Moon in Aquarius for some time. With both his Sun and Moon in Aquarius in the 7th house, he was the archetypical loner. Holding the cards, he could see himself in the scientist peering down into his laboratory—humanity. Instead of feeling himself reflected in the Moon's mirror, he identified with the barren surface of the Moon and said that he had always found dealing with emotions extremely difficult. Walking the Moon-Pluto opposition, more of his painful mothering story emerged. After the death of his adopted parents, he had traced his birth mother only to find himself, as he experienced it, rejected once again. However, the experience had thrust him deep into himself and had helped him examine his relationship to his adopted mother more fully. After the demonstration was over, I asked Edward if he would like to contribute to this book. We kept in touch over a period of two years. This is his story:

I was born at the end of January and taken to the care of my adopting parents at the end of March. My mother was only 19 at the time of my birth, having had a love affair with a man a couple of years her senior. Her pregnancy shocked the family, who bungled [sic] her off to an understanding aunt some distance away from her home. She was told adoption was the only possibility and I believe that parting with me caused her much distress. My adopting parents died in 1977 (father) and 1983 (mother). They were always very kind to me and spoilt me quite badly at times! I was brought up as an only child.

A few years later I was able to search for and easily find my natural mother. She was delighted to hear from me and a meeting was quickly arranged. Even her husband, who knew of my existence, was happy about the situation. My half brother and sister did not know of me, and had to be told, but they accepted the situation wonderfully. Visits were only occasional as we lived at different ends of the country. They went pretty well for a time, but my upper middle class upbringing made it difficult for me not to create a class barrier. My adopting parents were very class conscious and much of it rubbed off on me.

Our relationship broke down when my natural mother became jealous of what I had, and the education which she could not have given. For my part, I had been guilty of behaving in what must have seemed an overbearing and superior sort of way. I was not sufficiently sensitive to the practical difficulties it would have created for her

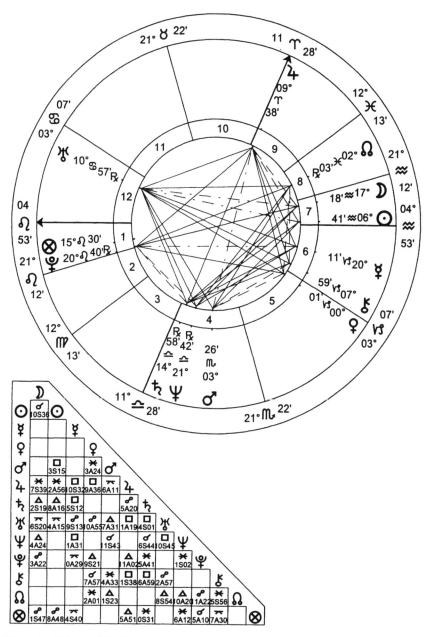

Chart 11. Edward. Placidus houses. Birth data withheld for confidentiality. Source:
Natural mother's memory.

Figure 11. Moon, Pluto, Aquarius, and Leo cards from The Zodiac Pack (published by Findhorn Press, 1997, used by permission).

to have me suddenly appear on the scene. On what turned out to be the last visit [progressed Moon squaring the Moon-Pluto opposition and forming a wide fixed-cross with transiting Pluto in Scorpio] she let fly at me for having led a very sheltered life and not having to work for what I had. This was very hurtful to me because it tapped into a feeling of guilt. When, a little later, she moved closer, I attempted to telephone only to find her number was ex-directory and I interpreted this as a signal that she wasn't too keen to hear from me. In fact, it may simply have been an over-sight. [That defensive Moon opposition to proud Pluto in Leo would be quick to see a potential rejection and step back to avoid the hurt that might come.]

Since then we have exchanged Christmas cards as I try to keep a foot in the door until such time that I felt I had developed a sufficient sense of self-respect to be able to meet her again. I feel I have that now, and hope that I am perhaps a little humbler than I was six or seven years ago.

A month later, when sending him the karmic reading I had prepared, I asked for a progress report:

> *Unfortunately there does not seem to be an obvious means of contacting my natural mother. I sent her a card, but she has not replied. You were right, of course, to say that I was expecting far too much from her when we met (natal Moon trine Neptune). I would very happily settle for a great deal less now.*
>
> *You asked particularly which of my mothers carried the devouring dominant archetype. It was without doubt my adopting mother. She was a strong dominant personality. Her power came over in her tone of voice when I was younger, "You just don't do that sort of thing . . . it's just not done." She disapproved terribly of anyone she thought was out of the right social class. Her disapproval, as far as I was concerned, registered without her having to say a word, and yes I felt limitations in who I could bring back to the house. It was not a coincidence that soon after she remarried, following my adopting father's death, I cleared off to Kenya for three years and didn't resettle in the UK until after she died.*
>
> *The previous incarnation which you mentioned was very interesting. [As a medieval crusader who was "rescued" from captivity by a strong mother-figure, he had protested about atrocities perpetrated by the crusador army and had been imprisoned by his own side.] My mother's actions and treatment of me as the crusader knight and the feelings it left go a long way perhaps to explaining some dreadful problems I've had with low self-esteem. It is much diminished now, but I came across an old diary a couple of years back that I kept when I was in my late teens. It was quite a shock to be reminded just how bad it was at that time.*
>
> *The other interesting thing is that the only past life regression I've had that I feel really gave a genuine insight into a past life was one where I was chained up in a dungeon/jail. The incredibly strong feeling I had was that, for some reason, I was not being allowed to speak out on something. I did not, at the time of the regression, have any idea of who I was or exactly where I was, or when it took place. But it now seems to tie in with being imprisoned for protesting about what was being done during the crusades.*
>
> *I hope I haven't given the impression that my adopting mother was like the devouring medieval mother. The archetype really only came out as far as I can see in the context of social class. In other respects I got a lot of praise and support in whatever I achieved. My departure for Kenya was not met by rejection, and, indeed, the red carpet was really rolled out when I got home on leave. There was a hint of the illness of which she eventually died at the time I left, and this was deliberately kept from me at that time in order that my decision to go would not be affected.*

By the time we checked in with each other a year later, Edward still hadn't heard from his natural mother. But things had certainly taken a turn for the better in his self-esteem. The progressed Moon was now conjuncting natal Pluto and transiting Pluto had just edged into Sagittarius to throw a little light into a previously dark place—his karmic purpose. Transiting Pluto would soon square his nodal axis, helping him to move out of the entrenched past and bringing up insights for his transformation:

I suppose overall what I really have now that I didn't have a few months ago is a feeling of inner strength and knowing the time has come to go out and live and say what I really believe—and take any flak that might fly around as a result.

I had sent him a tape to help him cut the ties with both his mothers, and some Australian Flower Essences to help the process of disentangling himself:

I think just recently I began to see what had really been going on between me and my adopting mother. It came to me with the help of a book called Behind the Masks *by Jean Bond, and also through being involved in a close relationship with a woman for the first time in years [transiting Pluto was exactly semi-sextile his isolated natal Venus bringing relationship issues to the forefront]. It came to an end partly perhaps because we were not truly compatible, but also because I couldn't handle someone getting as close as she wanted to get [Moon in Aquarius pushing away the possibility of finally getting its needs met].*

I can see that my mother made me the center of her happiness, and that involved doing what she wanted and behaving in the way that she wanted! [Libra on the 4th house cusp plus the Hades Moon effect]. And I can see now that is what I was always trying to do because at the time I suppose I would have seen my security depended on it. I think that it must be very close to the "If you don't do as I say, then I won't love you" syndrome that you identified in that earlier life.

I doubt very much that my mother would have been aware that this was the game she was playing any more than I was, but I can see it now and at times I feel quite angry because it seems it may be partly responsible for my always behaving as a "people pleaser" [indicated by the Sun and Moon in the Libran 7th house reflected through Aquarius], finding it very difficult to say no. That came out in this recent relationship. I had reservations, but somehow I just kept on going, thinking I must do everything to please her, when I should really have been saying—hey, hold it a moment, this is going too far too quickly for me—and the whole thing fell apart and she got hurt more than if I had been honest about what I felt in the first place!

In fact, I am now having to deal with the whole question of the rejection issue brought about by my adoption, and I have found a hypnotherapist locally who is helping me. It was suddenly finding myself having a woman in love with me and realizing that I couldn't accept that, that made me realize that I had to seek help and deal with the issues.

The healing for any kind of loss and abandonment is to go deep down into its center and face the fear, to find that one does not, after all, die. This is the gift that mothers who have to give up their children offer to that child. It is the potential to break old patterns, to find a new way through. Pluto is the survivor. In the depths of such trauma, he brings to light the possibility of nurturing oneself and finding new life. Likewise, the only way to resolve rejection is to take that risk, to open to intimacy, to forgiveness, and love, to go into a relationship undefended, ready for whatever may come. This is the positive side of the Hades Moon.

GENETIC SEXUAL ATTRACTION

In the mythology of the Great Mother, there are many coital references. When she was not playing the over-protective maternal role, Demeter was the mother who copulated with her son. In the ancient religion of the Earth Mother, there were sexual practices which mirrored the fertilization, fruition, and decay of the vegetative year. Mother mated with son, son was killed, and his body used to fertilize Earth. This sacred drama was played out by priest and priestess, or priestess and victim (willing or otherwise), and mothers sacrificing their sons at birth.

Life has a way of mimicking myth—and myth reflects life. Oedipus (a rejected, abandoned, wounded child whom we can safely surmise had a Hades Moon) has passed into psychoanalytic parlance as a synonym for parricide and incestuous desire for union-with-mother. Metaphorically, this is the son who so desires his mother that he fantasizes killing his father, the arch-rival. But there is another part of the story. Oedipus is rejected because his natural father has been told that he will be killed by his son. The father nails Oedipus' feet together and exposes him on a hillside. The child is rescued by an old shepherd, but is lame thereafter. Oedipus is adopted but his origins are withheld from him. Having been told by an oracle that he will kill his father and marry his mother, he goes into voluntary exile. That is, he separates himself from his adopted family and his perceived destiny. But! One cannot so adroitly avoid Pluto. His fate was waiting on the road to Boeotia. When Oedipus, having killed his real father by accident, meets his (unrecognized) mother, he is so drawn to her, he marries her and they produce two sons. (This being myth, he does of course have to perform an heroic task to win her hand). Having discovered the truth, Jocasta hangs herself from shame and grief, and Oedipus puts out his own eyes and goes into exile with his daughter. His sons, in an argument over their inheritance, commit fratricide.

Oedipus, unlike so many men who are drawn into emotional—or physical—incest, did not know Jocasta was his mother. Nor did she recognize him. But this myth embodies not only a deep psychological truth, but a physical one as well. Sons do want to fuck their mothers. I had one client, then middle-aged, who had a Pluto in Leo to a Taurus Moon opposition to Venus in Scorpio, who started every regression session with me by fantasizing that he was, as he put it, "screwing his mother." I learned that, if we wanted to do any real work, this was what would precede it. Although his mother was by then in her 70s, to him she was as desirable as she always had been. He would not have dreamed of acting out his wishes physically, but his imagination ran wild. Other men "fancy" their mothers. Lincoln, whom we met in chapter 3, had a powerful attraction to his mother. The taboos of society normally contain this desire. But not always. And certainly not in cases where mother and son have not grown up together.

Mother nature has her own way of holding mother and child together—something which is genetically programmed to take place at birth. A mother imprints on her child in the first few hours after birth as part of the bonding process, and vice versa. Disrupt this, and child and mother never quite feel they belong together. Smell and shape play an important part in the recognition process. In

Britain, mothers had to remain with their babies who were put up for adoption for the first two weeks or so. The breaking of that early bond, and the consequent lack of an imprinted mother figure, account for the vague (and sometimes extremely strong) feelings of "not belonging" within the adopted family that so many adoptees report, even while they are not consciously aware of having been adopted. This, and the need for a sense of identity, impel them to find their birth mother. When they do, to their surprise, the innate recognition may manifest as adult lust. After all, this is the woman they have yearned for all their life. So common is this "pull to the mother" (or other members of a separated family) that a name has been coined for it—Genetic Sexual Attraction.

With true Plutonian synchronicity, as I was writing this chapter, I spoke to a friend, Janet Thompson,* whom I had not seen for some time. I knew she had traced the sons she had to give up for adoption when she was a teenager, so I asked her how the relationship was faring. She said the contact with the younger one had been what she expected. But what had happened with the older one had taken her totally by surprise—although fortunately she had been warned of the possibility and so managed to resist temptation. As a result, she had just written a piece on Genetic Sexual Attraction (GSA), but it had been rejected by the newspaper. It went beyond the bounds of what they were prepared to publish. While they had already printed articles on brothers and sisters who had been separated at birth being drawn into sexual relationships when reunited, the prospect of mother and son doing the same broke too many sexual mores. Janet (Pisces Moon inconjunct Pluto) offered it to me for this book.

> Recently I heard about GSA. The letters stand for Genetic Sexual Attraction. I had never heard the term previously, but I have certainly experienced the feelings and emotions. In August 1965, I gave birth to a baby boy, whom I named Arron [Moon conjunct Pluto in Virgo opposite Chiron in Pisces]. He was with me for the required two weeks in hospital and was then given up for adoption. I was just 18. In 1966, I got pregnant again, and in December 1966 gave birth to a second son [Moon in Gemini square Pluto], who was adopted into the same family.
>
> On November 30, 1994, I met again my eldest son who had been adopted thirty years previously. The meeting was arranged through Ariel Bruce, a charming and compassionate independent social worker, who runs a tracing service. After the phone call telling me she had found them, my sons and I exchanged letters and photographs. A couple of weeks later I was invited to Ariel's office to discuss arrangements for the first meeting with Arron—to take place the following day. The adopted parents had changed both boy's names, but to me he will always be Arron. Ariel suggested that if we both felt comfortable once we had met, it would be fine for us to go off and have dinner together. She then looked at me very seriously and said:
>
> "I am going to give you a piece of advice that I want you to listen closely to. You're an attractive woman; you don't look your age; you are not that different in age to your son. Don't fuck him, if you do, you will never retrieve the relationship. I will also say the same thing to him."

---

*This is not the author of several titles published by Weiser!

And she did. At that time I had little understanding of the very strong feelings that would surface after our meeting. During dinner on our first night together Arron, looking across the table at me, rather sheepishly said: "You know that thing that Ariel said." Understanding his reference immediately, I replied: "What, not to fuck you, you mean?" And we both laughed at the thought.

The following night I had invited Arron to accompany me to the opening of a film I was appearing in. Walking down the Haymarket holding his arm, alarm bells began to ring. I had the first inkling of Ariel's warning. Suddenly it felt like I was out with a young lover. This stranger on my arm could have been any one of the younger men I've known over the years. I felt young and free with this handsome blue-eyed boy. His obvious delight in my company, and mine in his, grew stronger as the weeks went on. It was like falling in love. I found myself thinking about him constantly and wondering what he was like as a lover, wanting to explore his body and in my mind doing so, all the time knowing that it was inappropriate, but unable to curb the thoughts and feelings. The forbidden nature made it all the more thrilling and tantalizing—it was something only we two knew about.

Whenever we parted, he would make a point of walking me to the car, away from other people, so we could hug each other close. Secretly and surreptitiously I wanted to feel how his body felt under my hands, aware of the impact of his thighs as they pressed hard against mine. Nothing wrong with all of this, after all we were just two people saying goodbye. Our mouths would stray from the cheek and linger on the lips. Although we were able to talk about how strange the feelings were and that it was like being in love, I didn't speak about how I felt physically nor try to stop the close and intimate contact between us. Thoughts of incest and the forbidden shockingness gave the experience an added charge of excitement. The problem was exacerbated because Arron was soon leaving to spend a year in Australia. So, having found him, I was very soon going to lose him again.

The feelings and emotions that we shared I now know are common to people who have been reunited with a loved one. Not only adopted children meeting birth parents, but siblings separated through the breakdown of relationship. A reunion is likely to be a highly charged event and people carry expectations they are not always fully aware of. Body smells and physical similarities play a big part in the attraction. Suddenly finding someone with whom you belong can be a powerful and disturbing attraction. Sex can be a powerful channel to explore primitive emotions. Both parties in the adoption process can suffer from "low self-esteem," the mother from having given up her child and the child from being rejected. To be forewarned of the dangers and possibilities gives some understanding and there is less likelihood of losing control.

Exploring the bonding process thirty years later with a grown man was not easy, and finding the balance between being a magic mother and a real person is like trying to walk on snow, trying not to disturb it. Saying "No" as a birth mother is tricky, as to express denial might be seen as further rejection—when what you want is to make up for the lost years. With time, my son and I have found interests and values in common that give us a different, more appropriate kind of intimacy. I met my second son in February 1995. The relationship with him was quite different, there were no sexual feelings, and although we are affectionate, this time there was no complicating undercurrent.

Arron and I didn't allow our relationship to overstep the boundaries and now three years further on, the intensity of the feelings has lessened and we are able to enjoy a happy and loving friendship. Our story might not have had such a happy outcome had it not been for Ariel's timely and very specific advice.

What I found particularly significant about Janet's account was that, knowing nothing about her meeting with her sons, I had previously done a karmic synastry reading for her in which I had seen Arron as her lover in a past life, but saw her second son as her child. With electric each-way Moon-Uranus inter-aspects between the charts, Janet and Arron had old freedom-commitment issues, but the sexual attraction had, as so often happens, clearly jumped lives helped by a Mars-North Node contact. Arron was born at the time of Janet's Nodal Return, so they have conjunct Nodes in Taurus. This indicates that they are traveling in the same direction; they have the same karmic purpose—finding inner security rooted in

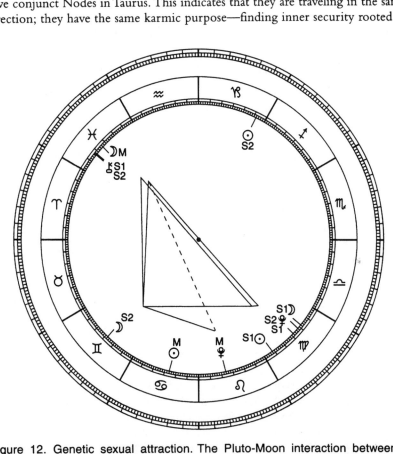

Figure 12. Genetic sexual attraction. The Pluto-Moon interaction between a mother and the two sons she gave up for adoption. M = mother (Janet); S1 = first son (Arron), S2 = second son. Birth data withheld for confidentiality. Source: mother's memory.

the piece of eternity that is their spirit, soul, or true self. They had put their names on a register to trace each other at the same time. A one-way aspect from Janet's Moon conjuncting Arron's Chiron and opposing his Pluto-Moon conjunction, showed the rejection-abandonment issues they would face in the present life, but these had not been carried forward from a previous life (see figure 12, page 133). However, in the synastry with her second son, who was initially reluctant to meet her, there were repeating each-way Moon-Pluto, Moon-Neptune and Moon-Saturn inter-aspects. The karmic issues here clearly related to replaying heavy symbiotic mothering patterns so that they could be transformed through a one-way Uranus-Moon opposition.

HEALING THE FAMILY TREE

Rejection and alienation between parent and child can be resolved. But it takes time and work. In the process, the ancestral line is healed and this healing projects forward into future generations.

Jan's family is typical of the enmeshed issues that interwine down the years. Her mother, Clara, who was adopted, did not know her father. Her son, Peter, has married a woman who was herself adopted and has not traced her family. Jan was brought up by her paternal grandmother, as her mother worked, and Jan's own children were raised by their paternal grandmother. Each-way inter-aspects between the charts show that there is personal karma between characters in this archetypal drama. Notwithstanding, the lack of Pluto-Moon interaspects between Jan and her sons shows that, although they are acting out the family karma by Jan "abandoning" them to be brought up by their paternal grandmother, and also acting out their own expectations of "abandonment," indicated by their natal Moon-Pluto aspects, this was not a repeating pattern of personal interaction between them. There are, however, other mothering issues across the charts. It is sometimes easier to heal a family pattern if you have not been deeply immersed in that pattern *with that person*, yourself, in the past.

The Moon-Pluto aspects across the charts of maternal grandmother, mother and sons form a mutable cross (see figure 13, page 135). Mutable cross aspects are karma which, although it has arisen before, has not become so entrenched it will be impossible to heal. It is a challenge for the family to change the way the patterns manifest. As she is an astrologer, Jan has an understanding of the planetary dynamics that underly the family contacts (although for clarity and brevity I have kept these mainly to the Pluto-Moon contacts). Her speciality is Chiron, but I asked her to look at her family in the light of a repeating Moon-Pluto pattern and to see how that affected mothering. She, unknowingly, picked up many facets of the Hades Moon with which we are by now familiar:

> The first thing I have to look at is my mother's chart. Mum [Clara] (Moon in Capricorn opposite Pluto in Gemini) never knew who her father was. My maternal grandmother had to put Mum in an orphanage when she was 4. From what I can gather, they were basically thrown out into the street by my grandmother's brother because

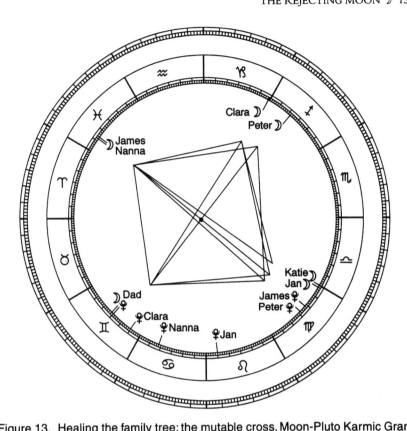

Figure 13. Healing the family tree; the mutable cross. Moon-Pluto Karmic Grand Cross, extracted from the charts of maternal grandmother (Clara), mother (Jan), and her two sons (Peter and James), Jan's mother-in-law (Nanna) Jan's father (Dad) and Jan's granddaughter (Katie). Birth data withheld for confidentiality. Source: All data from family records.

> *Gran wouldn't divulge who my grandfather was. At that time Mum's progressed Moon was conjunct her natal Chiron in the 10th house. My Mum used to say, "I'm like Topsy [in* Uncle Tom's Cabin*], I just growed.*

Apparently, Jan's mum was traced by her mother to the house where the child, Clara, was staying. But the people were out. Her mother never came back for Clara (something over which Jan's mum was very bitter but which would be healed by Jan's reconciliation with her own children). Jan's mother was then adopted by a man the family call "Uncle." He has a bucket chart with an isolated Sagittarius Moon conjunct the North Node as the only planet above the horizon. As far as the world knew, he had no blood ties with his adopted daughter. But Jan feels there is a family secret lurking here:

When I started to research Uncle's chart, I came up with the theory that he knew more about my mother's father than he ever told Mum. His Pluto is inconjunct Mum's Moon and his MC is on her Moon. Mum's Pluto is widely conjunct Uncle's South Node and conjunct his IC. If you look at her wedding photograph and look at both her eyes and Uncle's, I am sure you, too, would feel there has to be a blood link, not just an adoption link. I don't feel he was my grandfather, but I bet he knew who my grandfather was and took the secret with him to his grave. No proof, just a strong "gut feel."

As Jan was being christened, Uncle's wife (her mother's adoptive mother) died in the churchyard outside. Someone came into the church and said: "Hurry up, there's someone dying out there." Jan's mother was never really sure whether Jan had been christened or not. Jan became convinced that she was, therefore, a child of the devil—which may have, in part, contributed to the psychiatric illness she later experienced. When she became interested in astrology, she had herself christened again, "Just to make sure I would not be an agent of the devil."

With a Sun in Leo that had been obscured for many years by having the Ascendant, Moon, Mars, Neptune, Mercury and North Node in Virgo, Jan needed to be recognized:

My chart also tells a story and I feel I need to share it. The Moon-Neptune conjunct the Ascendant is where I've always felt exceptionally sensitive emotions/antenna but over the years, because of the emotional abuse, I stopped trusting them, listened to other people and became totally confused. My progressed Moon crossed this conjunction earlier this year. After that aspect, houses 2-8 are devoid of planets, showing my years in the wilderness with no help from the universe or my higher self because I had lost my way. But now I have transformed myself. This autumn I intend to symbolically bury my old self in California (too far away for me to ever fall back into old habit patterns). When I've done this, and am finally in control of my thoughts and emotions rather than letting them control me, my Sun conjunct Chiron will really shine and I shall be a Chironic Astrologer, writer, philosopher, and whatever else the universe has in store for me. Not only that, but I can finally honor all the sensitivity and emotional honesty which has been hidden in that Moon conjunct Neptune and sextile Pluto, and become a true Leo, not one bogged down in negative energies.

For the first four years of her life, Jan was totally doted upon (Moon conjunct Neptune):

As you say in your books, Leo's are here to learn the lesson of specialness. Trouble was, I was too special, i.e., the only daughter, granddaughter, niece, etc. Because I was so loved, no one taught me discipline or boundaries, apart from Uncle.

"Uncle" was the bane of Jan's young life. He had moved in with his adopted daughter when his wife died and he was the only person who tried to control the young child. He was emotionally and physically abusive, constantly telling her to "shut up." Jan was absolutely terrified of him and he scarred her deeply. As Jan said, he was so dominant that her father, who was a quiet, gentle man mutually besotted with his daughter, was lost in the background somewhere.

But, the "disengaged father" is, as we have seen, all too typical of the Hades Moon. The "chosen child"[6] is equally hadean. So utterly loved and so totally engulfed by the family, the child has no opportunity to develop a separate sense of self. It can be as heroic a task to separate oneself from being the chosen child as it is to leave behind the rejected child. When Jan was 4, her mother went back to work full-time and Jan's world fell apart. She felt totally abandoned. Her progressed Moon was in Scorpio. Her paternal grandmother, whose house was close by, took on the role of mother. Jan asked:

> *Was she devouring, because my dad has Moon conjunct Pluto in Gemini? [Well, let us say she certainly carried the archetype for Jan's father who only moved round the corner from his mother when he married.] Gran's Pluto in Taurus sits in my eighth house yet we were great mates. Her Moon in Pisces was on my South Node [an old soul connection]. My Pluto is inconjunct her Moon in the first house. After talking to you last night, it suddenly came to me. Has Gran been with me before, possibly even as my mother?*

As we have seen, the Hades Moon can well signify that a beloved grandmother may be an old soul contact who will incarnate to help the child through a difficult childhood. Typically, Jan's mum found herself looking after her husband's mother as she moved in with the family when Jan was 14. This event followed closely on Uncle dying. So, as Jan says, her father never really regained his place in the family.

Jan has a natal Moon-Neptune-Ascendant conjunction that sextiles Pluto-Venus. She has recognized that the men of her generation have their Pluto conjunct her Venus, which she finds hard to handle. As she sees it "men of my age squash my femininity/sexuality." Any such contact brings up the "emotional black hole" neediness of her own Venus. But it also activates her mothering issues through the wide contact between the Moon and Pluto. Her perception of the family pattern of "mothers rejecting their daughters" was that it was due to Moon-Neptune, and that Pluto related to the men in her life, although she felt that her Sun conjunction to Chiron may signify "the males in my life, most of who have vanished for various reasons." Clearly her Sun-Chiron combination shows wounding around fathering, and a wounded father—although she idolized her father and was devastated by his early death. But, as we have seen, the Hades Moon correlates as much to the absent father, as it does to the rejecting mother. A Neptune Moon contact tends to indicate a mother who is idealized, "wonderful," but somehow *unavailable* when needed.

Jan married and had two sons; she also suffered from depression and mental illness. Eventually she was hospitalized and given ECT (electro-convulsive therapy) treatment. Uranus was at work and something went wrong. She was given an enormous jolt of electricity. She was in a coma for a week. At the time, the transiting

Moon sextile Pluto was setting off her chart. She returned to the family home but soon afterward her husband walked out on her. She had her young children during the week; her husband had them during the weekend. On a day when the Moon, trining Pluto, exactly opposed her natal Pluto, Jan decided to opt out. That suicide attempt was one of the lowest points of her life. Her husband took the children full-time and his mother, "Nanna" (who has no Moon-Pluto aspect), became their surrogate mother. Jan's son Peter has the Moon square Pluto, and her other son James has Moon opposite Pluto. They expected a devouring and, quite possibly, rejecting mother but Jan has never seen herself in that role, although she felt guilty for many years over giving them up. When the Hades Moon works well, it is the mother who is able to do what is best for her children while understanding the very deep emotions that will be triggered, and who can guide her children through the pain. However, Nanna has her Moon conjunct James' Moon and square Peter's Moon so she could equally well play the role of devouring or empowering mother for them.

> I now understand that I had to give them up and let their Dad and Nanna physically nurture them, otherwise I would have tried to control them, plus all the other negative Pluto "stuff." By giving them up and making this sacrifice (very Chironic), I have become their wise "old" mentor, rather than a controlling, devouring mother [although a great deal of healing was needed on the relationship before they reached this stage].
>
> However, there is another, far more karmic reason for letting them go which has only just come to light. Recently I felt impelled to take Nanna (with whom I had maintained a close friendship) to a local psychic fair. The information we received feels so right for both of us that it has to be true.
>
> It seems my James should have come through Nanna, not me. He should have been her son and John (my husband)'s brother rather than his son. Nanna miscarried between the birth of my Peter and James. She never told me this until after the psychic reading. It turns out that James is actually her miscarriage. Because she was very ill after her miscarriage, James couldn't come through her, so I was his only entry into the family. No wonder I went down the garden to talk to John one evening and said to him: "If Peter wants a brother, tonight's the night." We went to bed and that night James was conceived. No wonder it felt so right to let James go to live with his dad. But not Peter. It was only because I believed you couldn't split brothers that I had the courage to let them both go, yet I felt so guilty afterward. If you believe, as I do, that Peter has been my father in a past life (no proof, just an inner knowing and some interesting Saturn-Nodal interaspects) then you will understand why it was such a wrench.
>
> I know John and I came together just to bring those boys into the world and all of this must have been planned when we were in spirit. The chemistry between us when we met was unbelievable. Yet by the time James arrived and the boys had lived their formative years in a united family, John and I started to "dissolve" [they have conjunct Neptune-Moon conjunctions].
>
> When I look at the interaspects between James and Nanna, I feel something very karmic is afoot. I may not have tried to control and devour him, but I feel

Nanna's chart reveals that she could (her Pluto is conjunct his Ascendant) and James, being very intuitive, would be aware of this. Yet it must have been hard for him to "fly the nest" because he has Cancer Ascendant, Nanna a Cancer Sun, and they share conjunct Moons. My sons both have amazing charts (no, this is not a doting mum speaking) and in James' chart, the angles and nodes form a Star of David. Something tells me that he is going to star on the world stage one day.

Despite all my past suffering, I am so lucky these days. The boys have both told their Nanna that I have nothing to forgive myself for over letting them go and at long last all the guilt is behind me. For I now understand that I have been a much better mother by tutoring them from a distance and they've been so lucky having two mothers to cherish and nurture them. Nanna nurturing them physically, while I nurtured them emotionally, mentally, and spiritually. They were like me in that respect (having two mums). But my Mum and Gran weren't aware of what was going on. So, with all this love and attention, it is hardly surprising that my boys have matured into healthy, wealthy, happy, and wise individuals (a very rare and precious combination). The whole family has come a long way since that day when Peter was 8 and the divorce solicitor asked him when he wanted to see his mum again and he said, "We don't want to see our mum again, ever."

In Melanie Reinhart's book on the centaurs,[7] there is a report of my discussion with her at a seminar. We are looking at the stewardship of the generations and I am talking about how, now I am the "grand matriarch" of the female side of my boy's family tree, I feel I have the responsibility/stewardship of the generations in my hand. Because I am aware of this responsibility, I feel "the buck has stopped with me" inasmuch as it has been my role to clear the family line. I feel I have cleared out the family line for the seven generations that have gone before and the seven generations still to come (providing they don't mess things up). But I have one even more special, "gut feel" reason for doing this. One day I feel I shall come back into my family through Peter's family line. He's been my dad before and will be again, inasmuch as he'll be my granddad, or great granddad. Wow! I've recently discovered Peter's wife [who was herself adopted and never knew her parents] is pregnant again with their third attempt at parenthood (they lost the previous two by miscarriage). The baby will be a Capricorn. I feel that, knowing my family as I do, the lesson the baby will be able to learn is to find the balance between materialism and spirituality. No wonder the baby has chosen me for its grandmother. I should be able to help her.

Peter and his previous girlfriend aborted a baby, so I feel this is a reason for the two miscarriages. Yet I thoroughly understand why they had to go through the abortion. I feel they were both very brave to make the decision at the time without consulting the family [that she felt they should perhaps have done so is indicative of the enmeshed Hades Moon at work]. I sensed what was going on, although I couldn't understand it at the time [the psychic Hades Moon at work]. I felt as though something tragic was going on. And it was, for I was sensing the loss of my grandchild.

As with so many Hades Moon babies, this one arrived following the death of a family member. Jan's aunt, a Capricorn, died soon after the conception. The new baby, Katie, is a Capricorn with Virgo Moon sextile Pluto. Her Moon conjuncts Jan's Ascendant, Neptune and, most importantly, her Moon. A Moon placement shared between grandmother and granddaughter indicates strong links from the past as well as a genetic, and emotional inheritance through the family. The family Grand Cross was powerfully activated by her birth. It will be interesting to see whether Jan's work will be sufficient to change the family pattern for the new generation.

CHAPTER 5

THE RAGING MOON

The best reason to love our enemies is that "they" hold up a mirror in which "we" may see the reflection of our disowned self. Our enemies hold the secret, the missing dark treasure, that we need to become whole and true.

—Sam Keen[1]

HIDDEN IN THE DEEPEST layers of the Hades Moon is an unresolved rage and frustration that has traveled through generations. This is where the collective karma of war and repression lies. It is also where individual rage and resentment festers. It may be fueled by Mars, but it is inherent in the Hades Moon. Whenever an emotional eruption occurs out of all proportion to the trigger, the Hades Moon is at work. Whenever passionate conflict explodes, whether between individuals or on a global scale, the root energy is the raw power of the primal rage of Pluto focused through the instinctual forces of the Moon.

This primal energy is not of itself constructive or destructive. It simply is. It is how we plug into that energy, where we utilize it, and the moral judgments and values that we place on it, which make it "good" or "bad." If we access it creatively, then it fuels our endeavors. However, when the energy becomes blocked, we see it thrust itself into consciousness, violently and with overwhelming force. Blockages occur through repression, by non-acceptance of the emotional needs behind the aggressive urge, and by consigning our "unacceptable" or unlived out energies into the shadow. This arises collectively and individually. So often this century, Pluto changing signs is foreshadowed or accompanied by war breaking out: Cancer, World War I; Leo, World War II; Virgo, the Suez Crisis, and so on. In virtually every war I looked at which had a specific start date there was a Hades Moon aspect on the day the war began bringing unresolved rage and frustration to the surface. When North Korea attacked South Korea, precipitating the Korean war, the Moon was in Scorpio—a Hades Moon. Traditionally, war is ruled by Mars. Mars, however, is immediate, impetuous, and over in a flash. Astrologically speaking, Pluto is the higher octave of Mars. In wars such as Vietnam, the start cannot be pinpointed to a certain day as internal conflict emerged gradually, and of course all wars have contributory factors which may span decades or even centuries. This is where we see Pluto at work. Pluto acts much more deviously than Mars. Its effects are hidden until it erupts from the depths. By then the conflict is serious stuff. The collective dimension has been hooked in and the unresolved, festering rage and paranoia that lies beneath the surface is activated. This is the instinct

141

to war. The Moon is the "planet" governing instincts, and war can be seen as the shadow face of the Moon's nurturing quality. As the collective (the Moon) tends to be the stronger force, many individuals find themselves swept up into a conflict which, on the surface, has nothing to do with them. However, we must always remember, "as within, so without." The cosmos is mirroring back to us all the antagonism we feel, but we do not own. So, war and conflict show us where forgiveness and reconciliation are needed in our own lives.

I am not suggesting that Pluto and the Moon are the only planets involved in war, but aspects between the two appear with great frequency both in significant dates and in the charts of personalities involved. War is clearly playing out Hades Moon themes.

Once I started researching this aspect of the Hades Moon, I was surprised how often the Cancer-Capricorn axis came up. I had already explored these signs as the Gate into Incarnation and the Gate into Initiation (see chapters 1 and 10). I had always seen them as the point where the masculine and feminine met in the chart; and the axis that indicated the Cosmic Parents—Cancer, the cosmic mother, and Capricorn, the father. Now, as I looked more closely at war they began to take on a life or death struggle. They signified two of the entrances to Hades, the place where unresolved rage and frustration could reach out and pluck the unaware into the Gates of Hell.

THE HARVEST OF THE DEAD

C. G. Jung called World War I "a veritable witches sabbath."[2] Pluto moved into Cancer at the end of May 1914. On June 28, 1914, the Archduke Ferdinand was murdered. Murder is a Plutonian act. On that day, Pluto was sextile the Moon in Virgo. This particular act set in motion a harvest of the dead, many of whom died on Flanders Field. Out of the mud and death of the trenches came millions of poppies, giving rise to the Remembrance Day Poppy. Poppies, naturally, are a Persephone flower. Trenches are a Plutonian place, a crack leading into the sinister shadows of the Underworld, the abode of the dead. We will look a little later at the effect that war had on one man, the poet Wilfred Owen and at his chthonic experiences.

On August 1, "the Fatherland," Germany, declared war on "Mother" Russia and World War I was launched. Early that morning, the Moon was in freedom-loving Sagittarius, inconjunct subversive Pluto. An inconjunct (150°) is a karmic aspect and the causes for World War I stretched way back into history. Cancer is strongly attuned to the past and the war was led by the old guard, the Kaiser Wilhelm and the Tsar Nicholas (who was to perish in the upsurge of communism at the end of the war).

Communism in its pure form is another Cancerian energy, the State is acting as mother to her children; none need go without. However, in true Plutonian style, much more goes on underneath the surface and the State becomes a domineering, controlling parent who brooks no dispute or dissension (Capricorn), exactly the qualities we see in the devouring Moon-Pluto Mother. In communism, Plutonian paranoia and secrecy reached its greatest depths, and its secret police were much feared by the very people they were supposedly protecting. This is a typical Plutonian turnabout, the collective forces of bureaucracy taking over and controlling the power of the individual.

We can also see, in America's response to the Cold War later in the century, a projection of the Moon-Pluto paranoia onto the enemy "out there." In the July 4, 1776 birth chart for the USA,* the Moon in revolutionary Aquarius is exactly semi-sextile Pluto in Capricorn. The revolution that preceded the setting up of the USA was, of course, yet another struggle against the overbearing mother country, and the established society and ideals of Capricorn. Minor aspects, such as the semi-sextile and semi-square, are most often projected onto, and lived out, by another. So, having rebelled and become the norm, society then sees the enemy "out there" living out the revolutionary ideals that could change the world again, and yet, because this is not integrated as an inner drive, it is perceived as posing a threat to life and liberty.

The Bolshevik revolution began with a meeting on the evening of October 23, 1917. The Moon was in anarchic Aquarius, inconjunct seditious Pluto in home-loving Cancer. Here again we have the karmic aspect of tension, the 150° quincunx, bringing together two very different energies, this time bridging the revolutionary fervor of humanitarian Aquarius with the caring and concerned, and yet deeply ingrained, attitudes of Cancer. For the first time, a group of people took power not for personal reasons but to put into practice a carefully conceived theory which would change society as a whole.[3] The established government of the time had been "battered into helplessness" by the war that was exacting a huge toll in lives, but the revolution had been fermenting for much longer and was a challenge to the old feudal system symbolized by Cancer. Karl Marx (whose Pluto in Pisces semi-square Moon in Taurus challenged established credos, but brought in a fixed idealogy of his own) believed that capitalism polarized society into a small group of the extremely rich, and a much larger group of the poor. His ideal was equality for all. Lenin, who has been called "one of the greatest world-shakers in history," not surprisingly has an Aquarian Moon (although there is confusion over the actual date of his birth). Aquarius is always light years ahead of its time and is concerned with the good of humanity. No matter what his actual birthdate, he would have Pluto in Taurus, and was of the generation that was challenging the accepted norms regarding money and possessions, and was therefore seeking a new form of material security and a redistribution of wealth. He took the view that the organization of the proletariat was the main task of a revolutionary party that was aiming at a coup d'état through conspiracy (a Plutonian theme). Two weeks after that fateful Bolshevik meeting, a new State and a new society were proclaimed. Here again we can see both the Aquarian Moon and the forces of Pluto at work:

> The overthrow had happened with dreamlike ease, against a background of turbulence, discontent, suffering and futility. They thought themselves on the verge of a vast ground swell that was about to transform the world; they expected to be caught up at any moment by similar eruptions and similar seizures of power through Europe and the world at large.[4]

Years of bitter civil war followed, echoing the divisiveness of the Pluto energy in Cancer: the womb of Mother Russia was being rent asunder by the birth pangs of a new era. A 1990s comment, made after Pluto in Scorpio had dredged previously

---

*Source: Liz Greene quoting Dane Rudhyar.

concealed evidence to the surface, says that Lenin ruthlessly suppressed cultural diversity and put in place all the practices that made the Stalinist State possible. Lenin (who died in 1924) felt by then that "the machine had gotten out of control": the collective forces of Pluto had taken over. His powerful position was taken over by Stalin, a man who had already had considerable covert power and controlled thousands of lives: he had been the hidden power behind the throne that is so typical of devious Pluto. On Lenin's death, Stalin "outmaneuvered, crushed and finally exterminated" all opposition. He came to hold total power, a true Plutonian dictator with a propaganda machine, secret police, and devastating purges to back him up. Stalin lived out the negative Pluto archetype and carried a dark secret—alcoholism.

Like Lenin, there appears to be some confusion over the exact date of Stalin's birth. I found reference to two charts for him. The secrecy and confusion surrounding the birth of these figures who rise up out of the collective unconscious to take on an archetypal, almost godlike role (and remember that communism replaced God with the State), is typically Plutonian. There are always several versions of the birth of mythological figures. Their origins are shrouded in Plutonian mystery. This is part of their role, it imparts a numinous uncertainty to their beginnings. We can see the Pluto shadow archetype taking over in both these men virtually at birth, as though fate had marked them out, and so their origins, too, were shrouded in mystery.

Stalin's connection with the Hades Moon is interesting in that in one of the charts given for him (December 21, 1879, Sun in Sagittarius), it is not apparent at birth. In that birthchart the Moon is conjunct Saturn at 7° Aries, but does not aspect Pluto in Taurus. However, by progression, when Stalin took over power that Moon had progressed to Scorpio, opposing both natal and progressed Pluto. When World War II started, the progressed Moon was once again in Scorpio, opposing Pluto. In the other chart, which I am assured has been authenticated (January 2, 1880, Sun in Capricorn), he has a wide square from Pluto at 25°46" Taurus to the Moon at 3°20" Virgo, so that he is bringing in the Hades Moon from birth. Certainly from the strong connection I have noted between Sun, Moon, and the Nodes in Cancer-Capricorn and figures involved in the war, it seems likely that the "dictator" energy is here associated with a Capricorn Sun rather than a Sagittarian one.

According to a British 1950s history book, Britain entered World War I because of "a plain instinct," the same instinct which had caused her to fight Philip of Spain, Louis XIV, and Napoleon: i.e., defense of the homeland, a Cancerian concept, and Cancer is, of course, ruled by the Moon. The Cancerian mother will fight to the death to defend her young, and once those crab's claws have caught hold, only death will force them to let go. War causes great emotional suffering to the family (emotion and family being linked to Cancer) through breakup and disintegration, and we can see the Plutonian energy at work in the grief and desolation that followed loss. Certainly, for many people involved in World War I, the Cancerian Gate of Incarnation brought them face to face with intense suffering. For Britain in 1914:

> An overweening military strength threatened the balance of power [Pluto] . . . on which depended alike our safety [Cancer], livelihood [Cancer], and ideals [Sagittarius] . . .

and war was the inevitable result. However the writer points out that:

> It would be easy to spread the responsibilities for this calamity to all
> mankind: to show that by offensive means Austro-Hungary was fighting a
> defensive war, or that the Slavs were defending a racial offensive, or to admit
> that British and French Imperialism often provoked a natural indignation.
> The chain of crime might be traced much further back in Turkish persecu-
> tion, the partitions of Poland, or the aggression of Louis XIV.[5]

Collective karma (a 12th-house matter) underlies war. We are, of course, looking
here at the darker side of Pluto: territoriality, imperialism, abuse of power, intimi-
dation, aggression, racism, persecution, genocide, festering resentment, etc. But we
are also looking at the shadow side of humanity rising up, foreshadowing the discovery of Pluto and the full flowering of the destructive urge in World War II.

Three weeks after the war began, there was a solar eclipse with the New
Moon in Leo. Eclipses have their strongest effect in the months leading up to the
eclipse,[6] although if they aspect a planet, the effect continues for another six months
after the eclipse. The light of consciousness was blotted out, the instinctual forces of
the proudly nationalistic Leo Moon could rise up and overwhelm the caring, concerned "home-loving" side of Cancer, urged on by fanatical Pluto. It overcame the
benevolent heart-centered energies of Leo, releasing the despotic dictator archetype
that lay beneath. It let loose the legacy of the unresolved rage of the Hades Moon.
Millions of men were fired up with the idea of war, believing that they were called
upon to fight "the forces of evil" and in Britain:

> Nothing . . . was more genuine, or in the long run more decisive, than the
> feeling we were fighting for causes much larger than our own. . . . This
> flooded the recruiting-stations in 1914, and produced from this unmilita-
> rized nation over three million volunteers. That voluntary sacrifice excited
> an idealism which helped to bring America to war, set up a contagion in the
> East, and bequeathed to the world of 1919 a short vision of a better world.[7]

Despite the idealism, however, it was nevertheless a nationalist and territorial war,
not an ideological one. As the United States Ambassador in London wrote to his
President in October 1914: "It is not the same world as it was last July." Pluto had
done its work. An epoch that had begun with the Renaissance had ended. The
world would never be the same again. Collectively, Man descended into the Underworld. Now it was Woman who was left to grieve as the Demeter archetype once
more walked the land and the world was made desolate. The position of woman,
too, would never be the same again; she gained a right and a freedom unknown before. An idealized picture of war perished in the trenches. By 1916 each side was
firmly dug into carefully prepared Plutonian positions "against which attacks were
brutal, bloody, and generally unsuccessful."[8] Over one million British men lost their
lives, and the Cancerian family, as Britain had known it, was irrevocably broken.

On Armistice Day, November 8, 1918, the German Foreign Minster was presented with the draft of a peace treaty which contained "ruinous reparation pay-
ments" despite that its stated aim was the reconstruction of Europe. Pluto can be

seen at work: "Its harshness and vindictiveness, however, caused widespread resentment and eased the way for nationalist extremists culminating in the rise of Adolf Hitler."[9] "It caused a grievance against the inevitable retribution; an ill-founded grievance in the circumstances, but a festering grievance nonetheless."[10] As one of the German ministers said, it could be summed up quite succinctly: "Germany gives up her existence." At midday on that day, domineering Pluto exactly opposed the Moon in authoritarian Capricorn. Neptune, the planet of ultimate surrender and devious ploys, was conjuncting Pluto. The overt war, for the time being, was over. The covert war was just beginning. Pluto would continue its subversive work away from the public eye, while the collective pretended all was well.

When I showed the draft for the above to Robert Christoforides—who has closely studied the events of World War I, he gave a rather different view in his response:

> As a historian and a Pluto subject, I feel that you have been too nice to the Hun! They had been sizing up and provoking the international community for over 50 years and were determined on war—a quick one certainly—so as to dominate everyone else by militarism. Most of the war was fought on others' territory and incredible damage was done as a result. In my view we let them off the hook. Germany unfortunately did *not* cease to exist and was able to mount another WW twenty years later. Unlike the French in the Franco-Prussian war of 1870, they were bad losers and brought the worst depravity to the world through the Nazis. Retribution then followed again. The jury is still out on the question of their future behaviour. I know that this isn't fashionable, nor politically correct; but there it is!
>
> In this respect, in psychic terms (and some astro-physicists are exploring the idea), the future can control the past. A psychic awareness of the "still-liveness" of the past's evils, (however deeply disguised and forgotten), and, thereby, a projection backwards to destroy or, at least, hobble them, enables victory over them or, at least, disables their capacity in the present and the future. Believe me, this is the case here. It is a demonstration of the crucial purpose of Plutonism—exemplified, for example, in aspects of Shiva, Durga and Kali. Those who are not of it of course see it otherwise; but the Plutonic subject never forgets and recognises no Statute of Limitations for crimes. This is not vindictiveness—it is due retribution and an always-attempt at prevention and to baulk repetition.
>
> On the other hand the Plutonic subject is a great exponent of resurrection and redemption—the two apotheoses of transformation.[11]

A DREAMER CAST OUT FROM SUNLIGHT

They were in one of many mouths of Hell
Not seen of seers in visions: only felt
As teeth of traps, when bones and the dead are smelt
Under the mud-trap which they help to sell,
Mixed with the sour sharp odour of the shell.
                                                —Wilfred Owen[12]

Wilfred Owen was a pacifist, a shell-shocked veteran who abhorred war and yet was awarded a Military Cross for "conspicuous gallantry and devotion to duty . . . [He] personally manipulated a captured enemy machine gun from an isolated position and inflicted considerable losses on the enemy." His war poems present graphic images of the horror of war and show the futility and inhumanity of such conflict:

> If you could hear, at every jolt, the blood
> Come gargling from the froth-corrupted lungs,
> Obscene as cancer, bitter as the cud
> Of vile, incurable sores on innocent tongues,—
> My friend, you would not tell with such high zest
> To children ardent for some desperate glory,
> The old Lie: Dulce et decorum est
> Pro patria mori.[13]

In the closing months of his life, Owen came to believe that it was his task to chronicle "the truth untold, the pity of war, the pity war distilled."

While Wilfred Owen's heroic death, in the last week of World War I, is known to within an hour or so, his birth time was not in any of the family records. In such cases I use a sunrise chart (Chart 12, page 148), symbolic of the karmic intent of the incarnation. I was asked to look at this chart (initially without knowing who the subject was) by a lawyer friend, Robert Christoforides. Robert has undertaken in-depth research on the manuscript fragments left by Wilfred Owen at his death and has produced a performing/reading version of Owen's previously unseen poetry. For reasons which will be apparent later, he knew Wilfred Owen and his poems intimately. When I read a just-prior-to-sunrise chart prepared from a dowsed time of birth, he commented: "Wilfred was a before-dawn person—dawn was seen by him as a glorious miracle—this is his personality." In his fragmentary poem "Sunrise," Wilfred describes "a large pearl more marvellous than the moon" looming over the horizon. This may well be an unconscious echo of his birth. To describe the Sun as a pearl is certainly a Piscean view of the fiery luminary.

The sunrise chart gives Pisces rising and a very wide sextile between a Pluto-Neptune conjunction in Gemini and the Moon in Pisces. As the day progresses, the Moon would come closer into orb. The Moon would also move into Aries with its links to heroism. Owen was an extremely sensitive man, and has both Sun and Venus in Pisces. In my researches into his life, and from his poetry, it seems certain to me that he has a Hades Moon. A wide orb allows a more objective perspective on the issues, transforming them into poetry. However, as we shall see, Wilfred Owen's life reflected both personal and collective experience of the Hades Moon. Although I have included his story here so that we can share his chthonic experience of those who went to war, we will also look at his remarkable relationship with Robert Christoforides and the synastric aspects between their charts. The repeating each-way Pluto-Moon aspects between them demonstrate a positive side of dark Moon contacts.

Wilfred had an extremely close, intensely passionate and symbiotic relationship with his mother. Mrs. Owen was the archetypal devouring mother. She kept

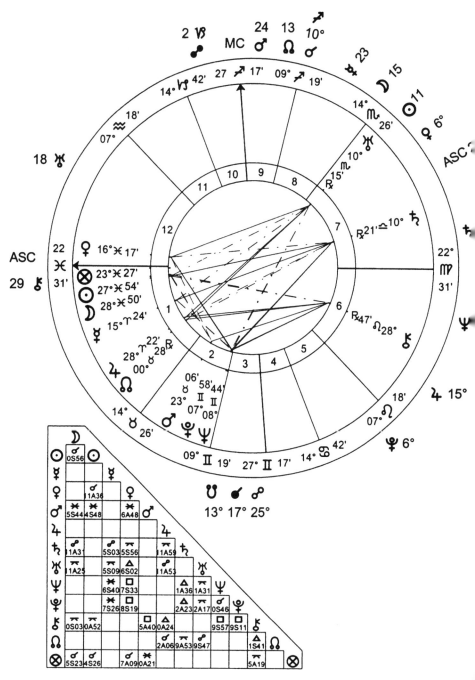

Chart 12. Pre-sunrise natal chart for Wilfred Owen. Born March 18, 1893, GMT 06.1
52N43, 002W45. Placidus houses. Date from Robert Christoforides via Dominic Hibbe
from family. No time of birth recorded. Outer ring: transits at death, November 4, 1918, O
France. Time of death approximately 6.47 (Army records are not specific to within an hou
Eclipse data has been added to the outer ring as follows: ☌ = 17' ♊ May 8, 1918; ☋ = 2°
May 25, 1918; ♂ = 10° ♐ Dec. 3, 1918; ☍ = 25° ♊ Dec. 17, 1918.

her son tightly bound to her. Of almost seven hundred extant letters written by him, the vast majority are to his mother. His last letter, full of "transcendental hope and comfort," was addressed to her. As his biographer Dominic Hibberd says: "the bond between them was suffocatingly intense; there are connections between it and the many images of (s)mothering and drowning in his poems."[14] It is clear from the published letters that Wilfred's mother connection was living out the archetype of the Hades Moon linked to Neptune. The psychic umbilical cord had not been severed. He was absorbed in her and by her, still in the ouroboric intrauterine state of a Pluto-Neptune contact to the Moon.

Because of this bond, he was set apart from the rest of the family. His "stiflingly respectable" father never understood the sensitive, poetic "mother's boy" whose leanings toward homosexuality would have so horrified the polite society of the time had they been made known. Wilfred had to keep a great part of himself secret, even from his beloved mother. He has the typically alienated and yet prophetic qualities of the Hades Moon. He was not cut out for war. A tiny figure of a man, he was, seemingly, not the stuff heroes were made of. His intense inner life set him apart, as did his sexuality. "His poethood began in secret darkness, born out of a tradition which had made the poet both the prophetic voice of the people and a solitary, damned figure, a dreamer cast out from sunlight."[15] He was no stranger to Pluto; at 19 he wrote:

And can men, plunging and writhing round this lightless, scopeless pit,
Breed and increase their woe a million-fold?

and he pondered:

How do the heavens rule my gloomy moods?[16]

Well, as we have seen, transiting Pluto squaring the Sun (and the Moon in the sunrise chart) can explain many a gloomy mood, and fueled, no doubt, by this transit, 1912 was one of Owen's most productive years. It was also the year when he decided that Christianity was incompatible with science and poetry, had a major breakdown, and was nursed back to health by his mother.

A Sun-Moon conjunction often blots out one parent. In Wilfred's case it was his father, although his volunteering for war and especially returning to the battlefield after he had been invalided out with shellshock, spoke of a deep need to prove to his father that he was "a man." The hidden, or disengaged parent, although seemingly the weak link, is often the most influential—a kind of negative inversion that may emerge after years of therapy, or with hindsight. Notwithstanding his symbiotic mother bond, Wilfred's karmic connection was with his father. His Sun was quintile to that Pluto-Neptune conjunction. A quintile is an aspect of fate or destiny, and in Wilfred's case it is linked to his Piscean tendency to self-sacrifice. He had to resolve the relationship to the father (archetypal and personal) and thereby to his self (the Sun) even if it meant becoming a sacrifice on the collective altar of war.

Despite being deeply religious in his youth—when he left school he became a lay assistant at a vicarage—like Emily Bronte, Wilfred had an almost pagan feel for nature. He speaks of his poetry as being "born," "nursed," and "suckled" in the solitude of the hills around his Welsh-border home. It came to full flowering in the Plutonian dugouts on the Somme. As Dominic Hibberd points out, even here there was a mother-son relationship, but Mrs. Owen had to be disobeyed in order that Wilfred could establish his relationship with his "other mother"—nature. Many of his poems were mythological in form and content. The seasonal cycle was a structure he used for several of his pre-war poems. Fragments exist of a never-completed heroic epic concerning Perseus and a descent into the Underworld, which Robert Christoforides feels is "spiritually and emotionally autobiographical."[17] Dominic Hibberd points out that below the surface of the poem is a "shadowy but insistent pattern, a secret myth which he seems to be making out of his own experience."[18] The fragments include scribbled references to those denizens of a mysterious Underworld—Pluto and Prosperine (Persephone). In an early fragment, the narrator, after a death agony that takes him into "hell's low sorrowful secrecy" meets an old hag who offers to be his lover. By the time Owen has been through his early war experiences, the poem has evolved into a saga of erotic initiation and subsequent rejection which takes him down into Hades.

Wilfred Owen himself literally took a trip into Hades. Having volunteered for duty, he was sent to France as a junior officer. After an interminable, but actually quite short, time in the mud and death that was the front line, he was tempted to submerge himself in a pit of excrement until he was dead. All his life Wilfred had suffered from the most vivid and unpleasant nightmares. In 1912 he wrote of the "despondency that shaped his nights in bloodiness and stains of shadowy crimes." He was also subject to congestion of his lungs: producing a feeling of drowning which is echoed in many of his poems. He had a deep fear and horror of paralysis and of drowning (linked to his Pluto-Neptune conjunction in Gemini) and yet, as a Pisces, he had this yearning to sink down into the primal slime, once again joining the collective dead.

In France, he had three near-burials in quick succession. He spent fifty hours "trapped" with his men in a dugout with rising floodwater and a roof that was threatening to cave in under incessant shellfire. One of the men was horribly blinded when a shell exploded close to the entrance of the dugout. Wilfred said of that experience that it was not safe to think or feel deeply, but he turned it into poetry:

> We'd found an old Boche dug-out, and he knew,
> And gave us hell; for shell on frantic shell
> Lit full on top, but never quite burst through.
> Rain, guttering down in waterfalls of slime,
> Kept slush waist-high and rising hour by hour,
> And choked the steps too thick with clay to climb.
> What murk of air remained stank old, and sour
> With fumes of whizz-bangs, and the smell of men
> Who'd lived there for years and left their curse in the den,
> If not their corpses . . .
>   There we herded from the blast

Of whizz-bangs, but one found our door at last—
Buffeting eyes and breath, snuffing the candles,
And thud! flump! thud! down the steep steps came thumping
And sploshing in the flood, deluging muck—
The sentry's body; then, his rifle, handles
Of old Boche bombs, and muck in ruck on ruck.
We dredged it up, for dead, until he whined
"O sir, my eyes-I'm blind-I'm blind, I'm blind!"
. . .
Those other wretches, how they bled and spewed,
And one who would have drowned himself for good,—
I try not to remember these things now.
. . .
Through the dense din, I say, we heard him shout
"I see your lights!" But ours had long gone out.[19]

Shortly afterward, he was concussed in a dark underground hole for several days. Then finally he was hurled off his feet by a shell and into a small hole with only the dismembered, decomposing body of a fellow officer for company. He was closeted there for several days. He was unconscious most of the time. When he emerged he was suffering from shell shock. His symptoms were uncontrollable shaking, stuttering, sweating, and a sense of suffocation. His worst nightmares were about caves, dugouts and a distorted landscape in which he met the dead, tortured faces of men he had been responsible for and who had been casualities of this unholy war.

Fortunately for Owen, the army recognized shell shock in officers as a specific disease (or dis-ease) of war and had set up a hosptial at Craiglockhart in Scotland under the auspices of several respected doctors. Wilfred was referred to Dr. Arthur Brock there. Brock believed that shell shock was the result of extreme severence from the environment. His cure was to immerse the patient back into his immediate surroundings, which included his own past experience. Brock said: "The individual is responsible for his own growth, understanding his past and open to his future, including its terrors, united with the future, as well as with the eternal world." A great believer in mythology, he likened his patients to Antaeus "crushed to death by the war giant." Antaeus was the son of the earth, Gaia, and the sea, Poseidon. He could not be overthrown in a contest while his feet were in contact with the earth. If he was raised off the earth, then his strength failed. Reunited with the earth, his strength returned rapidly. He was killed by Hercules, who held him up off the earth and crushed him. This myth resonated with Wilfred's experience, he too had been hurled off his feet into "death." Wilfred described some of his fellow inmates at Craiglockhart as "men whose minds the Dead have ravished."[20]

Under Brock's guidance, Wilfred came to look on his nightmares as "a purgation of the soul." It was Brock's belief that the past had to be confronted as quickly as possible and controlled by a conscious act of will. Once brought back into consciousness and faced up to, these experiences became grist for the creative mill. It proved to be so for Wilfred, his poetic abilities developed dramatically. No longer did he see his war experiences as something apart from his poetry. The hideous memories were transformed into poetic images of great power, and not a little Plutonian beauty:

> Whether we speak or yet are creatures
> and say our life is in the deepness of these craters;
> Yet we are waiting, till the burst earth gulfs for us
> And our door opens.[21]

As a reminder of his transformatory experience, Wilfred bought himself a small statue of Hermes (Mercury), the messenger who was able to pass freely between Pluto's realm and the world above. He took this back to the Front with him when he returned to lead his men into the last battle. With his medical history, he could have been given light duties, but he asked to be sent back. In a letter written to his mother from the front a month before his death, he explained:

> I came out in order to help these boys—directly by leading them as well as an officer can; indirectly, by watching their sufferings that I may speak of them as well as a pleader can.[22]

Having sat in muddy dugouts scribbling the lines that would become his most famous poems, on November 4, 1918 Wilfred and his company were ordered to cross a canal. Orders were clear: "There is to be no retirement under any circumstances." It was a scene straight from hell. The thick mist was further obscured by gas and smoke. Bullets thudded all around, casualties, many dismembered, lay where they fell. In the midst of this the small, calm figure of Wilfred Owen went among his men, encouraging them and giving them heart. As far as can be ascertained, he died trying to take a raft across the river. Appropriately for such a lunar Underworld figure, the dowsed times of his birth and death are just before sunrise. It was a new Moon in Pisces and then Scorpio, it was also Moonrise. The Sun, ASC, Moon, and Part of Fortune were conjoining in life and death. Wilfred stepped onto Hecate's Moon-boat to make his transition to the other world. He is buried in the corner of a vast war cemetery. On his gravestone his mother ordered a misquote from one of his poems:

> Shall life renew these bodies?
> Of a truth, all death will he annul.[23]

The actual poem has a question mark at the end of line two. After his death, the family covered up many of his secrets, destroying his papers and editing his words, even forging a new citation for bravery. "Capturing prisoners" was deemed rather more suitable an activity for a poet than killing them en masse.

When Wilfred was killed, transiting Chiron was at 29° Pisces, conjuncting the Sun, Moon, and Ascendant in the sunrise birthchart. The transiting Sun was conjunct his natal Uranus in Scorpio, and the transiting South Node conjuncted his Pluto-Neptune conjunction, pulling him deep into his karmic sacrificial redemption. In May there had been be two significant eclipses at 17° Gemini and 2° Capricorn (almost on the midheaven of the sunrise chart). As we have seen, eclipses can bring out the inherent issues in a chart *in the months leading up to the eclipse*. In the middle of May, Owen took the poems he had been working on to friends in London. A few of these poems had been published in *The Hydra*, the house magazine of Craiglockhart. Other poems, such as "Spring Offensive" shared with his fellow sufferers the experience of seeing one's friends killed and yet surviving oneself:

> But what say such as from existence' brink
> Ventured but drave too swift to sink.
> The few who rushed in the body to enter hell.
> And there out-fiending all its fiends and flames
> With superhuman inhumanities.
> Long-famous glories, immemorial shames—
> And crawling slowly back, have by degrees
> Regained cool peaceful air in wonder—
> Why speak not they of comrades that went under?[24]

His friends, including fellow poets Siegfrid Sassoon, the Sitwells, and Scott Moncrief, agreed to have them typed up and sent to a publisher. These were the insights Wilfred had gained during his time at Craiglockhart and which subsequently become deeply intense poems. Although that Gemini eclipse was close to the natal Pluto-Neptune conjunction, it was even closer to the Moon conjunct South Node in the solar return chart for 1918. When Wilfred returned from London, he drafted out the preface and contents of a book. He was determined to bring the truth, and pity, of war out to the public. In June he was graded fit for active service but not on the front. His father sent him a message: "Gratified to know you are normal again." By the time the poems were almost ready for this wider public dissemination of his inner life, Owen was dead. The December eclipses were at 10° Sagittarius (solar), opposite the natal Pluto-Neptune conjunction and 25° Gemini (lunar)—right on the Solar Return Chart Moon. On the day of his death, transiting Mars opposed the Gemini eclipse. Consciousness was wiped out. The collective slaughter overwhelmed the individual. But his voice could still be heard:

> It seemed from my dull dug-out, I escaped
> Down some profounder tunnel, older, darkly scooped
> Through granites which nether fires and plutonic wars had groined . . .
> Yet also there encumbered sleepers groaned,
> Too fast in thought or death to be bestirred,
> But, as I probed on, one sprang up, and stared,
> With pitious recognition in fixed eyes
> Lifting distressful hands that loomed as if to bless
> And, by his smile, I knew that sullen hell—
> By his dead smile I knew we stood in hell.
> With a thousand pains that vision's face was grained;
> Yet no blood reached there from the upper ground,

And no guns thumped, or down the flues made moan.
Strange friend, I said, here is no cause to mourn.
. . .
I am the enemy you killed, my friend.
I knew you in this dark: for so you frowned
Yesterday through me as you jabbed and killed.
I parried, but my hands were loath and cold.
Let us sleep now
Foreheads of men have bled where no wounds were.
. . .
But not in war, strange friend, I said,
. . .
Earth's wheels run oiled with blood—Forget we that.
. . .
We two will stay behind and keep our troth—
Let us lie out and hold the open truth
And fall out—from fleeing from futurity:
Beauty is yours, and you have mastery,
Wisdom is mine, and I have mystery:

Then, when much blood has clogged their chariot-wheels,
We will go up and wash them from deep wells;
For now we sink from men as pitchers falling,
But men shall raise us up to be their filling,
The same whose faces bled where no wounds were,
Even from wells we sunk too deep for war,
And filled by brows that bled where no wounds were,
Even the sweetest wells that ever were.

These lines come from a performance version compiled by Robert Christoforides from the fragments and rough drafts that Wilfred Owen left behind. "Strange Meeting," completed perhaps as late as June 1918 shortly after the eclipses, has been published as an Owen poem, but Robert went back to the original drafts—under the direction of Wilfred Owen—to produce these Pluto-Neptune versions, one which has been scripted for actors and music.[25] The poem is believed to be based on an out-of-body experience Wilfred had during his first round of service at the Front and then at Ripon Cathedral when he was on convalescent service and spent time meditating in St. Wilfred's (634-c.709 A.D.) Cell which has two underground passages. A deeply psychic person, he chronicles many such experiences throughout his life. So, in writing the poem, he reworked one of the most traumatic experiences in his life into a Plutonian descent into hell in which he is reconciled with his enemy, an image of perceived enormous power, but, in reality, much like himself.

Robert Christoforides first encountered Owen's war poetry when he heard Benjamin Britten's "War Requiem" many years ago. He was deeply moved, but thought little more of it. But, several years ago now, he became aware of the presence of Wilfred Owen as a discarnate being who made it clear that he wanted to work on the fragments of poetry he had left behind. In time, the fragments became a book. Robert and I then worked to help Wilfred, who had been frozen in time, move on. As Robert said:

> It is of course possible that I knew Wilfred Owen in a previous life—I have remembered my death in that life when I was killed crossing a field with a comrade in that war so, it would appear, I was not with Wilfred Owen when he was killed, but I believe I knew him well.

The synastry between the charts confirms a deep karmic connection. When I first looked at the synastry, not knowing the circumstances, I told Robert that he was living out for this man (whom I knew only as Wilfred) something he had been unable to complete in his own life. I felt very strongly that Wilfred had died feeling that he had left much undone, and a great deal unsaid. Little did I know then that a book of over seventy poems and a performance play would be the result. I had assumed that Wilfred was a member of Robert's family as I sensed a deep connection between them. The connection may, however, have been on a more subtle level, that of old friends and comrades reunited.

They share common issues. Both have Neptune in aspect to Venus, a karmic need to develop unconditional love; and Pluto in aspect to Venus, that deep black hole which is so needy until it finds an inner source of love and sustenance. Each is dealing with the change/maintenance dilemma of Saturn in aspect to Uranus—in Wilfred's case a semi-sextile that manifested all around him in the chaos and death of war. The interaspects are unusual in that each man's Pluto closely squares the other's nodal axis, urging transformation as fulfillment of karmic purpose. They can enter into a shared mythical landscape, peopled with characters from a joint past, and find there the catharsis that will release the Plutonian treasure out into the world.

Robert, a Gemini with an 8th-house Sun and Mercury, is a perfect amanuensis for Wilfred, a ghost-writer par excellence. Their psychic communication is facilitated by repeating Moon-Neptune inter-aspects across the charts. Their shared minds have no limits. Robert has a line into Wilfred's head that permits him to understand the creative genius in a way open to few others. While Robert, whose analytical Moon in Virgo has been capable of exemplary scholarship when researching the Owen archives, has no Moon-Pluto contact in his own chart, nevertheless there are repeating Moon-Pluto aspects between the charts (aspects which hold good wherever Wilfred's exact natal Moon placement might be). Wilfred's Pluto squares Robert's Moon, his Moon trines Robert's. It is quite possible that, in earlier lives, these two had been mother and son. It is equally probable that they had been lovers. Their metaphysical union was seminal. The creative birthing (or rebirthing) of the Owen poems that has resulted from their Plutonian collaboration is truly a child of the Hades Moon. But that, the work complete, Wilfred was tempted to linger is also part of the Hades Moon. He was enjoying his ersatz life too much to want to leave. With a little help, he was persuaded to depart for the equally Plutonian realms beyond death.

DEATH IN A WIDER ARENA

World War I was fought mainly on European soil; it was a war "close to home" (Cancer). The Battle of the Somme, for instance, could be heard on Hampstead Heath in London, and many a local village cricket match was played on an English green to the background of gunfire across the Channel. When Pluto moved into Leo in June 1939, the theater of war became worldwide, and Britain faced the threat of having her boundaries breached through invasion.

The move into Leo came just in time for World War II, which arose directly out of the inequities of the 1918 peace treaty. A new generation reaped the collective karma of its forefathers. According to the jingoistic, leonine, rhetoric of a 1950s textbook, Britain resisted war (while Pluto was still in defensive Cancer) and followed a policy of appeasement until "interests vital to the Commonwealth's very life were at stake." This gave time to "husband our strength." Throughout the 1930s Pluto remained in Cancer. For Britain, and its leaders, the main goal was the protection of its Commonwealth family in accordance with Cancerian principles.

Britain's Prime Minister, Neville Chamberlain, had his Sun in Pisces, a gentle, often confused sign that tries to be all things to all people, so appeasement came naturally to him; but he also had both Pluto and the Moon in dogmatic, bull-headed Taurus: no wonder his "Peace in our time" was rapidly followed by outright war. It reflected his own inner confusion and conflict that, once flowing down its own path, could only believe that his interior worldview was the right one. Taurus, unlike Pisces, allows for no changes of mind, but Pluto forced realization upon him.

In April 1939, just after Germany invaded Poland, there was a solar eclipse in the warrior sign, Aries, followed by a lunar eclipse in Scorpio, the sign ruled by both Mars and Pluto. Appeasement was abandoned. In Europe, preparations for war were begun. Pluto moving into Leo brought in a different energy and signaled a period of national pride, a struggle for world domination, with the shadow energy of the dictator quickly emerging from the Underworld in both Russia and Germany; and a "hero" later emerging in Britain to save the country. The major players in the drama resonated to the Hades Moon archetype: Adolf Hitler had the Moon at 6°37 Capricorn, inconjunct Pluto at 4°39 Gemini in the 8th house. The "hero" Churchill also had Pluto in the 8th house at 21°24 Taurus, square the Moon at 29°40 Leo. Stalin, as we have seen, had either a wide square from Pluto to the Moon, or had the progressed Moon in Scorpio opposing Pluto in Taurus.

Both Hitler and Stalin had, of course, been covertly developing their hadean roles during the 1930s. As Hitler said: "The man who is born to be a dictator is not compelled. He wills it. He is not driven forward but drives himself."[26] The Pluto shadow archetype was once more visible in the Upperworld. This sideways, sidling approach is typical of Cancer, too. The crab never directly approaches an objective, it scuttles about and then, suddenly, it is there: Pluto has moved into autocratic, despotic Leo. The Pluto shadow archetype once more rises into consciousness. The Stalinist purges arose out of a "demonic war" against "evil," trumped up charges of espionage being the excuse for execution or imprisonment. Stalin had set up a totalitarian state with himself as absolute ruler, once more an echo of Plutonian shadow values. Hitler meanwhile had been developing his ideology of a leonine master race who would rule the world, with himself as absolute overlord, and was preparing for the Holocaust which would bring millions face to face with the Lord of Death. All very Plutonian.

THE BEAST FROM THE ABYSS

In esoteric astrology Scorpio/the 8th house is the place where Avatars are born, as we have seen. Adolf Hitler, with an 8th-house Pluto, was acclaimed by many of his followers as a Savior of the German people, the mythologized Germanic Messiah who had been prophesied time and time again. By his enemies, and at least one of his biographers, he was identified as "The Great Beast," the Anti-Christ who seeks to destroy the world. Seen by many as the epitome of evil, seemingly it was through Hitler that the "collective powers of darkness" were let loose in the world. He was a perfect mirror for "collective evil," a channel through which all the repressed shadow energies could rise up. Most commentators look at Hitler's Saturn-Mars aspect and Pluto conjunct Neptune in the 8th house to explain his psychopathology. As far as I am aware, no one has linked his Pluto-Moon aspect to his formative years.

In a statement made by one of Hitler's boyhood friends regarding Hitler as a 19-year-old "drop out" in Vienna, we can catch a glimpse of the Capricorn Hades Moon at work: "He just did not fit into a bourgeois order. . . . In the midst of a corrupt City, my friend surrounded himself with a wall of unshakeable principles which enabled him to build an inner freedom. . . . He remained a man alone and guarded in monkish asceticism the 'Holy Flame of Life' [August Kubizek]."[27] At the time, he was living in a doss house amongst drunks and junkies, thieves and dropouts. This is a most Plutonian abode, highly descriptive of the alienation of his 8th-house Pluto to the Moon contact. And yet, this was the period Hitler was later to say taught him the profoundest lessons of his life, laying the foundations of his philosophy and preparing him for running the Nazi Party.

We can see the collective 8th-house energies, and the creative daimon, taking over in a 15-year-old boy who suddenly finds his mission. Hitler, at this age, was no stranger to the loss and pain of the Hades Moon. His father had died when he was a child. His mother, who brought him up in abject poverty, had died of cancer after being devotedly nursed by her son. He was totally alone. It was a performance of Wagner's *Rienzie*, the story of a Roman tribune's meteoric rise and fall, which was the trigger for a Plutonian revelation: "Adolf Hitler stood in front of me and gripped my hands . . . I felt from his grasp how deeply he was moved. The words did not come smoothly from his mouth as they usually did, but rather emptied hoarse and raucous . . . It was as if another being spoke out of his body and it moved him as much as it did me. . . . [Pluto-Neptune in the 8th house] I felt as though he himself listened with astonishment and emotion to what burst forth from him with elemental force. He conjured up in grandiose inspiring pictures his own future and that of his people. He was talking of a Mandate . . . he would receive from the people to lead them from servitude to the heights of freedom—a special mission that would one day be entrusted to him."[28] As Trevor Ravenscroft, who quotes Kubizek's eye-witness account, says: "He had poured forth the prophetic words which were to be fulfilled with such a staggering concreteness."[29] We are, after all, dealing here with a Sun-Taurus personality who would embody all the atavistic potential of that metaphysically-orientated Hades Moon.

Other people were to witness this same "taking over" of Hitler by something seemingly outside him. Depending on your point of view, this kind of "demonic possession" is where the energies of the most negative Pluto archetype [or collective evil] poured through the 8th house, or where he meets the Christianized Pluto, Lucifer, or the Devil, and is tempted to the power Christ, supposedly, rejected. But it may also be where his daimon is able to surface, to break through from the unconscious. "His face was flushed and his brooding eyes shone with an alien emanation. . . . His whole physiognomy and stance seemed transformed as if some mighty Spirit now inhabited his very soul, creating within and around him a kind of evil transfiguration of its own nature and power" (Stein). "Some people believe, from having experienced in his presence a feeling of horror and an impression of supernatural power, that he is the seat of 'Thrones, Dominions and Powers'. . . . Where do the superhuman powers he shows on these occasions come from? It is quite obvious that a force of this kind does not belong to the individual and indeed could not even manifest itself unless the individual were of no importance except as a vehicle of a force for which our psychology has no explanation" (Denis de Rougement).

Not every witness perceived this as an evil force; Lucifer (the beautiful fallen angel) is, after all, the Light Bringer: "Listen to Hitler and one suddenly has a vision of one who will lead mankind to glory. . . . A light appears in a dark window. A gentleman with a comic moustache turns into an Archangel. Then the Archangel flies away and there is Hitler sitting down, bathed in sweat with glassing eyes" (Gregor Strasser). Such "Luciferic possession" could well be diagnosed as schizophrenia, or as the alienated Pluto archetype we met in chapter 2 taking control, but it could equally well be a rising up of the creative force.

Dr. Stein, who knew Hitler intimately, wrote the first description. The "overshadowing" happened when he stood with Hitler looking at the "Heilige Lance," Hitler's talisman of power. Trevor Ravenscroft, a pupil of Stein's, says that during Hitler's Lost Years in Vienna, Hitler was studying mythology and folklore when an event occurred that was to change his life. Hitler was in the Hapsburg Treasure House when he happened to overhear a guide say that whoever held the Spear of Longinus (the Heilige Lance), and solved its secrets, held the destiny of the world in his hands for good or evil. This ancient talisman apparently activated in Hitler "inherent instincts of tyranny and conquest" and set him on the long search for occult power. It was this, said Ravenscroft, that fueled the events of World War II. A Plutonian "hidden agenda" lay behind the facade of overt power. When Stein went with a youthful Hitler to see the lance: "It appeared to me that Hitler was in so deep a condition of trance that he was suffering almost complete sense-denudation and a total eclipse of self-consciousness."[30] That Hades Moon is deeply psychic and capable of tuning into other realms.

That day there was a lunar eclipse at the beginning of Aries square to Pluto at 0° Cancer (Pluto being just into Hitler's philosophical 9th house where it would

stay until the outbreak of war). Pluto had ventured briefly into Cancer before re-
treating back to Gemini to await World War I. The Gates to Hades were open wide
at that moment. Arian self-consciousness was extinguished. Pluto reached out and
plucked Hitler into another dimension. Hitler himself was later to say: "I move like
a sleep-walker where Providence dictates." Pluto is often perceived as a demonic
energy, an agent of evil forces but it may also be divine providence. It all depends
on one's perspective.

The "question of evil" was one which, apparently, occupied Hitler greatly
during his hidden years in the dosshouse. He spent his time reading in the University library. One of his "mentors" was the philosopher Schopenhauer, who denied
the existence of good and evil and thought that the only reality open to human beings was the physical experience of Plutonian willpower. According to Alan Bullock, in *Hitler: A Study in Tyranny*, Hitler's forceful personality did not come
naturally but was purely the product of "an exertion of will." "No word was more
frequently on Hitler's lips than 'will,' and his whole career from 1919 to 1945 is a
remarkable achievement of willpower."[31] Mars in Taurus has, with the possible exception of Scorpio, just about the strongest will in the horoscope, but so too does
an authoritarian Capricorn Moon.

Schopenhauer's ideas on will sprang from another of Hitler's early heroes.
When he was 15 he had read Nietzsche's *Genealogy of Morals*, a hadean proof that
so-called evil is good, and so-called good is evil. Nietzsche believed in the will-to-
power. It was from Nietzsche that Hitler learned his virulent hatred of the Jews,
whom Nietzsche called "the most catastrophic people of world history." However,
this was not, as had been the case historically, based on seeing the Jews as "Christ-
killers." For Nietzsche, and Hitler, Christianity was a natural, and diabolical, consequence of Judaism. However, it has also been suggested that part of Hitler's
hatred may have stemmed from the fact that he had Jewish blood and was trying to
eradicate this family secret (symbolized by Pluto-Neptune in the 8th house) by
projecting the dark side of himself "out there" onto these collective scapegoats. It
was Nietzsche, and Wagner, who pointed Hitler toward his Teutonic antecedents,
the "proud and unspoilt Germanic tribes." This, combined with Wagner's *Der Ring
des Nibelungen*, a dramatized myth cycle of operas chronicling the early history of
the German peoples, fueled Hitler's fanatical, and highly Plutonic, propaganda of a
master race, on which Hitler came to power, propaganda which was to spill out
through Hitler's 3rd-house Hades Moon conjunct Jupiter.

What motivates Hitler seems to have been both an overwhelming lust for
power (Sun on the Aries-Taurus cusp and the shadow side of the Libra Ascendant)
and an all-consuming, passionate hatred which is the distilled essence of the negative Hades Moon combined with the shadow energies of Taurus, Leo, and Libra:
"Hitler is full of resentments. . . . Hatred is like wine to him, it intoxicates him. . . .
he would have men against whom he had a grudge tortured to death in the most
horrible way" (Rauschning). His hatred was, in typical Plutonian 8th-house style,
inextricably linked to his sexuality: "It is to women's encouragement that he owes
his self-assurance. Women with more than a touch of hysteria [i.e., Moon-influ-
enced women] are selected before all others" (Rauschning). An 8th-house Neptune also widely inconjuncts the Moon. "Most of all Hitler is the reeking miasma

of furtive, unnatural sexuality which fills and fouls the atmosphere around him, like an evil emanation" (Rauschning). "Nothing in his environment is straightforward. Surreptitious relationships, substitutes and symbols, false sentiments and hidden lusts—nothing in this man's surroundings is natural and genuine, nothing has the openness of a natural instinct."[32] An apt exposition of 12th-house Uranus in Libra inconjunct Venus and Mars in 7th-house Taurus combined with the Hades Moon.

In true 8th-house fashion, this breaking through of the collective energy could be communicated to others. He touched the collective shadow energies: "Hitler's gestures and the emotional character of his speaking, lashing himself to a pitch of near hysteria in which he would scream and spit his resentment had the same effect on his audience. He succeeded in communicating a passion to his listeners, so that men groaned and hissed and women sobbed involuntarily, if only to relieve the tension, caught up in the spell of powerful emotions of hatred and exultation from which all restraint had been removed" (Bullock).[33] Otto Strasser said Hitler acted like "a loudspeaker proclaiming the most secret desires, the least admissible instincts, the sufferings, and personal revolts of a whole nation. . . . His words go like an arrow to their target, he touches each private wound on the raw liberating the mass unconscious, expressing its innermost aspirations, telling it what it wants to hear." And, in turn, reflected the underlying need. It was this underlying rage and frustration, "the raw wound," and the collective resentments carried forward from World War I and Teutonic history, that would propel Germany into war once again.

But, for Hitler, World War I was a crucible that led to rebirth. At the start of the war, transiting Pluto was sextiling his Sun and would shortly oppose the Moon: an optimum time for metamorphosis. For Hitler, the "black hole" of a Pluto transit manifested physically all around him. One night he awoke shaking on account of a vivid dream: his bunker had been hit by a shell and he had been buried alive. He went rushing out to get some air and at that moment a shell landed in the bunker behind him, all the occupants were buried alive. This contributed to his sense of special destiny. "The Adolf Hitler who emerged from the blood and slaughter of the trenches of the Western Front was no longer a pathetic entity. He had become a figure of almost superhuman pride."[34] Hitler himself said in *Mein Kampf*, "I sank down on my knees and thanked providence in the fullness of my heart for the favour of having been permitted to live in such a time." He was one of 300 out of 3500 men who survived the battle of Ypres. He appears "to have relished this rude baptism of fire,"[35] for which he received an Iron Cross.

He remained at the Front throughout the war as a runner, an extremely dangerous thing to do, as he was constantly exposed to enemy fire. "Amidst this daily scene of death and desolation, Adolf Hitler deafened his ears to the human frailty of his comrades and stemmed all natural emotion so that he could be born anew with that super-personal strength and resolution he would need to fulfil the mandate which the Gods of German Folklore had ordained for him." In the last month of the war he was caught in a gas attack and temporarily blinded. Now he really was in Hades and he found its treasure. While his eyes were recovering, he apparently had a mystical experience of "the magical relationship between man and the whole universe."[36]

When Germany was defeated, Trevor Ravenscroft says that "far from feeling that everything with which he identified himself had been defeated and swept away" [transiting Pluto was now opposing natal Moon], as Hitler had said in *Mein Kampf*, he actually "was loyal only to his own lust for power. . . . The poverty, humiliation and chaos of a defeated nation in the aftermath of war offered him his one and only road to political power. . . . His future success would come about entirely by exploiting with unequalled political cunning, the very consequence of the nation's defeat and surrender."[37]

Hitler's last contribution to World War I came when a Soviet Republic was declared in Munich and Hitler remained behind in an act of Plutonian espionage. He circulated freely among the soldiers supporting the revolution. When the regime was brutally overthrown, Hitler walked down the assembled ranks of soldiers pointing out the ringleaders, who were taken away and shot. He was then assigned to a course of "political education" and his future was assured. He joined the Press Bureau of the Political Department "the very centre of subterranean activities, of espionage and propaganda." He had found his hadean home.

Shortly after, Hitler met Dietrich Eckhart, a founder member of the Nazi Party. Eckhart was head of the Thule Gesellschaft, a powerful occult organization "responsible for much of the terrorist activity, race hatred and most of the cold-blooded murders which were an almost daily occurence." When Hitler met Eckhart he said: "[He] is a man I can admire. He appears to know the real meaning of hatred and how to demonstrate it." Eckhart said of Hitler: "Here is the one for whom I was but the prophet and the fore-runner."[38] In 1921, with transiting Pluto still opposite natal Moon, and Eckhart behind him, Hitler became undisputed head of the National Socialist Party. When World War II began, Pluto moved onto his 10th house cusp, squaring the Sun. The rest is history.

Hitler may appear to be an extreme, isolated example but this is not so. Everytime abuse, misuse of power, resentment and even "road rage" surface in ordinary people, the Hades Moon is there. We meet it day after day.

"THE PATHS OF GLORY LEAD BUT TO THE GRAVE"[39]

When war was declared by Britain and France on September 3, 1939, the Moon was in Taurus, square Pluto. A month later the eclipses were in Libra and Taurus. Appeasement and keeping the peace at all costs are Libran attributes, but now that the collective cooperative forces of Libra were brought up from the depths, a partnership was entered into to support war. Taurean security and material values were threatened, but the heart energy of Leo had to reach out to protect others. This eclipse cycle was the period of the "phony war," Poland had fallen and Britain and France found themselves fighting in Plutonian isolation. At the time, a defensive Libran strategy was adopted when an attacking policy might have better served the allies. The individual heroic courage of Leo was aligned to the Plutonian collective, particularly when Britain battled alone against the might of Germany. The military alone were not fighting the war. This was a period when death might literally fall from the skies, when civilians were buried in the ruins of their homes; when blackout was the order of the day; and Britain faced the threat of invasion: all Plutonian situations in which the Underworld could suddenly reach out and pluck the unwary into Hades. This situation was to become all too familiar in Germany, too. Many people in England literally took to the Underworld, camping out in bomb shelters and Underground railway stations for many months and meeting Pluto, the Lord of Death, face to face in his realm. A Moon in Scorpio square Pluto in Leo woman was born to her Cancerian Hades Moon mother in the bombed ruins of an apartment block in Hamburg. They were entombed, buried alive. It was three days before mother and child were dug out of the rubble. That child's life had literally begun in Hades and was indelibly marked. But, like all Hades Moon children, she knew she could go into hell and survive to tell the tale.

Once again, Demeter walked the devastated earth. Men, women, and children were mobilized for war production, and promises of social change were dangled by the world leaders as an inducement to the populace at large to continue to support the war effort. War was a time when "the masses" on both sides had to reach inside themselves to find reserves of courage and resources they did not know existed. The hidden "treasure" of Pluto was brought out and shared. The collective shadow was "out there" for all to see. On each side, the people were united in fighting a common enemy, and the energy could be harnessed for change and transformation amid the devastation.

However, in typical Plutonian style, the experiences of war for many combatants, and civilians, went underground. In a BBC Television program titled "Not Forgotten," a World War II veteran described how "he and countless others continue to suffer for their country five decades later." They constantly struggled with memories of the past. The program went out as the Moon in Capricorn exactly sextiled Pluto in Scorpio. As the introduction said, the program "powerfully evoked the twilight world of those who have repeatedly to relive terrible events from the past." A psychologist on the program explained that "they kept it bottled up for fifty years and couldn't talk to anyone." Participants in the program graphically described how they were unable to speak about their experiences, especially to their wives, when they returned home from the war. They did not believe that anyone else could understand what they had been through. They certainly did not receive help from the military doctors. One man, who had been in a Japanese prisoner-of-war camp and returned home weighing six-and-a-half stone, was certified fit and discharged immediately on his return to England. It took fifty years before he was able to discuss his symptoms in counselling organized by a veterans' association which was becoming increasingly concerned at the number of men who were experiencing distress. A psychologist on the program believed that 25–35 percent of veterans would suffer from the resurfacing of the trauma with increasing age. Then the memories "came back with a vengeance." One man said, after therapy, that "the effect was like coming out of a black hole, having a door opened and coming out into the light."

It was estimated that 30 percent of soldiers suffer post traumatic stress disorder (PTSD) from combat. It was pointed out that in World War I (Pluto in sympathetic Cancer) "shell shock" was a recognized disorder, as we saw when we looked at Wilfred Owen's life. However, no such "dis-ease" was accepted during World War II (Pluto in proud Leo), adverse reactions usually being put down to cowardice. It was

not until the Gulf War (Pluto in insightful Scorpio) that PTSD was again acknowledged. And then, perhaps, it was used as a cover-up for a much more devious disorder: the effect of secret nerve gases and other biological poisons used
indiscriminately to assess what the effects would be on civilian and soldier alike.

In World War II, it was not just the military who suffered. The civilian population were caught up in it, too. A letter to my local paper pointed out:

> Before we all become emotionally moved by November 11 [Remembrance
> Sunday], may I comment that prior to D-Day more civilians had been ex-
> posed to gunfire and bombing than the military forces in England. The civil-
> ian death and injury toll was horrific.
>
> Before I was 15, I had witnessed the Battle of Britain and the bomb-
> ing of London Docks. I had been evacuated to Bedfordshire, only to be
> chased down a road at St. Neots by a Dornier looking for RAF Tempsford.
> Returning to London, I was subjected to the daylight "hit and run" raids of
> 1943–1944. And as if this was not enough suffering, I lost my home in Kent
> to a V1 and another subsequent home to a V2 . . . [and several other inci-
> dents]. The scars of a lost childhood are still with me today, but fortunately
> they are kept at bay by a strict mental discipline.[40]

As I could hear many echoes of the Hades Moon in this letter I wrote to its author.
Captain Roddis kindly gave me his date of birth. A Sun in Gemini, he has Mercury
conjunct the Moon in Taurus sextile Pluto in Cancer (a somewhat gentler manifestation of the Hades Moon). One can see that Pluto-in-Cancer energy at work in
his being torn from his family, and having his home quite literally destroyed around
him not once, but twice. His Mars in Aries square Pluto, combined with the Hades
Moon, may well hold the key to his particularly Plutonian experiences during the
war. This combination tends "to attract" violence, and his iron mental control since
that time bears witness to the fact that the Pluto-Mars will is an exceedingly powerful one. He also has the North Node in Taurus and appears to have learned that
the only security he can take with him is the internal one of being grounded in a
piece of eternity within himself.

When I wrote to him for permission to quote, which he freely gave in the
hope that it may help someone else, he told me that his technique for coming to
terms with trauma is not to let the "mental gramophone record" play too much.
[Excellent advice for a Sun Gemini with Mercury in Taurus so long as the trauma
is moved on from rather than repressed.] Also, you must pass "A" level Survival.
[He has the South Node in Scorpio which always passes this test with flying colors,
as well as the Hades Moon.] He later told me that the manageress of his local doctor's surgery was the unwitting key to his "trauma control": "She sees many patients under stress and the common denominator in all of them, be it war, divorce
or natural bereavement, is the inability to put the event behind them, and get on
with life in the 'land of the living.' All of life is dangerous and the only people who
do not accept change are the dead."

When the War in Europe ended on May 8, 1945, the Moon in Aries was
widely squaring Pluto and opposing Neptune. The end came for Adolf Hitler when

he (seemingly) committed suicide in a bunker beneath the smoldering ruins of the Reich's Chancellery in Berlin. Transiting Pluto was inconjunct his Capricorn Moon, creating a Finger of Fate with the natal Moon-Pluto inconjunct. The lunar eclipse in June fell on Hitler's Moon, but by this time the light of this peculiarly hadean consciousness had already been extinguished.

Peace had been signed in the early hours of the day before the end of the War, the Moon then being in Pisces and trine Pluto, a most apt aspect for surrender. In June, the lunar eclipse was at 3° Capricorn, inconjunct Pluto. This time it was the lunar instinctual forces that were blotted out, allowing the light of consciousness to rise up. Since agreement on the peace terms proved to be impossible and the old rage remained, the seeds were sown for the Cold War that was to last for another three decades.

"A Vast Door Slamming in the Depths of Hell"

However, it was an even more Plutonian event that brought the war in Asia to a close. On August 6, 1945 (with the Moon in Cancer) an atomic bomb was dropped on Hiroshima and "the practice of war changed convulsively and irrevocably. . . . No one saw the bomb, only the blinding, inconceivable flash that seared consciousness. . . . As a four-mile-high mushroom cloud formed over the leveled city, the world entered the Atomic Age."[41] The cathartic Pluto energies had been loosed on the world, energies that would respect no territorial boundaries: nuclear fallout travels where it will. Like Pluto it is invisible, and quietly lethal. It remained to see whether the fires of hell would be purifying, or would rage out of control. Warning had been given to the Japanese people in July, when the Moon was entrenched in Taurus, squaring Pluto and inconjuncting Neptune: "We call upon the government of Japan to proclaim now the unconditional surrender of all Japanese armed forces. . . . The alternative for Japan is prompt and utter destruction."[42] We can see some of the Taurean shadow qualities in that destruction but clearly no one in Japan could conceive of the Plutonian wasteland which was to follow that ultimatum. It must indeed have felt like burning in the fires of hell:

> The fire that followed was fed by thousands of little charcoal cooking fires burning in the flimsy houses that collapsed in flames in a circle three miles across. Those trapped in the wreckage died as the fire storm grew. Those wandering—blinded, scorched, with the skin peeling off them and their faces in shreds from the first horror of that flame—died in the fire storm also. But most of those in the center were killed by the blast itself. It is believed that 78,500 people perished on the first morning. How many died later is unclear; people are still dying from causes attributable to the blast.

As David Divine, the author of this horrific description says:

> The horror of the first atomic bomb lies not in the death and desolation of Hiroshima . . . but in the scientific and technological potential that it unleashed. It made possible the unthinkable. The involvement of the twentieth-

century world in the consequences of nuclear physics, the extravagances of missile technologies, the phenomena of lunar and planetary exploration, and the possibility of total destruction, are the moral issues arising from Hiroshima.[43]

One of the official observers to the first British H-bomb test commented: "It sounded like a vast door slamming in the depths of Hell."[44] All the unresolved rage and frustration of past generations and the paranoia of the current one would pour into the nuclear arms race, bringing mankind face to face with the Great Destroyer. Not until Pluto was transiting through Scorpio many years later and the collective energies were once again on the move, would a real attempt at reconciliation be made. Even then, a scientist interviewed on BBC radio in 1993 gave his opinion that, despite the apparent end to the arms race, we should continue to explore all possible developments in nuclear weapons. It was our duty. Indeed, he said, we had an obligation to subsequent generations to do so. What would they think of us, he asked, if we did not pursue to its utmost the potential for exterminating our enemies? *"After all, you never know when we might need it."* I wonder just what inner demons he was projecting out onto an unsuspecting world?

THE LADY OF THE BLOODBATH

We can learn a great deal about primal rage, and the reconciliation and healing that follows forgiveness, from Egyptian mythology, and particularly from the Goddess Sekhmet, who can be seen as a female face of Pluto. Set and Osiris, whom we will meet elsewhere, are the male faces. Sekhmet is the dark, destroying face of the goddess Hathor. The "Eye" of her father Ra (rational, differentiated solar consciousness), she has the instinctual ability to see behind the facade, to delve deep into the unconscious, to truly *know*. She is a solar goddess, part of the principle of self-individuation and differentiation—consciousness becoming aware of itself in all its facets so that it can be integrated and made whole once more. She is the goddess of war and vengeance, and birth and healing, Sekhmet is the power aspect of Pluto and shares with him the property of retribution and new life. It is Sekhmet who carries the ankh or symbol of life. And it is Sekhmet who punishes the damned in the Duat, the Other or Innerworld. She is the guardian of the second Gate to the Duat:

> The goddess who guards the second pylon
> is treacherous and her ways are devious.
> Lady of the Flame, whore of the universe,
> with the mouth of a lioness,
> your vagina swallows men up,
> they are lost in your milky dugs.[45]

This is the *vagina dentate* ("the vagina with teeth") that swallows men whole (a great fear of men with the Hades Moon and Pluto-Venus aspects). It is the place out of which man emerged; he spends his life separating from this. It is the place of primal fear, the lunar birth canal to the other world. At this gate we must confront the apparent duality of the dark goddess: that what grants life, and individuality, can also take it away. We must recognize that one is the shadow face of the other, that, without one, we could not have the other.

The Duat is the place of transformation. One innovative commentator has seen it as the story of spirit incarnating into matter, the Duat being the body. For me, it is the place where the collective unconscious resides, but this "place" could well be the body and the spirit consciousness. But the standard interpretation is that it is where the soul passes after death and prepares for rebirth. However, in Egyptian thought, although man was born of flesh, he had the potential to become spirit—a god. "The sacred science of Egypt amounts to a setting out in detail the stages of this process of transformation—of the carnal or material into the spiritual."[46] At each gate, consciousness, or mind, must pass through a series of initiatory tests which amount to a stripping away of all that has gone before so that something new can emerge (the equivalent of a Pluto transit).

This journey is graphically told in the guides to the Duat that form the so-called *Egyptian Book of the Dead*, guides that are full of symbol and allegory. The second gate is where barley, the "dead grain," miraculously turns, through fermentation, into living beer. The second hour of the night or Duat, is the hour of magic. As John Anthony West says: "Magic was the principle underlying the world of transformations that, in fact, comprises our experience. The Word becomes Flesh through an act of will or command. But the agency through which this transformation is possible is Magic. . . . To cover up its ignorance, our science calls that force Evolution and thinks it has dispelled the mystery. The ancients knew better."[47] The Goddess Sekhmet is the principle of "the spiritual arising out of the material and the temporal," a place of death and rebirth.

Hathor and Sekhmet are a depiction of the dual goddess "split" into two, one the acceptable face and the other the shadow. Sekhmet is usually shown as a lion-headed woman, and Hathor as a cow, or as a beautiful woman wearing cow's horns. For the Egyptians, each "god" had complementary qualities which were incorporated into a goddess "wife," someone who carried the feminine qualities for him. So, Sekhmet in her capacity as both destroyer and life-giver is married to Ptah, the creator god who made man on his potter's wheel.

In the earliest Egyptian text, Hathor is depicted as being created at the same time as Ra and taking her place in the solar boat alongside him. In Egyptian myth the solar barge, consciousness, descended into the Underworld, the unconscious, each night. There its occupants had to overcome the powers of darkness, including the serpent Apep, symbol of eternal chaos, and other denizens of the Duat. This was the encompassing of the opposites within the whole.

Hathor was the patroness of women and the goddess of love, music, and dancing: her rituals feature musical instruments and dancing girls, and her temples were "places of intoxication." Hathor is where rapture is used to make contact with the gods, and we will meet her again when looking at addiction. The beer was, however, brewed in honor of her "sister" Sekhmet. Hathor is also "Queen of the West," the protectress of the Theban necropolis, the abode of the dead. It is she who welcomes the dead to Amenti, "the Other Side" which is the equivalent of the Elysian

Fields. She is the Egyptian Persephone. Depictions of Hathor are in stark contrast to the statues and representations of Sekhmet, who is almost always shown in her awesome aspect. In one extremely powerful wall painting at ancient Karnak, Sekhmet is shown with an erect phallus. Here she is the side of the feminine energy that contains its own generative and procreative power. She is the dark side of the great earth mother, the creator and destroyer of life by her own powers, the feminine side of the Hades Moon.

Legend portrays Sekhmet as the avenging "Eye of Ra," the Sun God. In his declining, Saturnine years, Ra, losing his powers, was mocked by his people, the Egyptians. The god was no longer honored by his subjects: anarchy, or chaos, was returning to the land. Consciousness was splitting off, "cosmic awareness" was being lost. Angry, Ra plotted revenge. His daughter, Sekhmet, in the form of a rampaging lioness, was sent forth to destroy Man (his own creation) and quickly discovered a delight in killing. Her blood lust could not be sated and she massacred everyone she met. Ra, feeling that his vengeance had been completed, and regretting total annihilation of his creation, mankind, asked her to stop the carnage. But Sekhmet, who had divine power and could overrule Ra, would not be halted. "By the life," she answered him: "When I slay men, my heart rejoices."[48] The Nile and the land of Egypt ran red with blood.

There is, however, another point of view which may shed a different light on Ra's reason for sending Sekhmet out in the first place. The Russian mystic philosopher, G. I. Gurdjieff, believed that when Ra masturbated mankind into existence he ruptured the primordial oneness that had previously existed. In many of the myths, man is spoken of as "springing from the tears of Ra," and Gurdjieff felt that Ra experienced a need to expiate his "sin" of separateness. It may have been in a fit of remorse that he sent Sekhmet out to destroy his creation and return the universe to a state of primal oneness. In either view, we can see what happens when the repressed instinctual forces are loosed, when rational control, the Solar energy, runs amok. Ra, the Sun God, and therefore symbolic of rational consciousness, feels that limited punishment is required for his disobedient subjects (who can be seen as "split off" facets of consciousness itself). Sekhmet, the uncontrollable instinctual rage that lies beneath solar constraint, cannot be reined in that easily. Once this energy is unleashed, as has been found in war after war, it takes on a life of its own. Something else has to intervene.

Ra sent his messengers to Elephantine Island, at Aswan in Upper Egypt, to gather together the fruit of the mandrake, the juice of which is blood-red and has a powerful sedative effect. In other versions of the myth pomegranate juice is used instead. This is a fruit associated with the Underworld—the one Pluto used to entrap Persephone—and its magical powers were used in the mystery rites symbolic of death and rebirth: we may be seeing here an ancient acting out of that rite, as both mandrake and pomegranate are associated with death. This is one of the great myths of death and regeneration.

Women brewed seven thousand gallons of beer, mixed it with the mandrake juice and poured it out on the earth to form a lake of blood. When Sekhmet passed by, she drank the lethal brew and went quietly to sleep. When she awoke, the Moon-god Thoth led her home in peace, telling her humorous tales to help her forget her hangover. Forgiveness and gentleness were at work healing the archetype. She was reconciled with her father, and, to honor her, thousands of gallons of beer were brewed each year at the festival of Hathor. As with Athene and the Fates, this dark aspect was given honor and transformed. It is when this primal rage energy is accepted, reverenced, and allowed to consciously become part of life that transformation is possible. Part of the shadow was embraced and accepted and therefore lost its fearsome energy. Clearly a metamorphosis took place, as from then on Sekhmet is depicted as a healer goddess, one who watches over initiation and childbirth.

Thoth (the Greek Hermes or Mercury), is the personification of wisdom in Egyptian mythology, but this is not rational, intellectual wisdom. He is a Moon-god. His wisdom is a "knowing" that is instinct functioning at the intuitive level. He is the Egyptian Mercury and, like Mercury, could pass freely between the worlds, entering the realm of the unconscious at will. The myth of Sekhmet is a transformation myth. It depicts a necessary truth of human life and of the psyche. There is a hadean part of each one of us that could run amok and kill. The myth encompasses that energy, epitomizes a universal truth, and contains it through its mythic character. By acting out the destructive urge in mythological time, and acknowledging that universal truth, the psyche is spared from acting it out in actuality. This is the purpose of myth and sacred drama. As Thomas Moore says: "Atrocious acts in fiction are not of the same order as atrocious acts in life."[49] The Sekhmet myth, by encompassing the dark energies, depicts the growth of wisdom; the "conquering," or "sublimation," of the instinctual, destructive Hades-Moon side of life, which is transformed by its acceptance. It reveals the consequent flowering of the higher octave of that energy: Sekhmet becomes the healer who presides over initiation into higher states of consciousness.

Sekhmet, like Pluto, is the archetype to contact when courage is needed: "the strength of a lion," when action has to be taken, when transformation is called for, or the reconciliation of opposites undertaken. It is Sekhmet who can ruthlessly cut out all that is decayed in our life. If we are in the grip of an overwhelming instinct or obsession, such as self-destruction, contacting Sekhmet will help to attune to the positive benefit of that archetype: destroying the old so that the new can arise, for instance, or creating from the non-biological level. As Sekhmet understands betrayal and humiliation, she is an archetype to contact for healing old abuse of any description. She, like so many aspects of the feminine, has the power to take us deep within ourself, to meet our shadow, and to birth the sacred self.

PROJECTION

As we have seen, the shadow energies, whether individual or collective, are so often projected onto A.N.Other (or, just as often these days, Mother); someone "out there" is seen as unacceptable, or overly-aggressive, or somehow the cause of all our problems. This works most clearly in war or conflict, but it occurs every day in a minor way, especially for those with the Hades Moon. We are all only too familiar with the effect of having a bad day, a day when every little thing niggles and irritates us, but we suppress that anger because we are too afraid to acknowledge its source. Indeed, we do not usually recognize that the source is actually within us, the resentment has been held onto too long without being accepted as "mine." We wonder: "Why must they be so stupid? Why can't they get it right?" If we are astrologers, we look at our transits and say, "Oh yes, that's Mars doing. . . ," or whatever. Then, we have an accident or someone explodes at us. We can then feel righteous anger: it is "their fault." For most people on first looking at their mothers in therapy (or astrology), the feeling is "she did it to me." It is only by taking this projection back and owning it as *ours* that we can begin to transform the energy and reaccess the pure creative powers of primal rage. We cannot heal the unresolved rage of the whole world. But we can heal ourselves. If we, each one, accept and integrate our own dark places, then the collective is healed. It is only by saying: "Yes, in me, too, there is a murderer lurking," that we can heal this old rage. It has taken a long time for me to acknowledge it, but there have been at least two occasions in my life when my rage was so great that I could have murdered. This does not mean that I gave in to the impulse, or would have done had things been different. But I can recognize this impetous in myself.

Much of my insight and acceptance came about through having Sekhmet as a guide in my psycho-synthesis work. I had made a powerful contact to her in an Egyptian temple on my first visit there (in this life!) but was surprised to find her accompanying me back to England. She was an interesting companion to say the least. Fortunately she rarely manifested in her awesome aspect, although this came in extremely useful when I came under psychic attack from a man whose Mars conjuncted my Hades Moon as we will see.[50] I met the playful side of the archetype many times. It is difficult to remain terrified of a goddess with whom you have enjoyed an exhilarating slide down an unexcavated Egyptian tomb and landed in an undignified heap at the bottom,[51] but I still respected her. She took me, symbolically and in actuality, into many other dark places and offered me illumination.

So now I can say: "Yes I too share this energy," and accord it due honor. I no longer have to hide from it or feel embarrassed to acknowledge it. I have also noticed that now I am no longer afraid it will shatter my fragile stability; I feel much more in touch with life and my own power as a woman. As a result, the impulse no longer festers to emerge at some other, inappropriate, moment; and I no longer get angry at someone "out there" who reflects back to me my own rage. Instead, I turn my attention inward to find its source. Like the Hydra, old rage and resentment can only be dissolved by lifting it into the light of consciousness.

LANCING THE BOIL

When working with old rage and present anger, there are two simple decisions that will allow release. Either accept the situation and let it go, or do something about it. Either way, getting the energy moving in a physical way helps the release. For Angela, the old rage erupted, briefly, as physical violence. But it is vital to find some healthy way of bringing the energy into the body, and discharging it in an appropriate way. Other people have found that going to the Bottle Bank and hurling old bottles, or pillow-bashing, are excellent ways to pummel "the enemy." Anger often emerges from regression sessions. I have an orchard full of stinging nettles and brambles. Clients are always welcome to go down there with the scythe to "hack and slash." Roger Woolger, in his past life therapy, uses pillows and a mattress for clients to "kick the anger out." All report feeling much more alive as a result. Ronald, in chapter 1, found running and football physicalized the rage energy for him and made it accessible. Movement or the martial arts can be useful. One friend swears by the "Fuck you" mantra, repeated over and over, often accompanied by foot stamping.

Stamping and shouting both give the energy voice and direct it into the earth, grounding it into the body. I was amazed at the effect of fifteen minutes stamping and shouting "No" in a workshop. Jupiter was transiting my Hades Moon at the time. I felt I had moved energy that had been stuck since the Plutonian birth of my daughter. I had been strung up in stirrups for many long hours. As a result, the base of my spine was fused, trapping a great deal of old rage from the powerlessness I had felt during the delivery. This was released in those fifteen minutes, and the creative energy it had once held was channelled into this book.

In that same workshop, I had the experience of "standing in my hoop," finding the calm, peaceful place that was my center, while the rest of the group raged around outside. They shouted and screamed, stamped and jeered. The whole room throbbed to the energy of rage. I found that, while I could defend myself against the incursion of their anger, it took effort and energy to hold it off. But, when I allowed their rage energy to vibrate through my body in waves, it moved into my center (physically located in my lower belly) and was transmuted. It somehow became primal rage and then creative energy, which in turn fed my lower chakras. So, through accepting their rage, I became empowered. This experience allowed me to release the old Hades Moon rage I had been storing in those same chakras.

A week-long group I was "shepherding" found, seemingly by accident, a way of releasing some very ancient energies. The old house we were staying in had a labyrinth of cellars beneath it. The owner had casually remarked these were "a great place to howl in." The group went down with drums, huge Tibetan gongs and bowls, and one candle to light the way for the wary. The darkness down there was palpable—primordial and atavistic. The rounded, domed shape was a womb or a tomb depending on how you looked at it. It was an elemental, chthonic space. Thirteen people howled, drummed, and danced in a primitive rhythm. Old tables were brought into play as make-shift percussion, pipes were beaten, feet stamped. All inhibitions were thrown aside. Graceful, multi-armed shadow Avalokitesvaras were created by the light of the candle, evoking memories of archaic rituals in caves and other dark places. Solid waves of sound from the gongs traveled around and around the labyrinth—and up the metal drainpipes of the house, although we did not know this at the time. It was a powerful, primitive release on all levels, and some of the group could not take it. One lady, a born-again Christian, saw an "evil entity" and fled. Her own inner, unacceptable, energies were projected "out there" (although it was clear that ghostly shades who had been imprisoned in the building were released). It was a cleansing on a grand scale. As one man said: "It cleared my energies in a way that no amount of visualizing or theraping could have done. I feel reborn."

"The howling" was repeated on several evenings, gradually incorporating quieter moments, and then we danced around a bonfire out in the open air, bringing the transmuted energies up into the light. By this time, the group had accepted the hadean energies as "ours." Many of the group have since said that their lives changed following that raw, primal experience of pure energy. When I looked at the charts for the group, not surprisingly the Hades Moon figured strongly, as did Scorpio and early Sagittarius Suns. Even less surprising, on the first night of the howling, the Waning Moon was in Scorpio.

It is not always necessary to rant and rage. Some people find writing letters to the people they feel have wronged them very helpful. This technique is also useful for communicating with a departed parent or in asking for forgiveness or reparation. It is not always necessary to mail these letters. I use a ritual of consigning the letter to the Plutonian fire, which transmutes the energy. At times it may be helpful to confront the person directly. When Anne, whom we met in chapter 1, was worried about her niece visiting Anne's father (a child abuser), Anne's counsellor said: "Talk to him about it." She did, and was not only able to express all her old feelings, but also, she believes, was able to prevent her niece going through the same pattern. So, she became a "lineage breaker," who confronted and changed the family secret.

I often use a technique of talking to the person in my mind. It is my inner picture I am addressing and the dialogue helps me to focus on the real issue. However, a word of warning: I know from my own experience that simply throwing all our rage "out" onto the person who seems to have been provoking it can have powerful consequences. A therapist once encouraged me to express all my anger at my, then approaching teenage, daughter. Mixed into that was all the rage I had felt over her birth and the early death of her father, and many of my childhood issues as well—the full weight of my Hades Moon in Scorpio was triggered. I felt catharted, which was his intention. But, when I arrived home, I found my daughter prostrate with migraine. She had picked up all my anger and it pole-axed her. I had been trained as a spiritual healer and was used to sending absent healing energy to people, often without really thinking about it. I had to recognize that negative energy could also be sent. This is an important lesson for anyone with a Hades Moon, which is a sign of the immensely powerful healer. I realized that, powerful healer that I may be, I was also a destroyer. Now I put the other person in a protective bubble and talk to my inner picture and not the actual person.

This lesson was reiterated for me when Mars was transiting my Hades Moon. I triggered the long-festering rage in someone whose natal Mars was conjunct my Moon and squared my, and his, Pluto. From dreams I had, and from repeating aspects across the charts, it appeared to be karmic, and indeed, taking my Nodes into account, the synastry formed a karmic Grand Cross. He was someone who used his explosive, abusive Plutonian anger to empower him, but paid a heavy toll for being stuck in his rage rather than using the creative energy that lies underneath it. As Clarissa Pinkola Estes says: "The fieriness of rage is not to be mistaken for a substitute for a passionate life . . . after a time it burns interminably hot, pollutes our ideas with its black smoke, and occludes other ways of seeing and apprehending."[52] He had a T-square involving that Scorpio Mars opposite the Sun in Taurus, square Pluto in Leo, and suffered badly from arthritis, a sign of explosive anger acting inward on the body. I was told at the time that I had to "lance the boil for him," but I was unprepared for the vitriolic eruption that burst forth. It was totally toxic, one-pointed, focused rage projected out onto the enemy—me. Unfortunately, it did not have the purging effect that would have healed it as he did not own it as *his*. Perhaps I should have taken into account that in his chart the asteroid Lilith, who represents repressed anger and conflict resolution, sits exactly on my Pluto—an implosive combination. As Demetra George explains, Lilith "forms an intermediary step in the octave progression between Mars and Pluto. Because of the primal resentment that arises from being rejected, Lilith contains a tremendous amount of repressed anger. This suppressed rage, when activated, has the potential to erupt in sexual domination and violence."[53] Certainly I experienced an attempt at domination, and considerable verbal violence.

For a month or two my whole energy was involved in holding off the psychic attack he, and his cohort, directed at me. They were both powerful healers and he threatened that he would destroy me. I did not really believe he had the power, but I seriously underestimated the depth of his hatred and that their combined energies were formidable. I took another trip into Hades. I had to face my old Hadean Moon persecution issues. Instead of dying, I met the place where that energy still resided in myself. But, the actual person was still there, not everything can be resolved internally. In the end, I resorted to magic. Several one-hundred-and-twenty-foot high Sekhmets were despatched to patrol the space between us. I withdrew my defensive energy and the healing love I had been sending, which I realized had been fueling the battle through that close contact across the charts. My instinctual lunar energy was picked up by his Mars–Pluto, fed on, and flung back at me. Invoking Sekhmet for protection utilized a direct connection to primal energy without my going on the attack. (I felt that, if I had attacked, I would have had more karma to deal with in the future.) By withdrawing my energy, I was no longer connected, and he was rendered impotent. I had no more trouble, but it did remind me to review my techniques for psychic protection! Such techniques are essential for anyone with a Hades Moon because at the instinctual level we are very much "one" and open to both collective and individual rage. However, Pluto offers us gifts as well as challenges. The treasure at the heart of this Plutonean experience became apparent when I wrote a best-selling book, *The Art of Psychic Protection*, as a result, and this book helped hundreds of people deal with similar situations, which made my own experience doubly worthwhile.

At times, just to be with the primal energy for a while is what is called for, especially if anger has been denied over a long period of time and has festered. Underneath most depression, addiction, and grief lies anger. Acceptance is a vital stage of the healing and cannot be rushed. So often anger is "withheld knowledge" and we need to know what lies behind it. If we are too quick to express it cleanly, or to heal it, we can miss out on the vital knowing it holds for us. A sympathetic counsellor or a good friend who will simply be there with us is extremely helpful, as is an astrologer who is not afraid of the Pluto energy, and who will encourage us to accept it as a natural part of the cycle. Knowing that it is "right" to be in the depths, as when Ronald (chapter 1) went to see Howard Sasportas, makes it much easier to allow the energies to flow as they will.

If the energy has become stuck, however, there are ways of getting it moving again. We have already looked at the physical level, but the mind is a great mover and healer. If the energy has festered down into a general resentment, then using creative visualization to draw out the energy and disperse it is helpful. I use the "bubble" of charged light technique to absorb the energy from the body (at all levels). It then floats off and pops and is harmlessly dispersed. A "dark light" can also be passed through the body to draw off the toxic energies. I also use fire rituals, visualized or actual, where symbolically everything that we no longer need is collected together and placed in the fire. The energy is then transmuted and can come back into the body as a purifying, creative force. When working with these images, something new needs to be put in place, as otherwise the old energies will rush back in to fill up the spaces. I use healing light but I try to allow the right image to emerge from my client rather than my arbitrarily imposing an image. I have also found that clearing out cupboards and recyling the discarded content of our lives is therapeutic and leaves room for new energies to move in. This work is supported by the vibrational healing power of flower essences (see page 175).

"To Fill the All with Harmonies Caressing"[54]

Two of the greatest healers for old rage are using it constructively—putting the energy to work in our lives in a positive way, and forgiveness. Sometimes the forgiveness has to be for ourselves. At other times we need to go "out there" to forgive or receive forgiveness. Like grief, forgiveness has different stages and many levels. It does not have to be completed all at once. When working with "cutting the ties," I always ask a client to let love and forgiveness flow whichever way is needed. Some people can do this easily and fully. Others can only allow, or receive, a little forgiveness at a time. But it is setting the process in motion that matters, not that it be completed there and then. For the Hades Moon, completing is a task that will probably take the rest of this lifetime and may involve other lives as well.

Clarissa Pinkola Estes has identified four stages of forgiveness—foregoing, forebearing, forgetting, and forgiving[55]—that closely accord with what I have observed over the years:

1) Foregoing—I call this letting it go. Refusing to dwell on it for a while, what Estes calls "taking a vacation from it." This creates a space for the healing to begin. A place where the wounded psyche can become whole again rather than spending time apportioning blame and planning revenge.

2) Forebearing—to refrain from punishing. This is the point where we can make the decision not to become resentful and hostile. We do not induce guilt in the other person, or succumb to guilt ourselves. Practicing instead a generosity of spirit from which we benefit as much as the other person. This moves us into the constructive, therapeutic side of the Hades Moon.

3) Forgetting—letting it go from our memory, laying it to rest. If we constantly churn things over in our mind, we can never forgive. By making an

effort to consciously forget, to put it out of our mind, we create a space for new energies to emerge. Learning not to dwell on things is vital for the Hades Moon which can otherwise spend many hours obsessing over the past and wrongs both real and imagined.

4) Forgiving—to give up feeling that we are "owed" something or that someone else is responsible for our pain. In forgiving we set ourselves free. We know when we have forgiven because we have nothing left to say, we may feel a little sorrowful but we no longer rage. We can give up our coldness and our defensiveness around that person. We may not like them, we may choose not to spend much time with them, but we no longer actively make them suffer "for what they did." We have compassion and understanding. We can thank them for the part they have played in our growth. There is nothing holding us to the past. We can move forward free and unencumbered.

As with the stages of grief, these stages of forgiveness do not necessarily occur in this order; nor do they happen all at once. Some people will have more difficulty with one part than another. For the Hades Moon, forgetting is often more difficult than forgiving, which itself may be conditional "until next time," or limited. Reconciliation is a difficult process, but not an impossible one. It is in learning to let go of the past that the Hades Moon grows and the energies are transmuted. It is important to remember that forgiveness, like unconditional love, is not a blanket invitation for the other person to walk all over us. A Hades Moon needs to set limits, to be self-protective, to know when to say "No" and mean it. But it also must let go of the grudges and the feeling of "being hard done by" which demands reparation or restitution. To forgive, all we have to do is *feel*.

One of the greatest gifts we can give to ourself is forgiveness. We may feel that we ourselves have wronged another person and that we need to free ourself from the weight of the past. If it is not possible to approach that person directly (and so often when we do, we find that they have forgotten all about it long ago), then we can write a letter or create the person in our mind's eye and talk to that person there. We can picture ourself receiving forgiveness and opening to that person's love. If the forgiveness we need is less specific, the Hades Moon being prone to a kind of existential guilt, then we can close our eyes and visualize ourself receiving forgiveness from a radiant light that is all-loving and all-forgiving. I frequently end regression sessions with this all-embracing light, letting it wash away the past.

So often for the Hades Moon, the deepest forgiveness of all is forgiveness of self and of the family who carried the pattern. When we can bring the festering secret out into the light and look on its bearer with compassion, we break its hold.[56] When we can let go apportioning blame, we are healed. When we can see our experiences as part of our soul's growth, we can pluck out the essential learning and let go the rest. When we can cease to expect the worst, or to feel we deserve it, we are transformed.

We can arrange for reconciliation wherever it is needed in our life regardless of where the original split came from. However, we can also allow the other person to make his or her choice whether to accept it, or not, without going back into the old pattern. Forgiveness *is* letting go.

VIBRATIONAL HEALING

Homeopathy and flower essences can aid in healing old rage and associated conditions. Ignatia (a homeopathic remedy) loosens old grief, moving onto the next stage in the grieving process. Dagger Hakea (Bush)* and Willow (Bach)[†] release resentment. Dagger Hakea is especially useful when a relationship has ended. Mountain Devil (Bush) is for angry feelings based on jealousy, hatred, or envy; as is Holly (Bach). Sturt Desert Pea (Bush) relieves old hurt and Fringed Violet (Bush) lifts disease present since a traumatic event or loss. Sunshine Wattle (Bush) aids those stuck in a difficult past, releasing negative expectations. Wisteria is for sexual abuse. Crab Apple (Bach) cleanses feelings of self-loathing arising from the past. White Chestnut (Bach) closes off the mind, letting us forget. These gentle remedies are Plutonian in the extreme, but they show the healing, regenerative power of this often maligned and misunderstood planet.

---

*Australian Bush Flower Essences.

[†] Bach Flower Essences. Essences are made from flowers soaked in water and exposed to the Sun. They work on a vibrational level of healing. In the USA they are available from many health food stores. If you cannot locate them easily, try Centergees, 2007 Northeast 39th Ave., Portland, OR 97212 (E-mail: centergees@mcione.com). In the UK try The Living Tree, Milland, Liphook, Hants. GU30 7JS (E-mail: flower@atlas.co.uk).

CHAPTER 6

THE KARMIC MOON

Pluto's task seems to be to bring to the surface the past effects of a person's actions and conduct during the successive phases of his existence.

—Joy Michaud[1]

NO MATTER WHAT the aspect, the Hades Moon shows us some of the more deeply entrenched karmic issues we have carried from incarnation to incarnation over a vast period of time. It shows us where we react in fixed patterns, and how we project our expectations onto others, seeing in them what we cannot face about ourselves. It indicates where we act out unresolved problems over and over again. It also shows us where we can transform our actions and change our perspective, letting go of the past, where we can take up our unlived life and unfulfilled potential and bring this to fruition. Pluto in aspect to the Moon highlights our credits and deficits around how we have handled powerful emotions and other lunar issues in the past. Not that time is in any way linear or chronological, especially when it comes to dealing with our karma, but we need the concept of a past (the Moon) in order to make sense of the present.

Karma is not static; it is something that is evolving and changing all the while. We reap the rewards of our karma as well as making reparation, and we create our future karma every day. The incarnating soul, which carries the karmic imprint, is on a journey of evolution *back* to its spiritual roots. Having separated to gain independence of action (free will), it is moving toward wholeness once more. In doing so, it carries a karmic purpose that embraces the collective as well as the individual—what is learned by one soul enhances all souls, what is healed by an individual contributes toward the overall well-being at the soul level.

Some people incarnate with the intention of clearing collective karma in addition to working on their own personal stuff—indicated especially by planets placed in the 8th and 12th houses and in Pisces, but also by personal-planet aspects to Chiron and Pluto. The Hades Moon has a transpersonal quality to it that allows collective issues to surface and be absolved by the actions of a single human being. While squares, oppositions, and quincunxes bring that karma into sharp focus, it also manifests through conjunctions, sextiles, trines, and the minor aspects. In synastric contacts, the Hades Moon highlights our emotional interaction, mothering "history," and power struggles from the past.

We can look on the fixed signs as showing firmly entrenched karma, the mutable signs as karma from the last life, and cardinal signs as "karma in the making," but this does not always hold true for the Hades Moon. We need to be flexible in our interpretation. We may be having a different experience of an old pattern, learning to handle it another way; or we may be digging ourselves deeper into the mire. It may feel easier, simply because it is all so familiar. Or we may struggle to overcome an inborn tendency. It all depends on how much we are conscious of our soul's purpose and how much we blame on our fate.

The Hades Moon placement will show us how our past colors the present, the innate expectations we bring with us (see chapter 10), but it also shows our potential for change and Plutonian transformation. This chthonic Moon indicates where our power issues lie, and where we need to eliminate the past. It brings to the surface all our struggles and compulsions, our obsessions and imperatives; and points out to us where these have to be adapted to a new view of the world. Knowing what went on in our previous lives can be an enormous help in adjusting to the challenges of the present life.

Perhaps above all else a Pluto-Moon contact shows our "mothering karma": how we have been mothered, how we mothered ourselves, and our experiences around birth and incarnation. Many people with the Hades Moon are reluctant to incarnate again, knowing the issues that have to be faced and the traumatic emotions that are waiting below the surface. There are people who bounce back so quickly into incarnation that they do not have an opportunity to gain a more objective perspective on the life they have just left. They have a sense of unfinished business. The result is usually a replay of the past. As we have seen, there are deeply ingrained expectations of loss and rejection, abandonment, and persecution together with ancient rage and resentment. But, the Hades Moon is also the psychic Moon. There is healing and metaphysical knowledge to draw upon. The intuitive faculties have been developed, as has the ability to be with someone as they journey through their own consciousness. One of the most positive attributes of the Hades Moon is an instinctive understanding of the workings of the psyche. The Hades Moon helps us to be at home in our own Underworld—and that of others. It shows us that if we haven't been down into our own darkness, if we don't value what we find there, then we cannot help others to shine the light of understanding into their own being.

CONNECTING TO THE PAST

While the patterns and intentions of the past can be read from a chart,[2] in my experience the detail of other lives is only available from either reconnecting to that life yourself or having someone read it for you. I have never found that the "such and such a degree or this or that aspect equals a particular time and place" approach actually correlates with people's experience of their past lives. It is my belief that astrologers who find it does are probably using their own psychic abilities, as I do, to reach back into the past.

Personal recall can come about in several ways. Spontaneous reliving, a sense of *deja vu*, dreams, or past life regression (whether hypnotic or not) can all bring about experiences ranging from a graphic reliving to hints and vague recollections of what could have been.[3] Although not all regression therapists have the Hades

Moon, it is an enormous help in doing this work. Its psychic potential and connections to other levels of consciousness enable the therapist to enter into the regressee's space with him or her. Helen Wambach, one of the early pioneers of hypnotic regression therapy had the Moon at 12° Leo, semi-sextile Pluto in Cancer. Roger Woolger, one of America's most experienced therapists has the Hades Moon, as do I. You only have to see Roger work to know that he is totally tuned into his patient. They are connected on a soul level.

Quite a few of my clients contact me because they have had a glimpse of the past and want to know more. Or, they feel that it must be something from the past they are struggling with because they have explored all they can in the present and still have not found the answer. I look at the chart to see the broad karmic outline and then connect to the person's higher self to obtain the precise details of relevant lives. If appropriate, we also explore the issues through regression to relevant lives. As part of that work, I often find that a "piece of soul" has become detached or fragmented and remains stuck in the past. Reconnecting to this fragment changes how the energy connected with that memory functions in the present life. Shamanic practitioners have used soul retrieval for thousands of years. As Caitlin Matthews explains: "Soul retrieval breaks the tape loop of an inherited story or a traumatic accident, allowing a [person] to take up [his or] her own story, free from the burdens of nightmare or ancestral reenactment."[4] Soul retrieval is one of the inherent karmic skills of the Hades Moon, although not everyone with a Pluto-Moon connection will choose to use it in this way. But people who are caught up in the past, especially in the traumatic issues of the Hades Moon can benefit tremendously from reconnecting to the lost fragments of their soul.

In the Hades Moon stories that follow, I have deliberately chosen examples that have arisen time and time again. Each person's experience is subtly different, especially in how the feelings are handled and in outcome, but the basic story holds good. It is as though these stories are generic, or archetypal, and cross cultural boundaries. We do not have the space here to pursue why this should be, but I have explored it at length elsewhere.[5] Roz's story, which follows, is typical of people who go to a place and pick up on the atmosphere of what went on there before. But, as we can see, below the surface, something more was stirring. Roz, although she did not realize it at the time, was getting in touch with her own past.

IN MEMORIUM

I was asked by a friend, Marjorie, to look at an experience Roz had undergone when she visited Dachau in Germany, and also to see "where she goes from here." Roz was leaving her Mediterranean home and returning to England but could "see no future." As it happened, Roz (Chart 13, page 179) died of a brain hemorrhage when she reached England a few days after Marjorie's request—on my birthday, which I felt was rather significant. Appropriately, it was her second Saturn Return, in the 8th house of death and transition (Chart 14, page 180). Marjorie asked me to continue with the reading and to use the material in this book to honor Roz's experience.

Initially, Roz was not sure whether this was a reincarnation experience, or whether she was tapping into the shared memories of the collective unconscious.

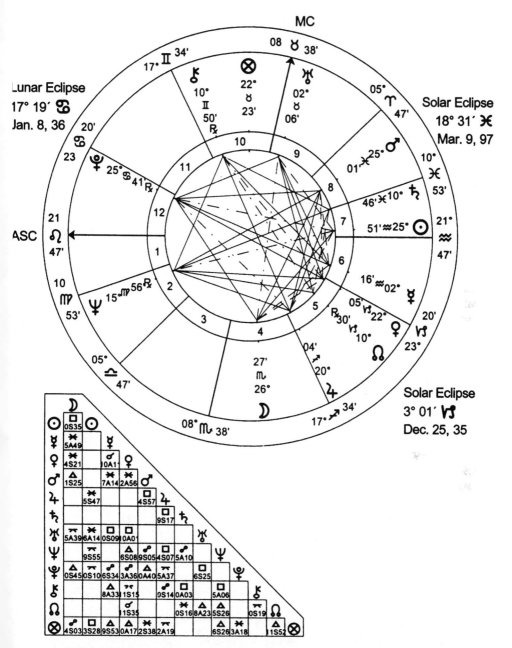

Chart 13. Roz. Placidus houses. Birth data withheld for confidentiality. Source: mother's memory. Outer wheel indicates the placements of the Solar Eclipse (March 9, 1997), the Lunar Eclipse (January 8, 1936), and the Solar Eclipse (December 25, 1935).

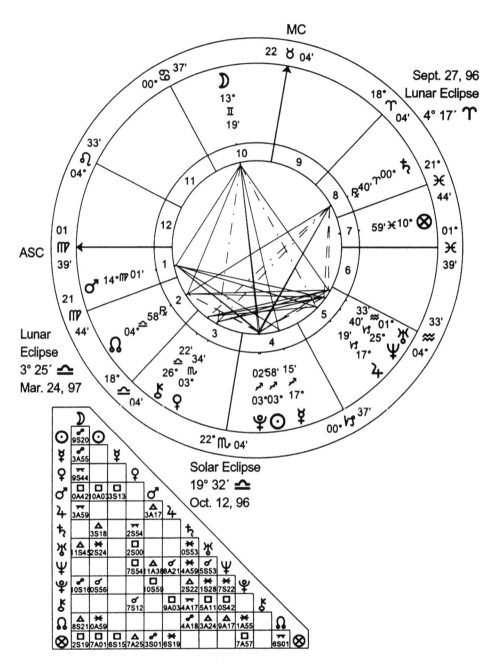

Chart 14. Roz' death. Placidus houses. Death data withheld for confidentiality. Source: time from a friend who was present. The outer wheel indicates the Lunar Eclipse (September 27, 1996), Solar Eclipse (October 12, 1996), and the Lunar Eclipse (March 24, 1997).

Or indeed, with her extreme sensitivity, she questioned whether she was simply tuning into the memories held by this particular place. With a 12th-house Pluto in Cancer trine Moon in Scorpio in the 4th house, and Mars in Pisces in the 8th house, it seemed that all possibilities were equally likely. Mars trine Pluto indicates old abuse and misuse of power, whether as victim or perpetrator, and both the 8th and 12th houses have a strong connection to the collective karma of the past. The doubly Hades Moon is adept at tuning into people and places but also indicates an experience of persecution in the past. Scorpio, of course, is the sign that penetrates where other signs fear to tread. That Roz may well have been personally implicated in the power issues was shown by her exact Sun-Pluto quincunx and Pluto's placement in the 12th house. As her Sun was in Aquarius, she had both the detachment and the humanity to work on behalf of the collective. A Grand Trine in exact aspect has enormous potential for the resolution of an issue, whether personal or collective.

That Roz had a particularly strong karmic purpose in incarnating was shown by her pre-birth lunar eclipse falling on her South Node in Cancer, and pre-birth solar eclipse on her initiatory Capricorn North Node semi-square to the Sun and Moon. With the North Node on the midpoint of the Sun and Moon, she was trying to reconcile the past with the present, to find the karmic point of balance. This highlighted her Capricorn need to work for society, and to find her own inner authority. But Capricorn can also act as the scapegoat in dealing with collective karma. Roz's life, and death, took some old darkness out of the world.

A post-death solar eclipse was on the Mars/Saturn midpoint in the 8th house, signifying the need to resolve the collective abuse of power. It fell in Pisces, a point where we can transcend karma or make a sacrifice on behalf of the collective. Eclipses work retrospectively, having their strongest effect before they happen, so this was the work she was doing in the six months prior to her death. A pre-death lunar eclipse conjuncted a South Node-Saturn conjunction in the 8th house in her death chart (Saturn being the Lord of Karma and the South Node the past), and a post-death lunar eclipse conjuncted the transiting North Node (karmic purpose). The Sun was conjunct Pluto in the death chart, indicating that she had resolved the natal quincunx, and transiting Moon on the natal IC showed that she was returning home.

Roz's story is best told by her graphic letter to Marjorie and her diary extracts:

Postcard from Munich

Love it here in Bavaria—lots of trees and green space and food and beer are great.

Letter to Marjorie a week later

When I was in Wimbledon, I bought a book called Rune Power *by Kenneth Meadows. It went into the history of the Runes and especially recent history, and specifically the misuse of the Runes by the Nazis. So, there I was, taking to Germany this book which chronicled the Nazi involvement, and also spoke of one of the German Runic authorities having spent the war years in Dachau in order that he would not speak about the involvement of certain Nazis in occult work.*

When I got to Kathy's [friend], I discovered that she had just bought and be-gun to read a book by a Jewish guy called Daniel Jonah Goldhagen, who had written of ordinary Germans and the holocaust, Hitler's Willing Executioners, *in which he puts forward a very convincing and well-documented argument that Hitler did not "force" Germans to discriminate against and vilify the Jews, that those feelings were already there, he simply fueled them. The extermination came later, but was also in the main, carried out by ordinary Germans who did not lose sleep over what they did, firmly believing that the Jews were the origin of all that was wrong in Germany. Well, of course I began reading this book, too, and there were many graphic accounts of the atrocities both in and out of the concentration camps. Dachau was, of course, mentioned quite frequently.*

My trip started in Munich. I didn't know that the Nazi movement began in that city, I thought it was Berlin or Nurnberg. But Hitler went to Munich from Austria when he was 19 and lived there for many years. It was where he wrote Mein Kampf *and did his plotting! He was tried and sentenced in the courthouse there when in the 20s he tried an abortive attempt to impose his Nationalist Socialist Party.*

And Himmler [Pisces Moon, Libra Sun, Gemini Pluto], who created Dachau in 1933 (the first of the camps) was Chief of Police in Munich.

Now we come to my visit to Dachau. I had no idea, initially, that Dachau was anywhere near Munich, but in fact it is only about ten or fifteen miles away. The town of Dachau itself is a delightful place, really pretty, with a river and lots of greenery. Dachau, the camp, was originally an armaments factory in the first World War and fell into disuse afterward. It was this ready-made site which Himmler decided would make a good venue for incarceration.

Well, I was VERY keen to go to this so called "Memorial Site," thinking that it would be quite something different to do—and how!!! Kathy took me on the Sunday. The main feature of the place is the huge museum, housed in what was one of the original buildings. The museum is a pictorial history of the coming to power of the Nazis and the formation of Dachau and other camps, together with what went on in them. That in itself was harrowing enough, but then there was the original, unrestored building which had been the prison block where prisoners were tortured etc. (Part of the museum building had housed the notorious showers.) The site itself is still surrounded by barbed wire fencing, the ditches and sentry towers. Just outside the site "proper" are the ovens (I found this most distressing) and the gas chamber which was never actually used—prisoners were sent elsewhere to be gassed—but plenty were killed at Dachau by other means. What I found quite strange and also made me angry were the several small churches and religious memorials which have now been erected on the site of the camp itself. I just thought, "And where the hell were all YOU when this was going on? Turning your faces to the wall!"

Walking around the museum was horrific, and I felt quite nauseous at times, and sometimes near to tears. But walking around the grounds where there were less people was in some way even worse. I kept looking at the sentry towers and imagining being a prisoner, and perhaps being so desperate that one would want to walk on the forbidden grass strip near the ditch and get mown down by the sentry's gun. But the worst of all were the buildings with the ovens in them, and it was one in particular which made me feel awful, and that was the oldest and smallest of them, with a tall metal, old fashioned type of chimney. It was really weird to be walking about where such terrible atrocities took place. It made me grateful that I'm alive now.

When we left, we went back into Munich to the Olympic Park (made from the war-rubble of Munich) and sat outside in the sun for cakes and a drink, and hopefully some of the awful vibrations disappeared from us. But that night when I got into bed my mind went straight back to Dachau and I couldn't clear it away. Also I developed pains in my lower back and legs, which I didn't at that time associate with my visit to Dachau.

The next morning I went swimming and I put my neck out in the most painful way. I was quite ill for a couple of days, and then it eased a bit, but I knew that I really needed some treatment as I was still having awful headaches, etc. My friends found this very nice chiropracter/acupuncturist/homoeopath. I had two treatments with him and on both occasions he gave me six injections at the top of my spine where it went into the base of the skull. These consisted of a dental anaesthetic and some homeopathic preparations (more on the relevance of this later). After my injury I set about looking at Dachau and my reactions to it, as I felt that what had happened to me in the pool was a result of my visit in some way.

What I felt most strongly was that by making a commemorative site out of Dachau. those awful vibrations, and all the terrible things that happened there are not only being kept alive but being STRENGTHENED by all the people who go there and experience what happened.

I did quite a long visualisation in which I pulled the whole place down, burned what was burnable, broke up into small pieces what wasn't, and made sure there was nothing left standing by bulldozing the whole site. Then I planted trees everywhere, and scattered grass seed and wild flower seeds, and imagined the whole place being taken over and cleansed by nature. The perimeter of the camp was no longer distinguishable, it was all just one natural site.

Then, I thought I needed to look at my own life and see where I have made commemorative sites in my mind and emotions of things from the past which needed to be completely obliterated from any sort of "remembrance." I needed to bulldoze those to the ground and return them to nature to be recycled.

When I returned home, Jacky asked me to tell the Thursday metaphysics class about Dachau, which I did. Then Melinda, who had been in the process of doing my chart, using it to look at past lives, and had felt that there was something else she needed to access and couldn't, suddenly said that I'd been in Dachau myself, and had been with Greta [Roz's daughter who has Pluto in Virgo square the Moon conjunct Neptune in Scorpio] who had been my twin. We had been experimented on, and had been injected as part of these experiments. (Hence my re-living those injections this time around with the chiropracter, and Greta with her heroin addiction.) Jacky said that she also felt this was so. She also said I had been there with Natasha. Natasha had been told on two previous occasions that she'd been a Jew and had been persecuted. A Kinesiology guy had asked her whether she was allergic to dental anaesthetic as that had shown up in his testing, she said "No." On further reflection he said that it was the nearest thing to the cyanide gas used in concentration camps, and he felt that her brain still carried memories of that!

Diary extracts

Thursday: After having so vividly in my mind and emotions the dreams in Germany and being sure that I needed to do some inner work to find out the connection with Dachau, I was switched completely to Greta after Melinda's comments. I felt that my meeting with girl twins yesterday and talking to their mother, and reflecting myself on what it must feel like to be a twin, and how they coped apart, etc. etc. was a confirmation of what Melinda told me.

Saturday: By the afternoon I was "connected" again and started to work on Dachau full of feeling.

First of all querying the dates: I was born in 1936—there was only three years of Dachau before that—I wonder when the experiments started?

"The experimental station of Dr. Rascher was set up in early 1933 in Block 5, where high pressure and exposure experiments were practised on defenceless prisoners . . . many of these experiments resulted in death."

Comparing this to my symptoms in Germany this time—

- Great pressure on my head and top spine caused by cold water—and the Doctor emphasised the factor of the cold (which "infected" my structure);
- Injections in the base of the skull;
- Felt out of control in the Doctor's surgery because of the language barrier; I was "helpless";
- Great fear before each visit—because of the pain I was in and also because I was going into the unknown and an "alien" doctor and practices.

Did a visualisation with Greta and the camp, and went into the infirmary block where the experimental station had been. Also visited the crematorium where I had been particularly horrified by the older and smaller of the ovens. Again I come to the time factor—could I perhaps have been aware of Greta's cremation there after 1940? If she had survived me, then perhaps part of my consciousness had stayed with her and registered all that happened to her, and I had experienced her pain, fear, and suffering, too? Is this why I "came in" this time around with those ghastly nightmares which persisted for much of my lifetime and still occasionally visit me, although the content is different, but the fear remains—also the migraines.

Visited Gertrude in hospital. This took me back to the fear and pain of my own similar experience. I was dreading this as I have a fear of hospitals anyway. I can remember my operation to remove my tonsils when I was 9 years old—that was when the war ended. I was fully conscious when I was taken into the theatre and put on the operating table—I can still remember the mask going over my face. And I recall some days after the operation a nurse talking to someone and saying that I was the "worst one in there" (and as a child I thought she meant the worst behaved or something). The same thing happened when I had my hip operation, quite conscious being taken into the theatre and transferred onto the table, but no mask. I also hate hospital machinery—e.g., bone scan. With the work I had just done re Greta and I and the experiments, I was led to look at my visit to Gertrude in a different light. I thought it might be an opportunity to change some of my energy and connection to past fearful experiences. So, two areas to work on: connection to Dachau and my own experience in St Lukes.

Tried to prepare myself mentally before I went. Then I decided to look at the different way that I was entering the experience this time:

- Going as a visitor and not a victim/patient;
- Taking with me gifts of flowers and fruit.

When I arrived I had to wait in a queue and got angry about this and also very angry when I couldn't find the way once I got inside.

Sunday: Hadn't slept properly the night before and was very "weepy" first thing. My right hip/thigh were hurting/aching—same as night of visit to Dachau.

Sundries:

When I was 20 I spent some time in London and lived with some German Jews who had come to England before the war began. At the same time I worked for Victor Hochhauser's wife (he was an impressario), they were orthodox Jews and I learned quite a bit about the religion and became very interested in Zionism.

Although there was so much of the Nazi past in Munich, I liked the city very much and felt happy and at home there.

Greta:

I have been involved and connected to her while she was injecting heroin, and also when she was doing "cold turkey." Both of these situations were traumatic.

She has said to other people that I had "abandoned" her when she was about 13 (I had left home for about six weeks). This quite understandable feeling in this lifetime may of course also be linked to the past if I died before her.

Kathy:

I wonder whether my constant need of, and return to, her is to do with a subconscious need for a twin?

When I looked at Roz's chart and did the psychic reading for her, I felt that she was correct in her assumption that she had been interned at Dachau, but had died very early on, leaving her twin (now her daughter) behind. They were powerfully connected, and the contact did not end when Roz died, but carried over into the present life and pulled Greta to her as her daughter—there were very strong Pluto-Moon contacts across the charts and Neptune inter-aspects with the personal planets. It is possible to backtrack when incarnating, to actually be born before death in the other life, which leaves very strong "cross-threads" between the two experiences. I also felt that Roz had agreed to incarnate again quickly so that she could be mother to Greta at the appropriate time.

One of the most notorious of the concentration camp doctors, Joseph Mengele (Libra Moon, Pisces Sun, Pluto in Gemini) was particularly interested in experimenting on twins. In 1934, the year when Roz believed she went to the Dachau, he joined the newly founded Institut für Erbbiologie and Rassenhygiene (Hereditary Biology and Racial Hygiene) but so far in my research I have been unable to confirm that he actually worked at Dachau. From 1943 onwards he was at Auschwitz, but when he escaped from the Allies, he went underground at Rosenheim near Munich, so he was certainly familiar with the area. I felt a strong connection between this man and what Roz had undergone at Dachau.

As we can see, Roz had considerable metaphysical experience and was able to resolve her experience by looking deeply into her own life and making connections and appropriate changes, as well as using imagery to reframe, and thereby to put some healing into, the whole Dachau experience, not just her own part in it. When her karmic task was completed, she moved on.

Many people "remember" being in the concentration camps (particularly those born with the Saturn-Mars-Pluto conjunction in late 45 and early 46, but any combination of these planets can carry the memory as well as the Hades Moon). Applying Roz's method of working could alleviate and heal the pain of that experience, for victims and persecutors alike.

In Marjorie's letter giving me permission to use this material, she expressed the hope that publishing it would encourage us to make Dachau a garden of remembrance and forgiveness instead of focusing vibes of horror and negativity there. She said, "I am continuing to visualise Dachau as a place of peace and love, festooned with wild flowers in full bloom." Please do likewise.

LEARNING THE LESSON

Karma is not an eternal damnation, an endless punishment; it is an opportunity to learn. Sometimes this entails living a life which is the opposite of what has gone before—or watching someone else do so. Karma also means that we bring our gifts with us—the talents and abilities that we have developed in other lives. Our karmic purpose may entail using these, although we do not always do so consciously.

When I did a reading for Anna, I saw her mother in her previous life living very frivolously. She was an English "Raj" wife who had gone out to Ceylon, and found little to occupy her time and so turned to genteel gambling and discreet drinking, which got out of hand as addictions tend to do. When Anna wrote to me afterward she said:

> *Your description of the mother figure who gambled and wasted money really struck a cord in me. As a young child I never saw anyone playing cards, but I vividly remember the visits to the cinema with my aunt. Whenever there was a supporting feature in which cowboys, or the like, gambled, playing poker, I felt physically sick, and the apparent waste of money really horrified me. I used to wonder, as a child, if I had gambled in a past life, and thought it unlikely.*
>
> *In my present life, my mother died suddenly from appendicitis only ten months after I was born. I'd like to tell you of the circumstances because I do feel that those parents in Ceylon were probably my parents in this life. My father came from a poor family of Welsh origin. He, and his mother and sister who looked after me, left school at 12 and disapproved of anyone sitting down reading (particularly women). My mother's family were educated, talented, and Irish.*
>
> *When my mother and father met, he was about 30 and she was 19. It was in 1919 after the first war. They were secretly engaged for eight years, saving every penny to buy a house outright, without a mortgage. That was difficult, but they seem to have learned their lesson and never drank or gambled. In fact, my mother kept account books in which she recorded every farthing she ever spent. The year after they married,*

I was born and the following year my mother died. My father was a widower for forty-two years, and would never alter anything in the house. He was like a tyrant and I was afraid of him.

I found it very difficult to break free from him, as he played on my sympathy all the time. I never told him I had a healing gift and sometimes, in my sleep, found my-self at people's bedsides. I didn't travel deliberately; it just happened. After my father's death, I felt free to join a Spiritualist Church. Well, that was when I discovered how very cruel, treacherous, and manipulative my [dead] mother could be. For about seven years, in many churches, I received constant criticism and even ridicule from her, and she tried to block me in various ways, telling mediums I was not psychic and could not heal. I kept receiving frightening warnings and predictions, as though to keep me in a state of fear and apprehension. Even now, I find it hard to meditate as I feel she is al-ways around.

Anna not only had the Hades Moon herself, with Pluto near the Ascendant squar-ing the Moon in the 4th house, her mother did also (together with a Jupiter-Saturn opposition signifying the gambling and the penny-pinching lives—Jupiter the spendthrift and Saturn the miser), and there were repeating contacts across the charts. Such contacts do not end at death. Her story demonstrates how the "de-vouring mother" does not have to be around physically in order to make her pres-ence felt, and how cutting the ties might well be necessary after someone has passed on, especially when the bonds extend into another life.

Anna's healing gift clearly traveled across lives, too. When doing the reading I had had a strong impression of the Japanese invasion and prison camps, etc., but knew that this was not Anna's own experience. I mentioned it to her in case she could throw any light on it. Her reply was that she wondered if it could have hap-pened in her sleep, although she was only 13 or so at the time, as she had been told by mediums from time to time that one of her "tasks" here was to visit children in refugee camps in her sleep, and that she had been to Vietnam during that war, al-though she had little memory of it. This kind of ability was taught in the temples of Egypt and Greece and could well be a carryover from training in those lives. Many people find themselves doing in a sleep state something which does not necessarily belong to the present life. Both healing ability and psychic potential are positive at-tributes of the Hades Moon, and as such would be talents Anna had to use as part of her karmic purpose.

REWORKING THE PAST

In chapter 4 we saw the close links that the Hades Moon has with loss and rejec-tion. This is a pattern that continues down through many incarnations until the soul feels that it simply must be resolved. When Grace contacted me, she felt she was be-ginning to integrate some insights she had had a long time ago. She had been helped by the traumatic end of a relationship. Grace (figure 14, page 188) has the North Node of the Moon in Leo in the 12th house, indicating that she is trying to move beyond her karma and go deeply into her own heart. She had to move be-yond the detached Aquarian perspective and put her insights into practice on a

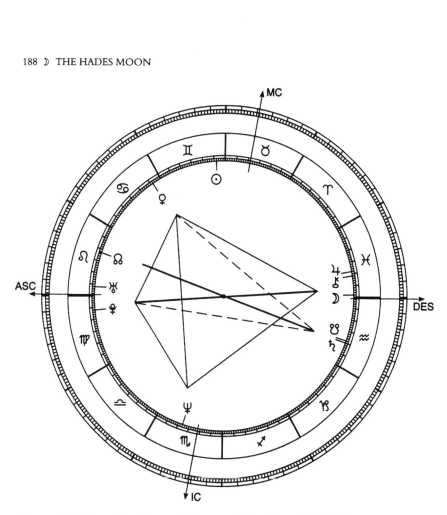

Figure 14. Reworking the past. Grace. Birth data withheld for confidentiality. Placidus houses. Chart used by permission.

one-to-one basis. As her South Node conjuncted Saturn, she was easily pulled back into the past karmic pattern.

The 12th house Pisces Node takes on an extraordinary amount of other people's karma, the stuff that no one can really claim. No one can say "this is mine, this is yours." It is cumulative, collective stuff, and there is a lot of that floating around at the end of an astrological age. We have to clean up the mess from Pisces before we can move into Aquarius, so Grace was one of the people who are doing this as part of her karmic purpose. Grace describes this as "a compelling motivation to clear things and progress." Pluto in Virgo is in the 1st house opposite the Moon in Pisces in the 7th house. Pluto also aspects Venus. Not only did she have the mothering karma of the Hades Moon, but she also carried very powerful patterns of abandonment-rejection and abusive relationships through several lifetimes:

The pattern in my life has revolved around loss and rejection by others. Coping with the loss of a partner is a situation which brings up an unbelievable amount of terror and futility—it reflects the ways in which I seem to lose my centredness and give power away—and yet in most other areas of my life, I feel I am powerful and successful. I feel that despite the devastation I have just experienced, I am working toward breaking the final link in this patterning, and intuitively feel that I have integrated a major lesson in this area. The man I assumed was my father left when I was 6 and I do tend to choose distant men with little fire or passion [the absent or disengaged Hades Moon father], and the more intense I become, the more they withdraw, eventually fleeing. I'm sure, despite my life-long protestations, that I've been addicted to this sort of pain until this last experience. The wound does go very deep [Chiron in the 7th house].

Grace has the kind of background we have come to expect with the Hades Moon:

My mother was very rejecting—she had some sort of post natal breakdown when I was 3, and myself and my siblings found ourselves in and out of various institutions for the next thirteen years. During the times I was at home, my mother displayed a fairly virulent hatred of me—as the outsider in the family [Hades Moon, Moon opposite Uranus and Neptune in the 3rd house feeling an "alien" in the family]—and I have got in touch with some past lives we shared together that shed some light on this. I encountered a great degree of suffering, deprivation, and physical/emotional abuse living with my mother. She eventually committed suicide.

I lead a strong spiritual life—but have found until recently that although I can firmly believe something intellectually, it's often difficult to live this as a reality, e.g., I know that loving myself, and not looking to the next relationship for my salvation, would be a good idea, but it's only in the last couple of months that I've begun integrating this. I often experience this type of dissonance, and also a major feeling I've found difficult to shake off since childhood is a desire not to be here, and the feeling that life is futile. I recall wishing I was dead for most of my childhood—even when things were fine. My spiritual beliefs and understanding of karma now mean that I am here for the duration, but I did make two childhood suicide attempts. Wanting to give up and opt out has held quite a pull for me, but since I've worked with addressing my emptiness and this has improved.

Grace told me that she wanted to find a way to integrate her healing talent and abilities into her work. When I looked at her chart, I told Grace that I felt that she had chosen an incarnation where she had brought together everything to focus it and to really go into overload so that she broke through—indicated by Pluto on the Ascendent, Pluto aspects to Moon, Sun and Venus. and the 12th-house Node. I said that my experience with this was that, initially, it could be horrendous. I could not find another word for it, and yet once the breakthrough was made, the energy that was released was in even greater inverse proportion to how far "down" people have to go initially, so that the healing that is available and then the energy that can be put into other people is enormous. What I have found was that it is usually the mid-30s, or even later, before all of this energy reverses. (So she was looking to her approaching Chiron Opposition as a focal point.)

When I examined the basic energy of her chart, I explained that the Moon was the instinctive, instinctual approach to life that she had built up over many life-times. A Pisces Moon, even one that had only just slid in at 0°, was the "great es-caper" of the zodiac which got trapped in victim-martyr-savior scenarios very very easily. The difficulty with the Pisces Moon comes from an inability to let go of the present, the past, people, and emotions. To let go of the desperate urge to merge and become one that is so Piscean. It is the illusion of that merging being possible that tends to keep Pisces in relationships, in situations, long after other people would have let go. This Piscean illusion is powerful, as is the lack of boundaries and the absence of any sort of sense of individual self that Pisces can have. Pisces is a sign which will sacrifice itself for somebody else, hence the tendency to want to be the savior, but very quickly that turns into the victim or the martyr and becomes trapped in the situation. So there would be lives of self-sacrifice, of religious ideals, all the things that are Piscean, behind that Pisces Moon.

There was also an incredible amount of karma with the mother, not just her physical mother in this present life. Notwithstanding—as her Moon was in the 7th house—I would say that there was a personal karma between them in the past, in-cluding possibly having been married to her mother at some point. A 7th-house Moon indicates either that the present life mother has been a partner in the past, or that the daughter has acted as parent to the mother at some time in the past—or may do so in the present life. There were the Hades Moon archetypal moon-mother issues to consider as well. The Hades Moon dominated the chart and so there was mothering karma in the widest possible sense of the word; issues of re-jection and abandonment, death in childbirth, death of or as a child, etc. Difficult birth is often a feature because coming back is so painful. A tremendous reluctance to incarnate leads to a sense of "not wanting to be here." This archetype, and Grace's chart, carries an incredibly painful mothering experience which goes so deep, especially the devouring and rejecting mother experience which Grace's let-ter expressed so well. It goes through so many deep dark emotional traumas it is almost impossible to get to the bottom of it. The focus has to be on letting go and healing. But underneath all of that trauma and drama, there was a very deep heal-ing potential.

Grace told me that she had a compulsion toward healing. The Hades Moon is extremely psychic and very intuitive. It has innate healing power, and that comes out of the old mystery-fertility religions where there was an attunement to the cy-cles, the seasons, the rhythms, the earth-as-mother. I told her I feel that everyone who has the Hades Moon is here to undertake the healing of Earth. That may be the physical entity that is Earth, it may be the esoteric and etheric components of Earth, or the people on Earth. It expresses itself in different ways, but the urge, the need, is there to heal the Earth level of existence. There are old skills, knowledge, and abilities which can be tuned into and used very powerfully for that purpose. There is always the old priestess in the background waiting to come forward.

Grace's square from Pluto to the Sun showed karma around projecting her power onto other people, especially men, with the need to own her own power, but also there was the so called "easy" aspect, the sextile, to Venus which could not be ignored. The "emotional black hole" was emphasized by the Cancer placement of Venus. Grace did not believe she could ever get enough love and so she constantly recreated a situation which confirmed: "I cannot get love." Her father leaving, her mother going into the institution, men fleeing from her, was a classic Venus-Pluto-Hades Moon story created from the chart.

When Grace first contacted me, she was coming up to the conjunction of Chiron to her natal 1st house-Pluto opposite the Moon and this was a time when the issues would come into focus and a shift would be made. When Pluto was triggered, all the karmic issues were set off as there were so many Pluto aspects. It would reverberate right around the chart and around her inner self. Hopefully that would be the moment of resolution when the old suffering was given up and the healing took place.

The way for her to turn her old pattern around was to learn to love herself (Saturn aspect to Venus). It was vital. Until you love yourself you cannot love anyone else, but with Venus-Saturn as part of a Finger of Fate (with Saturn-Pluto on the other side and the Nodal axis as the outlet), moving into her heart was essential. That was the healing route. She needed to go into her inner being, the part she got thrown out from whenever relationships broke up, and in that center to find the point which is all loving, all giving. Whatever name we put on it, God, the cosmos, divine love, it is within us. When she was centered around that and filling herself up from that source, it would never run out, unlike fallible human love. When you are attuned to that, you can give out love with no fear that it will cease. You then get love back, but Grace cannot do it on that basis because that would be manipulative and that was part of what she was trying to give up.

The old pattern of Venus-Pluto is to have manipulated, maneuvered, accepted anything that passed for love even if it was abusive or dependent, because of the need for love. She had not looked at the quality of love or what was really going on (Pisces Moon). It was a dependent placement, but it was possible to break the cycle. I suggested that she look at codependency and find help to break out of that cycle.

The key to feeling fulfilled was to find an outlet for the Finger of Fate through the North Node. The work that she did on cosmic clearing, work that would be done *en masse* and yet in a very heart-centered, individual way, may involve a partner and may not. It was not important for the focusing of the energy.

As she had Jupiter conjunct Chiron in the 7th-house, this would help with her relationships. As well as the painful, wounded relationships, she had also had experience with "good" relationships in the past and could use these to expand beyond her current situation. At the moment, it was feeding "over-the-top" energies and so as soon as she got into relationship all the Pluto obsession came in. When she had dealt with this, then Jupiter could become the expansive heart and she would grow through her relationships. Chiron shows us where we have to give up our suffering, and it shows us where we wound ourself as well as others, and relationships would be a powerful focus for healing her sense of self.

Grace had a Grand Trine in water planets, with Pluto forming a kite (figure 14, page 188). This configuration is deeply emotional, very compassionate and caring, and extremely sensitive, and the addition of Pluto did mean that whatever she did would be intense and deep, but it could be transformative as well. Pluto always involves death and rebirth as well as destruction. It has to let go of the past to make fertile compost for the present. In allowing what must be to be in its cycle and in its season, healing comes. This was Grace's outlet.

I pointed out to Grace that, along with the "devouring mother" expectation, she also anticipated "poor" fathering (Sun trine Saturn) with its consequent loss of self-esteem and lack of self-worth that entails; and that the devouring mother is often accompanied by the absent father. But she also intended to learn to parent herself. It was not that she arrived and then was terribly disappointed that the beautiful vision did not work out, that the father tumbled off his pedestal, but that she expected it to happen. Simply knowing that she had made that choice would change something. It is when you feel the victim (Pisces), the "Oh, poor me, what did I do to deserve this?" that it is at its worst, its most destructive. But when you are able to say: "I did choose this, this was my learning experience. I needed to let go of the illusion of fatherhood (Sun inconjunct Neptune), I needed to let the expectation that I would not get fathered go, and somehow come to a much deeper understanding because of it."

The placement of Grace's Sun in the 10th house indicated previous karma with her father. Typically with the Hades Moon, these fathers who have not taken responsibility before, who have died, disappeared, done whatever in the past, do agree to come back with that child again in the hope that they themselves can actually work through that karma and can learn about fatherhood. But of course when they get here they forget their intention, and wriggle out of it, and away they go, and therefore the situation repeats. So Grace actually offered her father the opportunity to reverse something that had happened before but he was not able to take it. He fulfilled all Grace's expectations and propelled her into the pattern she was trying to overcome. So it could be a question of thanking him for the lesson and letting it go so that she would not have to go through it with him again. From her point of view, either experience was equally right, and whichever one she got she had agreed to prior to incarnation.

When I looked at her past lives, I felt she had a "cluster" of difficult and painful lives which were closest to the surface. Therefore, I would look on those as having the greatest effect on the present life. I told her that we all go through a period when we go deep down into the emotional side of life as part of our learning process on Earth—Earth being the only plane of existence where you can have the deep emotional experiences and are able to hide emotions. So she was immersed at the bottom of the emotional cycle and this was the breakthrough point where she could move out of it. Therefore, there were a lot of lives with the pattern of abandonment and rejection, desperately seeking love, not feeling worth anything, and a slave-experience where she was literally owned by someone else.

That life was very contradictory. She was then a small boy who was petted and pampered. He was a beautiful mixed race child with long lashes, brought from Barbados to England by a woman who lost all her children due to fever. She had returned to England for the good of her health. Grace was obviously her substitute child although the boy was a slave. He had been born into slavehood, and was most probably the husband's child (which the mother may or may not have admitted to herself). The child was about 3 and was taken away from his natural mother, and so felt abandoned, although there was a black woman who was brought over to be the nanny, but she resented the child deeply. She hated England, blamed the child, and went into a deep dark depression. In England she was looked on as the lowest of the low while the child was elevated and pampered. I felt there was a strong connection between that nanny-figure and Grace's present life mother. In that life the nanny literally pined away and died, she thought herself into death. The child was left at age 4 with a housekeeper and servants, all of whom adored him. The child was educated but as he grew older he was more and more aware of having no place because, although at 15 he was extremely handsome and very attractive to women, no one would allow him to marry their daughter. So he became deeply unhappy because he could not have a physical relationship with anyone due to the class and color barrier. He would always be an outsider.

He asked desperately to go back to his country, where his natural father was happily living with his real mother. His father would have taken him back and given him a place on the plantation. But when he returned, after his surrogate mother's death, he had his creamy-olive skin and black curly hair, and this made life difficult because the society out there was stratified and rejected the half-and-half child, and he did not fit in with his mother's people either. So he went to live in America instead. There he was able to have a business and be a part of the rigid strata of society to which he "belonged" according to the thought of the day. He was able to marry and have children.

Nevertheless, inside something had died with the rejection of going back to his birthplace and not being accepted. Deep down inside, he felt wrong. The wrong color skin, the wrong place. He felt unloved, especially as he had been pampered and petted and not loved for who he really was in the first place. Also having been torn away from his natural mother, he felt he would be going back to her love, but she rejected him because he looked way above her slave-status and he was beyond her reach. She was still a slave while his father had given him his freedom. Part of her had been very hurt by what happened and now here was a stranger coming back whom she could not accept, and therefore she lashed out from her pain.

So although he then had thirty or forty years of apparently happy life, the pain was underneath and the underlying problem did not heal. While he was living in New Orleans, he had many affairs with white women. With his striking appearance he looked like an adolescent (the eternal puer), which seemed to be symbolic of his arrested emotional development. It was the fashion to have a colored "toy-boy" and he was passed around between friends, but was not seen in public with any of them. He lived a double life which did not add to his sense of worth. Many patterns crystallized in that life, and he was unable to break out of them.

I also saw Grace as a kind of "Voodoo priestess" somewhere in central America, someone with a lot of power, a lot of knowledge—of not only herbs but hypnotism, metaphysical practices, different states of consciousness. She was trained for extensive trance work. She died young, just when she was getting into her powers. The reason she died seemed to be due to someone else's jealousy. Some forgiveness was needed for that person because all Grace's potential was cut off by that death.

I had to go "back" a long way before I could find an incarnation where she had both a deep spiritual practice and a fulfilling relationship. That woman, ironically, wanted to know about these other things. As she sat in the Temple and listened to people describe jealousies, pains, lack of self-worth, etc., she felt, "I don't know about these things. I need to know because how else can I help these people. I cannot feel it from my heart because I haven't been there." And therefore she made the conscious decision to experience all these things. But she didn't intend to get trapped in the cycle for so long. Had we been working in Past Life Therapy, I would have asked Grace to trace these incarnations herself and to connect to what made this particular relationship work. We could have amended that decision to empathize with people by joining them in their pain so that it was limited to a prescribed period only. As it was, this was something she had to work out for herself in the current lifetime.

When I checked back with Grace two years later, she told me that she was continuing to do personal growth work to heal any past wounds that were still running her. She had half-written a book concerning her childhood and later experiences and was finding it a healing journey. She was still working through that karma of loss and rejection, but appeared to be at the end of a karmic cycle. She had been told by a channeller that her last partner, as with several others who had abandoned her in this present life, had gathered for a karmic resolution. She was told that she had been a Taoist monk and, at various times, when those men came for guidance the monk had used them for sexual gratification. The guide said, "Understand that now the whole pattern has been released. All pain is healed, all connections repaired. I hold both imprisonment and freedom in my hands. The key is turned, the door is open—you may fly free." All of this had strengthened her spiritually, and she had made a conscious decision to reach for joy. She said:

> What my last relationship made me aware of was that the destructive relationship I had with my mother left me with an addictive drive to fill the inner void in me with any relationship that would distract me from my sense of empty incompletion. My work with A Course in Miracles showed me that the sense of exile I've always felt probably goes back further than my mother, and is a deep spiritual wound in which I mistakenly believed that I am separate/lost from God. Among other things, I'm currently working with John Bradshaw's books and tapes, which involves reclaiming and championing one's inner child.
>
> If it's true that we create our own inner reality, that people simply mirror back to us our opinion of ourselves and trigger us where we are still damaged, then my mother offered me the gift of journeying back to self-love through childhood adversity. Perhaps that was just my Soul's process this time around, yet, my sense of justice and humanity tells me rightly that each child deserves to be loved and cherished. What is important to me is that I've found a path to empowerment. I've begun to sprout and refine a Good Mother inside me, and she will extinguish the generational legacy of maternal wounding, a belief my future children will one day hopefully testify to.

She finished:

> I have connected with my mother on a number of occasions, and in various ways since her death twelve years ago, and I have a growing sense that she is evolving well. I hold only compassion for her, and send her light, while hoping that we never have to repeat the mother-daughter dynamics of this incarnation.

As we have seen, Hades Moon people often experience alienation and isolation, leading to a sense of being the outsider. When she read this piece, Grace (who is of mixed-race Irish and West Indian parentage) commented:

> I have been the subject of a lot of racism this lifetime. My mother, a white woman, was the worst offender, very verbally abusive in this vein, which did somewhat affect and wound my self-esteem. But the older I got, the less split and better I feel about my identity and the less attached to it.

In at least one of her other lives, Grace experienced the rejection that comes from not fitting in because of color, but she was not persecuted because of it. Other Hades Moon people experience persecution for a variety of reasons in their past lives and we will look at the karmic effect of this in chapter 7.

ATTUNING TO A JOINT KARMIC PURPOSE

The relationships in the karmic case history we are going to look at next go way back into other lives, and weave a tangled web indeed, drawing four people together. It is a complex example of karma working through synastric aspects and highlights how issues are "pulled in" by contacts with another person's chart. The story concerns Lenny, an adopted child, Dana his adopted mother, Simon, his adopted father, and Petra who had to take on the role of surrogate mother. Richard Idemon says, "People born with a natal Moon-Pluto aspect carry around some kind of tape or myth with regard to nurturance."[6] In Lenny's case, this myth was reworked to give a happier ending than he had been used to in other lives.

When Petra met Dana, who was then a working colleague of Simon's, Dana told Simon that she had met just the woman for him. As Simon and Dana were, as he thought, happily married, Simon dismissed this. But shortly after he and Dana split up (at Dana's instigation), he met Petra again and the two started an intense but quite difficult relationship. The situation brought up many old patterns for Petra which she worked hard on changing. When they began the relationship, she did not expect to end up mothering Lenny. But this seemed to be what fate, or was it karma, had in store.

Lenny was born to a heroin addict, under a "Place of Safety Order" (a legal order made by UK social workers to protect a child) and was fostered as soon as he left the Special Baby Unit in which he had to be treated for a heroin addiction at birth (with six planets in earth, coming into a body was difficult and toxic). At fifteen months he was taken from his foster parents and given into the care of Dana and Simon, who intended to adopt him. Shortly afterward, Dana ended the marriage, but Simon continued to live in the house and to care for Lenny. Sometime later, Simon met Petra again. Eventually he moved out of the ex-marital home and he and Petra had Lenny on weekends. Once they had established a long-term relationship, Dana asked them to take Lenny.

If we look at the charts, Lenny has a wide quintile (72°) aspect between the Moon in Capricorn (conjunct the MC) and Pluto in Scorpio. This is a karmic aspect

of fate or destiny, an aspect that Jeff Green says is part of a process of creative transformation in which the new evolutionary purpose is being individualized, although
he points out that, due to the pull to the past, this is still somewhat difficult.[7] Lenny
has the North Node and Jupiter in the 12th house, showing that he is here to work
on collective karma as well as his own as part of his karmic purpose, and has priestly
training to back this up, the karmic inheritance of Jupiter in the 12th.

His chart also shows Saturn square the Sun and semi-sextile the Moon. He incarnated with expectations of "poor" parenting and emotional deprivation, which
he was seeking to overcome. He needed to learn to parent himself, and to find parents who could help him in this task, bolstering his sense of self-worth and his ability to nurture himself. Dana has an unaspected Moon in Capricorn, which widely
conjuncts Lenny's Moon. This Moon represents a mother who can be distant, patriarchal, somewhat judgmental, not able to show emotion; not having the ability—the gift—of sharing emotion, and therefore appearing rather remote and cold,
but nevertheless working hard to meet the material needs of the child. That reflects
in Lenny; he has those qualities of withdrawing from close emotional contact at
some very deep level, not really being comfortable with it and needing to learn
about being nurtured and nurturing as a balance to that cold Capricorn side, and so
getting more into the earthy nature of Capricorn. With his natal Moon right on the
Midheaven, the mother was the carrier for many of Lenny's lessons and experiences. Lenny's natural mother had, of course, not seen him since birth, bringing in
all the Hades Moon issues, but that was exactly how it should be. It fitted his pattern and put him into a place where healing was possible.

Dana's Pluto is quincunx Lenny's Moon, showing a tension around mothering in the present life. The only significant repeating each way interaspect between
their charts, indicating old karma, was the Sun conjunct Saturn, and then Saturn
quincunx the Sun. Their Nodes were conjunct. These two had an old debt or duty
to each other, a promise they had agreed upon, and their karmic purpose was in
harmony, but the pursuit of self (Aries Node) may interfere with that. With four
planets in Virgo, Lenny could well feel that he was the cause of the situation that
had arisen between his adopted parents, and he needed reassurance that he was still
loved and cared for (Saturn-Sun, Saturn-Venus).

Dana had been very disappointed when she and Simon found they could not
have a child. This was attributed to the adhesions blocking the fallopian tubes that
had resulted from appendicitis when she was 16. An operation failed to correct this,
and Dana insisted on making three attempts at invitro fertilization. Simon had felt
that it would be better to accept the infertility, mourn, and adapt to the situation.
The marriage was running into difficulties into which he did not want to bring a
child. But Dana was adamant. She applied to adopt, asking Simon to make a commitment to take a full part as a parent, although he was reluctant to adopt under the
circumstances. When the process of assessment started, Simon told Dana that he
was glad she had sufficient faith in the relationship to feel it could support a child.
He thought she was jesting when she said she would stay with him until she got the
child and then leave. As it turned out, she wasn't joking. Within a few months of
Lenny joining the family, Dana told him she was leaving as she had fallen in love
with another man but had no plans to live with him. However, as it turned out, she

stayed in the house which she split with Simon. Lenny was upset by the split but was reassured by having his father's presence. As Simon saw it, Dana had manipulated him into giving her the child she wanted.

Between Simon and Dana the main karmic issues were to do with Pluto and Neptune inter-aspects with Venus so there was a very old closeness and symbiosis, but with one-way Uranus interaspects, a need to separate and see each other clearly was very important.

Simon felt that Dana controlled Lenny by threatening to leave him if he was not compliant (the devouring mother syndrome). Although she was clearly devoted to him, she found it difficult to understand his feelings. Often conflict between her and Lenny would escalate because she did not understand that he could be provocative to get attention and that very little attention would suffice.

Simon's synastry with Lenny was more personal and karmic. His South Node conjuncted Lenny's Moon-Neptune. His Saturn squared Lenny's Nodes and his Neptune conjuncted Lenny's South Node. These were old soulmates with a strong emotional and psychic link. Each would instinctively know what the other was feeling. Neptune pulled them back into the past, but Saturn said this time you have to face up to the responsibility of what is going on here. Stephen has a natal Moon-Pluto sextile. His Moon quincunxes Lenny's Moon, Lenny's Pluto quincunxes his Moon, a most unusual occurrence. This indicated old mothering issues, probably a mother-child relationship in the past, one that may well have tension, rejection, and abandonment in it. Clearly these two had come together again to work on nurturing issues and to heal the abandonment and rejection issues Lenny faced in incarnating. Simon had agreed prior to incarnation to come in and take responsibility for learning a lesson he had avoided in the past. Lenny needed to learn that here was a father who would be there, even if in an unconventional way. The support and strength would be there for him while he dealt with his own issues.

To his surprise, Simon got on well with Lenny, having a loving relationship and good communication with emotional understanding (actually not at all surprising looking at the synastry). He felt that he had a remarkable and very lovable son. As he says, Lenny has a strong and determined, intelligent character. At nearly 4, Lenny could be "quite adult in his pertinence of rapport and his ability to share mood" (something common to all Hades Moon children).

Social Services, who were monitoring the situation regarding the adoption, suggested to Simon that he should adopt Lenny himself, but he did not feel this was appropriate. As he said: "I am trying to adapt to the situation of having a son I did not seek and finding that now I have had him I miss him when I'm not with him."

The initial surprise when looking at the synastry of this complex situation was the number of each-way contacts Petra's chart made with Lenny's, indicating something that was planned before incarnation. Petra has a Moon-Pluto bi-quintile (encompassed within the quincunx if an 8° orb is used). She had strong Hades Moon issues herself. Her Moon sextiled Lenny's Pluto, and his Moon inconjuncted her Pluto—there was an old mothering issue of separation going on here. Three of his planets squared her nodal 4th-10th house axis (the parental axis of the chart), showing he would be instrumental in moving her deeper into her karmic purpose. They had more repeating each-way inter-aspects than any of the other chart combinations. Her Moon squared his Nodes. This was a soul she was here to nurture. She was working through both individual and joint karma with him. What happened helped her to nurture him, but it was nurturing in a different way, a much freer way, than was probable in the past. She could also understand this child at a soul level. With Neptune contacts she had a line into the child's head. She could love him unconditionally, for what he was, and not have to change him and make him different. It was very important that this child be loved in that way and be allowed to develop in the way he needed. This was a gift she could offer him. When Petra wrote to me, she said:

> My relationship with Lenny has developed gradually over the last year. He visits me with Simon most Sundays and has recently stayed overnight. I have never had a child of my own and am now 44 years old, so it feels a great privilege to be a significant person for Lenny. He and I have a relationship in which he is able to play fantasy games—killing the bad monsters but saving the good ones and the babies is current favorite. He is also able to openly show his aggressive feelings toward me. Simon and I are both aware that I can be seen by Lenny as not only someone who can enter into his fantasy world, but also as someone who takes his Daddy away. I love Lenny and am committed to supporting Simon in his continuing relationship with Lenny. I am committed to a relationship with Lenny in whatever form that may take.

She ended up mothering Lenny when Dana, unable to sustain the relationship with Lenny, asked Simon to take him. It certainly looked as though this was something that had been arranged prior to incarnation, and that it formed part of the karmic purpose of all concerned. It also seemed as though Petra had agreed to be part of the "back-up system" put in place as a safety net for Lenny so that if Dana was unable to continue, Petra would be there to give Lenny what he needed from a mother, and to support Simon in offering Lenny the parenting he had opted out from in the past—something that the psychic past life reading confirmed.

There may be a great deal of "between-life" (or interlife) planning behind an apparently random meeting and the drawing together of a group, or indeed behind an intractable or conflict-prone situation. We draw toward ourselves exactly the people and situations we need in order to both overcome our difficulties in the past and to find ways of maximizing our potential by integrating the lessons of the past into our present life. The following story was a great learning experience for me. It drew on the skills I had brought back with me, and on the new insights I had developed in this present life. The relationship with Mac, who started out as a client and became a friend, still continues despite his recent death, and never ceases to bring new facets of old soul contacts to the fore. My work with him always stretches me beyond the known and familiar. He is one of my karmic teachers.

THE PRIESTESS OF THE MOON

Mac, whom we met in Ronald's story in chapter 1, has a Chiron-Sun-Mercury-Pluto-Mars conjunction across the Cancer-Leo (5th-6th house) cusp, opposing his Moon in Capricorn in the 11th house, which forms the point of a Kite Formation involving all his planets except Venus on the IC. His Moon is tied to Pluto through the conjunction, and he is extremely sensitive to Pluto transits and to his Moon progressions (figure 15, below).

Mac was my first professional client, both for a karmic reading and for past life regression. The one arose out of the other although some time elapsed between the two. He was very aware of the issues of rejection and abandonment he carried, which surfaced both in his relationship to his mother and to women in general, but he wanted to know whether there was anything else underneath that. He had an enormous fear that, if he loved someone, he would lose that person. Anyone he loved would die or be killed in some way. He was sure this related back to the past. When I did the reading, I saw him as a nun with a withered arm. She felt that this arm was a punishment from God for a love affair she had had. She was full of guilt. I could also see him as a priestess of the Moon but I felt that he needed to person- ally experience the life that went with that, so he came for regression.

It is a session I will never forget, and neither will he. He still speaks of it as though it were yesterday, although it was well over twenty years ago. It was one of

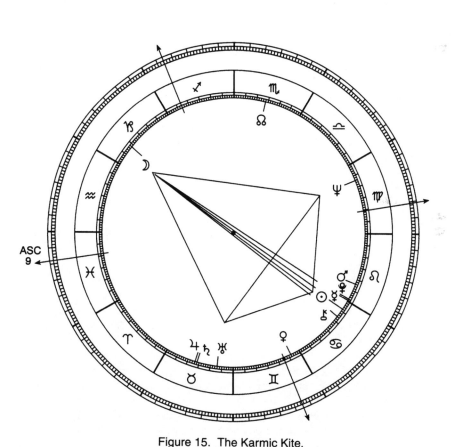

Figure 15. The Karmic Kite.

the most graphic "reliving" experiences I have seen in all that time. This was long before video cameras were available, but it is one regression that I wish I could have video'd for teaching purposes. Here was a man, a stocky, down-to-earth Yorkshire bricklayer, moving into a woman's body and becoming female (without adopting a funny voice or anything like that). I already knew that Mac was extremely psychic and had strong healing powers, so it was no surprise that he went so deeply into the regression.

I use an induction method which involves imagery for past life work. After deep relaxation and consciousness-expanding exercises, the regressee goes down some stairs, opens a door and steps into another life. Some people see it rather like a film; some experience being in the life but still have a sense of detachment; others are totally immersed in the feelings, the sights, the sounds. They are in that life, in that other body.[8] Mac was one of the latter. When Mac went down the stairs, he was a male in his late 30s. When he stepped through the door, he was a young female, a priestess of the Moon goddess. She was sitting in a cave by a deep, still pool of water. The cave was lit by flaring torches around the walls. She was dressed in a simple robe, with flowers in her hair and silver jewellery around her arms and neck. There was an enormous sense of anticipation mingled with dread. She was awaiting a lover. It was a religious ceremony, but she was so afraid that she would have to kill the young man who would come to her, to sacrifice him. The fear and the anxiety were so clear I could almost smell them. But the excitement that was intermingled was powerful, too. This was a woman who was waiting for a sexual encounter that was very important to her, and to her people, as it would ensure the fertility of the crops for the year ahead. But intuitively she knew it was important to her in a personal way, too. She had loved a young man, but had been parted from him so that she could take up her place as a priestess. Now, unbeknown to her, they were to be reunited.

Suddenly, the young man appeared, walking down from the cave entrance high above. It was the man she knew, the one she was deeply in love with. Together they ate the ritual meal that was set out for them. The food had great symbolism attached to it. Then they disrobed and went to a place where furs had been laid out on the cave floor to make a soft bed. They made love with great feeling and care for each other, but the ecstasy was tinged with sadness. Both knew that it was the one and only time they would be together. They wanted to make it a time to remember as well as honoring the goddess with all due respect.

Then, as they dressed again, the young man vanished. She was left alone, suddenly bereft. She thought the Goddess had called him. Although she was intensely relieved at not having to kill him herself, she feared that this was exactly what the priests were doing at that moment. Deep emotion shook her. She was supposed to make her way out of the cave to the waiting people. But it was impossible to move.

Fortunately, it is possible to intervene in a reliving, even one as graphic as this. I asked Mac to let his consciousness move away from his body and to follow the young man to wherever he had gone. To Mac's amazement, the young man was being feted by the priests, not killed. He had been led down a concealed passage and through the mountain. He would then be sent to another temple far away, although the priestess and the people would be told he had been killed. In reality, an animal was sacrificed and its blood substituted for his in the ceremonies that followed.

Mac started to laugh with relief. He was so sure that the young man had been killed after the lovemaking. The laughter went on and on, but I knew it was releasing tension that had been held for centuries. Eventually he quieted and returned to that other life. The priestess was joined by the priests, carrying the bowl of blood. They went out and showed it to the people. It was then spread on the fields, along with blood and semen from the no-longer virgin priestess, under the new moon. Ceremonies to honor the goddess went on for several days, with the priestess as the focal point. She never saw the young man again. But at least Mac now knew that he had not had to kill his great love, nor had a death followed their sexual union.

Feeling that there was even more beyond this, I asked Mac to trace the line of that incarnation back into the ancient past. He traveled back 6000 years. Again it was very graphic. This time he was a young man, and full of anticipation, he wound his way up a spiral mountain path to a cave near the top. Then he went deep down into the cave. There the Moon Goddess (as he saw her) was waiting for him. She was a mature woman in her 50s. It was his sexual initiation. First of all they bathed together and carried out a ritual. Then she took him over to a stone couch. She laid him on the stone and mounted herself on him. As the initiation progressed, he was "working her" and she was "working him." Their energies united. He became her, felt all her feelings as well as his own. It was a true inner marriage, a union of masculine and feminine energies, of the god and the goddess. Afterward, they ate a sacred meal together. Standing up, she took two goblets of red wine, which she told him symbolized death. She threw them over him and told him he had been reborn. Once again, he started to laugh. But this was healing laughter.

Mac's North Node is in Libra in the 8th house. His karmic purpose will be played out through relationships. Shortly afterward, Mac entered into his first serious relationship. Synchronistically, he "chose" a woman who was on a two-year "Mother Divine" course and who was supposed to be celibate during that time. She used to sneak out of the meditation center and join Mac in the woods. As he said, they honored the goddess under the moon. The relationship lasted some time, but eventually she said goodbye. This brought all his rejection issues to the surface and he worked on these for several years.

Mac went to the island of Majorca in the Mediterranean Sea. To his surprise, he found "his" convent, Santa Clara, and spent some time sitting in the courtyard reconnecting to the nun with the withered arm and letting go of the guilt and forgiving the person he had once been. Then he went over to the north side of the island and found his mountain. Although the cave had been filled in, the entrance was quite clear.

While he was on the island, he went into a relationship that was deeply karmic. It began by him helping his girlfriend to clean up, literally and figuratively. She was living rough, drinking, and taking drugs. He felt called upon to come to her aid. Eventually she joined him in England.

His partner, a sensitive Cancerian who was strongly psychic and had a Pisces Hades Moon herself, was told by her guide that they were working through the karma from seventeen different past relationships. That they included Pluto-Moon issues was clear from the quincunx from her Moon with his Pluto, and his trine from the Moon to her Pluto. This was an intensely symbiotic relationship, with enormous power struggles beneath the surface. Part of the lesson was to separate and find their individual identities instead of being pulled along by their joint karma. Her North Node conjuncted that stellium around his Sun, propelling him into his destiny. Her South Node conjunct the Sun sat on his Moon, confirming that they had an old soul link. When they finally parted, each felt that they had worked through as much as was possible in one lifetime. They looked forward to a different, and better, relationship in a future life.

It is these ingrained karmic patterns that have to be eliminated and the energy transformed in a new creative urge. One of the most powerful tools I have found for aiding this transformation is flower essences. *Boab* (Bush) was specially created by Ian White to break ingrained family patterns. He also makes a *Relationship Essence* to enhance the quality of relationships and help with forgiveness. Findhorn Flower Essences offer *Karma Clear* to help release from the past, and there are many other essences available.[9]

CHAPTER 7

THE CATHARTIC MOON

The dark phase of cyclical process is the womb of the soul.
—Demetra George[1]

S O OFTEN WHAT the Moon-Pluto contact needs is a catharsis, a clearing out of all the festering rage and resentment. I have always thought of it as a deep, deep well, full of the mud and muck of the ages. But, way down inside, there is a spring of pure clear water, which is the positive Hades energy. If the muck can be cleared out, then the creative energy can flow again. For some people this clearing is a painstakingly slow job. Bucket by bucket it is hauled up in therapy, dreams, or daily life. For others, the cleansing is swift and uncontrollable—a true catharsis.

PURGING THE PAST

Some time ago a client of mine, Angela (Pluto in Leo square Moon in Scorpio), entered into a particularly Plutonian relationship. She met a man whose own Moon-Pluto opposition sat firmly on her Moon-Pluto square to form a T-square. It also formed a "double-whammy," an each-way aspect across the charts from Pluto to the Moon, indicating an old karmic interaction between them. His Sun was conjunct her Moon. They met as transiting Uranus crossed his Venus and transiting Pluto approached her Moon. There was a powerful attraction at first sight, but the relationship was difficult. He was an alcoholic who was struggling to recover, and his unresolved mothering issues intruded into their relationship—with that Pluto-Moon square she was the ideal hook for his mothering projections. When transiting Uranus retrograded back across his Venus, he met a "spiritual friend" with whom he had an intense, alcoholic relationship, but with whom he did not have sexual contact—not from choice, his "friend" refused. She had Sun and Venus conjunct Pluto in Leo square the Moon in Scorpio and played suitably strange emotional games. Her Moon was conjunct Angela's in Scorpio so the "double whammy" was in operation between all three charts (see figure 16, page 204).

With his detached Aquarian Moon, her partner could not understand why Angela objected so strongly to his other relationship. "After all," he said, "I'm not screwing her. The relationship is a spiritual one." For Angela, the fact that her partner was having an intense relationship with someone else was what mattered. She felt that the other woman was always present in the relationship. It also activated, as she realized later her own "unavailable father" issues.

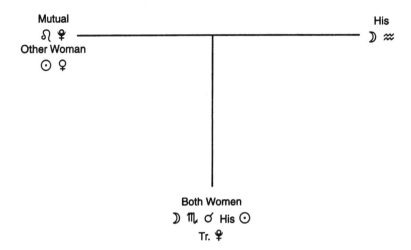

Figure 16. Catharsis. Angela, her partner, and the other woman: Mutual Pluto-Moon-Sun-Venus aspects.

Her partner would set off to see his mother, a pretty powerful lady of whose displeasure he was terrified. Unfortunately he had to pass his "spiritual friend" on the way. Inevitably he would drop in, go on a drinking bout with her and fail to make it home to mother, who, of course, blamed Angela for the fact that she "never saw her son." Eventually he would turn up again at Angela's, full of remorse and asking his "surrogate mother" to forgive him.

Although Angela recognized that some deep emotional game was being played out, the situation went on for many months. Angela wanted to end the relationship and yet somehow she always took him back. Eventually, transiting Pluto reached her Hades Moon. Angela blew. All the power of her repressed rage erupted out into physical violence, something she had never done before. She found herself beating this man, while he cowered in a corner, saying in true Aquarian fashion: "I don't want to be here." Angela, normally a quiet person, found herself shouting that she would no longer be his mother, she would not stand for having a third party in the relationship, she wanted someone who was fully "here," she wanted what was possible between them to have a chance, etc., etc. Each statement was accompanied by another blow. She was physicalizing, and discharging, energy that had not moved since her childhood. When all the rage was exhausted, Angela was sobbing, but said she finally felt "clean inside, like everything had been cleaned out." It was a catharsis.

She insisted that they go to see the other woman, whom she had never met. She surprised herself by walking in and saying: "Fuck him or leave him alone." The friend, who was coming down off a drug high, protested that she didn't want this, all she wanted was someone to drink with and talk over the spiritual ideas that interested them both. To Angela's amazement, she found herself offering Bach Flower remedies to help with the withdrawal and suggesting counselling help. They talked for four hours.

Her partner made one or two more visits, but somehow the energy had gone out of the situation. He went into a successful treatment program for his alcoholism. Angela, who had already worked extensively on her mothering issues, went back into therapy and started to deal with the "absent father" who had emerged. (And she, too, had Sekhmet as her "inner guide" for the work. The Sekhmet archetype appears for many women regardless of whether they know her story.) Angela began to work as a drug and alcohol counsellor "to put something back." The spiritual friend was in and out of several clinics for her addictions, with little success. She lived out the disintegration of the Pluto transit, but somehow never made it to the transformation. From time to time she would phone asking for "the only person who understands what I'm going through." One day he was not available. "Never mind," she said to Angela, "you'll do instead." When Angela reported the conversation to her partner, he didn't say anything. But he did not visit again. Angela and her partner now have a strong, mutually supportive relationship that has stood the test of time.

THE VALE OF SOULMAKING

In the preceding chapters we have seen a great deal of the pain and anguish of the Hades Moon. At this stage, you will no doubt be asking yourself whether there is anything positive about this aspect at all, and why it is associated with so much emotional trauma. Well, the answer is that there is a great deal of positive and constructive energy connected with this Moon. Nonetheless, it does seem as though this chthonic contact acts as a crucible for the soul.

If we look at it in karmic terms, it is as though all those things that were not finished, or were avoided, or were endlessly repeating patterns are picked up once again with great intensity. This is not as a punishment, but so that the incarnating soul simply has to deal with the issues—in other words, to evolve. The pain and anguish come first, compelling people with the Hades Moon to go deep into themselves to find their authentic self. It is a catharsis, a purging of the soul. When the breakthrough has been made, the insights gained, then it gives an added dimension to life—and to consciousness. Such breakthroughs are usually accompanied by a spiritual awakening, an entry into a different mode of consciousness. If the spiritual awakening does not happen, then we will fall back into the instinctual realm once again and the karmic wheel will turn until we again have to face these issues.

As we have seen, breaking out of the pattern, letting go of mother or child, dealing with unresolved rage and resentment, remembering our isolation and fragmentation, are all archetypal and universal experiences. They cross time and space, and cultural boundaries. In chapter 8 we will explore the myth of Isis and Osiris, the death and resurrection mystery, a myth that is very pertinent to the Hades Moon. Isis is a Moon goddess, but she is also a foreshadowing of the mature Persephone. She is the magical, "wisdom" part of the Moon, the part of the archetype who has experienced it all before, who is cyclic and creative. Her sister Nepthys is the much more emotional and instinctual side of the Moon. Together they are an emotional wholeness which can evaluate before acting rather than being totally caught up in the feeling of the moment. Osiris, the conscious ego, together with his dark twin Set, the unconscious shadow, can be looked on as one of the former incarnations of Pluto. (The Egyptians differentiated between the bright face of the creative, life-renewing side of the Pluto energies and the destructive, death-dealing part of the archetype.)

There is a sub-plot to this myth, which it would be relevant to look at here. Isis and Osiris have a son, Horus: the divine child. Horus was conceived after Osiris' death. Isis brought her husband back to life just long enough for him to impregnate her. In this ancient Egyptian myth, which spanned at least three thousand years, the Sun, Moon, and dual Pluto dance in an intimate quadrille of death and renewal. We see the death of the Sun each evening, and the cyclic appearance and disappearance of the lunar Isis. But within this, there is a division and distinction between different manifestations of the Sun, i.e., consciousness. Horus is the new, young solar principle, Ra the old solar lord. Horus is "the lofty spirit of aspiration" and Set is "what drags it down or tries to oppose it,"[2] the shadow. In other words, this is also part of the duality of Pluto, Horus being that part of Pluto that is aiming for transformation, and Set that which sabotages it. The story of Horus is an allegory for the development of the different modes of consciousness and of the self. He is also the divine child in us all. Horus symbolizes spirit becoming manifest on the physical level—consciousness of self. "Set is unevolved desire, Horus evolving desire."[3] Horus is having a lesson in using and controlling power. Horus and his shadow, personified by his uncle, Set (animal vitality and unspiritual matter, chaos and death), battle out the succession to Osiris, the fertility god who has been sacrificed for the collective. These are initiation rites. The adolescent Horus seeks to challenge the energy of the Sun god Ra "the source of eternal creativity, of self-generating and self-renewing spirit,"[4] who has allied himself with Set, death and decay. Horus must integrate and transmute the negative power of Set, his own violent libidinal Plutonian energy and utilize the light of the Sun to create himself anew. In so doing, Horus experiences blinding and defeat. He is pushed to look inside himself. "Horus comes to life . . . in the pit of the netherworld. That is where inspiration begins."[5] What he has to overcome and integrate are the shadowy, instinctual forces of Pluto and the Moon. He takes on many of the turbulent and violent attributes of his uncle but is eventually transformed to take his place in the solar barque. When Horus is triumphant, he captains the solar barque across the heavens and through the Underworld (the unconscious). He is captain of his own ship, freed from the controlling forces of the past. He has emerged from the undifferentiated consciousness of the collective, the instinctual realm, and attained individual self consciousness.

Notwithstanding, before he can deal with Set and Ra, Horus has to confront his maternal history. He is the product of a one-parent family and son of a devoted mother who fought tooth and nail for his survival. The bonds with Isis are extremely strong. It is Horus' relationship with his mother which most concerns us here. As part of his battle with his Set, he cuts off Isis' head, and rapes her (that is, takes her feminine energy for himself thus reconnecting to his anima). This is the violent separation between mother and son, the cutting of the ties that bind them together. It is necessary for Horus to find his own self, but it also releases the shape-shifting Isis into a new phase of her being. As Alison Roberts explains:

> The necessary, if brutal, rupture between Isis and her raging beast of a son means that Isis too is transformed . . . She is no longer solely a "Mother" concerned with the needs of her son. . . . She has been made to relinquish that part of her maternal instinct which prevents growth in her son, and in doing so, both mother and son have been given the possibility of new life.[6]

Having broken free of his mother, Horus goes on to vanquish Set. Set is not killed. He is metamorphosed; the shadow is integrated. He takes his place in the solar barque to protect Ra—consciousness—from his enemies. Thoth, the wise and magical Moon god, restores Isis to life. Later, mother and son are reconciled, but have a new relationship to each other. Cosmic order has been restored, the fragmented self has become whole, but the destruction which preceded it was a necessary process:

> The Moon Eye had to be shattered, to go to pieces in the struggle, before it could be recreated and made whole again. Importantly, too, its loss and subsequent restoration were extended to other fragmentations in which an equalization of parts was relevant. . . .[7]

In other words, order and chaos, destruction and creation, aggression and beneficence, illumination and ignorance, expansion and entropy, individual consciousness and the collective unconscious, instinct and reason, eros and thanatos are all brought together and balanced within the one being. The tension of the opposites is held and healed. No longer is there any chance of creation running amok, nor will destruction get out of hand. The collective unconscious will no longer rise up and take over. The power is finely balanced and can be utilized as needed. The soul has integrated all the facets of consciousness and become whole.

THE DESCENT INTO THE UNDERWORLD

When I was contemplating this book, Jayn Ingrey (see chapter 9) told me how her mother, Judy, had dealt with having cancer. Cancer is, of course, one of the gateways into Hades. As with all serious illness, it takes you deep inside yourself to face your own mortality, and it can be where you find your immortality. Not everyone who has a Hades Moon will suffer from cancer, but many do. In the Western world, it, and death, are two of the great taboo areas of life left to face. When confronted with these two "no-go areas," the Hades Moon imparts a particular kind of courage that comes from knowing, on a deep level, that the soul can survive.

Dis-ease: A Crucible for the Soul

Attitude is everything. Some people—rarely those who have the Hades Moon, unless the Moon is in Pisces—simply fold up, feel like a victim, and allow everything to happen to them. Other people fight the disease furiously, harnessing all their willpower. Some go with the flow, allowing the experience to take them where it will. Many Hades Moon people intuitively believe that such an illness is either a learning experience, or a karmic one, or both. This Moon has the strength to overcome the "dis-ease" that underlies such an illness, but it also has the courage to surrender to the process when this is more appropriate. As I believe attitude plays an enormous part in how people recover from life-threatening illness, I spoke to Judy. She is an extraordinarily strong woman: Virgo Sun, Moon in Aries square Pluto in Cancer, a typical Jewish mother who lives for her children and her husband, without totally overpowering them. When Judy was 40 she discovered she had a lump in her breast. It was exactly six weeks before her son's bar mitzvah. The transiting Moon was conjunct her natal North Node sextile Pluto. Transiting Pluto was inconjunct her natal Moon. Her progressed Moon was on her natal Ascendant conjunct Mars and Mercury. She says for those six weeks she did not want to know one way or the other. She did not worry, she simply put it out of her mind. All that mattered to her was that her son should have his special day.

At the bar mitzvah, she showed the lump to her brother-in-law who was a doctor. He sent her to hospital on the day the transiting Moon in Scorpio conjuncted her South Node. On the day of her operation, the transiting Moon was conjunct her natal Saturn and inconjunct natal Pluto. The doctors had asked for permission to perform an exploratory operation and, if appropriate, do a mastectomy. When she awoke from the anaesthetic, a nurse told her she had had her breast removed. She says it did not bother her in the least. Her family background was such that an aunt had had a similar operation, but this was never talked about. It was "the worst thing in the world that could happen to a woman." Judy was determined to treat it another way. It was what had had to be; she surrendered to the process and did not allow fear to overtake her.

While she was in hospital she "bucked everyone else up." Her positive attitude was such that one woman actually asked Judy to tell her husband that she, too, had had a mastectomy because the woman could not face telling him herself. Judy's operation was followed by radium treatment—appropriate for a Plutonian illness. What can burn and cause disease, can also heal when used wisely. Judy says this was the worst part. She could not wash and the irritation was terrible. She then spent three months at home feeling physically weak but mentally she was very calm. From then on she felt extremely well. A year later she had to return to hospital to have a lump removed from under her arm. After that she had no further trouble.

When I asked Judy, twenty-five years later, what had helped her to get over her time in Hades, she said it was something inborn, an inner strength and a positive attitude of mind. Although she was not a religious person, she had not been afraid. Indeed, she wondered why people were so frightened of cancer. She felt that the experience had brought her closer to her family. Her powerful motivation for living was that she wanted to see her daughter married and her grandchildren grow up. I felt that, with her Hades Moon, she was fearless when entering Hades realm, her natural home. This was what gave her her strength.

As we have seen, the Hades Moon can have a strong "death wish," a desire not to be in incarnation at all. My friend Mac (figure 15 on page 199) whom we have met several times throughout this book, felt recently that he had done all that he had to do, that his time on Earth was over. With his Cancer Sun and no place to call home, he was suffering from a dis-ease of the soul. He had also been diagnosed as suffering from manic depression as he had "gone over the top" several times. To my eyes, he seemed rather to be in the grip of out-of-control psychic experiences (the collective level having broken through) which he did not want to channel into a constructive pathway, nor would he accept that they were inappropriate (see chapter 8). Having been clairvoyant for most of his life, he was used to "his voices," but of course orthodox doctors assumed that he was suffering from paranoid delusions—especially when he started talking about world conspiracy theory. So, he had spent a few years in and out of psychiatric hospitals and the drugs they had given him had exacerbated the situation (a typical response of a 6th house Pluto-Mars placement). With no family, his friends all scattered, and living in half-way houses himself, he yearned to go back to "Spirit" (which he called his true home). He felt he would better continue his evolution elsewhere.

Mac had been a heavy smoker for years and quickly developed lung cancer. He believed that his karma was such that this was an experience he needed to have to clear past negativity. He had strong past life memories of being a powerful Jesuit, someone who had abused and misused power to achieve what he wanted—a memory which had been supported by the regression experience of a woman friend who knew nothing of his belief but who saw him as a "very frightening black-robed figure with powerful, piercing eyes. He just has to look at me to make me do what he wants." Mac had often said that his healing work in this present life was to make reparation for the Jesuit life, but he felt something more was needed.

Mac came to the conclusion that he had to embrace his pain. He had abused his body quite considerably in this present life and now needed to feel compassion for his body and what it was going through. What could also have helped him was to see his body as himself, but this he could not do. He was strongly polarized between his spiritual self and the body that he used but did not really inhabit. As he had had several traumas in this present life, not to mention his previous lives, he seemed to be suffering from "soul loss." He had become fragmented. This was reflected in both his mental and spiritual state. In the past we had retrieved several soul fragments and he had taken flower essences for years to heal his emotional dis-ease, but he had never really integrated all the different parts of himself into a coherent whole. He always wanted to escape through his Pisces Ascendant into the spiritual realm. He was like a homing beacon for lost souls from the astral plane and suffered several attachments, particularly when he "went manic." However, this was not necessarily a negative experience. We cannot judge from the viewpoint of Earth what is happening on a spiritual level, and it seemed that he was working with these lost souls on another level, a level which, unfortunately, so disrupted his earthly life that from time to time he lost all contact.

Paradoxically, as he became physically weaker, so he became much stronger spiritually. His Hades Moon energy had carried him through an earlier cancer, which he had fought with willpower (Mars conjunct Pluto square Saturn and Jupiter), visualization, spiritual healing, and deep work on himself. But, in his healing work he had been drawing some particularly dark energies from those with whom he came in contact. What he failed to do was transmute this energy at the conscious level, nor did he clear the energies from incursions which happened without his knowledge (such as when he was "out of it" on drugs, prescribed or otherwise). With a Pisces Ascendent, he acted like a psychic sponge, soaking up all the dis-ease around him. He was also suffering from his own inner dis-ease as well. Now, he no longer wished to fight that dis-ease.

With Chiron conjunct his North Node and Pluto trining itself and sextiling his natal Moon, he began to consciously practice Tibetan "transmutation" to release any remnants of his own negative karma, and also to help humankind deal with its pain. In a relaxed state, he would feel his own pain, having compassion and love for what he was going through. Then he would let himself become aware of all the people around him (he was in a hospice) who were going through that same pain with their own cancers. He would picture the pain leaving them. Then he would draw their pain into himself as dark smoke which went into his spiritual heart center. There, through love and compassion, he would transmute this pain into spiritual energy which he would send back to them for healing. In doing this his own spiritual and karmic dis-ease was healed.

TRANSMUTING THE PAST

The drawing in and transmuting another's pain comes naturally to the Hades Moon. It is not always done consciously, as we shall see, and may be a deeply cathartic experience, as Barbara's experience shows:

Being born during the war it was inevitable that my father would go away while I was a child. My mother began a relationship with a G.I. with whom, I am told, I had a very very close rapport. When he contracted VD, it was passed to my mother who, in fear of passing it to me, wrote to my paternal grandmother and asked her to bring me up (her own mother was an alcoholic and so deemed unsuitable). After a short time, I was reclaimed by my mother—who came to fetch me back accompanied by a policeman of all things [Barbara's Moon is in authoritarian Capricorn]. My father was informed of all that was happening by his mother, and he duly received special leave to deal with the situation. As my mother was now pregnant by the American, a divorce was granted and a Court Order made for my return into my father's custody.

All this I eventually found out when I traced my mother forty-odd years later. She also told me of my reluctance to go back to my paternal grandmother's house. (At that time I had no recollection of any of the events.)

I was taken to live with my grandmother as my father's work took him away a great deal, and eventually he moved down south to live permanently while I stayed with his mother [So, as well as not being allowed to see her mother, Barbara also had an absent father.]

During my life I formed several relationships, some of which led to marriage, but all of them failed. Outwardly I was very strong and confident, but I now recognize my constant need and "testing" of my partner and my friends. When I attended a regression course, I re-experienced the moment my mother took me to my grandmother for the last time. I must have been about 3 (when her progressed Moon had come to exact inconjunction with natal Pluto). It was emotional, painful, especially the recognition of my protests being hopeless as she left me there. I could feel her pain as she left me, but there was nothing she could do, as she had been ordered [by a Capricorn au-

*thority: the Court] to leave me. From that age on, I was afraid of the unknown. I be-
haved as though I had no choice over anything, other people shaped my life. I projected
all my pain onto anybody and anything. I was desperately needy. After the regression,
I changed, but I cannot put into words what has happened. I feel more accepting and
more understanding of other people now.*

*Recently I watched a program called "The Dying Rooms" about the aban-
doned girl children in China. Although it was tragic, I was able to be detached enough
to endure the harrowing scenes. Only at the end, when I saw the girl called Mai Mei
(No Name) who was deprived of food, water, light, and human contact, and upon
whose death there was denial of her existence, did I feel it. Suddenly I was gasping for
breath and distraught, feeling the full pain of abandonment.*

*I rushed for help to a mediumistic friend [who, interestingly enough was not in
and so she had to stay with the pain until the next day]. It was explained to me that
in feeling and recognizing the pain I recognized my own abandonment and the abandonment of those children. In doing so, I helped to transmute the energy. (It has taken
over fifty years to do so.)*

Not surprisingly, Barbara has a wide opposition from Pluto in Leo to the Moon in
Capricorn. When she came to the regression workshop (on her Pluto trine to natal Pluto, Pluto being her chart ruler), she missed the introductory session, prefer-
ring to spend the evening with her new manfriend (the transiting Moon was on her
Descendant). I had warned her this might put her outside the group. She laughed
and said: "I've been the outsider all my life." When she arrived, she fell immediately
into the "lost little girl" and was extremely demanding of my attention. Indeed, I
felt like I had a very needy small child clamped to my left nipple all the time. It was
clear that she needed to go back to when her mother left her, but it had to unfold
in its own time. Eventually, when the transiting Moon in Cancer was opposing her
natal Moon, she found the place where she had left so much of herself. (She described it afterward as "when I fragmented.") She then worked to re-integrate this
part of herself. Then, she had to feel all the feelings she had cut off from for so long.
"The Killing Rooms" was the catalyst and the catharsis for this. When she rushed
to her friend, she wanted to get rid of the pain. But, she had to remember it for as
long as necessary, to feel it within herself.

Now, Barbara is realizing that rather than desperately grabbing at someone out
there to provide what she needs, she has to mother herself. She is a powerful healer
who specializes in working with the remnants of childhood. In keeping with her
Scorpio Ascendant, she travels into some very dark places indeed. She says that she
is often conscious of the mothering energy coming in when she gives hands-on
healing. "It is as though having found it for myself, I can share it in my healing
work with others." In recognizing her own pain, she is able to honor their pain and
join in their transmutation process. She is then able to aid her patients in re-attun-
ing to the universal mothering energy.

MURDER MOST FOUL?

There is something murderous at the heart of the Hades Moon. But it is murder for
a purpose, killing off the old so that something new may form. Horus has to break
free from Isis. Self-awareness has to flower. His adolescent potential has to find its

own pathway. Isis, too, has to be released from motherhood so that her psychic and healing abilities can blossom. Nevertheless, this urge may become twisted and compressed into a different course. Those with the Hades Moon may become stuck in the fascination of death, rather than breaking through into a new way of being. The urge to destruction may arise out of the collective and take over. Both physical and soul murder can result. Not all murderers will have the Hades Moon, but a significant number do.[8] The aptly named Billy the Kid, who killed his mother and many others besides, had a doubly Hades Moon, for instance. Not all homicides take place on a physical level. As we have seen, a mother who will not let go her child murders his soul just as surely as if she had plunged a knife into his breast.

The vast majority of killings take place in the home by someone known to the victim. They are the result of a moment's breakthrough of the shadow energies, a snapping of the bounds of convention, a plunge into the jealousy and rage of Pluto. These are the murders that are founded in personal rejection, animosity, a sudden flare up of hatred, an uprising of the shadow. But there are other murders that are a reflection of primal angst, of the killing instinct run wild. It has been said that serial killers are constantly trying to resurrect themselves anew (Billy the Kid's Moon was in regenerative Scorpio), that the murders they commit are somehow a Plutonian purging of the past. And yet, serial killers can be seen to be compulsively playing out a fixed pattern the origins of which are buried deep in the past.

To any victim of homicide, and the victims' family, the murderer is acting out a Plutonian role, pulling them deep into Hades, a place where transformation is possible. At the same time, the murderer, too, is plunging into Hades. If conventional religion is to be believed, the murderer will be consigned to hell. If reincarnation theory is correct, he or she will be called upon to make appropriate and sufficient reparation for the deed, which does not mean being murdered in turn. If we look at the karmic root of murder, it is unlikely to be the "eye for an eye" scenario of a murder victim then killing his tormentor. There have been instances where a murder's victim has come back as his or her child—or parent. There may be deeply convoluted karmic reasons behind the act. It may be that, through what seems to be the most heinous of crimes, a lesson is being offered to those who are pulled into Pluto's realm. The answers may not be worked out in one lifetime. Although forgiveness is possible, it is quite likely that another lifetime with the murderer making some kind of reparation will be necessary before it is resolved.

Murder may also be a deeply symbolic act carrying an archetypal enactment of a collective urge or a personal compulsion. It can be projected onto a person who "acts out a role," something which may seem almost preordained, i.e., Plutonian fate. It may even be a sacrifical act on behalf of the collective—as in ancient religious sacrifice, or an act of personal redemption. A participant on one of my workshops, Cornelia (4th-house Scorpio Moon conjunct the IC and Mars), shared with us her experience with her son David (Aries Moon on the 12th house cusp exactly quincunx Pluto in Virgo and sextile Venus and Neptune in Scorpio to form a Finger of Fate, the outlet point for which was the North Node conjunct the IC in Libra):

1991 was a very difficult year, to say the least. It began promptly with David killing his close friend and landlady on the 4th January in the wee small hours of the morning. Her body was badly mutilated. A great deal of anger had gone into the killing.

At his trial, the verdict was diminished responsibility. It has not been verified that he was schizophrenic but he had pre-crime similarities. As the lady was my age, I have quietly worried that it might have been "something" against myself. Later in the year, it was discovered I had a tumour in my right kidney which proved malignant, but fortunately removing it has cured me of cancer.

In Chinese medicine, the kidney is the organ that carries fear. The right side of the body is the masculine side. So, the cancer could well have been her fear for her son manifesting physically. It may also have had to do with her overwhelmingly powerful and controlling husband. (She has the Sun conjunct a 12th-house Pluto, her karmic pattern would be to project her power onto men, and at some point in the present life to have to face her need to regain her own power.) To have the cancer removed and the dis-ease healed could well have been symbolically clearing something she had been carrying for some time (most probably back into a previous life). Dreadful though it was, the murder was cathartic.

After some months in a high security hospital, David made remarkable progress with medical help and today I feel I have my son returned to the land of the living.

She went on to give something of David's background and we can see the reflection of the Hades Moon in his birth:

One of the karmic factors was that I didn't want David—I already had a baby of nine months [karma can accrue from the present life as well as a previous one]. Birth control wasn't allowed by his father, not that I was aware what to do about it at that time. I was emotionally immature and married to a very strong Taurean man twelve years older. I had four of my five sons within the first seven years, plus two miscarriages. At birth, I was disappointed David was not a girl, having a son already.

He was an induced birth, by some six days and against my will. I cried in protest and trembled physically [which can indicate that past life trauma is being triggered] through the one hour twenty minute birth.

My husband and I separated in 1977. David soon became involved with the Moonies. He was with them for several years and after leaving was never the same— sort of lost. By the time it was realized he needed medical help, he had disappeared and "locked" himself away with her and the rest is gruesome. I have a huge lump in my throat at the moment.

The experience propelled her into astrology. She needed to understand what was going on. The astrology group felt that it was something highly karmic and preordained. The workshop Cornelia attended with me was on karmic astrology. After the workshop she wrote to me:

I love David, obviously, though I am very sad, and it was all very distressing, well frightfully traumatic! At the moment I feel less blameworthy, as his mother, than before this past weekend and I hope the emotion lasts awhile longer!

We had talked at the workshop about Hades Moon issues, including the mothering side of things and David's anticipation of a "devouring mother," as he was so tuned to that archetype from his past experience of mothering. We could see that Cornelia's initial rejection of him, or what might be construed as rejection, fitted perfectly into his expectation. So, she was providing exactly the maternal ambience he needed. Cornelia's fear was that it was a "surrogate murder," that his angst was really with her, and not the woman who was murdered. With that Neptune-Moon inconjunct, he would never see his mother clearly and could well project his issues with the archetypal mother onto her—and anyone else who could provide a hook to hang them on. But equally Cornelia could blame herself without cause. We had also looked at how a small incident could trigger the enormous rage of the Hades Moon, something out of all proportion to whatever had been said, and which usually indicated that a past life trauma was being activated. Unfortunately we did not have David's lady friend's birth data so we were unable to look at the synastry between murderer and victim. But we could look at the interaction between David and his mother, and at the transits at the time, which would be reflected in the external events.

Cornelia's North Node is conjuncted by David's Sun, her Saturn conjuncts his South Node. This is an old karmic interaction which will feel very familiar. With that Sun-Node connection, he may well feel like a "soulmate," especially as her Moon is conjuncted by his Neptune and his Moon is conjuncted by her Saturn. When the murder happened, transiting Saturn was opposite Cornelia's Sun, and the transiting Sun was conjunct David's Saturn. The transiting South Node was on Cornelia's Sun. This was a karmic event. David's Moon is trine Cornelia's Pluto, so she carries some of the devouring mother archetype for him, but its effect is more gentle. It did not indicate a previous devouring mother experience between them, so she might well have been helping him to heal his ancient pain around being mothered. With an each-way repeating Neptune-Moon contact, indicating a very close, idealized past life mothering experience with her, he may well have idolized Cornelia and projected the "bad mother" out there onto someone else, someone who had to be "killed off" as she represented a part of himself that he had violently rejected, and which then turned back on him and overwhelmed him. It was a literal acting out of what could have been an inner, psychological process of integration and resolution of an ancient pattern.

While this is an horrific act, from the soul-evolution perspective it may be just what he needed to learn. To know that he could "kill off" something he needed to break free from would be enormously liberating. In my experience, *very occasionally*, two souls will agree to come back into a situation like this in order that one of the souls can learn a lesson that has perhaps been locked into (and struggled with) through many previous incarnations. So, the woman who was murdered may actually have agreed to this before the incarnation took place. (That David healed so quickly could be an indication that this was indeed a catharsis for him.) In the greater scheme of things, what seems to be an extreme act that accrues huge amounts of "bad karma" may be exactly right for that soul at that particular time. David is at the stage the young Horus is when he beheads his mother. He has stepped into violent power, but the act of murdering his "mother" tames and transforms the energy. David may find that, like Horus, he becomes imbued with new life. Indeed, having suffered soul loss with the Moonies after the breakup of his parents' marriage, he regained his soul within the environment of a high security hospital after the murder and, like Horus and Isis, was reconciled with his mother. When people have suffered soul loss, another person can then "hook in" to that vulnerable lost part of the self and take yet more soul—psychically vampirizing them (a Plutonian act). This woman may have been powerfully controlling, or acted the little girl. Either of which would trigger the archetypal rage which had been so long suppressed. Whether or not this was the case, we cannot say for sure. Given the transits, it is likely that David's ladyfriend was acting in such a way, and the murder may have been the only way his disturbed mind could seize control back. It was his first step in taking back his self.

Cornelia, too, found herself. Like the naive young Persephone, she had given away a great deal of herself in her marriage. She, too, had suffered soul loss and needed to regain her true self. The murder was a catharsis in which she had to face her deepest most unconscious fears, but she had a deeper trip into Hades to come, the confrontation with her cancer. Its removal taught her that she could excise what was, on the inner level, killing her. Transformation was possible. A born survivor, her Scorpio Moon knew that it could go down into the depths to find there the insights she needed, not only for her own healing, but those of the people who would then be drawn to her. There was also an enormous lesson for her around mother love and the need to separate the person from the act. She could be horrified by the act, while still loving her son. It was also a huge challenge for forgiveness and unconditional loving (she has a Neptune square Venus, which brings this issue to the fore).

The Hades Moon was particularly strong at the time of the murder. By progression, the Moon had returned to its natal place in Scorpio conjunct the IC in Cornelia's chart. Transiting Pluto was sitting between her natal Moon-Mars conjunction in Scorpio; and transiting Pluto was also squaring the transiting Moon conjuncting her natal Ascendant. David's progressed Moon opposed his mother's natal Scorpio Moon. The transiting Moon was widely conjunct his natal Pluto. The Sun, Uranus, Neptune and Saturn were conjunct his IC. Something was about to erupt. Things were stirring in the depths of the unconscious. Catharsis was imminent. Transformation, although deeply disguised, was afoot.

IN THE PIT

When aspects between the Moon and Pluto or other significant planets are too wide to be considered in orb, a Pluto transit pulls in the connection. If there is an indirect contact, it suddenly crystallizes. In figure 17 (page 216), Anne has Pluto conjunct the North Node of the Moon in Leo opposite Venus widely conjunct the South Node in Aquarius. Venus then inconjuncts the 4th-house Moon in Cancer. A Hades Moon connnection is indirectly fed through Venus. Her Sun trines her Moon and inconjuncts Pluto, forming a pair of "angel's wings" in the chart. In my experience, such a configuration usually implies great potential waiting to unfold.

A Pluto Venus connection often accompanies the Hades Moon, adding yet a further emotional dimension to the issues of abandonment and rejection. I have always referred to this aspect as "the emotional black hole." It takes in all the love, all

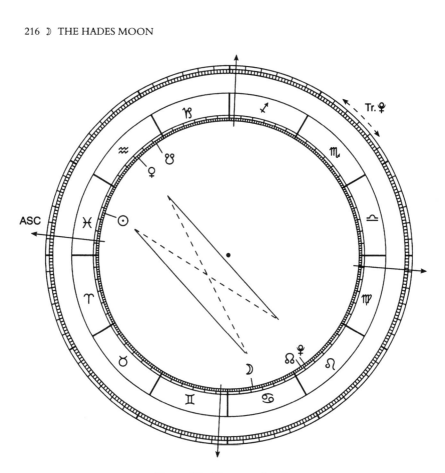

Figure 17. The angel's wings.

the caring it can get, but it never feels loved enough. Its greatest fear is lack of love, and this aspect will manipulate and maneuver to stay in any relationship that is passing for love, be it collusive, abusive, or dependent. Just as with the Hades Moon, there is considerable karma attached to the Pluto-Venus connection. The karmic lesson is to let go of old relationship patterns, to stop looking for love outside oneself, and to go deep within to make the connection to "divine/cosmic" love, a source which can never fail or run out. Once this connection has been made, the insecurity of the emotional black hole is transformed into a powerfully healing love for oneself, and others.

Anne is an extremely intuitive astrologer and now has a clear grasp of just what was going on when transiting Pluto trined her natal Moon and squared her natal Pluto: a transit which was part of a much larger, complex pattern of transits. At the time, however, she simply had to go down into Hades, what she calls "the black pit":

That was definitely the feeling, like being in a black pit and every time I tried to climb up out of it someone was up there with hobnail boots treading on my fingers so I'd fall straight back, and it just went on and on. It felt just like a void. Like swimming in treacle. I just didn't get anywhere. It was all thick and black and I couldn't see in any direction. It was just that horrible feeling, doom. . . .

Her experience was similar to Ronald (chapter 1) in terms of effect, but the underlying cause was different. With Sun in Pisces and the Moon in Cancer, this was a lady who had always been swamped by her emotions and who was symbiotically connected to her family. She had always felt everyone else's pain as her own. The issue for her was how to separate and become her own self. Like Ronald, the trigger was a Pluto transit:

That was the day I met Robert [who has Taurus Moon exactly trine Jupiter/Pluto in Virgo]. In a way, he was my Pluto transit because when the transit finished, he vanished. Transiting Venus was on my natal Pluto-North Node that day. It was all very involved, very karmic, like it was supposed to be happening.

I think that was the point where my life started to crumble. Pluto had got to the middle of my 8th house. It was forming a Grand Trine with my Sun and Moon, and Robert's Descendant was forming a synastric kite. I had a square from Pluto to Venus, then a quincunx to Mars and other transiting aspects. It got highly complicated and I didn't really know what was Pluto and what was everything else.

Anne and her husband, William, had "always rubbed along together." She says it wasn't too bad as "it hung together for almost twenty five years," but this could well be Plutonic and Piscean denial—living with a virtual alcoholic could not have been easy. It may also be the Pluto-Venus tendency to justify staying in what passes for love rather than risking real love itself. When her daughter Frances went off to college the whole family seemed to collapse:

William spent all his nights down at the club. My son was in his bedroom playing records and I used to sit in the kitchen and study astrology every night. Frances had held the family together and when she went, it all fell apart.

And Anne plunged into all the grief of the desolated Demeter archetype:

Two friends of my daughter's, one of whom was Robert, used to come round nearly every night and "unlonely me" as they called it because they knew I missed Frances a hell of a lot. My husband didn't like me doing astrology if it involved going out to a group; he had started to get really jealous—he had transiting Pluto on his Sun and a natal Moon-Pluto quincunx. So it all got very Plutonian, very jealous, very possessive.

I started to go crazy. I think I went mad but no-one realized, the pressure was unrelenting. It built up and built up. I had a breakdown and didn't know. Nobody diagnosed it. It got to the pitch where I was feeling so hemmed in, like in a prison, that something had to give. I wasn't sleeping and I was having fantasies about things and I was literally pacing the garden half the night crying. I moved into the lounge and slept on the floor for months. I had three years of the pressure of it. I think the worst thing about it was fighting it, because I really did hang on to it.

With a chart like hers, it is not surprising that she hung on so long. Both Pisces and Cancer are loathe to let go, and the Venus-Pluto fear is that, if what passes for love is let go of, there will be nothing else. I asked her what it was like having the Moon in Cancer, as this carries the archetype of the Smother Mother and is somewhat similar to some aspects of the Hades Moon:

> When I started doing astrology, I realized that my Moon is extremely strong, because not only is it in Cancer, it is also in the 4th house. Because it is under the layers, not conscious level stuff, I hadn't realized what I was doing. My two air sign children told me I was smothering them to death: I was over-protective. I had to know who they were with, everywhere they went. I took them to school every day right through their school lives. They said, "Oh you're always breaking into what we're doing, you're always treating us like babies, you're always being a martyr." When I read what my Moon represented I thought, "My God, this is me, they are not kidding." So, I did a lot of work on myself then and I let go quite a lot.

She is highly aware of her split between being the smothering mother and the great need she also had for emotional freedom:

> I've got this hugely possessive bit and this very intense bit, but I also want a lot of freedom so it's a fight all the time to balance it out. Venus is 11th house in Aquarius, with the South Node. I think I want to let people be free, but at the same time I want to be part of what they are. I don't actually want to own them; it's more I want them to care about me as much as I care about them. I think it is the Pluto opposition to Venus with the Nodes and then the inconjunct to the Moon, that seems to be most important.

Her ambivalence about emotional relationships was reflected back to her through Robert, her "Pluto transit":

> In 1989 things came to a head with Robert. We fell in love—loads of links between our charts, and he had transiting Pluto right on Venus in the middle of Scorpio. It couldn't really go anywhere because he wasn't old enough (he was just 21 at the time). Early in 1990 he had this big turn around, and decided he couldn't cope with the age gap—Pluto was retrograding over his Venus. He said, "I can't handle this, we can only be friends."

This brought the incredible pressure she was experiencing both internally and externally, to a head. Her painful emotions became too much to bear:

> I was in such a state by then that I raided all the drawers in the house for all the pills I could find. That day there was a lunar eclipse opposite my natal Jupiter, which made the eclipse virtually conjunct Venus, with transiting Pluto widely squaring it. Looking back I don't know if it was a suicide attempt. It was just a case of trying to stop the pain. I just wanted everything to stop and give me a rest because I was so tired with all this Pluto stuff piling up. Whatever way I turned I couldn't see a way out; it was just like a prison. It was the most horrendous month of my life. My mother was des-

perately ill in hospital. I really thought she was going to die. We had a big crisis at work and my job got very rocky. My father was freaking out and I have never got on with him [he sexually abused her when she was 13]. He drove me mad. It was like everything that could break down was breaking down. The pressure just built and that's why I took the pills. But, somehow I survived.

In May Robert said, "Get out because you are not going to survive if you stay." He'd always been the one to say don't leave David [her son]. Now he said, "For the sake of your own sanity, go. I'll stand by you." And I really trusted him. It took me till August to find a room. On the day I moved I had transiting Pluto, which was still trining the Moon, exactly square Venus. That was the day everything ended.

At this point she felt that Pluto had literally stripped away everything:

I had left William. David, my son, didn't speak to me for thirteen months. Robert helped me move, but just never came back. It went from bad to worse because I had nobody. People I had known for twenty-five years, all my neighbors, turned their backs. The job literally did collapse, so I was financially in trouble. Two months after I moved, even the car collapsed. Robert had head injuries in a car crash (which is how I lost my youngest brother) and I couldn't even visit to see if he was okay. That was hell! I just kept telling myself "nothing else can happen, nothing else can possibly happen." I was so down. I just sat in my room and didn't talk to anyone. I couldn't concentrate, the pain was there all the time. That was black stuff, and it colored everything I tried to do. I couldn't block it long enough to do anything else; I was living inside it. I was so miserable. I really did think about suicide then, because it felt that everything had gone, what was the point in going forward. I went to the lowest ebb as they say. I was totally on my own for the first time ever. So really it felt like the Pluto transformation started but didn't actually produce anything to take its place, because I wiped everything out. I waited and waited for the new start but it didn't happen. I didn't know why it was but perhaps it was because Pluto is so slow moving.

About a month after she left home, she went into therapy as the result of a coincidence. She went into the Citizens Advice Bureau for financial advice and came out with a counsellor. At first all she could do was to be with the energy and allow the therapist to mirror back to her what was happening, just like the small beings who were made from the dirt under Enki's fingernails. But gradually she was able to explore all those years of smothering motherhood and the powerful rage that lay behind her relationship with her father:

To start with, I couldn't talk to the counsellor because I thought she was going to judge me and say how evil I am because I have run away from my family, my responsibilities. I thought she'd judge, but she never did. She used to make me talk for about an hour and then she'd take all the bones out of what I said, take away all the rubbish, and just give it back to me and I could see what I'd been saying. It took a couple of months before I opened. I had to go into all the family relationships, how I got on with everyone, what happened, and, oh yes, the Scorpionic and Plutonian stuff I had to deal with was what had happened with my Dad. [She was abused at 13, when her mother was in the hospital having her eighth child. When she tried to tell her mother, the mother refused to listen. Her father was eventually arrested twice for offenses against other girls but never came to trial.] I had buried that for thirty years because I felt I was wicked because I couldn't love my dad, but actually it is because he's not lovable—it took me thirty years to find that out, my God [laughter]. She actually got me to say he's evil, I hated him, he should not have done what he did, and I ended up in a total heap on the floor screaming. But after that I felt I could deal with my father a lot better. I have accepted that I'm never going to like him, but I don't think I should like him now, I don't feel guilty anymore.

Even in the darkest days, she was given a clue as to what was happening, but could only recognize this after it was all over:

During the transit, when things were really black, I meditated to try to find a way out (any way out!). All I was given was a single word which I didn't know and had to look up in the dictionary. It was catharsis. *The dictionary said, "an emotional release in drama or art; the process of freeing repressed emotion by association with the cause, and elimination by abreaction; purgation and cleaning." Yep. Quite an accurate description of the transiting Pluto effect on the poor little sensitive Moon, I think.*

Gradually she came out of the pit, although the seductive pull of the past and how she had been still had a powerful hold:

After that I met a lot of new people. I got into workshops and developing that side of myself, but I bitterly resented that. I just wanted to go back to how I had been and I fought it every inch, which was probably why it was so painful. I didn't want to let go of the past; I didn't feel ready. It was what I valued and it all went.

It has taken a long time to do the rebuilding that I've managed so far. But I'm definitely coming out of it. Other people can see a difference more than I can, especially the people who knew me when I first left home. I must be out of the pit. One of the good things about it is that I went through so much then, it might sound a bit melodramatic but the pain was so bad that I literally just survived it, I didn't conquer it. But I feel like a survivor and I don't think I will feel that bad ever again. If it didn't kill me that time, then I'm strong enough and I'm not frightened. That's a real plus for me because I went through the whole of my life being frightened of something or other, being the doormat type. So it has taught me a lot in that way. I have become a lot more of what I should have been all along.

Anne's deep dark family secret was her abusive father, no doubt a pattern that stretched way back into the past. One of the ways in which such family patterns can be healed is by "telling the secret," another is by confrontation. Anne had tried to tell her mother at the time, but her mother had not wanted to know. So when Anne heard that her father was spending a great deal of time with her 13-year old niece (the age Anne had been when she was abused), it took great courage to warn her sister and confront her father. Having done so, the family secret lost its power. And so did Anne's father. She began to recognize him as a rather pathetic, lonely old man. She still did not like him, but she repaired her relationship to him as her father. She was also able to forgive her mother for abandoning her when she had most needed support. The family dynamic changed.

Anne is now using her extremely powerful psychic gifts to give astrological readings which go beyond the usual dimension. She takes her clients into a healing space where they can accept themselves as they are. As her creative energies expand, she is beginning to think seriously about writing. She has many deep insights to share with her potential readers.

CREATING WITH SOUL

When the Hades Moon energy is worked with consciously, then it is deeply creative but may still bring Plutonian issues to the fore. In its old sense, catharsis was a purging by drama. Sacred drama formed part of the rites of many religions. To watch a Greek tragedy was cathartic. To enact the sacred drama of ancient Egypt purged the soul. To live a myth cleanses the archetype. Sometimes a person may instinctively know that a catharsis is required and this can be woven into life in a creative way.

Sir Arthur Connan Doyle (Chart 15, page 222), who created perhaps the best known figure in literature, the brilliant and eccentric Sherlock Holmes, had the Moon in Aquarius square Pluto in Taurus. His creation, Holmes, was deeply Plutonian and overwhelmingly successful. He, Dr. Watson, and the arch-villain, Professor Moriarty, seemed to have a life beyond the written word to such an extent that there was no space for anything new to emerge. Conan Doyle's publishers, and his public, wanted more, more, and still more of the same. When Conan Doyle killed off his hero there was considerable Mars transiting the 12th-house planets activity in his chart, including a conjunction to Pluto activating the Hades Moon, and his progressed Moon was semi-sextile Pluto. The shock reverberated around the world. It was meant to be a catharisis for his soul—or perhaps a retrieval of his soul, which had been so taken over by this alter ego. Certainly the semi-sextile aspect is one which projects what is going on inside oneself out onto others for them to act out. He needed to kill this part of himself, which had taken on separate life, so that he could regain his own soul.

Notwithstanding, public demand was such that he had to resurrect Holmes. It took an ingenious mind indeed to rescue Holmes from the void into which he had fallen, together with his arch-enemy, the evil Moriarty. Shades of Pluto here in this plunge into oblivion and mist-shrouded deliverance. Holmes' return from the dead is Plutonian, too. He hovers on the edge of consciousness, a mysterious half-seen shade dwelling on the moor who only reveals himself at the last moment to the ever-faithful Dr. Watson.[9]

Like Pluto, Conan Doyle and his alter ego, Holmes, take the reader into some dark places indeed, places with which Conan Doyle was intimately familiar. Sherlock Holmes is a cocaine user, a depressed genius who springs to life only when confronted with a mystery to unravel. But this reflects a side of Conon Doyle which was a closely guarded secret. With his 12th-house Pluto, he, too, had his addictions and depressions, and his own dark secrets. He may have been trying to cathart this side of himself when he killed off his hero. But it was not to be. The

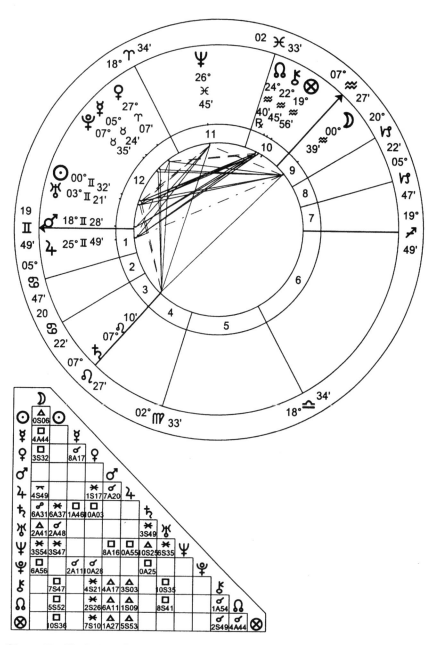

Chart 15. Sir Arthur Conan Doyle. Born May 22, 1859, GMT 04.55, 55N57, 003W11. Placidus houses. Data from AA Database. Source: birth certificate.

resurrection of Holmes was the start of the end for his creator. Sometimes it is like this, a creation takes over and sucks the life from the one who gave him birth. Holmes, Watson, and Moriarty became archetypal figures in their own right. Over a hundred years later, "Holmesmania" still exists. It has become a cult with special societies dedicated to Holmes in New York, England, and other parts of the world.

Conan Doyle had another Plutonian interest, one which was much less well received by the public. He was a founding member of a society pursuing psychical research. He was a psychic, and yet deeply rational and scientific man in accordance with his Aquarian Moon; he was fascinated with life after death. It was a virtual obsession which started with the death of his son from wounds incurred in World War I. He spent much of the latter part of his life promoting the cause of Spiritualism. Perhaps he was hoping that, after his own death, he too would find new life.

SEARCHING FOR SPIRIT

Many addictions originate in feeding or soothing the body when it is the soul which is aching.

—Caitlin Matthews[10]

We briefly met Hathor, the goddess of music and intoxication, in chapter 5. As we saw, she is the "light, bright" face of Sekhmet, the propitiated, beneficial face of rage. Alison Roberts, who has studied Hathor extensively, says that to Hathor belong gifts of radiance, fertility, love and sexual attraction.[11] She is rather like an Egyptian Aphrodite (Venus) and yet she has an affinity with the Hades Moon through that part of her which is connected with the Underworld. She also partakes of Neptune. In her honor a festival of drunkenness was held each year to honor the return of the life-giving waters of the Nile. In this respect she is the Moon with her attunement to the great life cycle of birth, maturity, and death. She is one of the goddesses of transformation. She can be "wild and terrifying" and then of "radiant, shining beauty." Through ritual, music, intoxication, and trance dance, Hathor led people into a unity with the bright spirit of the gods. They experienced the numinous through an expanded state of consciousness. To achieve this state, they surrendered control to the goddess.

As Matthew Fox says, addictions come from looking for spirit in the wrong place—"in the wrong bottle" as a friend of mine says. Addiction arises out of spiritual emptiness; a yearning for something other, for the numinous radiance that filled the worshippers at Hathor's altar. The "drug of choice" strips away control, but, all too often, it also renders the person senseless, unconscious, adrift from life. For addicts of all kinds, a catharsis is needed, a merging into the sacred drama of Hathor to restore the spirit. Events happen which take the addict down into the Underworld, down into Pluto, Osiris, and Hathor's realm. This is where the healing can begin.

While working as a drug and alcohol counsellor, I had access to over 1500 birth dates for addicts. I did not have birth times, so the research I could do was limited. However, from a noon-chart base, over 85 percent had major Moon-Pluto aspects and virtually all had Neptune-Mars aspects. This is not surprising as Pluto has such a compulsive quality to it and Neptune is the great escaper. Richard Idemon feels that the Moon is one of the key planets underlying addiction, and that it becomes addictive when unfulfilled emotionally,[12] especially on the inner child level. He goes on to explain that "Moon Pluto gives a deep hunger which can lead into addictive forms of behavior. People with Moon-Pluto aspects need to live a deeply erotic life, and since most of us are not programmed to live this way, they look for some other means to deaden their hunger or ease their pain."

The center I worked for also had quite a large number of family members and partners in counseling, and here again the Hades Moon showed up strongly, often, but by no means always, in a more "gentle" aspect. It was as though the addict acted out the addiction for the family and/or partner. In other words, there was a degree of projection going on. Of course, in many cases, the addiction was one of the family secrets that passed on down through the generations, so that whoever showed up in counseling could be seen as the lineage-breaker for that family. Moon-Pluto aspects, and Venus-Pluto aspects were extremely common in cases of codependency where the partner or parent could be seen as "addicted to the addict," sharing many of the emotional issues that lie behind alcoholism, etc. In codependency, the core self is surrendered to meet the needs of someone else. Boundaries are sacrificed as is self-image and self-need.[13] And yet, as Linda Schierse Leonard[14] points out, a co-addict can be "a martyred wife, devouring the partner through control, guilt and judgments and putting the partner down as weak willed." A typical manifestation of the Hades Moon. We must always bear in mind that addictions come in many shapes and forms, and do not relate solely to alcohol or drugs.

Clarissa Pinkola Estes, a Jungian analyst and storyteller, has defined addiction as "anything that depletes life while making it 'appear' better."[15] Shamaness Caitlin Matthews says, " Addictions and compulsive behaviors spring up to fill a vacuum. . . ."[16] Astrologer Richard Idemon sees addictions as "pain corks," an "attempt to deaden hunger and pain,"[17] while Jungian analyst Marion Woodman[18] views addiction as a form of abandonment of the self. Dr. Bruce Lloyd, a human relations counsellor, states that: "Addiction is the result of a split or separation of an individual from the blueprint he carries within his soul."[19]

In these definitions we can begin to catch a glimpse of why addiction should be so closely linked to the Hades Moon. They give the soul something to fill its empty spaces, a "false god" to subdue psychic yearning. They overcome feelings of alienation and abandonment in the spurious bonhomie of the alcohol, drug, or chocolate haze. They are a substitution for nurturing, a surrogate mother perhaps. Or, they may be an attempt to kill off the voice of the overwhelming Mother.

When I asked Lincoln (chapter 3) why he had taken to drink and drugs, he said:

For me, it seemed to offer freedom. Even as a teenager, I had no desire to grow up and join in the semi-detached 9–5 world. I couldn't see the point. I wanted something more. I needed to find something to save me from the coma of endless days. Everyday life seemed shallow and pointless. Something in me yearned for strangeness, for intensity. When I wrote songs and played them, I felt alive, really alive. But then I had to go back to the everyday world. But when I found drugs and alcohol, particularly

amphetamines, I felt like I'd found what I was looking for. I took off and I felt like I
could go on forever. I wanted to go on forever. And I liked the way the drugs and al-
cohol disorientated me: I felt free. I felt like the sluice gates were opened and my an-
gels and demons were let out and inspired my songs. Except they were all demons and
the songs were dark and bitter. And, in time, the drugs and alcohol took over and
deadened my creativity.

Today it is a different story: I'm clean and sober. Now there are angels in some
of my songs. And now I've seen that I've got a God-shaped hole in me that only God
can fill.

For Lincoln, his addiction took him close to death. He head-butted a car and was
left for dead in the gutter. He was in intensive care and then in plaster for six
months. As Erich Neumann says: "our time and our destiny . . . strike us in the
face, perhaps also in order to fling us into the void of center, which is the center of
transformation and birth . . . facing death, is inherent in creative transformation."[20]
For some people, the compulsion to face death is obsessively acted out through the
drug of choice as a way of destruction. For others it is a creative act, a way of
touching the spirit:

In a culture that doesn't understand initiation, drugs and alcohol become initiations
for young men. . . . Jim Morrison son of a disengaged father, rebellious, spiritually
hungry for real manhood, sought initiations by Native American Medicine Men in his
visions. Drugs and booze, the tools he ultimately relied upon for initiation, for vision,
for breaking through to the other side, destroyed him.[21]

THE SHAMAN'S SONG

Jim Morrison, lead singer of The Doors, had the Moon in Taurus square Pluto
conjunct the North Node in Leo (Chart 16, page 226). He has become a mythic,
cult figure. He carries the archetype of Pluto and, like Pluto, he is hidden from the
world. His public image is a projection of what his public wants to see. He is a man
who invented a wild, orgiastic performance as a rock-star. He was the embodiment
of the erotic life. But behind that, he had the soul of a poet. "Jim turned language
into mystery, into a priesthood. He was the conjurer, wearing the cloak of the
shaman, weaving a magic carpet of words that soar and sail and swing and fly. He
was constantly a practicer of charms and talismans to help all of us travel to our
metaphoric destinations."[22] He is a modern-day Dionysus, that endlessly recreated
dying and resurrected god, who provides an orgiastic bridge to another world.

Indeed, Morrison patterned his life on the ancient shaman who gets his powers through visions and trance. One of the shaman's functions is to act as the psychopomp who accompanies the dead on their journey into the other world. He
himself travels extensively in that otherworld, to heal and to retrieve fragments of
lost souls. On stage, Morrison would put himself into trance by frenetic movements
and the beat of the music, entering into the shamanistic state with the intention of
providing a catharisis for his audience. Morrison was a Sagittarian, and Sagittarians,
as we know, are on a life-long vision quest. They ask the great universal questions

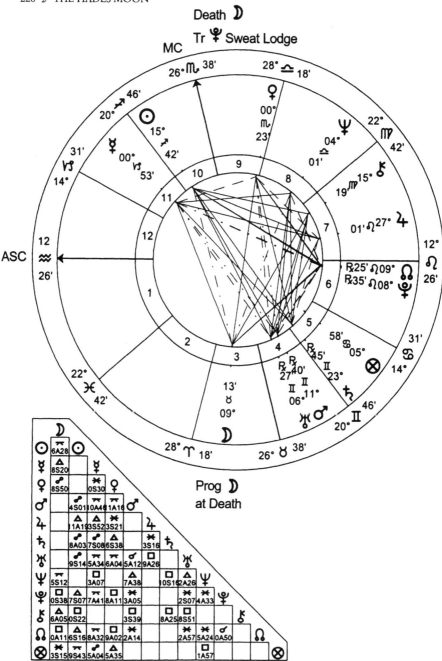

Chart 16. Jim Morrison. Born December 8, 1943, GMT 15.55, 28N05, 080W57. Placidus houses. Data from German Astrologer's Database. Source: birth certificate. Outer wheel shows the Progressed Moon and the Death Moon, and transiting Pluto at the time John Densmore called on Morrison's spirit at the Sweat Lodge in 1985.

of life. As James Riordan and Jerry Prochnicky say in their aptly named biography *Break on Through*, this is the man whose questions of what life and death are all about will never go out of style.

Morrison was the "perfect tragic superstar," a man who had the hubris to challenge the gods. The Doors drummer, John Densmore, said that anyone who came into close contact with Morrison would find himself "under the fringes of darkness."[23] His vision quest took him into the Plutonian places. As he was to find, drugs tend to "blow the mind" in rather a different way to how the term is normally used. We all have psychic gates (or doors) to protect us from incursions from the other world. Shamans and channellers learn how to open and close the door to the otherworld at will. But drugs blow that control; Morrison became open to incursion at any time. He used drugs to travel in the other world, there to find his music. He had always written poetry, but the drugs took him to a different source of creative inspiration. In so doing, he left himself wide open to the instinctual forces of the collective unconscious. He drank for another purpose. Like so many people with the Hades Moon, he was constantly in touch with another dimension of the shamanic world, one of "demons, ghosts, and spirits begging for release." His use of drugs made it impossible to close the door. Frank Lisciandro, a photographer and close friend, says that Morrison drank, not for inspiration, but for peace, to blot out the ceaseless clamor of those denizens of hell.[24] Unfortunately, when he drank, he changed "from angel to devil." A much darker part of his psyche was unleashed, fueled perhaps by those demons of hell (he was raised a Catholic) and maybe by the repressed parts of his own unconscious.

His metaphysical experiences started early in life. When he was about 4, he and his family came upon an automobile accident in which a truck load of American Indians had been hit by a car. They were scattered all over the road. This was the day he discovered death. He said that, seeing with a child's eyes, all he saw were people lying around covered in funny red paint. But, at a deeper level, he could feel the vibrations of the people all around him and realized something serious was going on. Then, as he described it, the souls of one or two of the dead Indians who were "running around, freaking out," just jumped into his soul. He saw himself as a sponge, waiting to absorb it all. To his mind, he was possessed by the spirit of a dead shaman, a shaman who took him to the edge right through his life. The incident gave him a lifelong fascination with death.

The belief that he was possessed by the soul of the shaman shaped his life. He felt this was something he had been called upon to do, a vocation. But he was not an initiated shaman. A shaman goes through death, is dismembered, and then is reborn. No matter how compulsively he lived out his confrontation with death, Morrison had not made the controlled journey into death. Initiation shapes the forces, brings the power under the control of the shaman himself. In Morrison's case, the forces controlled him, the power drove him. He saw the shaman as a scapegoat, someone who could take the projection of other people's fantasies on board and become those fantasies. But, as he perceptively realized, people could also destroy their fantasies by "killing" the bearer. They could release their own psychotic impulses through attacking Morrison. His fans, on the other hand, released their inhibitions and found catharsis through his shamanic onstage performance. He believed he was an exorcist for the collective, but, in the end, the unconscious engulfed him.

And eventually these forces destroyed him. At his death, the Moon was in Scorpio, opposite his natal Moon and forming a Grand Cross with natal Pluto and the Nodes. His progressed Moon had returned to its natal position. Once again, transformation was afoot. Death, at some level, was an inevitable precursor to change. Morrison left an enormous creative legacy behind him in his songs. When his biographers looked at this legacy they said, "He took the fear that accompanies the explosions into freedom . . . and, after first making it even more bizarre, dangerous, and apocalyptic than anyone thought possible, diffused it all by turning everything we were taking so seriously into a big joke midstream."[25] This is the real shaman at work, the trickster who stands things on their head, who turns "reality" inside out.

Typically for such a mythic figure, Morrison's death was shrouded in mystery. The death certificate gave the cause of death as heart failure, but this has been questioned many times. Was it due to a heroin overdose? Or the result of an injury he sustained previously? Had he committed suicide? Was he dead at all? After having been taken to court in Miami for alleged indecent exposure on stage, he had exiled himself to Paris, to write, to reflect, and go within, but seemed to descend into massive depression, aided by alcohol. He wrote to a close friend that he was "standing on the downslope of a dark, angry void." He was hovering at the entrance to Hades. He was approaching that great astrological watershed—the Saturn Return. The time of reassessment of one's life. Did he look inward and find it wanting? Or did he shirk the soul searching? Was he unable to face the vast gulf between his public persona and the man he really was? The monster he felt he had become? Or did he feel it was time to continue the quest someplace else, to make the journey through the Egyptian Duat? We will never know for sure. One thing we do know, the woman who found him, with whom he had had an apocalyptic relationship, said, "For the first time he was at peace."

Five years later, The Doors had a resurrection. Morrison had left behind a recording of poetry made on his 27th birthday, seven months before he died. His producer and recording engineer got together with the remaining members of the band, new music was written, and the final album emerged. *An American Prayer* brought to the public Jim Morrison the poet. An autobiographical exploration, it has words that "devour and liberate." It explores Morrison in his many facets: child, dreamer, libertine, sex-idol, shaman. As the singer/poet Patti Smith says: "[It is] the cocoon of the lord, he is sleeping . . . awaiting the changeling and the elegance of his change."[26] Is Morrison waiting his next metamorphosis, his next manifestation of the creative spirit on Earth?

In a sweat lodge with the poet Robert Bly in 1985, The Doors' drummer, John Densmore, called on the spirit of Jim Morrison.[27] He wanted Morrison to help him understand his death, which had haunted him for thirteen years. Densmore says he was possessed by "the black-leather Lizard King" as he called Morrison, who cast a giant shadow over him. He wanted to get out from under and find his own creative energies once more. At the sweat lodge, one of the participants asked to be healed of his alcoholism. Densmore called on Morrison to "use his knowledge of alcohol, another 'spirit'," to help the man, who was sitting on the other side of the circle. Transiting Pluto in Scorpio was by then opposing Morrison's natal Moon and forming a Grand Cross with his Pluto and the Nodes. It was an opportunity for Morrison to undergo further transformation. Densmore comments that the alcoholic "seemed to get a jolt"—a common phenomenon when a piece of soul is being returned home. Had that old shaman, Morrison, been able to journey to the Underworld to retrieve a part of this man's soul, and in so doing redeem his own? He certainly redeemed John Densmore, who found not only his creative energies again after that sweat lodge, but also his spiritual self.

Many deeply creative people are also addicts of one kind or another. As Linda Schierse Leonard explains in *Witness to the Fire: Creativity and the Veil of Addiction*, "there is a parallel process occurring in the psyche of the addict and the creative person. Both descend into chaos, into the unknown underworld of the unconscious. Both encounter death, pain, suffering. But the addict is pulled down, often without choice, and is held hostage by the addiction; the creative person chooses to go down into that unknown realm, even though the choice may feel destined"[28] (i.e., Plutonian fate). With the Hades Moon, the journey may be compulsive, but the Scorpionic quality of this Moon enables the addict, the shaman, and the newly dead to find Pluto's treasure, and to arise again. To find new life. It is in the depths that we touch our soul: "When the energy of the soul is recognized, acknowledged, and valued, it begins to infuse the life of the personality. When the personality comes fully to serve the energy of its soul, that is authentic empowerment. This is the goal of the evolutionary process in which we are involved, and the reason for our being."[29] The Hades Moon teaches that, when we are in touch with our soul, we find spirit within ourselves, not in a bottle.

WALKING IN THE VALLEY OF THE SHADOW OF EVIL

Paranoia is a standard habit of mind for citizens of the realm.

—Sam Keen[30]

There is something deeply paranoid about the Hades Moon. Paranoid in the sense of suspecting there is more going on than meets the eye, or the ear, or the written word. In the sense of having "knowledge on the side," a knowing that is not intellectual, or even conscious, but which emerges from the depths. Of course, at its extreme, paranoia may be delusions of an enemy being "out to get me," a projection of inner demons out onto a hostile world. The emphasis, and how well it will be handled, will depend on other planetary aspects which support or neutralize the effect of the Hades Moon. Paranoia may also be a way to avoid living life to the full, of evading being fully present to the demands of life, taking refuge in the good self and projecting the "evil" self out-there onto someone else.

When my friend Mac, with his Sun-Mercury-Pluto-Mars conjunction opposing the Moon, flipped, he fought Maggie Thatcher (then Prime Minister of Britain and a woman who has the Moon in Leo semi-square Pluto in Cancer) on the astral plane. She was a perfect hook for his projections as her Pluto opposes his Moon and widely conjuncts his Chiron Sun. He was convinced she was the personification of evil. His energy was flying around his Grand Trine with enormous power, but with no outlet other than the Moon it took him deep into his own unconscious and the shamanic Underworld. No wonder he "went over the top"—aided by a Jupiter transit. He believed that the Conservative politicians were practicing black magic and turned themselves into owls who attacked him in the dark. (A rather interesting metaphor this one. Owls are symbolic of wisdom and the mind in Greek thought, but in Egypt the owl symbolized death and the realm of the dead sun, that Underworld through which the Sun passes at night and which the owl can so easily traverse.) Mac drew on his considerable metaphysical talents, and fought back with arcane ceremonies and much muttering and incantations. It was a cathartic drama of great intensity. Mac liked using candles, and had already "accidentally" set fire to one home. Now there was more than a passing possibility that he would do the same again to the place he was being forced to leave so that it could be renovated as housing for the homeless. It was ironic that the squatters in this section of town were, for the most part, builders who had already worked hard on the houses. Under government policy, they were not allowed to remain.

Mac, not surprisingly, identified with the homeless, especially those who were unemployed, who were turned out onto the streets when the large psychiatric hospitals closed, or who lost their entitlement to state benefit because they were under 18 and "should be at home with their parents" according to the Iron Lady who seemed to have no insight into why the young should have to leave home. In this, she was a typical Hades Moon "mother" who could only see things from the perspective of her own background, a background alienated from Mac and those on the streets. When Mac's somewhat bizarre behavior came to the notice of the police, he was hospitalized. When he came out, Mac practiced forgiving Maggie Thatcher, saying she was his "sister." He made his peace with her for quite a few years. But then, as his death approached he turned his attention to her once more. His "friends in spirit" told him that she, along with anyone else who had not taken up the opportunity of spiritual evolution, would be "consigned to the sun" so that they could not incarnate again. As Mac pointed out there are many other channellers who have said much the same thing. He asked whether we are to assume that they are all mad? Or have they glimpsed a great truth; that we need to purge and burn out all that is outworn and outgrown before we can move into a new astrological age? I would ask: Are they seeing as concrete something which is a metaphysical metaphor? Confusing catharsis with eschatology? Mac believed in the latter.

Mac's experience is an extreme manifestation of the paranoia of the Hades Moon, and may have been more than a little inflated by the other aspects to Pluto. When I speak of the "paranoid Hades Moon," I am focusing more on an everyday sense of something that is just out of sight, hovering over the shoulder, or a vague feeling of something not being quite right. Quite often this is "knowledge on the side," information coming from beyond the five senses, what Thomas Moore calls "an unreflected, uncultivated dark suspicion that there is more going on in the world than we are aware of."[31] This is the stuff of oracles. It is an intuitive *knowing*, but it can be difficult to pick up the message clearly. The language of the unconscious does not communicate with words, and many of these vague feelings come from that deep part of ourselves that has an instinctual knowing—which is why all oracles had their priest, or priestess, to "interpret" for them (something which could of course be much abused). Now, when I start to feel paranoid or "got at," I pay special attention. It is most probably not what it seems, but there will be *something*, some piece of information, some clandestine activity of which I need to be aware. It may be some inner piece of me, but it may well be something in the outside world to which I need to turn my attention. In such circumstances I tend to ask the universe (higher consciousness) for guidance.

When I came under psychic attack[32] (see chapter 5), I became obsessed with finding out what was going on. Close friends began to think I was suffering from paranoid delusions. And then I discovered that a woman who was close to the person I had inadvertently upset, and who was perpetrating the attack, had rung places where I was working to sow seeds of doubt. They had blocked reviews of a book by informing magazines that I had broken trust and used personal, private readings. This was manifestly not the case—I had permission—but it took some time for me to find out what was going on. Once I was aware of it, I could counteract it. But I had been receiving obscure signals from my unconscious for some months before this perfidious behavior came to light.

Then, as time went on, I became aware that I needed to practice metanoia, to turn round and face the darkness within my self once more, to reclaim my projections. Metanoia means "change of mind." I desperately needed to gain a different perspective. Sam Keen[33] says we have to repent of our self-righteousness as an ongoing discipline of the spiritual life. A hard one this, for a proud Leo Ascendant conjunct Pluto and the North Node. I practiced his "game" in which you pretend that everything you say about someone is false (but is true of yourself), and what they say about you is true. As he says, the harsh judgments we make about other people tend to say more about "me" than "them." For me, it was part of an ongoing process of reclaiming my soul. I became aware of just how much of myself I was giving away in my "righteous anger" at this person, and how unaware I was of the mote in my own eye. Catharsis was called for. Forgiving, him and myself, became a priority.

And yet, for the Hades Moon, such paranoid feelings can have great validity. It is just that they do not necessarily belong to this present lifetime. That feeling of being watched, spied upon, can so easily come from a persecution experience in a past life. The Inquisition flourished for a very long time, and there were similar organizations before that. Most people with psychic abilities will have passed through their hands at least once (which is why so many people with the Hades Moon are terrified of using their gifts). It is part of the training process. But we may need to differentiate between then and now. The problem is, deep down in the psyche, time has no meaning. It is all one. But then again, are we ourselves creating this Inquisition? Is a part of us standing in judgment on ourselves, trying to control the way we believe and act? And are there things for which we need to forgive ourselves that we have hidden so deep we can only see it projected "out there"? These things need the incisive eye of Scorpio; the searing glance of Pluto. Then we will forgive, and thank, our enemy who has pointed out this need to us.

The catharsis of the Hades Moon is, then, both a purging and an integration. The shadow energies, all those facets and figures of consciousness we are unaware of rise up into awareness. We have the choice. They can remain projected "out there," in which case the catharsis is empty, devoid of meaning. Or, we can bring them into our Self. We can re-member our soul. We can reconnect to our wholeness, our spiritual purpose, our "blueprint" for being here. When we do this fearlessly, with Plutonian insight, then we gain the spiritual riches that are hidden deep in Pluto's realm.

CHAPTER 8

THE SACRED MOON

To those who create the necessary conditions [the Moon] will draw close and help them to rise to a plane of heavenly wisdom . . . and to become aware of the divine plan which they, as servers of the great Mother, can help to fulfil.

—Joan Hodgson[1]

THE HADES MOON is without a doubt one of the most psychic and meta-physical of the Moons. It is a sacred Moon, a Moon dedicated to a specific purpose. Its links to the old priestess of the mysteries are exceedingly strong. The Moon is intuitive, and may be in touch with other realms, but when the Moon is touched by Pluto, arcane magic is afoot, and magic has always frightened those who do not understand it. This is a Moon that can manipulate powerful energetic forces, so healing is one of its potential skills. Its intense focus makes it unnecessary to be physically present to bring about change. Part of the healer's energy field can travel wherever it is needed to do its work. Distant healing and earth-energy-work are Plutonian attributes; so are soul retrieval and rescue, and inter-life work. Emotional release, regression, and catharsis are also part of this chthonic Moon. With its connections to the unconscious, it is a Moon that can "read" people at a very deep level. A psychotherapist or astrologer with a Hades Moon will know what a client is reaching for long before the client is aware. Attuned as it is to other realms, this is the clairvoyant Moon that can communicate with the "dead," other times, other places.

It is also the Moon with a metaphysical inheritance from other lives, old skills that can be called upon when needed, an intuitive knowing that "just is" and does not have to be learned, a sense of communication and connection to other realms, the ability to see spirits, to interpret dreams and portents, to heal the sick and accompany the dying. All are inherent in this ancient Moon. And all will break through with great intensity at some time in the life of a person with a Hades Moon. It may take a near-death experience, an emotional shock, a catharsis, a moment of sublime consciousness, before connection is made; but for many other people with the Hades Moon it has been there since childhood. It may have gone underground to hide from insensitive adults, but it is waiting to emerge. Psychic abilities of all kinds are a natural expression of the Hades Moon.

PITFALLS OF THE PSYCHIC PATH

The greatest pitfall on the psychic path is undoubtedly ourselves. An inflated sense of self may well accompany the Hades Moon. As the experiences are so intense, so *special*, and oh-so-accurate, they can be ego-inflating. We think we are the greatest healer, the most important past life figure, the best channeller that ever was—or card reader, astrologer, counsellor, whatever. We have all the answers; we are always right; in other words, the Hades Moon can be an arrogant Moon. A little (true) humility is called for here as hubris is so often followed by a fall from grace. I have always admired the mediums who could say: "No, today I am not getting anything, I am not tuned in," rather than those who were manifestly not tuned in but persisted in struggling on regardless. Or the astrologer who could say: "This chart simply does not speak to me, perhaps you should see someone else." Or the healer who can say: "It's not me who does the healing, it is something working through me, thank that." These are the people who have learned an essential lesson of the metaphysical Hades Moon: it channels power through us, it empowers us, but it is not us who do the healing or whatever; we are conduits.

For the Hades Moon to work well, psychic energy must be cleared and channelled correctly. If there is emotional baggage, it will contaminate what is intuited, seen, or felt. Many people will be familiar with card or chart readings that go compulsively into one particular area. A button has been pushed, but in the reader not the recipient. It may well be that the recipient has a similar issue, and the reading will resonate at that level, but this may not necessarily be so, and an incorrect emphasis may be put on the reading. If the reader or therapist is still hooked up in the issue, then nothing objective or constructive can come out of it. On the other hand, if whoever is doing the work has dealt with their own "stuff," then great healing can take place, because he or she will be able to bring energies back to balance or lost memories may reach the light of consciousness for reintegration. When healing takes place at such a deep level, the recipient may or may not necessarily be aware of all the work done but will surely recognize the energy change that accompanies it.

If psychic energy is not controlled, it will fly around, lashing out, looking for somewhere to land (as in adolescent poltergeist activity). So, if healing ability has not been recognized, for instance, the recipient of an angry thought might well find himself feeling quite unwell. Even people who seem to have the energy under control can let fly. When Mac, whom we have met from time to time, knew he was dying, he asked for his ashes to be scattered around the Buddha in the center of our garden. As the garden had become very overgrown, a friend of ours set about revitalizing it. I had told Mac that this was going to be done. "Don't move that Buddha!" he said firmly. Well, in order to weed, the Buddha had to be moved. As my friend lifted it, a wind suddenly whipped up out of nowhere. It caught the umbrella of a garden table, sending it flying. Two pots of stones had been on that table. My poor friend suddenly found himself showered with stinging gravel. Fortunately he is a healer himself, and recognized what was happening. "Don't worry," he told Mac in his thoughts, "I'm going to put it back but I just need to put it here for the time being until I've put these new plants around it and made a new base." The wind died down as quickly as it had arisen. When Mac saw a photo of the completed garden, he wholeheartedly approved. But, as he said: "For a moment there I got very angry to think of my favorite place being changed." His angry thought had traveled!

Many people who are psychic are wide open to everything that is around them on the unseen levels (especially if the Moon is in Scorpio or one of the other water signs). They draw in energy from other people, absorbing the "dark" equally with the "light" energies. So, they will draw in "dis-ease." They are not always unaware of doing this. Indeed, I have met many healers who feel this is their function. They see themselves as drawing off their patients' dis-ease. Not surprisingly, many of them end up depleted or suffering from cancer and similar illnesses because they do not transmute or let go of that energy after they have drawn it off. Even when they know they are psychic, and channel the energies accordingly, they may not be aware of taking this dark energy on board to this extent. So anyone with the Hades Moon needs to learn simple psychic protection and cleansing techniques[2] and needs to remember to do them (it is amazing how often we forget these things and then have a sharp reminder of how important they are).

Of course, one of the great pitfalls of the psychic path can be other people's misunderstanding or condemnation. So very many Hades Moon people have suffered persecution in the past. Psychic abilities are a greatly misunderstood gift, and what people misunderstand, or do not accept in themselves, they fear. Fear, as we know, provokes an angry, defensive response. When someone is standing in their power, using their Hades Moon at full wattage, other people can get very nervous. That fearless Hades Moon enters some deep dark places indeed, and can work miracles, and those who also have to make the journey may have a natural reluctance to go too far or too fast. The power of the Hades Moon was that used by the witches, and the Christian church has condemned witches for centuries (without ever really understanding what they did). Unfortunately, a great deal of that fear and condemnation lingers today. Pluto, being so intense, goes straight in there when maybe a softly-softly approach would disarm opponents.

I well remember, while doing my Religious Studies degree, talking to one of my tutors—a lay minister. My thesis was on Spiritualism, and I presented considerable evidence for the efficacy of healing, the validity of clairvoyance and precognition, the authenticity of past life memories, and the certitude of life after death. "My problem," said my tutor: "is not that I do not believe these things exist, and that you have these abilities. My difficulty is that if I accept that you can do these things, then I have to give you the same status as Christ, and that clearly is impossible." When I pointed out to him that Jesus had passed these precise gifts onto the disciples, and other members of the early church, and told them to "go out and do likewise," he spent an uncomfortable few moments. "Well," he said, "I'll believe it when I can do it." Some months later he went on a spiritual retreat. He had a "peak experience," a direct meeting with God. When he returned, he became a healer. Naturally, he too had the Hades Moon, but he would never go as far as to have his chart read. Astrology was still on his list of taboos.

PSYCHIC VAMPIRISM

A peculiarly hadean difficulty is with psychic vampirism. As someone with a Hades Moon is extremely powerful (whether consciously or not), it can draw energy from other people, leaving others severely depleted. This frequently happens with family, friends, or working colleagues. It is not limited to the prosaic, pragmatic side of life. It can also happen during spiritual activities. I have known this to happen during readings, therapeutic sessions, or healings. The psychic, healer, or therapist can unconsciously draw in the energy required for the work, from the patient or client, or anyone who happens to be around. As a result, the patient or client is exhausted, but is usually told that he or she is tired because of the cathartic release of the energies, or maybe that he or she is "blocking" or resisting in some way. Unless the perpetrator of the vampirism recognizes it, the energy will not be returned. On the other hand, people with a Hades Moon make good powerhouses. They can channel energy down from a higher source, or up from Earth, so that this can be used either by themselves or by others. It is not their power, it simply flows through them (an important distinction). This may be an innate ability, but it can also be learned. The important thing is to distinguish whether it is being done consciously, or not. If it is not, then appropriate training will bring this ability under proper direction.

It is possible to deplete your own energy. As Caitlin Matthews points out: "If a woman chooses to ignore her power, she submits it to a vampiric force which diverts her energy. . . . The tendency of women to eroticize power and to mate with their projections often helps to aggravate their situation."[3] Such leachings of power do not only occur with women. Men, too, can deny or restrict their own psychic power and so be vampirized. The Hades Moon person does often deny power—mostly out of fear—and the karmic necessity is to learn to access this power and use it wisely and creatively.

Bram Stoker, the creator of perhaps the best known horror-figure, the sinister and seductive vampire Count Dracula, had both the Sun and the Moon in Scorpio. His Pluto is in Aries, and may be quincunx his Moon (as is usual with these mid-19th century Irish births, no record exists as to time of birth so the precise position of the Moon is unknown). Bram Stoker was an extremely sickly child, he could not walk until he was 7 and he says that, more than once, he faced death. Maud Ellman, in an introduction to the Dracula story,[4] says that he was "more or less entombed" in his sickroom during his early life (a typical Hades Moon scenario). At age 7, his mysterious illness suddenly vanished. In his adolescence he became a strapping "red-haired giant" and went to Trinity College, Dublin. In 1878 he became business manager to the actor and theatrical impresario Henry Irving. From then, until Irving's death, he devoted great energy to promoting and serving Irving.

His relationship with Irving is interesting. The second time he saw the charismatic actor (Moon in Cancer square Pluto in Aries), he became "hysterical" during a recitation of poetry.[5] In his book *Personal Reminiscences of Henry Irving* he says: "I was no hysterical subject. I was no . . . weak individual yielding to a superior emotional force. . . . I was a very strong man . . . When, therefore, after his recitation I became hysterical, it was distinctly a surprise to my friends." He has been described as a "passionate idolator" of Irving[6] and it is possible that Irving drew on Stoker's energy. Certainly, after Stoker's death, it was commonly believed that he died of exhaustion, but Maud Ellman says that the death certificate hints at tertiary syphilis, an indication that Stoker lived a double life and had some dark secrets of his own.

While working for Irving, Stoker wrote *Dracula*, a somewhat turgid tale that is nowhere near as gripping as subsequent films have been. In the early hours of March 8, 1890, Stoker had a vivid nightmare.[7] This nightmare was repeated on March 14, and thereafter through the six years that it took him to write the book. The chart for the dream shows a kite formation, Mars opposing Neptune and Pluto, with a Grand Trine from Neptune-Pluto, Jupiter, and the Moon in Libra (Chart 17, page 238). In the dream, a huge crab rose off its plate and approached Stoker with open pincers. If we bear in mind that Irving had the Moon in Cancer, Stoker's unconscious may have been trying to communicate something to him.[8] (Certainly, according to Maud Ellman, the words Stoker used about Irving in his memoirs have echoes of vampirisim: "slumbrous energy," "ironic bite.") Somehow this crab metamorphosed into the figure of Dracula, aided, perhaps, by Stoker reading in Whitby Library about Vlad the Impaler, a bloodthirsty king of 15th-century Wallachia; and Elizabeth Bathory of Transylvania, a woman who allegedly had a penchant for bathing in the blood of virgins; and, of course, this was the era of that notorious serial killer, Jack the Ripper. All in all, it was time for such a horror to emerge from the collective. That an archetype might be at work is hinted at by the fact that the count arrives at Whitby from Translyvania in the aptly named schooner, the *Demeter*.

This figure of the vampire has a universal appeal—or horror. It is much older than Christianity, occurring in ancient folklore, but it is a myth perpetuated by Christianity with its blood ritual of the undead and hope of the bodily resurrection to come. As Maud Ellman points out: "The vampire itself is the demonic double of the blood-guzzling Christian whose body is destined to rise again."[9] She also points out that the Church contributed to the vampire myth with the notion that the souls of the excommunicated, the unbaptized, and the suicide would linger on as the undead. There is a fascination with this notion of something not dead and yet not fully living, a creature of the dark that can cross the two worlds. The vampire feeds on our fears, but it is also a projection of our fears. Like the shadow it is all that we deny in ourselves.

A great deal has been written about the archetype of the vampire, and about its eroticism. Dracula, his ancestors and inheritors, are particularly fond of young virgins. Do we catch here a glimpse of Pluto and Persephone? Are we hearing the echo of ancient blood sacrifices to appease the gods? It has been interpreted as relating to a whole gamut of taboos. The list Maud Ellman mentions reads rather like a biography of Pluto: sadism, masochism, rape, necrophilia, pedophilia, incest, oral sex, group sex, voyeurism, promiscuity, homosexuality, parricide, menstruation, and many more. This vampire is a shape shifter. Much of what is seen by late 20th-century eyes was not consciously visible to his creator or the initial audience. But, as psychology has unfolded and the notion of the shadow, or repressed energies, has arisen, the vampire has adapted himself to fit. As Maud Ellman has pointed

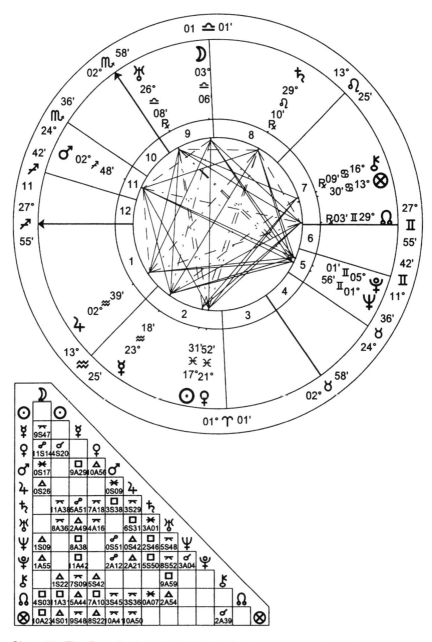

Chart 17. The Dracula dream that started the famous story. Date: March 8, 1890, GMT 03.00, 51N30, 000W01. Placidus houses. Bram Stoker's birth and death date are recorded on his tombstone. We do not have his time of birth.

out, "He [Dracula] stands for the return of the repressed, so the contents are ever shifting."[10]

A psychic vampire feeds on these repressed memories and the unstated needs of the deepest part of the psyche. A mother devours her child, for instance, because she hooks into the child's need for her. A man's need for a mother is fulfilled by a dominating wife who saps his energy while giving him the very thing he craves; or his need for a father comes out in a mentoring relationship that allows no room for his own expansion because he fears his power and projects it on the mentor. A psychic vampire is attuned to our darkest fears, and manipulates us through them. A psychic vampire also operates at the level of the higher energies of the psyche. It feeds on the lifeblood of the spirit—creative energy and soul. Notwithstanding, as with so much that we are taught to regard as "bad," a great deal of good can come out of the experience. The vampiric kiss may be an initiation into Hades, but, like the soul who traverses the Egyptian Duat, it does not have to be a death sentence. Some of those who are touched by the kiss of the vampire, who die to the everyday world, can arise to a new life nourished by the sacred lifeblood (which in olden days was believed to carry the "soul" or the spirit of life). At the end of the day, when the vampire emerges, all are one. The sacred encompasses light and dark. "Scared" can metamorphoze into "sacred," but only when we embrace the totality of our self. Then we will no longer vampirize ourselves. Nor, when we are totally centered in our own being, can we be vampirized by others.

THE DYING AND RESURRECTED GOD

In ancient Egypt, long before the Greek myth of Demeter, Persephone and Pluto came into being, Isis and Osiris, Set and Nepthys played out the eternal role of birth, death, and reconstruction, of the fragmentation and reintegration of the psyche and the different facets of consciousness. The story of Isis and Osiris is a lunar myth. Isis and her sister Nepthys are the Moon, and the attributes of Pluto are divided between Set and Osiris, although as funerary goddesses both Isis and Nepthys partake of Pluto's energies. Antiphonal and complementary, the four represent a duality, life and fertility set against death and decay. But the Egyptians understood the need for endings and change. In the early versions of the myth, Set is not an evil god, he is a necessary part of the process. In Egypt, where the division between the fertile land of the river valley and the arid desert is very marked, Osiris is the fecund plain and Set the burning, desolate waste. Each is honored in his own land.

Nepthys is the most mysterious of these four sibling gods. She represents our receptive nature and the "darker" energies of intuition and the unconscious mind. She is "the instinctual realm of feeling and emotion."[11] Some commentators see her as "the shadow" but this is also Set's role. According to David Lawson, she embodies the healing power of grief as well as guardianship over souls.[12] She is that dark phase of the Moon when we need to withdraw from the world to grieve, to reflect, and to receive our insights. But Nepthys is also something we have to transcend. She was the goddess of the wrapping of the mummified body, a guardian goddess who protected the body and its viscera. Mummification was seen as essential so the soul of the departed could return to an eternal home. And yet, for the soul to fly free, the deceased had to escape from "the tresses of Nepthys," in other words, from the body's bindings and the shackles of emotion. The passage through the other world could not be achieved without transcending the over-protective Nepthys.

Lunar Isis, Nepthys sister, is the archetypal devoted wife and mother, but she is much more than this. For a man, she represents the anima; for a woman, the intuitive self. She was one of the goddesses of power in whose honor a great mystery was re-enacted each year: that of death and resurrection. She used magic when necessary, and the power of life and death was an integral part of her myth—she brings Osiris back to life and also treats her son for a fatal scorpion bite. As with Demeter, the initiation rites of Isis included a symbolic death and return to the grave, from which the initiate would arise reborn; and her great yearly festival celebrated the annual fertility-bringing inundation of the Nile, indissolubly linked to the birth and death of the grain, and the prosperity of the land. She is the cyclic form of the Great Mother Goddess who underpins creation. The myth of Isis and Osiris is also one of the great statements of the core belief of the Egyptians—continuity of life after death.

Osiris is the great god of resurrection, but he is also the conscious ego. As the light of the world, he partakes of the divine nature of the Sun and the Moon, but he is also the "light of the conscious life," consciousness made manifest as an individual self. As such, he is fragmented and desires reintegration. He is that part of the self that must first disintegrate and travel through the Underworld to renew itself.

In the myth, Osiris, Isis' brother-consort, has a brother, Set whose sister-consort is Nepthys. Set, an ancient Upper-Egyptian god who, in the earliest myths, assisted the dead, became a dark twin in the later myths. He was torn from the womb of his mother, and so is associated with violent birth as well as endings. He is associated with natural phenomena that shut out the light of the sun, such as clouds, storms, earthquakes, darkness and, most terrifying of all for ancient peoples, eclipses. But he is also animal vitality and the part of the psyche that opposes transmution, the shadow.

Thus, Osiris and Set fragment and polarize the energies of the psyche and the dualities of good and evil, day and night, light and dark, growth and decay, life and death, all of which Isis ultimately reconciles. Their myth tells of a profound psychological truth, the death and dismemberment of the spirit into personality and the need to re-member who we are by traveling our own dark spaces and connecting to our own immortality. In Egypt, inner space (or consciousness) was not "in here," located somewhere in the brain, for instance; it was all around. The Egyptians lived, moved, and had their being within the spiritual world of which inner, psychic space, was an integral part.

According to the Osiris myth, Set became envious of his brother and desired to take over power for himself (that is, the dark, unrecognized parts of the psyche demanded their due). He plotted with conspirators who were also jealous of the power the incomer Osiris had gained in their lands (that is, the shadow and other subpersonalities inhabiting the subconscious realms resented the differentiation of the ego-self). In the later version of the myth, Set had a richly decorated chest carefully constructed to fit the measurements of Osiris' body and then gave a feast to welcome Osiris home. At the height of the feast, the chest was carried in and devious Set promised to give it to the man it would fit. Although many tried, no one could fill the stature of the king and eventually he was persuaded to try the box. No sooner had he lain down than the conspirators slammed the lid and nailed it shut. The chest was then thrown into the Nile.

In the earlier, unadorned, version of the myth, Osiris is hacked into fourteen pieces and scattered throughout the land. This is the allegory for the "death of the moon" as slowly, piece by piece, it sinks back into the dark of the Underworld. In this Underworld, the Moon must make the same journey as the Sun takes each night. The Moon, however, has the intuitive Isis for a guide. Isis re-members the Moon, in the body of her husband, and slowly, as she reintegrates his body, the Moon rises again. The story we are following here is a much-expanded version of this journey through consciousness.

Isis, an intuitive psychic, knew immediately of her husband's assassination and went into mourning. Full of grief, she set off to seek the chest. While on this journey she was told that Nepthys, her sister and wife of Set, had been seduced by Osiris and had borne him a son. Nepthys, terrified of what Set might do, had exposed the child immediately after birth, but the child had been rescued by wild dogs. Isis located the pack of dogs and regained her nephew, whom she named Anubis. He became the pathfinder who guided souls through the Underworld.

Isis forgave her sister, who left her husband and joined Isis in the hunt for Osiris. News reached the sisters that the chest had been washed ashore at Byblos and Isis went there to search for it. It had been thrown into the branches of a tamarisk tree, which grew around the chest and encompassed it into its trunk. This tree became famous for its wonderful size and beautiful flowers, and the local king had it cut down to make a pillar for his palace. When Isis arrived, she simply sat without speaking and the handmaidens of the queen, intrigued by the beautiful stranger, engaged her in conversation. Isis showed them how to braid their hair and make themselves beautiful, covering them in a sensuous fragrance (in other words, how to make the most of their feminine nature). When the queen heard of the beautiful stranger, she herself went to welcome her.

The queen's child was ill and Isis offered to heal him. Each day she would shut the queen out and place the child in flames to burn away his mortality. Unfortunately the queen was unable to resist interfering, but she recognized Isis as a goddess and the child became well. As a reward, Isis asked for the pillar that contained Osiris' body. She split open the tree, removed the chest and returned the pillar to the king and queen. She then began to lament for her lost lord, and so terrifying was her grief that one of the queen's sons died of fright.

Isis then loaded the chest onto a ship and returned to Egypt, where she immediately set about reviving Osiris. A beautiful Egyptian verse tells of her magic, which was able to warm and breathe life into Osiris's body long enough for it to impregnate her with her son, Horus. Set returns to the story and imprisons Isis, but she escapes and attempts to give birth alone, in the reeds. The birth, however, is a difficult one and ultimately two gods arrive, mark Isis with a cross of blood—the sign of life—and her son is born. As we have seen in chapter 7, Horus is destined to become the new solar lord, taking over from the old solar god, Ra. This birth takes place at the vernal equinox, the first day of Spring, when the young corn sprouts.

Isis is hunted by Set, and many misfortunes befall her while her son is little. At this stage she is a goddess who has lost everything including divine protection. She is like Inanna, going into the underworld of her sister Ereshkigal with everything stripped away.

Set, however, continues to be active in the story. This time he finds the chest with Osiris' body and cuts it into fourteen pieces, which he flings into the Nile. In one version of the myth, Nepthys joins her sister and together they change into kites who mourn without ceasing while flying the length and breadth of the land to seek Osiris. In another version, Isis sets off again in search of her husband and, after many trials and tribulations, she finds the missing pieces. Each time she finds a piece, she apparently buries it and builds a shrine, although this is a trick to fool Set. Only one piece was missing, the phallus (generative organ) of Osiris, which had been eaten by a fish. So, when she reassembled the body, it had a wooden phallus (in some versions of the myth, it is this wooden phallus which impregnates Isis with Horus).

Horus meanwhile has done battle with his dark uncle and vanquished him. This battle was, to Egyptian eyes, reenacted every night when the Sun vanished below the horizon to do battle with the forces of darkness. So the bright light of consciousness once again relegates the dark energies to the depths of the unconscious. But, this time it is different; Set has taken his rightful place in the solar barque. He has become a protective deity, the instinctual energies of the unconscious have been controlled by Horus, the divine child.

Horus then took his uncle's eye to where Isis waited with Osiris' body. He opened his father's mouth and gave him the eye to eat (the symbol of eternal life). Osiris was then able to ascend his shaman's ladder to the other world (the Duat, unlike the Greek Hades, was located above and beyond the horizon rather than below the earth). In the afterlife, it became his task to judge the lives of mortal men. If they, too, have overcome their instinctual energies and harnessed them to transformation, they move on to face the challenges of the Duat.

For three thousand years the mysteries of Isis were enacted as sacred drama, a spiritual catharsis. Egyptologist Rundle Clark[13] says that this myth was as useful to those who were still alive as it was as a guide for those who had died. It conveyed a "lasting vitality" and an all-embracing understanding of existence on all levels. For men, Isis was the anima leading them through the world of the unconscious, reuniting the dismembered and fragmented parts of the psyche, and guiding it through the spiritual realm. For women, she was a guide to the intuitive realm and to the mysteries of the feminine nature. Isis had a veil, which symbolized intuition and psychic powers. When a woman wore the veil of Isis, she too was possessed of these powers. For both sexes, it was a birth, death, and rebirth experience and included the sacred marriage of the god and the goddess (the masculine and feminine principles of the psyche). Each year at Philae Temple (the place where Sekhmet was subdued), Isis would be taken for a "honeymoon" visit to her husband on his adjoining island. The creative spark would fertilize the receptive soul, and the spirit of new life would be spread throughout the land.

In Greece, the mantle of the dying and resurrected god passed to Dionysus. In Rome, it went to Mithras. Both embodied different aspects of the hadean energies.

Mithras was the Martian energy, he was the soldier's god. Dionysus had a much more Plutonian feel—and more than a touch of Neptune. He was the god associated with ecstasy and delirium, but he had his warlike side. In the grip of Dionysus, his followers would make sacrifices that were torn apart with their bare hands—as we have seen murder can be a cathartic act. In all these death and resurrection rites, the aim was initiation and transformation. The partaker of the mysteries shook off the old persona and became a newly created whole, made sacred by intimate contact with the divine energies.

HEALING THE EARTH

In my long experience with Moon-Pluto, I have come to believe that everyone who has this aspect has, in some way, a karmic purpose to manifest healing for Earth. Some people will have the innate ability to correct areas of dis-ease in Earth—healing telluric power imbalances, such as "black" ley lines, clearing the energy at places where appalling slaughter has taken place and the memory lingers, cleansing spots where pollution of all kinds festers; or they may take up environmental projects. Other people will be able to help those who live on Earth, through counselling, healing, therapies of all description, and practical work. There will be those who fight for causes, and those who seek to overturn injustice. Each must come to their own way to bring renewed life to Earth.

Edward, whom we met in chapter 3, had always had a concern for the planet, even when he was very young. He says:

> I always hated to see anything wasted or thrown away. At university I was a member of one or two environmental groups. This became buried though by concerns over personal relationships, job training, having a good time, etc. It began to re-emerge strongly about ten years ago after a three-year job in Kenya. I was afforded the time to do much traveling and saw the effects of erosion and deforestation, over-cultivation, etc., for myself. I became tremendously aware of the various consequences of the rains failing (as they did once when I was there). I have always felt grateful for rain whenever it comes ever since!
>
> I began to get involved with numerous environmental organisations, supporting them financially, and did some actual conservation work, joined Greenpeace after the bombing of the Rainbow Warrior in 1985. I became increasingly concerned and saddened at the abuse of our fellow creatures. I am now actively involved in campaigning for Greenpeace and also the World Development Movement, an organisation that sees the link between the exploitation of the world's poor and exploitation of the earth. It seeks to establish fair trade, combat the arms trade, and eliminate the third-world debt. Most recently I have linked the practical side of the environmental movement with the spiritual aspect of the need for care for the earth and I now write to prominent people, and people in the media. I am dedicated to this and I'm delighted to say that I've had some very positive replies to letters.
>
> I now feel that I am one of those who are called upon to help raise consciousness, but presently I see myself having a practical role to play, too. In my own lifestyle I do what I can to try to "tread lightly on the earth." I restrict my car use as much as possible, no toxic chemicals in the home, garden managed with wild life very much in

*mind. Vegetables and fruit grown organically, investments channelled to ethical organ-
isations to help the earth. And of course, I belong to Fountain International (an or-
ganisation dedicated to earth healing).*

These are all practical ways in which those with Moon-Pluto aspects can harness
the immense power it possesses toward regenerating Earth and preventing further
abuse of Earth and its people.

THE INITIATION OF THE MOON

*To be illumined by the Moon produces a greater clarity of mind, but to be struck by
the Moon creates only lunacy.*

—Haydn Paul[14]

The word initiation comes from the Latin *initiare*, which means to instruct, to begin, or to introduce. An initiation is an introductory rite that sets things in motion;
it brings about an expansion in consciousness, opens up new insights, and *initiates*
changes. So often we find that, looking back, a Hades Moon experience or a particularly Plutonian trauma has been the spur that helped us to grow spiritually, to
expand our awareness past the everyday level of existence. The call to initiation may
come in dreams, in actual experiences, or through the telling of myth. It relates to
both the outer and the inner world—"The cellar, dungeon, and cave symbols are
all related to one another. They are ancient initiatory environs; a place to or
through which [we] descend to the murdered one(s), break taboos to find the truth,
and through wit and/or travail triumph by banishing, transforming, or exterminating the assassin of the psyche."[15] In ancient, and not so ancient, times death was a
prerequisite for initiation. The old had to die, symbolically or otherwise, before the
new could emerge. A boy died to childhood and emerged a man; a young woman
was initiated into the mysteries of menstruation and birth; a spiritual initiate put off
the old self and was reborn. Such rites of passage were a time of withdrawal, meditation, and insight, and then a coming forth into the new self. This process is no
different today. It may take place purely in the psyche, or parts of it may manifest in
the outside world. But the effect is the same, we die to the old and are reborn anew.

"WHEN THE MOON WAS BLOOD"

In pushing us deep down inside ourselves, initiation compels us to face our fears
and demons. It catharts the past, and ferments a new future, a future in which the
spiritual eye is opened. If the spiritual eye opens without this inner grounding, it
produces "lunacy." In times gone by, an initiation would be accompanied by a sacrifice of some kind. Blood would be spilled. It may be metaphorical blood, or actual. Nowadays, it tends to be psychic blood. Such ceremonies always took account
of the Moon. They occurred either in the five dark days of the Moon, culminating
in its rebirth, or at the Full Moon.

We have heard a great deal about Mac in this book. From the outside looking on, Mac's experience has been chaotic, disruptive, self-destructive, and yet, he

says he has grown immensely in spiritual understanding. His psychic abilities are enormous, the spiritual world is all around him. Not surprising really when he only has one toe in incarnation. In his experience of his chart, he had no way of earthing these experiences except through his sensitive Moon in Capricorn, which is opposed by the mighty combination of Chiron, Sun, Mercury, Pluto, and Mars. With his Kite (figure 15, page 199), he is flying high. He will explode or implode whenever the transiting Moon touches off either water, earth, or fire signs. Only when the Moon is in air does he find respite. With his comparative lack of air, he is all intuition and feeling, and yet, with the unaspected Venus in Gemini, he is not in touch with his emotions. He lacks rationality and the ability to analyze his emotional experiences.

He has plenty of earth energy in the chart, but none of it is comfortable. His Neptune is in Virgo, which can make a channel for the spiritual energies to flow down, but which may feel too heavily restricted by the boundaries of earth and want to escape. In Mac's case, his escape was drugs or continual conversations with his "spirit friends." In Taurus he has a Jupiter-Saturn-Uranus conjunction. This is like driving flat out on high octane fuel but with the brakes full on. When he worked as a healer, he was immensely powerful and, through his contact with his spiritual guides, could exactly pinpoint the emotional causes of someone's "disease," and prescribe just the right flower remedy. But, at the same time, he became inflated, believing he was the greatest healer ever. In abusing his body through the drugs, he opened the floodgates wide to invasion from the other levels. He had no control over his abilities. The energy flew around and around that Kite Formation, eventually bursting out through the Capricorn Moon in the 11th house, disrupting the society around him. "Authority" then stepped in to restrain him "in the interests of public safety."

In a different culture, Mac would probably have become an honored shaman, or an oracle. Cultures with a long experience of the divine energies have always prized those who were larger than life, "touched with the god." He had the potential to become a "medial man" who inhabited a point midway between the worlds of reason and imagination, thinking and feeling, matter and spirit.[16] As it was, he was the alien outsider. If Mac had been able to ground his experiences, to stay in his body while letting his soul touch the spiritual realms, he could have saved himself months of incarceration in psychiatric hospitals. But would he then have been following his karmic purpose? From the perspective of Earth, we cannot judge what his spirit's needs were. His North Node is in Scorpio. He has to explore the places and pathways other people fear to tread. He has to tread the byways of the Underworld. He needs to bring back his insights from these places. And, he believes, he had to make karmic redemption for the past. As part of his resolution of the past, he made peace with his brother, whom he had not seen for over twenty years. This was an enormous step forward for him, as he had harbored much resentment and bitterness over the breakdown of that relationship. Now, with forgiveness and love, the parting would be beneficial to both brothers.

When Mac decided to die, to surrender to the process instead of fighting it, the Full Moon was in Capricorn conjunct his natal Moon (which was, of course, opposed by the transiting Sun, which was in turn conjunct the powerful stellium of planets). His progressed Moon was approaching its natal place. Saturn would soon make its Return. As he was in the hospice and unable to do a ritual himself, I lit a candle for him in front of our garden Buddha (the place where he wished his ashes to be scattered), under the light of a blood-red Full Moon. I asked that whatever was appropriate for his soul growth would occur. In death Mac was looking for an escape from Earth, yes, but he was also seeking an initiation, a transition to the spiritual world in which he was certain he would continue to evolve. Mac would have agreed with a statement the poet John Keats (Moon in Gemini trine Pluto in Aquarius) made when he was facing premature death from tuberculosis: "I have an habitual feeling of my life having passed and that I am leading a posthumous existence."[17] Keats' poem "Ode to a Nightingale" expresses this Hades Moon readiness for death perfectly:

> Darkling I listen; and, for many a time
> I have been half in love with easeful Death,
> Called him soft names in many a mused rhyme,
> To take into the air my quiet breath;
> Now more than ever seems it rich to die,
> To cease upon the midnight with no pain.[18]

In surrendering to death, Mac became free. In being free, he was in control of life perhaps for the first time. He had gained a tranquillity he had never known. His only anger was that, according to the law of the land, he was not free to choose euthanasia as he would have wished. But perhaps if he had been, he would not have totally surrendered to the process. His death would have to be at the "right time" for his soul's growth, not when his ego dictated.

THE MEDIAL MOON

The Hades Moon is a medial Moon. This means that it acts as a go-between between the worlds of "consensual reality and the mystical unconscious."[19] Because the Hades Moon does not fear the depths, and is at home in the waters of the unconscious—but may, of course, have forgotten that and need to remember how to do it—a person with this Moon goes beyond the places where other Moons feel at home. This is why so many people with the Hades Moon experience soul dramas and traumas beyond the norm. The gift of the Hades Moon is that, having been there once, it is always possible to go again, this time without the fear that accompanies the initial journey. Having been there, it becomes second nature to move with ease between the different levels, higher as well as lower. Once initiated in this way in the full extent of consciousness, the medial person can perform this service for others. It becomes possible to birth ideas, dreams, intuitions, solutions, and manifest them out into the earth plane as concrete *substance*, substance which is touched by the gods and brings new light and new life.

CHAPTER 9

THE RENASCENT MOON

Encountering Pluto is like a touch of the Self, dying to the old and being revitalized as the new—becoming one of the twice born.

—Haydn Paul[1]

W HEN I WAS 24, I had the near death experience that was to change my life. At the time, the transiting Moon was sextile my natal Pluto and semi-sextile the natal Moon in Scorpio, activating my exact Pluto-Moon square. That transiting Moon was opposed by transiting Saturn. It certainly felt like I was meeting my fate (Saturn being the Lord of Karma). As mentioned in the introduction, I was in the process of giving birth to my daughter. Labor had been induced because I was suffering from pre-eclamptic toxemia and there was great danger to both the baby and myself. But, in what I was to learn was typical Moon-Pluto fashion, my labor did not progress well. Eventually, I became unconscious and the contractions all but ceased. At the same time, I found myself on the ceiling, looking down at my body on the bed. And I was also watching myself die in labor in rather different circumstances. I had died because I simply could not go on.

A guide was with me on the ceiling. He told me that I had opted out before and could do so again. But, I would have to go through everything I had been through before in order to get back to this point in another incarnation. He pointed out to me that I had had a purpose in incarnating, and that by dying I would not only opt out of motherhood, but I would also fail to fulfill my purpose. He told me that the traumatic time I had just been through (which had included being pregnant while cut off from access to the outside world during a civil war in the African jungle) was a "toughening up process" rather than a repayment of karma. He said it was part of my finding my inner strength. My decision to return and get on with the labor was not exactly positive. It was more on the lines of: "Well, I might as well try and get it right this time so I will avoid all this hassle next time." But return I did and, through sheer willpower, because I was too ill for a caesarian, I managed to have my child with both of us alive and well. Now, when I look back, that is the moment when I was born again, not in any religious sense, but with a spiritual knowing that was lacking previously.

Life did not immediately get better. In fact it got considerably worse. My husband died soon afterward. But it was a major turning point, the time in my life when, stripped down to the bare essentials, I learned I could survive. It brought all my psychic abilities to the fore—which had been stuffed down out of sight since childhood. By the time natal Pluto was sextiled by transiting Pluto, I had begun a psychological, astrological, and healing training, and had gone back to college, which enabled me to pursue my interest in metaphysics in much greater depth. I was working for my degree in Religious Studies when I met Howard Sasportas and he started to recommend clients for karmic readings—something which the guide had told me during the near death experience would happen "quite soon." I had met the Western mystic and metaphysician Christine Hartley during my time at college, and she had trained me in past life work. Mac, whom we met in chapter 6, had propelled me into working professionally as a karmic counsellor.

Christine Hartley believed in teaching her pupils how to fly free. But I had an enormous struggle to break from another mentor, who had taught me healing and psychic skills. She was a typically Plutonian matriarch, strongly controlling with rigid principles that had to be followed at all costs. I found that while I could use some of her tools, I was unable to follow her teaching slavishly—something that provoked a huge conflict between us. (An experience that has been shared by many of my Hades Moon clients. The struggle to break free from a mentor is a particularly Plutonian experience—and ubiquitous one that causes pain in a wide variety of settings.) But in making that break, I found confidence in my abilities. And so, my life changed dramatically.

I was completely at home in the Underworld. True to my Hades Moon in Scorpio, I could accompany people on the most traumatic and difficult journeys into their past and could move with ease between the different levels of consciousness. I could journey into the between-life state with my clients, and up to some very high states of awareness. With my acute sensitivity, I could feel what they were feeling, but I quickly learned to remain dispassionate and detached, as otherwise it was all too easy for me to be sucked down into whatever emotional trauma was around. But I was not afraid of the dark. Nothing fazed me. I seemed to know instinctively what was needed and how to guide people into contact with their own soul or higher self. Much of my knowledge of past life therapy came from this "hands on experience" and from the intuitive guidance I received, but I knew I was also drawing on other-life skills. I could also accompany the dying. When Mac was completing his transition, I accompanied him to help with post-death states that arose from a past life experience. We healed this so that he could move on into the light. I then returned my consciousness back to my physical body.

I wanted my clients to be reliant upon themselves, not me. It seemed to make little difference whether we used regression therapy, astrology, or psychotherapy, we reached the same place—a space where they could find the answers. This latter point was something which became very important to me. I was aware, with my Moon-Pluto contact, just how easy it would have been to force, or manipulate, people into the pathway I felt was right for them, to subtly suggest the "right" answers or program in false memories. But I was equally aware of just how deceptive a trap this was. It also became clear to me that I needed to be in ongoing therapy to transform my own emotions and instinctual reactions, as otherwise these could easily be projected onto my clients. I could become a "fixer" of all that was wrong with other people, rather than addressing my own issues. When I read Jeff Green's book on Pluto[2] in 1996, I turned immediately to the section on Pluto in aspect to the Moon. Within his first paragraph, he sets out the need to eliminate all external dependencies, finding inner security; to reformulate instinctive reactions; and to transform the self-image. He goes on to say, "Those with Pluto in aspect to the Moon have been learning how to focus the power of their Souls through their conscious ego,"[3] and points out just how single-minded and ruthless this aspect can be as a result. He draws out the many other dangers inherent in this aspect. These were all facets of myself with which I was, or was to become, familiar. But he sees, too, the positive, constructive nature of the Hades Moon, something shared by everyone who has this aspect. We all have the potential to be transformed, to fulfill our evolutionary purpose, to be reborn.

REBIRTH AND TRANSFORMATION

When the Hades Moon is working well, it can be exceedingly nurturing. It may well find new ways of helping the young, empowering rather than devouring them. This is true in both men and women. General (later Lord) Baden-Powell, who began the Boy Scout movement in 1908, had the Moon in Aquarius in exact square to Pluto in Taurus. Hedonistic Hugh Hefner, head of the Playboy Empire, also has a Hades Moon (Pisces Moon trine Pluto in Cancer). His Playboy Mansion has been described as a "strange, unreal, pampered womb,"[4] a suitable ambience for a Pisces Moon. When he was setting up Bunny Girls, he felt that they needed a "Bunny Mother" to take care of them, someone to whom they could take their troubles without having to deal directly with the male management. Whether or not you feel that he was a Plutonian figure exploiting women (the view of many feminists), he was concerned enough about his employees' welfare to make provision for a surrogate mother.

Hefner is a strangely hadean character who, when a stroke confined him to his mansion for ten years, became deeply introspective. Like so many other people, his entry into Pluto's abode transformed his life. He has said he felt as though he was tapped on the shoulder and asked: "Are you going to go on living your life like this for ever?" He married again, a woman thirty-six years his junior, one of his Bunnies. She put him on the road to recovery. In a 1994 interview,[5] he explained that his Playboy empire was contrapuntal to his Puritan background (he was an eleventh generation descendant of a Mayflower settler). Hefner also said, "You spend a lifetime working out the things that are laid on you as a kid." He explained that he had a very cold childhood, but had recently told his mother (then aged 99) that it was not her fault. She was merely repeating the pattern of her own childhood, and he felt that he had needed that particular type of childhood; it was what made him who he was. A typical Aries, he questioned: "What would a knight errant do without dragons, internal or other?"

• •

As we saw in chapter 3, Pluto-Moon aspects often indicate a difficult birth. Incarnation all too frequently begins in suffocation, near death or alienation—metaphorical or actual. So, if we are to heal the wounds of the past and move into the more positive and constructive side of the Hades Moon, it is with birth we need to start. Many people have found rebirthing to be an extremely useful tool, and others find themselves spontaneously reliving their birth, clearing the trauma and bringing in a new energy.

A participant in one of my workshops (a classic puer figure: Pluto opposite the Moon in Aquarius), experienced his birth most graphically during a regression. He moved down into the birth canal and then felt, rather than heard, his mother say: "No, that's it, I'm too tired to go on. I don't want this. Go back." Eventually, after a long struggle, he was born, but was not welcomed by his exhausted mother. He felt that this explained his lifelong emotional detachment and difficulty with intimacy, and his lack of trust. He rejected people before they could reject him. His wife, a psychoanalyst, who was also at the workshop, felt that it explained his attitude to his mother. She said that he was continually seeking his mother's approval and was deeply afraid of her displeasure.

In another session, he spontaneously reworked that birth, taking control of the process and facilitating his own arrival, which was smooth and easy. As his mother was not then worn out, she was able to welcome him into the world. However, he no longer felt reliant on her for his very life. As a result, he did not feel bound to please his mother all the time as had been the case in the past. When he checked back with his mother, she told him that she had got to the point where she really did want him not to be born. Then, when she had recovered from the birth, she felt so guilty that she spent much of her time trying to make up to him for that initial rejection. As a result, she became overprotective. After that conversation, she was able to let go of her guilt and allow him to go out into the world alone (aged 42!). He was able to manifest much more of his own self into his life, and to follow his own pathway.

Another participant, a woman with Moon in Libra sextile Pluto, realized that she would be born with the cord around her neck and would need to be resuscitated as a result. She was able to go back into the womb and lift the cord clear before her journey down the birth canal began. As she commented afterward: "I had always felt that my mother was like a weight around my neck, strangling me. Now I no longer feel that way. I feel like I have been reborn."

It is possible to plan a birth so that the best possible conditions are there for the positive side of the Moon and Pluto, whether in aspect or not, to manifest right from the beginning, as we will see from the following story.

SPLASHDOWN FOR NATHAN

Jayn Ingrey has the Moon in Libra in septile aspect to Pluto in Leo. Her son Nathan has the Moon in Cancer trine Pluto in Scorpio. An individual with a septile aspect has an evolutionary purpose that is linked to a a special destiny. Cancer, of course, is linked to motherhood and birth, with a trine being an easy manifestation of the Hades Moon energy. So it is not surprising that there was something rather special about Nathan's birth as Jayn's account shows:

I have been mediumistic since the age of 17, and about two years before Nathan's conception, I intuitively felt that a major change would soon take place in my life. Then, a year before conception, I knew that a baby was waiting to be born to us, I even saw his face—it was a boy with hazel eyes and mid-brown hair.

I became pregnant just after my 34th birthday (progressed Moon trine natal Pluto, transiting Pluto semi-sextile natal Moon). As it was my first baby and I was an "old mum" who is very overweight and only 5'1" tall, I took it more or less for granted that it would be a high-tech hospital birth. Also, I was frightened of pain and wanted an epidural!

It was a planned pregnancy and I had taken preconceptual care, eating a healthy diet and abstaining from alcohol. As well as preparing myself physically, I also tried to prepare myself spiritually and emotionally. I read The Secret Life of the Unborn Child *by Dr. Thomas Verny, which speaks of the fetus as a feeling, sensitive being, and Leboyer's* Birth Without Violence. *I learned that a pregnant mother's emotions and feelings affect her unborn child and that birth can be our most traumatic experience. Tests had proven birth to leave a very definite mark on the subconscious, which can last a lifetime, So I was determined to make my baby's entry into the world as gentle and beautiful as I possibly could.*

During this time I attended a jazz singing workshop where I met Jane Davies, who offered me a lift home. When I got into her car, she said: "I'll just move my midwifery bag out of your way." On learning that she was a midwife I, of course, told her that I was preparing for conception. Jane was then working for the National Health Service, but was planning to become an Independent Midwife as she wanted to give continuity of care. This sounded wonderful to me as Jane could be in charge of the delivery and provide ante- and postnatal care. I visualized the birth as an extremely special time and wanted to share it with someone with whom my husband and I had developed a relationship, and who would know our specific wishes regarding the baby's delivery.

Jane held regular social gatherings where her pregnant mums could meet mums who had already had their babies. There I met someone who had used a birth pool at home, to ease the pain of labor, and had then gone into hospital for the delivery. Jane said she had attended a few births where a pool had been used, as this provided pain relief without the need for drugs, as most of her clients wanted natural births. She said she had also delivered babies under water and said that this made the baby's transition into the world far less traumatic as he would be coming from fluid into fluid and would also be "cushioned" from light and noise before being brought to the surface. I could use a pool at home or hospital.

The idea of having a home birth where I could be in familiar surroundings with candlelight, soft music, and friends began to sound more and more appealing. My health was good and Jane was very pleased with the way my pregnancy was progressing. Jane works with a partner and assured me they would carefully monitor my pregnancy and labor and if there were medical reasons, or I decided on an epidural, I could go to hospital.

When labor began, my husband placed the birth pool in my favorite part of the house and created a lovely atmosphere with candles and music. Jane came around to make preparations for the birth. I went to bed, but the contractions were getting stronger and I could not sleep. I found remarkable inner strength and felt like a surfer riding the waves of each contraction. Between each contraction I would rest in a haven of peace in my own mind. I felt totally in control, and although I am usually very extrovert, I became totally focused within myself.

As soon as I had entered the pool, the reduction in pain was tremendous. The water completely relaxed me and totally transformed the labor. Also I had found it difficult to get into a comfortable position before, but with the water to support me, I could move about freely. Although I experienced some pain, it was very much reduced and quite bearable.

As soon as I felt the urge to push, Jane told my husband to get into the pool, as she knew the birth was imminent. I felt Nathan's head inside me before he was born and this is an experience I shall never forget. As soon as he was born, he turned, opened his eyes under the water and grinned at my husband. Jane soon lifted him gently to the surface and placed him in my arms. My first reaction was how beautiful he was. I knew that some newborns could look quite unappealing and, of course, having been born in water, he was clean! I welcomed him into the world and he seemed so peaceful and content, as if he was saying, "Hi mummy, I'm here and I'm safe." Jane told me to feel the umbilical cord and I was amazed at the force with which it was pulsating. As soon as the pulsating stopped, Jane clamped the cord and my husband cut it. I put Nathan to my breast and champagne was served.

After the birth, I seemed to forget about the third stage of labor. So, one-and-a-half hours after Nathan's birth, a syntometrine injection was prepared, as I had not yet delivered the placenta. I asked Jane and Tess if this was really necessary and they assured me it was. I asked them to wait for just a moment and I calmly prayed. I had come this far without the need for drugs and didn't want to give in now. The moment my prayer ended, I delivered the placenta painlessly into the bucket I was sitting on.

My husband and I were so impressed with the birth that, with back-up from the International Active Birth Centre, we started a service called Splashdown, which offers free information and advice, and hires out birth pools.

Jayn became such an expert in the field of waterbirths that she now speaks at international conferences. Her waterbirth service has helped hundreds of women to have a healthy, pain-free birth. In her own way, she became a priestess of the mysteries, dedicated to the service of that eternal mother, Isis, who watched over her work. Her son Nathan is a very confident and happy young man who shows no signs of negative Hades Moon traits. It will be interesting to see what happens to him as he matures.

REBIRTHING THE MOTHERING RELATIONSHIP

We met Louise in chapter 1. As she was a person who had made an extraordinary transition in her life, I wanted to share her story to show what could come out of an unpromising childhood that matured into a heroin addiction. Louise certainly turned her life around, as we shall see:

I think the fact that it is a trine has made my Moon-Pluto contact much easier, not only because what actually happened in its manifestations were undoubtedly easier and worked out better in the end, but also because I could see that part of myself in a more positive and accepting light. Being Sun Scorpio probably also helps me accept the Pluto feelings as natural. I have an innate understanding of the value of emotional crisis.

However, I have always had dark feelings—depression, self-destruction—and I still have them today, but not so frequently and not so powerful—I have learned to simply let them pass through. This pervading self-destructive tendency may have started in the womb, since my mother threw herself down the stairs to abort me (it didn't work, but talk about Moon-Pluto!). A few years ago I was regressed by a hypnotherapist to the womb. Immediately after she snapped her fingers (triggering the regression), I had an overwhelming wave of despair which passed over me and was gone in seconds.

My relationship with my mother is very colored by Saturn. I have Saturn in Scorpio in the 10th house, widely opposing my Moon on the IC, and a Capricorn Ascendant. My mother has the Sun conjunct the Moon and Saturn, in Capricorn, both opposite Pluto. So, we were never close (until very recently). I was actually afraid of her for most of my childhood. I had a vivid dream of her as a child where I was flying around this large gymnasium and she was standing in this black nightgown—like Morticia in the Adams Family—waving her arms and screaming at me to come down.

We became much closer in my late 30s. The turning point was when she wrote me a letter describing her own "dark night of the soul." She described to me how one terrible night, drunk and on pain killers from a recent hip operation, she'd fallen over from her crutches and broke her wrist. She had been an alcoholic for many years, but she felt that this night she'd really hit bottom, literally as well as figuratively. She stopped drinking forever. I was so moved by the courage and honesty of the letter that I wrote back and told her about my own successful struggle to give up a heroin addiction—something she'd known nothing about. Our relationship after that was much closer and more real. It seems that to achieve that rapport, we had to meet in the depths.

Just after Louise wrote this piece for me, her mother was diagnosed as having terminal cancer. Louise immediately went to be with her mother, who lived in the States. They talked and talked, covering all the years of silence that had been between them. They forgave each other for much past hurt, and became very close. Louise had to come back to England for her work, but then felt she must return to the States for what she was experiencing with her mother was too important to miss. She nursed her mother through her last weeks. When her mother finally died, Louise was with her all the way. When she returned to England, she held a ritual with her women's group to honor her mother's life. The experience with her mother changed Louise in a fundamental way. It somehow *deepened* her, brought her more into her spiritual self and enabled her to own her considerable power as an instinctual woman.

FINDING THE WARRIOR WITHIN

As we have seen, men who have a powerful mother seem to have an absent or disengaged father. As a result, they lose touch—or never come into contact with—their own male energies. We have met Lincoln several times through this book and, as it was nearing completion, I asked him what he felt had most helped him in his recovery, both from addiction and from the effects of his devoted mother:

One of the things that really helped me was ACOA (Adult Children of Alcoholics). Even though neither my mother or father drink, it was a dysfunctional household, i.e., "don't talk, don't trust, and don't feel." I reacted by rebelling, but in my rebellion I was still in chains, and still a child. I had to learn to re-parent myself, to bring the child in me out of hiding, to give myself what I didn't get while growing up, i.e., unconditional love. When growing up, I was only acceptable IF I kept my parents happy, IF I did my mother's will. Sometimes I felt that it was my job to make my mother happy. I grew up and became emotionally unresponsive, frightened of any real involvement because my mother's invasiveness had taught me that love is intrusive and love is a cage.

I discovered at ACOA that I was treating myself the way I was treated by my parents: I judged myself, and demanded perfection of myself, and I indulged myself. Gaining these insights was the start of my recovery. Then I had to start treating myself in a healthy way. It wasn't easy, but now I had help through ACOA, I learned that it's okay to be angry with people I love. I learned that it's okay to make mistakes, and that I am not on this planet to make other people happy. I learned that no one else can do my thinking for me, or live my life for me: that I am responsible for my recovery. I learned that as long as I am still blaming my parents, then I am still a child and still a victim. I learned that I can't control other people, but that I can change.

I also got a lot of help from a Men's Group I was involved in for three years. We spent a lot of time focusing on four archetypes—King, Lover, Magician, and Warrior. We did exercises to access these archetypes so that we could use them in our daily lives. For example, if you need to access the Lover, then you do something like smell the roses or look at the sunset, and really pay attention to it. If you need to access the Warrior, then you get up from the sofa and do something, anything: you get into action. I see healthy Warrior energy as being Mars at its best [Lincoln has Pluto opposite Mars], and it cuts through a lot of difficulties simply by standing up straight and acting. Warrior energy is focused, emotionally detached, and disciplined. It's motto is: "Today is a good day to die." It helps me get in touch with my masculinity. It helps me to set limits and do what I need to do. It enables me to project myself and to do whatever is necessary. Warrior energy is assertive, not aggressive. I learned to access this energy with a simple exercise: I stood up straight, feet apart and firmly grounded, my arms outstretched and pointing skyward, my hands clasping a sword or a staff. I would do this for five minutes, repeating an appropriate affirmation over and over. One that was good for me was: "I can take care of myself." I'm sure the affirmation wouldn't have had much effect if I'd been slumped in a chair, but standing in that position had a very powerful effect: it energized me. The affirmation worked.

I felt like a Warrior for the first time in my life, and it enabled me to cut through difficulties and to cut the ties that bind. I don't think I'd ever cut the apron-strings even though I might have seemed to have left home: I wrenched them and twisted them and tied myself up in their knots. I'd replaced one dependency with another, and spent thirteen years totally controlled by drugs. Now I was learning something new: how to empower myself, how to act decisively. I wish I could say that it happened once and for all, but it didn't. The difference is that these days I can usually recognize what is happening. I see now that I spent most of my life living out my Shadow side. I was compulsive, alienated, and unable to take care of myself. I did a lot of dreaming and not much real living. I was frightened of anything "soft"—Frightened of women; frightened of other men; frightened of life.

Now, when I get in touch with healthy Warrior energy, I am not identified with any fear I am feeling. I am increasingly able to detach, to see what needs to be done and to do it. After forty-five years of being obsessed and possessed, I'm learning to relate in a healthy way—to be connected instead of being overwhelmed, to be a partner, not a Siamese twin, to give of myself without losing myself. I cannot stop my mother trying to treat me like a child, but I don't have to play that game anymore. I can stop acting like a child. I can detach with love. It's not always easy, but it is liberating and it's always worth the effort. And, for the first time in my life, I'm in a healthy relationship.

I knew that Lincoln's partner had had her own cathartic experiences, including a car crash in which she had a near death experience. I also recognized that, as a Scorpio, she knew the territory of the Hades Moon intimately. But somehow, when she had spoken of her life, it seemed to flow more easily than many people. She seemed to be much more in touch with her intuitive energies. So, I asked her how the Hades Moon had worked for her:

I have the Moon at 17° Libra sextile Pluto at 10° Leo, and although this is a wide aspect, I have found it significant. Ever since I can remember, and from at least age 3, I have had archetypal dreams. I studied psychology and English and made a career in writing and teaching, concentrating on myths and legends. Now I am studying to become a therapist. I have always had access to my own unconscious and am very intuitive in regard to what is going on "under the surface" with others.

From time to time I have had flashes of past lives, especially when my progressed Moon activates this aspect. The first time this happened was in Jerusalem when I was 26-27. I had a past life flash showing me my then-husband and our past lives together, and also the actual medieval city of Jerusalem. This was very useful, as I "knew" my way around, never had to ask directions, and never got lost!

Secondly, when the progressed Moon has made contact with Pluto, even when this has been a square, trine, opposition or conjunction, I have had other past life flashes and received guidance in dreams. This occurred in 1992–1994, when the conjunction was forming. I saw past lives with Lincoln and was guided to come to England to find him—I was living in America from 1978 to 1992.

My mother died in 1995, shortly after I had married Lincoln. At this time my progressed Ascendant was 17° Libra, conjunct my natal Moon—activating the Moon sextile to Pluto and approaching Pluto itself. It was a peaceful death, she died in my arms as though falling asleep. But I feel that this has tremendous significance for my relationship.

THE LAST TRANSITION?

This ability to be with the dead and the dying is an inborn ability of the Hades Moon. This fearless combination can make the journey, and return. After all, this was one of the tasks of the priestess. I have a German friend who, as she matured, found herself caring for the dying. It was, we both feel sure, something she had done many times before in other lives. Freda, a Scorpio, has the Moon conjunct Pluto in Cancer in the 12th house. Knowing that she was a remarkable woman of deep faith which gave her enormous strength, I asked her to trace for me her evolution into a "wise woman" who nurtured people through this last great transition of life:

> I presume that my own mother must have had a Pluto-Moon aspect in her horoscope. She clung to me in a very special way, and I had to learn to free myself from her closeness and become independent. I am sure this was a necessary lesson for me to learn in respect to my own children. I have been a devoted mother and still, of course, care a lot for my boys—but over the years there has been growing a certain distance, a certain loosening, which I am content with.
>
> Outside my own family, I see the mothering aspect throughout my life mostly shown in spiritual and psychological assistance. In my early 30s, we had a number of au pair girls (English and French) living with us and helping with the children. Most of them had problems which they hoped to escape from by going abroad. This was the beginning of an intense caring for young people, which has been lasting up to today and seems to go on. Some of the girls had serious problems with their parents, often especially with the mother. I tried to support the girl's position and at the same time plead for an understanding of the mother's side, acting thus as a sort of intermediary. This, in some cases, lasted over years, and the relationships finally got mended. In two cases the mothers of those girls, at the wedding of the daughter, approached me very lovingly, thanking me for "the times when you have been more of a mother to my daughter than I have been." I explained then that I have never been working against them but for the family and the understanding. They must have known at the time and accepted it.
>
> In my early 40s, the assistance spread to adults, mainly male, the problems becoming more complex (alcoholism). In my mid-40s more and more artists of both sexes were looking for help—the assistance extended being mainly spiritual.
>
> I remember two men: we became close friends, and I am convinced that karmic relations played a major role in these friendships (entirely platonic). The only two visions I ever had in my life were connected with them and became reality. We were at times separated by thousands of miles of land and sea, and yet they both learned to feel my energy and receive it, even "having me present." Both had been without any contact to their church and none to their God, questioning the sense of living, one being a heavy alcoholic. Over the years, through intense talks and exchanges of letters, they found their way "home"—I am sure it was the power of the Divine Love that lit them, I was allowed to be the "transistor." I was asked to be present at the church service where one friend for the first time after forty-two years was bearing the candles and assisting the priest. I happened to be in New York just that weekend on my way from Panama to Bonn—one of those mysterious patterns of "The Plan," and surely one of many memorable moments in my life.
>
> In my early 50s I was entirely occupied by caring for middle-aged females with relationship problems. Having "covered" a number of fields of life, in my mid-50s, I turned toward assisting very ill and dying people in hospitals, most of whom were old. This work gave me a chance to experience the spheres between the here and the there. Knowledge was confirmed.

I first worked in a clinic, in the ward for internal medicine, once weekly in the morning for two to three hours. The doctors often asked me to stay with patients who had been transferred from old age homes to the hospital for various reasons. These people often were slightly confused, some balancing between consciousness and coma. I tried to learn wordless communication on a different level, reaching out into the world beyond ours in order to accompany the souls on their way to the thereafter. My presence sometimes had relieving effects on the patients. There was, for example, a very old, tiny, unconscious lady at whose bedside I had been sitting for a while. She was heavily sighing, irregularly breathing. I tried to transmit the idea of letting loose, letting go, when she suddenly started sobbing and crying, still in her unconsciousness. I took her in my arms and intensified my thoughts until she finally became very calm, breathing well. I stayed with her for another half an hour and then bid farewell to her.

Another patient at the edge of leaving this world was in complete harmony. She seemed fast asleep, so she had not seen me coming and sitting near her. All of a sudden, she sat upright, looked into my eyes and, with a radiant smile, asked me: "Did you see my mother?" Being convinced that her late mother's soul was coming to accompany her in her dying, I could but assure her of her mother's nearness.

In this clinic I was never present when a person actually passed away. It was a Catholic clinic and the Catholic priest made it clear that death was his domain. So after some months I changed hospitals and worked in the cancer hospital, there being asked to accompany a lady in her mid-50s who had only a few months to live. In that case it was more of a "preparing the house for departure" and helping her to be ready for reconciliation with her husband and daughter, and she made it. I worked with many dying people after that.

This hospital work so far has crowned my life. It fulfilled me. I miss it very much.

As Freda's Scorpio Sun was conjuncted by transiting Pluto, her husband was able to purchase his old family home in Eastern Germany. Freda had to make a transition of her own. She had been working in hospitals in Western Germany on a voluntary basis. As soon as the house was settled, and transiting Pluto neared its trine to itself and the Moon, Freda went to the local East German hospital to offer her services. Things were very different there. Under the old regime, no one had ever thought of volunteers going in to be with the patients. The hospitals were antiquated and badly stocked. A volunteer network would have to be set up from scratch. People would have to be educated in what it meant to give service of this kind. There were no counsellors, no one to work with the living or the dying. But that would have to wait until more practical matters had been dealt with. Freda waited to see what the universe required of her next, and moved into working within the community. Her heart-centered spirituality saw her through whatever changes were presented to her, whichever challenge called her to new growth. She evolved gently and inevitably. As she dealt with each moment as it arose, she had no need for catharsis or trauma. Her intuitive power grew as she flowered; she is a truly wise woman.

There is indeed a treasure at the heart of the Hades Moon. It offers the gift of empowerment and regeneration, the strength to face fearlessly whatever must be, to transform, transmute, transcend, but never to lose touch with the roots, with the ground of being.

CHAPTER 10

AFTERLIGHT

Pluto's house position and aspects to other planets demonstrate exactly what areas within each person have previously come under the evolutionary process.
—Jeff Green[1]

THIS CHAPTER is intended for reference when needed, not for ploughing through relentlessly in true Plutonian style!

THE HADES MOON THROUGH THE SIGNS

Any contact between the Moon and Pluto, even if it has a very wide orb or is a minor aspect, should be regarded as a Hades Moon. Pluto's influence tends to exaggerate the shadowy lunar qualities, especially if the aspect is conjunct, square, inconjunct, or opposite. I have concentrated particularly on this negative manifestation, as I believe that recognizing the effect is the first step in transformation. The comments below apply to the Moon in that sign aspecting Pluto no matter what the aspect may be. The sign and house in which Pluto is placed will further color the interaction. A Scorpio Moon, whether or not aspecting Pluto, should be regarded as a Hades Moon because of the Pluto rulership of Scorpio.

HADES MOON IN ARIES

The Hades Moon in Aries is a powerful instinctual desire to have one's needs met. Now. Headstrong and tempestuous, that urge demands instant gratification. This sign is highly passionate and cannot tolerate frustration on any level. The Aries' need for comfort and sex is strong and immediate. So, behavior may be fueled by unconscious sexual needs. In interaction with others, the dominant Aries Moon may be seeking self-oriented, ego-boosting experiences rather than any kind of emotional sharing. Someone with an Aries attuned Hades Moon may insist on having his or her own way, no matter what the cost, and, as the unconscious emotional triggers are very powerful, that "own way" may be self-destructive or without rationale. This can make the Aries Moon seem extremely selfish, or self-centered, and insensitive to other people. As Moon in Aries tends to be emotionally self-sufficient, when Pluto is involved there can be isolation from others. An unspoken message is put out: "I don't need you." When the pull from the unconscious has been recognized, the Aries Moon is capable of deep self-nurturing; and of caring for the needs of others.

With Aries, emotions and feelings flare up, and then die down quickly. Temper, for instance, blasts out without thought. This sign can be verbally abusive. But then it is over. This is not usually a sign to hold a grudge. However, the Hades Moon may well feel resentment that other people do not respond as expected or, even worse, expect an apology for certain Arian high-handed behavior. Aries responds badly to emotional challenge or demand, and the Aries Hades Moon, although it may be affectionate, may also subtly elicit alienation and rejection—and then feel terribly hurt by that response, wondering, "What did I do?"

Lunar food: Like all the fire signs, Aries needs to be recognized as somehow *special*, as being an important part of the greater whole. This is a sign that cannot merge into the background. The lunar food craved is admiration and validation; recognition of all the fiery courageous Arian qualities the Moon is displaying, even though this may be for self-gratification. Without this ego-massaging sustenance, the Aries Moon will become bad-tempered and sulky. With it, the Moon in Aries will shine. All too often, the person with an Aries Moon will become the heroic redeemer, either for the personal mother, for a partner, or for the collective. This Moon carries the archetype of the hero.

Mother: What the Moon in Aries seeks in a mother is a confident and ego-building caregiver, someone who is also fun and who will encourage her child to be independent and adventurous. What the Hades Moon in Aries fears is a dominating mother who will so fill the world, that no self-development is possible.

The archetypal mother symbolized by the Aries Moon is spontaneous and fiery. But, when linked to Pluto, the archetypal mother picture (and often the actual mother, too) can be domineering, egotistical, and self-centered. She may have limited time for her children as her career or outside interests may well come first. When the children do take priority, this is the power behind the throne, and woe betide the child who wishes to make independent choices. "I know best," is the motto of the mother symbolized by the Aries Hades Moon (no matter where her own Moon may be placed), who insists that the child behave her way or else. That "or else" may well include a total cutting off of love. Aries can be ruthless, and this is a powerful threat to keep a child toeing the line. Obviously this can create a conflict as the "child" with an Aries Moon is equally sure s/he knows best, especially when backed up by Pluto. Aries can be a blunt, tactless sign, and the mother symbolized by this Moon can make rather thoughtless remarks which can deeply wound a sensitive child and, unfortunately, the mother who is attuned to the archetype of the Hades Moon knows exactly where to strike for maximum effect. The mother symbolized by the Aries Moon may also encourage a competitive "Must win at all costs" approach to life so that the child will, in her eyes, reflect well on her. So, the child is aware of having to live up to great expectations.

The placement of the Sun in the "child's" chart mediates how well this mother archetype will be handled. Outgoing extroverted children will cope much better than introverted. They can attune to the positive, outgoing qualities of this archetype; but the cautious, withdrawn, imaginative energies of an introverted Sun will, however, baffle an Aries Moon mother—or child.

Healing: What heals the Aries Hades Moon is knowing itself intimately; accepting the totality of light and dark. In recognizing its own capacity for self-care and self-nurturing, the Aries Hades Moon is also able to initiate positive change for others. This placement needs to understand that the apparent difference between the seemingly polarized qualities of dependence and insular independence is in fact two faces of the same underlying separation from one's self. It needs to explore the positive benefits of interdependence. The person with the Aries Moon can then choose how and when to be in relationship, and when to be self-sufficient.

Potential: To be centered around one's Self, aware of and able to meet one's own emotional needs, at the same time recognizing that other people have feelings too.

HADES MOON IN TAURUS

The Hades Moon in Taurus has a strong drive toward security and maintaining traditional values, such as home and family. This leads to fixed habits and a strong degree of control. With those entrenched values, there can be an almost uncrossable generation gap dividing the family. This is the placement that will frequently dig itself into a rut so deep it becomes a grave. So often a square peg in a round hole, dependable Taurus will hang on in there, trying to fit in, resisting at all costs the Plutonian call for change. The Taurus Hades Moon may not even mourn the pieces that have to be shaved off in order to fit. After all, doesn't everyone give up something in order to stay safe? So what if the job is boring, the marriage stultifying? There is always the house: home means a great deal to this Moon. And if depression sets in, well life holds nothing to be joyful about anyway. Except perhaps food. Food is always an emotional experience for a Moon placed in Taurus. It is comfort, nourishment, and sensual pleasure. This is where the Taurus Moon heart is. When Pluto is involved, compulsions, obsessions, and addictions may well center around food as a substitute for love.

With the Taurus Hades Moon, letting go of what passes for security is that much harder. Resistance sets in as the inner energies push toward a cathartic crisis. It is an irresistible force meeting an immovable object. All the endurance of Taurus will pass into holding off the crisis, and all the power of Pluto will compel it into being. At the same time, the Moon holds onto toxic emotions, past patterns that have decayed and festered but cannot be released. Physical breakdown may result as, although Taurus has the constitution of an ox, the pressure has to go somewhere and the physical body becomes the battlefield for the emotional dis-ease. If security has been invested only in the outer world, then the Pluto effect often centers on job, home, and place in society. So, for the Taurus Hades Moon, breakdown may well be total; a stripping away of all that is held dear.

Taurus is an earthy, sensual sign and one of its most powerful drives is the sexual urge. But this is not simply for sex. It is sharing and touch that create the pleasure for the Moon in Taurus. Taurean sensuality is legendary, from sensuous clothes to the stimulation of the senses by perfume, massage, and myriad bodily sensations. This extends to a love of the earth and most Taurean Moons are firmly rooted in the soil. This is a sign that is attuned to the fertile, and patient, Demeter archetype. But, like Demeter, the Taurus grief is dark and devastating, especially when it turns inward.

Lunar food: The Taurus Hades Moon craves affection and sense stimulation. If this is not met early in life, a deep sense of shame about the body develops. If Taurus does not feel at home in the body, then everything is out of alignment, and disease—emotional and physical—results. So often the lunar craving becomes a food addiction, comfort eating replaces the inner sense of rightness about life and one's own particular place in it. What is needed is a deep sense of inner security, being rooted in a patch of eternity: the one thing that cannot be taken away.

Mother: What the Taurus Moon seeks is a dependable and stable "earthmother" figure, someone who deeply values family life and the sense of continuance which children bring, someone who is there, no matter what. (It is unusual to find a Taurean one-parent family, as Taurus will stay in an unhappy marriage "for the sake of the children.") What the Taurus Hades Moon most fears is abandonment and rejection, or disintegration of its safe little world.

The archetypal mothering energy symbolized by the Taurus Hades Moon is dominant, overpowering, and symbiotic. This is the archetypal Demeter Earth Mother who will not let go of her child. The Taurean Hades Moon carries the archetype of "She who must be obeyed" and does not encourage the child to think independently. Possessiveness is the greatest problem with the Taurean Hades Moon mother. The mother believes she "owns" the child, and, somewhere deep inside, the child concurs. This is the mother archetype who expects her son to take over the family business, or follow in father's footsteps into a trade or profession. The Taurean mother places great store on providing a comfortable home. However, suitable gratitude is demanded. Woe betide the child who chooses a different lifestyle, Taurus is a stubborn sign and holds a grudge even against offspring. The mother symbolized by the Taurean Hades Moon's greatest fault is holding on too tightly. This is the sign that invented apron strings—and reins.

Healing: If the Moon in Taurus has, for any reason, become shut off from the body, a road to recovery is open through physical experience: massage and touch for instance. For many Taurean Moons, simply plunging their hands into the earth restores their emotional equilibrium. Healing the Taurus Hades Moon is a matter of reconnecting to the eternal self within, of being grounded in that piece of eternity. Once that connection is made, inner security follows naturally.

Potential: To develop an unshakeable inner sense of emotional security.

Hades Moon in Gemini

The driving force behind Gemini is communication. The Moon in Gemini can be so busy talking about feelings that there is no time to actually feel them. So often, a feeling or an emotion is rationalized out of existence. In any case, this airy sign is actually frightened of emotional trauma and drama, shying away from anything "dark." So, the alienation and isolation of the Hades Moon scares the pants off Gemini, who will hop into bed with anyone to avoid exactly those feelings. This can be an insincere Moon, one that chases frivolity and fun. What fickle Gemini seeks is lightness of being. So Gemini Hades Moon, lacking honesty, chases an elusive experience—true emotion. This is a Jekyll and Hyde Moon and some very dark emotions indeed can lurk beneath the surface. Oscillating swiftly between two poles, this is the sign that gives out double messages. As a result, Gemini skates over the surface of social interaction, endlessly talking but rarely sharing deeply intimate moments. A compulsive interest in other people often leads to a tendency to gossip, and Pluto adds in a certain lethal quality. Many reputations have been ruined by a Gemini Hades Moon—setting up karma in another life. The Moon in Gemini is acquisitive, but it is people and facts that are collected. Indeed, people are often treated like possessions, brought out to be admired—or for amusment—and then put aside until next time.

The Gemini Hades Moon is particularly likely to play out the Pluto archetype for other people. Here is the rapist who snatches the innocent girl, the rake who ensnares Persephone, the bigamist who does not decide between two women, the bisexual who cannot settle on one preference. There is little commitment in a Gemini placed Hades Moon despite its need for people. Add to this the Gemini tendency to float on the surface of emotions. Then slip in the Plutonian ability to see right to the heart of what motivates other people and to what they most desire. The result is emotional manipulation, blackmail. Undemonstrative Gemini flirts and stays detached, other signs fall under the spell.

Artless and guileful, Gemini has strong links with the puer archetype, an archetype that cannot be pinned down. Other people constantly experience the Gemini Hades Moon as "slipping away," shrugging off responsibility. The Pluto archetype's ability to withstand isolation supports this Moon in remaining detached, but sooner or later the Gemini Moon must face the repressed needs that lie behind the apparently insouciant facade.

Lunar food: The Gemini Hades Moon craves attention and mental stimulation, so friends are important. It is ideas that make Gemini come alive. So often these are a substitute for attending to real emotional needs. Whether in therapy or relationship, it is attention the Gemini Hades Moon gets off on: finally someone is totally concentrating on my story—an elaborated, embellished, truth-skirting story to be sure, but mine nevertheless. If these needs are not met, if life no longer has meaning, the Gemini Hades Moon may well fall into the deep black depression that is characteristic of the sign. This is the door into the Underworld which may just offer the Hades Moon insights that will enable true communication of feelings, a mediation between the intellect and the instinctual emotional roots.

Mother: Gemini is a lively, spontaneous sign and what this Moon seeks is a communicative mother who enters into her "child's" adventures with zest and enthusiasm, and a wealth of information. What the Gemini Hades Moon most fears is that mother will smother.

The mother symbolized by the Gemini Hades Moon values her child for intellectual achievements. Difficulties can arise when the Gemini Moon child has a Sun sign that is practical, but not cerebral. The mother symbolized by this Moon is likely to want the spirited discussion which is life-blood to Gemini. If the child cannot respond, the mother may lose interest—permanently.

The mother symbolized by the Gemini Moon is mind- not feeling-oriented. This is not an affectionate mother archetype. The Gemini Hades Moon mother manipulates through words, knowing just how to play on her child's feelings. The inherent inconsistencies in Gemini can be perplexing for the child, particularly when this is mirroring his or her own inner contradictions. There is little stability expected from a Hades Moon in Gemini mother.

Healing: Healing the Gemini Hades Moon comes through allowing the feelings that have been suppressed for so long to emerge. Gemini holds a balance between the body and emotions, mediating through the intellect in order to recognize and acknowledge its own instinctual feelings.

Potential: To be able to recognize and communicate one's own emotional needs clearly.

HADES MOON IN CANCER

Nurturing and emotion are the driving forces behind the moody and overly-sensitive Pluto aspected Moon in its own sign of Cancer. This maternal sign is caring, compulsive, smothering, highly emotional, brooding, possessive and over-solicitous, especially when backed by Pluto. Terrified by its own vulnerability, the insecure Cancer Hades Moon desperately clings to what is known and familiar. This is the sign that will not let go, which cannot cut the ties with the past or with people. Most especially, the psychic umbilical cord to the mother is maintained throughout life unless a great effort is made to disconnect it.

Of all the signs, this is the one most governed by childhood conditioning and most influenced by Mother and unconscious emotional needs. It is a highly dependent Moon, and much adult behavior is directed toward meeting those needs that were unrecognized or unfulfilled in childhood. Cancerian behavior is often based on unconscious emotional triggers, triggers that go back into infancy and beyond. When the Hades Moon is involved, there may well be an old pattern of rejection to overcome; but fear of abandonment will motivate a great deal of Cancerian behavior, particularly the manipulation to which the sign is prone. Rejection, especially of Cancer's innate intuitive perception of other people's feelings, may well trigger hysteria. Sometimes this hysteria is simply over-wrought, out-of-control emotions, but it may also be a kind of nervous collapse in which the functioning of the body is disturbed. This disturbance used to be attributed to the womb as the seat of the emotions, implying it was a female complaint. But men, too, can suffer the hysteria of the highly strung Cancerian Hades Moon and its emotional implosion.

One of the problems for the Cancer placed Hades Moon is the tendency to look outside oneself for support and acceptance of one's inner needs. With such overwhelming emotional needs, there is a tendency to feel, "If my emotions are not recognized, then I don't exist." So, covert manipulation goes on, and the subtle message is put out: "You must love me." As most people tend to back off rapidly from any form of manipulation, the Cancer Moon then experiences rejection, and goes into an attack of the "Oh, poor me's," eliciting further nonacceptance. A vicious cycle begins which leads to a cancerous festering sore of unmet need.

Lunar food: The Hades Moon in Cancer desperately needs validation of feelings and emotional sustenance. Without an emotional response from other people, the Moon in Cancer cannot function. Emotional possessiveness takes over as Cancer fights to hold onto what it does not have. Cancer desires to be part of a family, to be included, to belong. If this is denied, then hurt feelings and isolation can quickly drive the Cancerian Hades Moon deep into its shell. Since Cancer needs to withdraw from time to time, to give an opportunity to process feelings and to recognize exactly what is going on inside, this can be a productive time, but only if the light of consciousness is brought to bear. Left in the dark, the unmet needs fester.

Cancer also needs somewhere to call home. Without a home, this Hades Moon is desperately insecure and deeply unhappy. With a home, Cancer will happily nurture others, providing food and emotional sustenance.

Mother: What the Cancer Moon seeks from a mother is nurturing, sustenance, comfort, and emotional closeness. This is the placement that expects to be mothered, or smothered. What the Cancer Hades Moon most fears is lack of love.

Cancer is the maternal sign, so here we have the archetypal Great Nurturing Mother. This is the sign of over-powering mother love and the mother symbolized by the Cancer Moon may use children as an excuse not to leave the home; nor will she allow the children to leave either. The apron strings remain firmly tied. Clannish and protective of the family unit, the archetypal Moon in Cancer mother tries to hold the family together at all costs, and puts "The Family" first. The result, emphasized by Pluto, is the "Smother Mother" who does not let her child breathe. Cancer can be a possessive sign, and may have a marked tendency to look back to the past. This mother wants things to remain the same forever, and so refuses to recognize the fact that children are growing up.

Paradoxically, for a sign that is so clinging and encourages dependence, the Cancerian Moon mother may be extremely ambitious for her children and may steer them toward a "good" career which will ensure material prosperity and status, rather than one which is fulfilling or particularly suited to the child's own personality.

Healing: The Cancer Hades Moon needs to disentangle the complex instinctual pull that this Moon exerts. The Cancer Moon, more than any other, needs to withdraw into itself cyclically for periods of solitude to go down into the Plutonian depths. In the inner silence, emotional experiences can be digested and assimilated, emotional insecurity can be overcome. Then the Hades Moon can emerge back into the outerworld refreshed and renewed.

Potential: To nurture and parent oneself as well as others.

HADES MOON IN LEO

Leo is the sign of the heart energy and this fiery Hades Moon placement has a warmth that naturally attracts others. That warmth, however, may soon turn to a conflagration. Leo is a powerful sign, prone to emotional games which, when Pluto is involved, can become compulsive and obsessive. The games center around who holds the power and control in relationships.

At its most destructive, the Leo Hades Moon is a drama queen given to histrionics and emotional exhibitions. Compulsively hogging center stage, this vain Moon, and the self-adulation that goes with it, is dominating and superior. The ego is easily wounded, and the Leo Hades Moon takes offense quickly. When the Leo pride is wounded, there is a fast retreat into dignity and standoffishness. However, the histrionics can be a cover to mask the deep insecurity of this placement, the lack of specialness which is so frightening for Leo. It is this inner lack of self-confidence that can make the Leo Moon susceptible to flattery and so desperate for external validation.

Lunar food: The dramatic Leo Hades Moon craves adulation and overt power. This is the sign that longs to be a star. Without acknowledgment of specialness, the Leo Hades Moon shrinks into itself and becomes merely petulant. If this Moon can learn to value its own worth and individuality, the unique qualities each one of us has, then self-empowerment follows and Leo blossoms.

Mother: The type of mother desired by the Leo Moon is warm and affectionate, someone who is slightly larger than life and full of exuberant energy—a playmate, an entertainer, a creative source, a mother who is proud of her child. What the Leo Hades Moon most fears is losing its place as the center of mother's world.

The authority which the archetypal Leonine Mother holds is embodied in the image of "The Queen Bee." There can be only one head of the household when she is around, especially when this is a Hades Moon contact. This is the Dominant Mother at her most mighty, and the needy mother, too. What the mother symbolized by the Leo Hades Moon cannot stand is to be "neglected." She demands constant attention from her offspring.

The mothers reflected in the Leo Moon set lofty standards for their children. They value both themselves and their children highly, taking an enormous pride in the family. They see themselves as having a place in the world which demands that they keep up appearances. Leo is an exuberant, affectionate sign which can, despite the fixed nature of the sign, be tolerant and easygoing with children—provided they do not overstep those clearly defined boundaries of "acceptable" behavor. However, with the Hades Moon mother, the insistence on "standards" may be so overwhelming that there is no room for individual expression. The outwardly happy family picture may also hide some very dark family secrets indeed. On the other hand, the Leo Hades Moon mother may overindulge a child: this can be the "chosen child syndrome" where a child is seen as so special that s/he can never match up to maternal expectations.

Healing: What heals the Leo Hades Moon is recognition of its own deep capacity for loving and natural generosity of spirit. When this Moon becomes centered in the heart, then it showers benevolent warmth on everyone, including itself. It knows that genuine love will replenish itself, being volitional rather than emotional.

Potential: To find creative ways of satisfying one's own emotional needs without looking to other people for validation.

HADES MOON IN VIRGO

Virgo is the sign of service and this Moon desires to serve. Indeed, the urge to serve may be a driving force that keeps the Plutonian Virgo Moon mired in unproductive servitude or servility. Or, this being a Hades Moon, service may be used to subtly manipulate other people and their opinion. So often this is not altruistic service. Instead, the unconfident Virgo Moon feels that, "If I serve, I must be good enough." "If I do this, other people will think I am worthy." Such service comes from a deep inner conviction that one is actually not good enough. This is the Hades Moon with a perfectionist streak, a perfectionism that is coldly critical of anything deemed unworthy of the extremely high standards that are self-imposed—and imposed on others.

The Hades Moon in Virgo has a pressing need to keep at bay the instinctual forces of overwhelming emotion. There is a deep fear that these forces will become uncontrollable, rising up to create chaos in what has to be a well-ordered life. With Pluto behind it, this fear becomes almost an obsession. Rituals are observed; time is carefully organized; rigid mental attitudes protect rigorously against any threat from the Underworld. The contents of the unconscious are heavily defended against incursion into consciousness. The Virgo Hades Moon will condemn and analyze out of existence any "bad" feeling that might arise (feelings that the Virgo Hades Moon has been taught to regard as "bad," but which are often natural feelings with no inherent badness in them).

Such bad feelings are often sexual. After all, Virgo is the sign of the harvest, and this is a fertile, fecund energy—when it is allowed to be. Instead, sterile purity has been imposed on Virgo. Whereas virgin used to mean whole and intact, one in itself, it has now come to mean untouched, undefiled. This is the Kore aspect of the Persephone archetype, the maiden who has to be ravished rather than willingly surrender to the energies of procreation. This sign has become prudish instead of a pure expression of the regenerative urge. This has damned up the creative energy, and driven the powerful Virgoan sexual urge underground into Hades realm. Denied access to consciousness, it produces a psychosomatic state of dis-ease, driving Virgo into workaholism or hypochondria. Often the Virgo Hades Moon gives out double messages based on deep ambivalence about sexual feelings and emotion: seemingly talking wittily and freely about sexual matters or feelings, but then revealing a revulsion; or hiding a tendency to nymphomania beneath a prim and prudish exterior.

Lunar food: This Hades Moon needs recognition and reward, especially for all the service rendered. An appreciation of all that Virgo Moon so quietly performs for others is solicited, but Virgo is too modest and self-deprecating (or too falsely humble) to ask for this directly. When the Virgo Hades Moon is appreciated, the service is unstinting and given from the heart.

Mother: What the Virgo Moon most desires is a mother who is perfect. What the Virgo Hades Moon fears most is not being a good enough child to satisfy mother's overpowering demands.

The archetypal Virgo Hades Moon mother is efficient but emotionally cool—on the surface. Below the surface are Plutonian fears. Although, like all Hades Moon mothers, she exudes a certain emotional neediness, she will not display her emotions openly. A great worrier, she is overly concerned for her children's health and well-being. She wages unceasing war on germs. She may have an obsession about health and hygiene that affects her child right through life. The mother symbolized by the Virgo Hades Moon is a critical perfectionist who has a very real concern for her children. Her deep need to be of service finds its outlet through the child. She will make endless sacrifices to see that her children get the best, and at the same time demands they meet her high standards. This mother archetype is attuned to intellectual energies and the child with a Virgo Moon needs to receive mental stimulation from mother. If this is forthcoming, then it compensates for any coolness in the feeling side of the relationship.

Healing: For the Virgo Hades Moon, healing lies in developing the ability to accept oneself as perfect *as one is now.* To allow into consciousness the totality of feelings and emotions, and embrace them all as acceptable and right. The Virgoan capacity for analysis may be turned inward to help in this process, but only if this is accompanied by loving acceptance, not criticism.

Potential: To become someone who serves from the heart, rather than out of emotional need.

HADES MOON IN LIBRA

The drive for the Moon in Libra is toward relationship. Self-worth is measured in terms of other people's opinion of oneself. It is a romantic Moon, much given to glamor and beautiful surroundings. Everything has to "feel right," Libra seeks harmony and avoids conflict—at any cost. In order to feel comfortable, the Libra Hades Moon will adjust, adapt, and compromise too much.

This is not a Moon that feels comfortable without a partner. The urge is toward someone who will "make a whole," someone who will complete the half-person who is seeking the relationship, a relationship which is by its very nature symbiotic. Even if the other person does not really "feel right," the relationship may continue with Libra trying to adapt and make it fit, at times with traumatic results. Although well disguised, there is something very, very dark indeed at the heart of the Libra Hades Moon, and it is usually projected out onto, and reflected back through, the partner. This Moon can become obsessive and compulsive, totally submerging itself in order to be in relationship, no matter how unfulfilling. What it most fears is being ostracized and cut off from social interaction. Because of its own unacknowledged darkness, Libra can often act out the Pluto archetype for other people, pulling them down into Hades to "meet their doom."

The Libra Moon is the people-pleaser. Born out of the need for other people to like them, Libra Moon people will put their own desires to one side. Eventually, of course, these unfulfilled desires explode into awareness, demanding to be met. Sensitive people trying to deal with a Libra Hades Moon will be aware of this hidden potential for violence, feeling that the Libra Moon's niceness is not to be trusted. There is an added Plutonian dimension, a "malignant niceness," about the Libra Hades Moon. The person with this fawning Moon will be whatever the other person wants, at the same time subtly manipulating and maneuvering the partner to gain support, approval, acceptance, or whatever. The fear is: "If my partner knows what I am really like, I will not be loved." Or, the fear is that if the partner does not feel good, then the whole world will collapse. This Moon is extremely uncomfortable with other people's darker emotions, and will do all it can to avoid dealing with them. Indeed, with all the indecisiveness of Libra, the Hades Moon in this sign will often let other people play out all that it has never got around to acting out.

Lunar food: What the Libra Hades Moon craves is admiration, adulation, and harmony, with success nourished by beauty. Everything must be "nice." Immersed in peace, Libra feels nurtured by partnership. But what the Libra Hades Moon most needs is to find those inner qualities which make self-nourishment possible.

Mother: What the Libra Moon seeks from a mother is peace and harmony in a beautiful environment. The mother, symbolized by the Moon in Libra, is pleasant and relaxed. She does all she can to provide a comfortable home. What the Hades Moon in Libra fears is that mother will turn out to be not at all nice.

Archetypally this is one of the "nicer mothers." It is Demeter before Persephone is snatched, or after she has been returned. We can, however, glimpse shades of the destroying face of Demeter in the darkness that lies at the heart of Libra. There is a peculiar selfishness: nothing is allowed to disturb the emotional equilibrium. It is important to the mother represented by the Libra Moon that her child is liked and accepted by everyone, which may mean that the natural tendency of the child with Libra Moon toward compromise is reinforced by parental approval. The child needs to be approved of, and so adapts to whatever mother wants. The Libra Moon mother archetype would much rather that the other parent dealt with unpleasant matters so that disciplinary threats are usually on the lines of, "Wait 'til your father gets home." By the time he does, peace and quiet has returned to the family, but nevertheless to a child with the Libra Hades Moon, the father may well be an ogre figure.

Healing: Libra Hades Moon healing comes in harmonizing and balancing one's own needs with those of other people, effecting a creative compromise that meets both sets of needs. It also comes through being a complete person in one's own right, not needing someone else to make oneself whole. When the Libra Moon finds personal inner equilibrium, there is no need for external approval. This Moon is then able to be honest and truthful in expressing feelings.

Potential: To become a whole person who can relate from a position of emotional equilibrium.

HADES MOON IN SCORPIO

The Hades Moon in Scorpio is probably the most challenging of all because it has a "double dose" of Pluto, and yet it is also the most rewarding and enriching. It is an emotional powerhouse, or a disaster area depending on how consciously it is being used. The rulership of Scorpio by Pluto intensifies the Hades effect, so much so that anyone with the Moon in Scorpio quite naturally has a Hades Moon even if there is no aspect from Pluto. Hidden behind an inscrutable facade, this is the Moon that is brooding, compulsive, paranoid, intensely emotional, and deeply repressed. It is also insightful, healing, and cathartic. The driving urge of the Scorpio Moon is to explore power and death, and to enter the taboo places where other signs fear to tread. This urge propels the Scorpio Moon into traumatic emotions, dramatic life experiences, and painful metamorphosis. This is a Moon placement that cannot live on the surface of life. The pull to Hades is too strong. This Moon is attuned to Pluto, Persephone as the mysterious Queen of the Underworld, and Hecate archetypes. It is in honoring these parts of the self that the Scorpio Moon finds its true expression.

The deeply mistrustful Scorpio Moon harbors old jealousies, resentment, pain, and passion. It suffers from ancient guilt and alienation, and may well elicit rejection as a defense against opening up to another person. Despite a craving for emotional intimacy, this Moon resists allowing anyone else "in." Its great fear is that, having access to these dark emotions, someone else will then be in a position of power. All emotions, pleasurable as well as painful, are held in an unrelenting control. As these seething emotions are so deeply repressed, from time to time they erupt in spectacular style with an energy out of all proportion to the trigger event. If the emotions do not erupt out, then there is a danger of implosion, an event that carries with it the possibility of physical, mental, as well as emotional collapse—propelling this Moon into Hades, its natural home. If handled wisely and guided by someone who understands the territory, the breakdown then becomes the catalyst for inner exploration and breakthrough into the mysteries of the inner self.

When relationships are entered into unconsciously, they are obsessive, compulsive, dominating everything else. The partner mirrors the dark and destructive energies of the Hades Moon. Something festers deceptively below the surface only to emerge later as addiction, dependence, or violence. Undertaken more consciously, there is an urge into merging, a mystical union of the emotions and, indeed, of the very souls of the two people concerned. Entering a Hades Moon relationship is like a descent into the Underworld, full of terrors and yet having the possibility of untold riches, too. The Hades Moon is an extremely loyal partner for those whom it trusts. Nevertheless, there is possessiveness, jealousy, and domination within the passion. This is an insecure Moon that will plot and manipulate to keep its "love." It fears endings desperately, and seeks to avoid the desolation of the death of passion. This Moon placement has experienced many betrayals, and plotted endless revenge. Vengeful and untrusting, the Hades Moon has a very long memory indeed.

For the Hades Moon, the past is an unsafe place to venture, and yet it is in the past that the key to understanding this Moon lies. There is an urgent need to explore childhood and beyond, to face the fears and traumas of past experience, to bring into the light of awareness all the secrets harbored by this damaged Moon. So often we find there the roots of the placement's fears, especially of abandonment and rejection, and an old persecution that explains the paranoid dread of the lurking but unnameable "them." This dread is recreated in the deepest recesses of the night; childish night terrors are so often founded on real experience for this wounded soul—as are adult nightmares.

This is a psychic and intuitive Moon, and people with this placement are able to tune into other people and instantly perceive their real feelings. As a result, in childhood, great confusion can arise between what is intuitively perceived and what they are told. They cannot trust their own intuitions and feelings, because someone else has declared them "wrong." So, they grow up not valuing this fey and witchy side of themselves, and will repress this if at all possible. Then, the "intuitions" become contaminated with emotional energies that have been strongly suppressed into the shadows. They make themselves known through dreams and premonitions. More fear and paranoia emerge, creating a vicious circle. Once these energies can be recognized as Pluto or Hecate's gifts, they can be reclaimed, cleansed, and put to use. This takes considerable pressure off the Hades Moon and releases its healing potential. As this Moon has the deepest traumas, so too it can reach the greatest heights.

Lunar food: For the Scorpio Hades Moon, power and intensity are sustaining. Power can, of course, be power-over or empowerment, and Scorpio experiments with both in its journey. If life, and relationships, are unfulfilling, then the Hades Moon tends to go for power-over situations. When the journey to Hades has been made and the insights gained, then this Moon becomes empowered and fed from its own inner reserves.

With this Moon, intensity is craved, in much the same way as an addict craves the drug of choice. There is a great deal in common between Scorpionic "love" and the psychological state of addiction. Both are emotional fuels. Each is a road into the Underworld, a pathway to understanding. Feelings, emotions, and moods may be obsessive and consume a person with the Scorpio Moon. This all-consuming passion turns them inside out, and brings them to that part of the psyche Jung spoke about, the world that is both the unconscious and the Underworld. It is the place of transformation.

Mother: What the Scorpio Moon is seeking in a mother is empowerment and insightful nurturing, with plenty of emotional intensity to it. Scorpio needs to know that it is cared for with passion. What the Scorpio Hades Moon fears is being devoured by mother.

Archetypally, this Hades Moon is the terrible, devouring mother, holding absolute power of life and death. This is the Great No-Sayer. It symbolizes the threatening mother who rigidly controls her child's life, and who lives out all her unlived life through that child. If the child dares to protest, then all the festering rage that lies behind this placement falls on the child. Annihilation is a distinct possibility, abandonment a real fear. This powerfully instinctual mother would rather kill than be thwarted. The psychic umbilical cord is kept tight, ready to strangle the child at the slightest provocation. Anyone with this archetype is liable to intense and powerful conflict with any dominant, rigid, control-oriented woman (or anyone perceived that way, projection is rife with the Hades Moon), as well as the biological mother.

The mother symbolized by the Scorpio Hades Moon can be passionately attached to her offspring, or pathologically jealous of the attention the child receives from the other parent. Scorpio is a difficult sign to understand, and the mother symbolized by the Scorpio Moon is no exception. The apparently calm, unruffled exterior gives no hint of how she really feels about children and there can be a strong love/hate relationship taking place below the surface, with extremely compulsive feelings involved. These mothers channel a great deal of their intense emotional energy into the care and control of youngsters. Unfortunately control may be the operative word, Scorpio needs to be absolute mistress in her own home, and the Scorpio Moon can indicate many clashes between parent and child. However Scorpio is a loyal sign, so children with the Moon in this sign expect support in the eyes of the community, no matter what goes on in the privacy of the home.

Healing: Healing for this Hades Moon comes through the journey into the Underworld, a journey which will involve confrontation with birth, death, and rebirth, and a recognition of the cyclical nature of the process. Eliminating the fear of death is the first stage of Plutonic initiation. Traveling to meet this Moon will necessitate an exploration of childhood and previous life patterns. It is only in accepting, and understanding, these powerful instinctual forces, and then integrating them fully into consciousness, that the Moon can access its rich inner resources of power and insight. In this way, it is possible to direct at source (that is, within oneself) the enormous power of the Scorpio Moon. This Moon has a primal connection to the creative life force. Once that journey has been made, this Moon becomes the guide and catalyst for other people's journeys.

It is also crucial for anyone with the Moon in Scorpio to encompass the "love-hate" dilemma and bring it into consciousness, to integrate the paradox that what creates can also destroy, or that which makes us feel alive can also bring us deadness, to recognize that both love and rage are irretrievably caught up in any relationship. They are not opposites, one of which must be eliminated; they are complementary forces that need expression. If each is given its own space, neither will go out of control and create destruction.

Potential: To integrate and accept one's own emotional darkness as a creative force.

HADES MOON IN SAGITTARIUS

The Hades Moon in Sagittarius has a driving need for emotional freedom. This is the Moon that cannot stand to be tied down on any level, and instinctively avoids an emotional pull. There is a deep fear of commitment. When Pluto is involved, escape may become compulsive. This is a dual Moon that can oscillate between two relationships, remaining committed to neither. It may prefer companionship to love. This is the courtesan's Moon, gregarious and dedicated to social pleasure, flitting along on the surface of life, but secretly enjoying hidden power. The Hades Moon in Sagittarius views feelings as irrational, and therefore not to be trusted, but is not above using them to manipulate a lover, or a child. When bored, the Sagittarius Hades Moon may well stir up a little emotional trouble to liven things up. It might even go so far as to act out a few histrionics. It then observes the results with fascinated interest, but fails to get involved at the feeling level. Whenever there is real emotional pressure, Sagittarius is "out to lunch." The response to emotional demands is to travel, preferably far and fast, but mentally will do if physical travel is out of the question.

When the Hades Moon in Sagittarius does finally get involved in relationship, this tends to be quickly and without thought. The Sagittarius Hades Moon is somewhat gullible, especially as it knows so little about intimacy. It can be easily taken in by attractive packaging and a charming manner, so it is susceptible to Pluto arising out of the night to snatch the innocent maiden, or puer youth, down into Hades. This brings the initiation into the darker side of life it has been avoiding for so long.

Being a head-oriented sign, Sagittarius enjoys discussions about feelings and what they *mean*. It is deeply curious about other people's experiences. With an overwhelming desire to understand, this Moon cannot really believe that other people may not share this urge to reveal all over the dinner table. This is the philosophical Moon that can tell you exactly the difference between feelings and emotion. But, ask about personal emotional experience and what you get is merely words. The Sagittarius Hades Moon is an expert in emotional self-protection.

Lunar food: For Sagittarius flattery and attention is nourishing, as is any kind of "mind fodder," especially intellectual or philosophical discussion. Like all the fire signs, there is a need to feel special, and perhaps of all the signs Sagittarius most wants to be one with the gods (indeed strongly suspects it is one of the gods). So, anything which makes the Sagittarius Hades Moon feel "out of this world," erudite, looked up to, is welcomed with open arms.

Mother: What the Sagittarius Moon seeks is a companionable mother, one who is able to enter freely into the imaginative world of childhood and play, one who offers freedom of choice and intellectual stimulation, but who also respects a child's space simply to be. What the Sagittarian Hades Moon fears is being consumed by mother and never breaking free.

The archetypal Sagittarian Moon mother is freedom-loving and spontaneous, yes. She is the opposite of the Great No-Sayer and yet, paradoxically, this may be a shadow element when Pluto is involved. Belief systems are important to Sagittarius, and the Sagittarian Hades Moon mother may strenuously impose her own particular brand of morality or philosophy of life, thereby severely restricting her child. As a sign, Sagittarians have great difficulty with routine and their own discipline, and the mother symbolized by the Sagittarius Moon may have equal difficulty in controlling wayward children—particularly as she so values the freedom to be herself and wishes to extend this to her children. For this reason, Sagittarian Moon mothers tend to be tolerant of behavior that other signs would find unacceptable, such as rudeness, lateness or untidiness. If this freedom is offered too early, before the child has developed any real sense of self, s/he is left without guidance. The child may grow up lacking a sense of boundaries, and find difficulty in being accepted in the world because of this.

Healing: The Sagittarius Hades Moon finds healing in experiencing life directly through the feelings and emotions rather than the head. By being involved, the Hades Moon learns that there is nothing to fear. In recognizing one's own instinctual lunar needs, and giving them space for expression, one can accept other people's desires. The Sagittarian Hades Moon then develops a philosophy of life that is open and trusting, which gives space to intuition and feelings, and gives true meaning to life.

Potential: To find true inner emotional freedom.

HADES MOON IN CAPRICORN

The Hades Moon in Capricorn has a strong sense of responsibility. This is the sign that carries the world on its shoulders. It is the Moon placement that takes life very seriously, indeed. It is the driving urge toward stability and maintaining the status quo, toward respectability and getting things right in order to deserve approval. Capricorn is somehow pre-programed toward carrying burdens, and this Moon meets its duties, and difficulties, early in life. This Moon often has a sense of mission, something that must be done, or a feeling that somehow the sins of the world have to be remitted. Such a messianic complex is difficult for an adult to deal with, let alone a child, and so often the Capricorn Hades Moon denotes the emotional scapegoat in the family or in life.

The Capricorn Hades Moon often has a particularly difficult childhood. A stultifying and emotionally repressed atmosphere is characterized by illness, poverty, duty, or deprivation of some kind. This deprivation may be emotional, intellectual, or physical. There is little emotional closeness in the restrictive Capricorn Moon home. Loss of a parent early in life is frequently experienced. For some children with this Moon, a parental preoccupation with wealth and status can lead to the absent father, or mother who is always working. In other cases, "duty" serves as an excuse for the Capricorn Moon placement (or the parent symbolized by this) to neglect the, for them, uncomfortable emotional side of life in favor of materialistic values. The child grows up feeling that the only worthwhile marker of progress is achievement and success. Self-worth depends on being "on top." This is a vulnerable and unconfident Moon at heart.

As a result, Capricorn is the sign of repressed emotion; feelings are negated in favor of value judgments about worth and status. Emotion is an unknown, and much feared, territory. The person with this Hades Moon can grow up to be coldly controlling, judgmental, afraid to express any emotion, and too cautious to trust life. A message of isolation and "approach with caution" is given out. Like all the earth signs, if the Capricorn Moon does not get in touch with pleasurable bodily sensation early on, or if physical closeness is frowned upon, then the result is shameful feelings about the body and its functions.

Fortunately for the Capricorn Moon, this is the placement where, paradoxically, one gets younger as time goes on. Somehow the burdens lift, or are grown into, so that they are not so heavy. The duties become less onerous. In maturity, the sardonic black humor of Capricorn can begin to see the funny side of life.

Lunar food: The Capricorn Hades Moon finds being in control and being successful nourishing. When this Moon feels that everything is in order, it can relax a little. When it is seen as successful, the validation makes everything seem worthwhile. What the Capricorn Hades Moon needs to learn is that it is possible to be loved for oneself, not merely for what one achieves.

Mother: With the Capricorn Moon, what is desired from the mother is materially comfortable surroundings and consistent discipline that leads toward maturity and self-control. This Moon needs a mother who provides boundaries and rules inside which autonomy can be developed. What the Capricorn Hades Moon most dreads is overly-emotional smothering or an out of-control mother who has no limits because she is immersed in her own darkness.

The archetypal mother symbolized by the Capricorn Hades Moon is authoritarian, cold and controlling, with a great emphasis on discipline. Another expression of the "Great No-sayer" archetype, this is not a placement that will allow experimentation by children. They are expected to conform. The Capricorn Moon will frown on any departure from the old-fashioned "norm." Too much discipline may annihilate the child's sense of self early on, or the child may be expected to act as a little adult. The mother symbolized by the Capricorn Hades Moon tends to push children to get ahead, and the emotionally needy child may suffer from the "cold love" offered in the place of genuine affection.

Healing: For the Capricorn Hades Moon, healing follows on after a secure material foundation for life has been laid. Once Capricorn has achieved some degree of success, there is much more readiness to trust life and journey inside oneself. The doubts and fears of childhood have to be explored, and the coldly rejecting archetypal parent rooted out. This Moon is then able to develop the self-love that provides a secure foundation for emotional trust and spontaneous expression of feelings. When this Moon is working consciously, it is steadfast, responsible and authoritative, offering dependable support.

Potential: To develop a deeply rooted sense of self-worth and personal autonomy.

HADES MOON IN AQUARIUS

The Hades Moon in Aquarius has a powerful urge for emotional space, and yet this is the humanitarian sign, with a drive toward revolutionizing the social order. This urge, driven by Pluto, can become anarchic and paranoid, or simply alienated from the rest of the world. Aquarius is the sign that fears commitment because it can bring the chaos of the emotional world too close for comfort.

This Moon, while being concerned about the whole of humanity, has great difficulty in one-to-one relationships, as though it is impossible to focus the vision down to just one person. Intimacy is alien territory. Other people, as individuals, do not mean anything and are somehow not even noticed. There is an exceptionally strong degree of independence with the Aquarian Hades Moon, which can lead to social isolation. So, this Moon has a non-close, distant, and formal pattern of relating and takes refuge in a very cold and lonely place whenever it is threatened with too much emotion. At times this Hades Moon, fueled by power-hungry Pluto, will use its strong connection to collective power to seek personal power. It becomes manipulative in a "magical" Uranian way. This is emotional sorcery at work, tantalizing and spell-binding its victim into compliance, all the while holding back on any emotional involvement. Traditionally seen as detached, this is actually a self-contained Moon that is out of touch with its own feelings. So, much Aquarian Moon behavior is motivated by deep instinctual lunar needs, and yet, because this sign lives "in the head," there is no connection made between these needs and Aquarian behavior. Once this connection is made, rational understanding combines with *feeling* to give an objective and yet caring perspective on all human behavior and interaction. Aquarius is capable of sharply perceptive insights into itself as well as other people. The lesson for this Moon is to recognize that detachment is being free from any need concerning a person or a situation, rather than being disconnected from, or controlled by, the need to be comfortable within a situation.

Unpredictable Aquarius is a curious, contradictory mixture of a progressive outlook (its Uranian ruler) and a fixed nature (its Saturnine ruler), and it must be remembered that emotional expression for Moon in Aquarius springs from this impossible combination. So, the Hades Moon in Aquarius may appear to be open and frank in emotional discussion, but it is strangely touchy and cannot bear criticism. Indeed, if there is too much emotional pressure, the rational Aquarian Moon will dissociate and retreat into theories or fantasy. Impersonal Aquarian Moon people can be so busy observing and reforming the world that they forget that they, too, are part of the human family.

Lunar food: The Aquarian Hades Moon finds nourishment in social contacts. This Moon desires friends who are intellectually stimulating but do not make too many emotional demands. And yet, deep down, the Aquarian Moon really longs for emotional intimacy with someone who can also allow space, someone who can appreciate the uniquely individualistic person who hides behind the Hades Moon.

Mother: The Uranian part of the Aquarian Moon would like a mother who is somewhat zany and unpredictable, a "live-wire." A kind of "universal aunt" rather than a motherly figure. But, the conservative, Saturnine side of the Aquarian Moon may well find this unconventional mother rather an embarrassment. Adding Pluto to the mix only creates more ambivalence. The person with the Aquarian Hades Moon fears that "mother" will cut off all personal freedom, dis-allowing the emotional space that this placement so desperately needs, and so breaks out into rebellion and eccentricity as a defense against being swallowed up in the devouring mother.

The archetypal Mother symbolized by the Aquarian Moon is detached and cool, caring but not overly concerned. This is the mother who puts the greater whole first, who may find it difficult to focus down onto just one child. The greatest difficulty with the unconventional Aquarian Moon mother may be that, having entered into an eccentric or avant-garde theory of child raising, when it clearly does not work or alienates the child from his or her peers, then Aquarius still sticks to the theory regardless. When Pluto enters the equation, mother's emphasis on theory may take on the qualities of an ogre. She may become all-powerful, totally dominating the child's world. The child does not dare to rebel in case she shuts off what passes for love. And yet she sees herself as "a friend," giving the child freedom. The problem is, the freedom is only to conform, or rebel, within rigidly controlled boundaries of what is acceptable to mother; it is not permission to grow.

Healing: Healing for the Aquarian Hades Moon means venturing into Pluto's realm and connecting to the greater whole. By allowing the deeply instinctual feelings to arise and be integrated into life, Aquarius can find true detachment, whereby one is able to stand in the middle, having emotions, feeling the feelings, but not being overwhelmed by them. It is in Pluto's realm that Aquarius can find the freedom from need which is true detachment. In Pluto's realm, too, Aquarius is able to plug into a rich vein of universal love. This love can then be expressed out for all humanity, but, it can also be expressed one to one.

Potential: To find emotional detachment and become the expression of universal love.

HADES MOON IN PISCES

The Hades Moon in Pisces has a driving urge to merge back into blissful union with the collective whole. It symbolizes a desire for self-immolation and individual extinction. Real life is a bit too harsh, so this escapist Moon spends many blissful hours engaged in fantasy and delusion, or communing with a bottle to find the ecstasy it so compulsively seeks. This is almost certainly the most unconscious of the Moons, the most swayed by any passing emotion, as the Pisces Hades Moon flows to and fro without control or volition. So Pisces, without knowing it, spends many hours in Hades.

It is a powerfully manipulative Moon, prone to enfolding other people in a beautiful fantasy of oneness: a shared delusion of perfect unity that lasts until the next sucker comes along. However, this being a dual Moon, the illusion of faithfulness is maintained, even while Pisces is happily involved in the next "perfect love" affair. The Pisces Hades Moon deceives itself into believing that it could not possibly hurt anyone, so it makes promises it has no intention of keeping, maintains two or more relationships at once, and goes its own sweet way, leaving a trail of destruction behind. Or rather, almost behind it. This is the Moon placement that has perhaps the greatest difficulty in letting go of past relationships and of separating from old lovers. Somehow the Pisces Moon never gets around to saying goodbye. And, somehow, with its tendency to victimhood, it is always the other person's fault. The Pisces Moon sees itself as having done everything possible to keep things going. So persuasive is this view that the partner often ends up feeling guilty. The Pisces Moon induces guilt with facile ease, even without the aid of Pluto. Nevertheless, the Pisces Moon is strongly sympathetic, kind, and considerate. Prone to over-empathizing with people, and so taking in all their pain, this is one of the Moon placements that really does care about other people. Until Pluto intervenes. Pitiless Pluto adds a dimension of self-centeredness that is, apparently, alien to Pisces; or does it simply bring closer to the surface an inherent selfishness? This is a question that the Pisces Hades Moon would prefer not to contemplate.

The Pisces Hades Moon has three scenarios that are all too familar. The first is the savior, the person who is out to save, most usually, another human being, although Pisces is addicted to lost causes and to sacrificial acts. This Moon is so sure that with just a little more help, a bit more cash, an added dimension of understanding, this lost soul can be helped—or forcibly changed, Pluto can be extremely coercive here. This scenario usually leads straight into scenes two and three—victimhood or martyrdom. The gullible Pisces Moon, having been taken advantage of time after time, still says: "How could I possibly see it coming?" "What did I do to deserve this?" "How could they do this to me?" This self-pitying Moon is prone to codependent situations where someone "other" lives out the most destructive Piscean patterns of addiction and victimhood.

However, the Pisces Hades Moon is equally capable of living out destructive patterns itself, usually through drink and drugs, but it may equally be emotional dependence, comfort eating, or sexual addiction: Pluto adds a powerful sex drive to the usually quiescent Moon. Here again, Pisces is "victim" rather than perpetrator. This Moon never means to take that drink, someone else insisted. It didn't mean to get into bed, it just happened. Nor was there any intention to see the object of their dependence again, s/he "simply came around." The excuses are many and varied; "I was only trying to blot out the pain," "I am so sensitive I just could not stand it," etc., etc. It is only when the Pisces Moon recognizes its own collusion that the pattern can be changed.

The Hades Moon in Pisces is a highly psychic and intuitive Moon. This is the natural medium or channel for spiritual inspiration. It is empathetic and aware of others' feelings to the extent of being telepathic and picking up intimate thoughts: indeed, one difficulty this Moon has is in distinguishing its own thoughts and feelings from those of other people. The problem is that unresolved emotional issues may well taint the impressions received, and this Moon lacks the discrimination to recognize this. What Pisces unconsciously puts out in the way of emotional needs is reflected back through the messages it receives from the subconscious, not from a "higher" level of consciousness. At its worst scenario, this combination goes in for emotional black magic. Knowing just how powerful psychic energy is, disingenuous Pisces quietly directs it toward the chosen victim. All the power is channeled in that one direction, and it is hard to resist its seductive lure. Those wide innocent eyes are batted, just once, and the spell is cast. The slippery Pisces Hades Moon, if challenged, denies it, of course, but this placement knows exactly what it is doing.

Lunar food: Other people are the lunar food demanded by this symbiotic Moon. It requires close, intense, but above all emotionally melding, relationships. The Pisces Hades Moon wants to merge into another, to be one, to extinguish self in the ecstasy of mutual orgasm—even in a social conversation.

Mother: The Pisces Moon desires a mother who is caring, sensitive, and sympathetic, a mother who empathetically encompasses the child in her imaginative world. What the Hades Moon in Pisces most fears is abandonment and separation from Mother.

The archetypal mother symbolized by the Pisces Moon is caring, sensitive, and sympathetic to children's needs, provided that the child is on their particular wavelength. The Pisces Moon mother finds great difficulty in recognizing children as existing in their own right, and therefore in comprehending that children can be different. When that difference is finally recognized, the child may be treated as an alien being, as the Pisces Moon mother has no way, other than her irrational feelings, to reach out to her child.

The darkest side of the mother symbolized by the manipulative Pisces Hades Moon is her guilt-inducing qualities. This is the mother who knows exactly which button to press to bring the collective guilt of centuries swimming up to the surface in her emotionally vulnerable offspring. Because she takes on the victim role so easily herself, she may subtly induce this approach to life in her child. Busy swimming two ways at once, Pisces has a great deal of difficulty with discipline, and with direction. Shrewd children soon learn to manipulate this to their own advantage and become used to getting their own way. This can lead to something in which the Pisces Moon mother positively wallows—martyrdom. "After all I've done for you," must surely have first been said by this mother, and she hasn't stopped saying it since. Add Pluto, and this is the tightly controlling mother who dominates through weakness, victimhood, and emotional blackmail. She desires eternal oneness with her child; her greatest threat is separation and loss of love.

Healing: Healing for the Pisces Hades Moon comes in voluntarily surrendering to the Underworld. By immersing oneself in the unconscious, one becomes aware of the source of feelings and motivation. In encompassing the darker side, lies healing and self-acceptance. In Hades, too, self-integration with the cosmos can begin. This is not a loss of self but rather an extension. With this added dimension, Pisces is then able to channel out unconditional love and acceptance to all.

Potential: To become a truly enlightened, whole being.

PLUTO THROUGH CANCER TO CAPRICORN

When considering the placement of Pluto in your chart, bear in mind its generational effect—what you share with your peers, its collective effect—the impact on society as it moves through a sign; and the personal effect pinpointed by Pluto's house position and aspects—your own unique experience of the plutonian energies at work.

PLUTO IN CANCER (1914–1939)

Cancer is where we plug into collective domesticity and nationalism. This is a nice cosy sign until Pluto sets up home. Pluto's subversive energy is potent in Cancer; as it works against the Cancerian need for security and frustrates its attempts to control the environment. This is where Pluto urges the collective into social change, but raises questions about the security of that change. The battle between communism (the "caring, concerned" side of Cancer) and capitalism (the aggressive cardinal side of Cancer that goes all out for material success) started with Pluto in Cancer. Pluto in Cancer also saw the Great Depression and the disintegration of families through World War 1. Initially, it also accelerated changes in the role of women, giving them more freedom and autonomy, but the Cancerian backlash after the wars forced them back into the home. We can also see the polluting effect of Pluto in that the Cancerian desire to grow more to feed the family, which led directly to the increase of chemicals in agriculture—chemicals that we now recognize destroy and mutate life—that often create the disease cancer.

The shadow side of Cancer is concerned with over-sentimentality and emotionalism, with idealizing the family and ignoring individual need. From here it is a simple step to fanatical nationalism. "The Country" becomes "the Family," and its needs lead to abuse of individual freedom. War is declared on anything that threatens the cohesiveness of the hive, especially on the collective shadow projected "out there" onto the "enemy."

Holding onto the past simply because it is there, Cancer can block progress or create conflict where none is required. Cancer could be where we learn lessons from the past, but this entrenched sign rarely lets go for long enough to take an objective look, subjectivity being a strongly Cancerian trait.

Defensive Cancer is the sign of emotional dependency, and it is also prone to fluctations of mood and emotion. Pluto in Cancer heightens these emotions, and forces us to recognize the shadow qualities and Plutonian fears that form the basis of so much of our behavior. Pluto "rocks the boat," bringing to the surface all the emotional insecurity and resentment we have tried so hard to hide. As Cancer is naturally a resentful and self-pitying sign, this spills over into a martyred, suffering shadow, a shadow that must be transformed to release the energy trapped within it. With so much energy tied up in security, Cancer is easily threatened. Paranoia can so quickly set in with Pluto in Cancer. Security is hard won. The Gate into Incarnation is not an easy one.

PLUTO IN LEO (1939–1957)

The "Me Generation" was born when Pluto moved into Leo. The Leonine need to be a unique, special individual could now find an outlet. Initially, during war, this was as a hero, but later Leo made its mark in many fields. The individual could separate from the collective, aided and abetted by Pluto. This is the sign that needs to direct its own life and destiny. As Jeff Green puts it, Leos need to be "in charge of their own play." This sign has a strong creative will. With Pluto behind that will, Leo can reach out and shape life "my way."

This generation was the first to have real leisure time, to experience sponta-neous moments of creativity. Not everyone was able to fulfil, through public recog-nition, this leonine need to be special, but the potential was there. Conversely, this is also the generation who first made it into the "big time." Mass adulation attended the Beatles and other pop stars born as Pluto moved into Leo. (Pop music came to birth as Pluto changed signs: the performers had Pluto in flamboyant Leo.) It is this generation who, as the century draws to a close, have been offered the opportu-nity to reach, and heal, that playful Leo child who is within each of us.

The Pluto-in-Leo generation was also the first to be recognized as "teenagers," an entity in their own right, and one that was to become influential in terms of pur-chasing power and influence on popular taste. Rock and roll, which ushered Pluto out of Leo, expressed the collective need to rebel (shades of the opposite sign, Aquarius). Many of the rock and roll idols were seen as anti-establishment figures who were given almost god-like worship by their fans. They provoked torrents of rhetoric, mainly from the Pluto-in-Cancer generation, which at times resembled the medieval inquisition (a most Plutonian affair). The main questions raised were: What the world was coming to? What had happened to moral values? And who had cor-rupted the young? Senator MacCarthy's paranoid anti-communist American witch-hunts also took place in the 50s, and were especially aimed at those in the entertainment business who had positions of "special influence." Pluto, being a god, could not be put in the dock. Had he been, he would no doubt have been pro-claimed guilty of the moral equivalent of treason. He was, however, merely raising the shadow of leonine idealism and omnipotence—persecution.

Leo is a sign that has to grapple with power—to own it and become empow-ered. But, at the same time, Leo faces the challenges of retaining humility. The shadow side of Pluto in Leo leads to self-aggrandizement and love of power, to megalomania and paranoia. Many countries were controlled by dictators, and devi-ous counter-espionage was undertaken "in the national interest." These measures were uncontrollable and took over as a collective machine (spawning the paranoia of conspiracy theory which surfaced as Pluto moved out of Scorpio). This era saw the birth of superpowers whose national pride came before anything else, leading to conflicts over territory and ideologies. It was when the world really polarized into "us" and "them." The Cold War became entrenched and there was no oppor-tunity for reconciliation because Leo pride could not back down over anything. "Them" was the Plutonian shadow projected "out there" onto "the enemy," who was perceived as everything that was evil and unspeakable, alien and foreign.

Individually, the Pluto-in-Leo need to be special can manifest as a "bottom-less pit," one that is desperate for flattery, attention, and what passes for love. Such a shadow is self-centered, with delusions of grandeur. It concentrates only on the individual at great cost to society in general. The danger is that what can create, can also destroy.

PLUTO IN VIRGO (1957–1972)

Pluto moving into Virgo brought people face to face with entrenched values about employment and health, and moral ideals of "perfection." This was the period when the development of birth control at last gave people control over their own fertility—a Virgoan attribute. But, before birth control became freely available, many babies were adopted, probably more than at any other time the secret fruits of fertility were "given away." This was the result of free love versus the traditional values of the Pluto in Cancer parental generation trying to maintain their standards at all costs, even if it meant depriving their child of her offspring and so going against all that maternal Cancer stood for. At the same time, the nuclear family broke up, and one-parent families, in the West at least, became the norm. In the eyes of the die-hard traditionalists, moral distintegration had set in.

Pluto moving into Virgo coincided with mass reconstruction and a vision of a new world. In both capitalism and communism, full employment and security of tenure after the horrors of war were the principles to which people clung. However, the shadow face of Virgo can be "cold," critically inhuman, the perfectionist. The vast housing estates constructed in Britain and the USA at this time proved impossible for human beings to thrive in, leading to the underground protest movements of vandalism and crime. Toward the end of Pluto's sojourn in Virgo, automated production replaced people with machines in the interests of efficiency. Virgoan craftsmanship was abandoned, as the leonine legacy of a generation demanding "more" was satisfied, and this demand would intensify when Pluto in Libra urged fair shares for everyone.

In a quest for perfection, food additives, pesticides, and chemical warfare all posed a huge, although unrecognized, threat to existence. This was the period when children received massive doses of pesticides. It would be several decades before the full horror of that legacy and other poisons would unfold.

The Virgoan ideals of service and duty conflicted strongly with Plutonian anarchy and subversion. The middle years of Pluto in Virgo, the 60s, were, in the West, a time of violent demonstration and protest—some were anti-war and against American imperialism, others were for civil rights, personal freedom, etc. The feminist movement started and strengthened as Pluto moved into Libra.

The yuppy section of the Pluto-in-Virgo generation, driven by ideals of the "get rich quick" philosophy drove themselves harder and harder, reaching for more and more as Pluto neared the end of Libra; only to come crashing down again when Pluto went underground in Scorpio. This is the generation that, in the 80s and 90s, experienced mass unemployment; and the fall of the yuppy culture, an offshoot from the "me generation" who brought their children up to believe they could have it all. It saw the disintegration of both the capitalist and communist society's godless way of life. They were also the first to hear openly the threat posed by the pollution of the planet.

Collectively, Pluto moving through health conscious Virgo opened the way for the hippy drug culture and free love (a return to the original Virgoan values); and for chemical pollution as more and more medical drugs were prescribed, fueling the enormous power of the drug companies. At the same time, ideals of welfare and health care were being realized, only to break down again in time for this generation to lose the benefit. (In Britain and the USA, when Pluto moved out of Scorpio and into the light of Sagittarius, "the Welfare State" became unable to support is responsibilities and "Mother Russia," the Soviet Union, broke down, leaving its citizens to fend for themselves.) Virgo rules health and especially psychosomatic illness. This is the generation that has the opportunity to break away from illnesses caused by emotional retention, repression and self-abuse, to move into the more gentle complementary therapies that treat the whole person rather than suppressing a set of "symptoms."

In the closing years of Pluto-in-Virgo, we took a "giant leap" to the Moon. While this was an expansion of outer awareness, it reawakened lunar consciousness. Collectively, the goddess energy was stirring and has emerged strongly since that time. Individually, Pluto-in-Virgo led to an expansion in consciousness and an exploration of inner space, although the shadow side of excessive self-criticism and over-analysis took its toll. However, many of this generation are now recognizing the need for self and planetary purification, and for a recovery of the practical skills and conservation methods that reconnect us to the earth.

PLUTO IN LIBRA (1972–1984)

Libra is the sign where personal, individual awareness begins its journey back to merge into the source. This is the first interpersonal sign, and it is in interpersonal relationships that transpersonal Pluto offers the greatest challenge. Relationships are, of course, where power struggles take place, where we experience the abuse and misuse of power and inequality. Pluto in Libra challenged the assumptions on which relationships—personal and collective—were based. On a personal level, this is the generation that is working to understand the place of the individual in society, and the one that is striving to make new, equal, relationships that work, overcoming the old Libran need to complete oneself through, or dominate in, a partnership.

When Pluto moved into Libra, there was a backlash against the leonine ideals of personal freedom. In some countries, harsh measures were taken against those who sought wider freedom—collective and personal. In the West, the permissive society came in, with subversive Pluto undermining the rigorous "partnership morality" of Libra, which valued marriage and heterosexual couples. Technology and big business multiplied and grew, as did the world population. This period, too, saw the rise of militant fundamentalism on all levels—Christian, Moslem, and Thatcher's Britain. All calling with Plutonian fervor for a return to "fundamental values" (Pluto in Cancer stuff), values which differed radically, and which were, of course, flawed and distorted according to the lens through which they were focused. The shadow side of Libra is fanaticism and self-interest, and Libra is the quickest sign of all to point the finger of blame.

The period while Pluto was in Libra was the time when we looked to the stars—astronomical not astrological. Exploration went out into deep space (it would move back in when Pluto descended into Scorpio). The space race brought us face to face with all our fears: would "the other" be the first to put space war technology in place? Would we have Star Wars? Would "they" establish planetary bases that would enable them to control the world?

However, the world was finally recognizing the urgent need for a sense of world responsibility, leading to greater cooperation among all nations. Peace conferences came, and went—Pluto was still at work and the old resentments surfaced—but gradually the Libran ability to compromise won the day. Nevertheless, Libra does compromise rather than work things out, so the karma of this would have to be harvested later as would the repressed issues breaking back into consciousness. Alongside this peace process world leaders were still vying to see who had the biggest weapon, who could shout the loudest, and who could pull off the most impressive espionage coup. Spying and underhanded manipulation were still the norm, and the shadow Libran need to dominate still held sway. Part of the Libran shadow is betrayal and lack of trust, energies that resonate to Pluto, as became apparent during this period. "Moles" were revealed in the highest echelons of the Secret Services. The Pluto-in-Libra generation is the one that is challenged to re-establish trust and honest diplomacy.

On the shadow side, the Plutonian Libran energies are dark indeed, and deeply repressed. This sign, which values partnership so much, is inherently selfish and will procrastinate rather than take action. On the surface all is sweetness and light, but down below ferments repressed rage. But it is projected "out there" onto the other person. Libra is "Fine, nothing wrong with me." The other person is to blame. We are back to the collective "them" who are at fault, especially as Libra is happy to play the peacemaker and advise everyone else how to overcome their deficiences. Sooner or later, this generation will have to look carefully at "me" and accept each and every person's part without blame.

PLUTO IN SCORPIO (1984–1995)

Pluto is at home in Scorpio. This is where Pluto confronts all the old taboos and sets them aside, unveiling all that is sacred and holy within and, paradoxically, revealing all that has been hidden and repressed. This was an opportunity to confront all the suppressed rage and resentment that has festered in the collective since time began. This toxic boil had to be lanced and allowed to drain, so that healing could take place. Pluto in Scorpio confronted the collective shadow and the egocentric power-drives that fuel abuse and misuse of power wherever they are to be found. Its natural ruler, Pluto moves through Scorpio with ease, offering the opportunity for inner exploration, a collective and individual visit to Hades. This placement signifies the urge for power, pure and unadulterated. It is how that power is used that is constructive or destructive—a challenge the Pluto-in-Scorpio generation will have to face.

When Pluto moved into Scorpio it accelerated the changes that were happening worldwide. This is the cathartic crisis energy that dredges up all that is unacceptable and repressed within society, and the psyche, and brings it out into the open. The choice, then, is acceptance and transformation, or we choose more repression and violent re-eruption until a cataclysm results. This is the period when the breakdown of communism and capitalism came to a head, when Germany reunified and met its "shadow" in the other half of the country; when the USSR disintegrated and brought the world face to face with the threat of nuclear weapons once more. This is the time when the world economy fell apart and recession struck; we saw environmental pollution at its height; when sexually transmitted disease including AIDS reached a peak; when starvation, natural disasters and diseases, such as cancer, killed more people than "natural causes."

This was when the world had to face its dark side, and make the choice for life or death. Collectively, there is a need to face, and accept, death. In the West death has been hidden for too long, and seen as something to overcome or stave off at all costs, and yet it is the one inevitable fact in all our lives, the one thing we all share. We all will die. In the East, it tends to be accepted as inevitable, fate, rather than something that can be taken hold of and used creatively. So the challenge is to accept death, and the Underworld, in all manifestations.

In the personal unconscious, as in the collective, the choice is life or death. We must face our own mortality, and thereby learn of our immortality. This is where we confront our own individual limits and transcend them. It is here we reconnect to the rejected energies of our shadow selves. It is here we come face to face with our darkest secrets, personal or familial. This is where we can renew and regenerate ourselves. This challenge is especially true of the Pluto-in-Scorpio generation who will be taking the world well into the twenty-first century. They are inheriting an ecological disaster which may have treasure buried somewhere within it, if only the key can be found.

The shadow side of Scorpio is concerned with mass manipulation and covert power struggles, with ruthlessness and power-plays that must win at all costs, with using psychological understanding to motivate and coerce others, and with control of all kinds. This is where power struggles arise, and resentment and rage fester. This is where the demonic forces lurk, where the "bogeyman" lies in wait for the unsuspecting innocent. This is what Pluto-in-Scorpio must confront and own; the challenge is to use this understanding constructively, to cooperate with Pluto in the task of transformation. Scorpio is the sign that has to master power. If we accept our own power, we become empowered. If we are prepared to explore the depths, we will experience the heights of consciousness, too. In other words, we change ourselves, so that the world in turn may be transformed, we recognize that we are all Avatars at heart.

PLUTO IN SAGITTARIUS (1995–2008)

Sagittarius is the sign that asks all the great questions of life: Why are we here? Where do we come from? What must we do to fulfill our purpose? So, Pluto in Sagittarius brings up the challenge of confronting the old, unworkable idealogies. It confronts us with the need to find a new way of formulating the religious impulse so that it incorporates spiritual values suitable for the Age of Aquarius. It challenges us to bring about global equality—now. It offers us a way to end the iniquity of one-third of the world having all the money and yet plundering and abusing the resources held by the other two-thirds. It gives us the opportunity of forgiving the massive third-world debt—and abolishing the concept of there being a somehow inferior third-world at all. It shows us where liberation and revision is needed, where we must re-educate ourselves to end corruption on all levels.

Pluto in Sagittarius pinpoints where we have to let go of outgrown patterns of being. Death will have to come out of the closet, and we may well find the world taking up the idea of merciful euthanasia and "living wills" as a way of coming to terms with dying rather than forcing people to live in a twilight world with one foot in Hades.

With Pluto in Sagittarius, there is no room for blind faith: Sagittarius has to know. Once Sagittarius knows, then being follows. Pluto says a way must be found to live out the inner vision. The great Sagittarian challenge is simply *to be*. This is where humankind must collectively confront belief systems, and eliminate all that is not working in religion, law, ethics, and morality. The new philosophy has to encompass personal freedom, and the liberty to believe as one will; while at the same time incorporating a global vision of humanity.

The shadow energies of Sagittarius include fanaticism and lack of trust. We may see a polarized battle between new ideologies and regenerated old religions. This may manifest through even more cults and "reforms" of accepted practice. It may also mean the fantatical clinging to old ideas that is so characteristic of the religious fanatic and bigot. Fundamentalism is, after all, founded on a Plutonian concept—purification and a return to strong moral values.

Pluto in Sagittarius has also brought "conspiracy theory" (a Scorpionic concept) to the surface. It postulates that a "world government" hidden behind the facade of individual countries controls our destiny. In this theory, a few shadowy individuals or organizations hold all the power, and there is nothing anyone can do—a highly Plutonian concept.

Sagittarius is fond of telling other people what they ought to do, without having any intention of doing this for itself, and those who preach loudest are often the greatest "sinners," as American evangelists and British politicians, among others, so often reveal to us. So, the challenge is to develop trust—trust in our own judgment, trust in our own self, and then trust in those "out there," that much feared enemy whose judgment and ethics we so mistrust. We fear because we have not yet recognized the dark, untrusting parts of ourselves, and we still project them onto others. Once trust is there, then Sagittarius unhesitatingly and fearlessly leads the way forward. Northumbrian astrologer Simon France says: "Sagittarius symbolises the path ahead, the future, the flight of the arrow towards its target. Pluto in Sagittarius indicates that the time is ripe for us to connect with our deepest and most profound vision of the future. Through our deeply held prayers, expectations and aspirations we truly touch the power within our being."[2]

The Pluto-in-Sagittarius generation is on a Grail Quest, a quest that can only be undertaken in one's own personal unconscious and, through that, the collective unconscious. The Grail is not somewhere "out there," it is within. The Grail is the inner light of understanding, of expanded consciousness, of intuition and inner knowing. This is "divine light." Once found, this Grail can then be offered to, but not imposed on, the world.

PLUTO IN CAPRICORN (2008–2022)

Capricorn is the Gate of Initiation, the start of a new evolutionary cycle. Pluto in Capricorn signifies conflict between conservation of the old entrenched economic and social structures, and the "old guard" who lead them, and implementation of the new political and social structures that will be needed as the Age of Aquarius gets underway and global responsibility takes over. The collective challenges here are to develop a new approach to constructive world government, to care about the planet Earth, to create interdependence for its people rather than the independence or dependency that underlie wars. A new authority has to be established, but this authority has to be based on autonomy, not authoritarianism and control.

The shadow side of Capricorn is strongly authoritarian, and frequently hypercritical. It is defensive, afraid to "give away power." Consequently, it is quick to act against any suspected usurping of power or position. Without social and emotional maturity, Capricorn turns to the rules and regulations in order to rule. It quickly becomes the dictator.

Equally, Capricorn easily becomes the scapegoat, taking the blame, or being blamed, for all the evils of the world. It is quick to scapegoat others. It was, after all, if the bible is to be believed, a Capricorn who died for "the sins of the world," although it is often postulated that Jesus, the mythologised savior, was a Pisces. The role of the scapegoat is to be a focus for carrying away other people's negative energy. Usually this is in a passive, Neptunian or Pisces "victim" role, but the Capricorn scapegoat can be more active and constructive, deliberately undertaking to release this energy on behalf of the collective. Whenever Capricorn goes against the accepted conventions of society, this scapegoat energy can be activated and this may be part of the challenge that the Pluto-in-Capricorn generation has to take on.

Capricorn, the opposite sign to Cancer, is where "God the Father" is polarized. In the past, this was an authoritarian, vengeful god who punished his creation harshly. Pluto in Capricorn says it is time to re-vision God—to integrate the male and female and reunite them in the divine. Entering the Gate of Initiation not only brings one face to face with the possibility of higher consciousness, it also introduces the notion of being a cocreator of the world. It is an opportunity to meet the divine within ourselves and honor it in those we meet, of being still and knowing that we are both god and goddess united in one being.

Initiation confronts one with death. The start of a cycle is also an end. How we meet the tests of initiation will determine our course when we enter through the Gate of Initiation. The challenge is to take up our spiritual heritage, to incorporate the "higher" consciousness with the "lower" energies of the unconscious, and to recognize them not as opposite polarities, but as complementary frequencies resonating together around everyday awareness, to form the whole.

PLUTO IN THE HOUSES

The following comments apply no matter what aspect the Moon makes with Pluto.

PLUTO IN THE 1ST HOUSE

In a Plutonian 1st house, the collective energies are expressed through either the Self or the personality. The personality is forceful, dominating; experienced by others as intense and Plutonic. The desire is for control, the compulsion toward domination. The Self has powerful connections to the archetypal realm and the urge is toward regeneration. Pluto gives a depth of insight that leads to true knowing. Pluto confronts one's Self in its totality. With Pluto in the 1st house, we meet our karma early in life, and continue to meet the results of our actions face to face. Much of that karma may result from the intense self-will of this placement. Life is rarely tranquil with Pluto here, and simply being born at all may entail an enormous struggle. Death may have to be faced at a very early age, indeed. Birth is frequently a near death experience for 1st-house Pluto. This life-and-death struggle is repeated many times, each renewal following on from the cathartic upheavals to which this placement is prone. Staying fully alive is the challenge.

Pluto gives an unusual intensity to interaction with the outside world. This is the placement of phobias and fears, compulsions and obsessions, the strongest of which is to understand oneself. The urge to self destruct can be almost as powerful. The face presented to the world may be enigmatic and self-absorbed, but a lot depends on the sign placement. Pluto in the 1st house is acutely aware of other people. "The other" (the opposite point to this house) is a collective mirror through which Pluto in the 1st learns to understand and define the Self. Once this has been achieved, Pluto makes an excellent guide for others who are making the same inner journey.

Pluto working positively in this house creates an unshakeable sense of eternal Self. An intimate connection to the great mysteries of life is expressed through that Self, with its accompanying manifestation of the processes of renewal and regeneration.

Crucial transformation: This is the person who must rebirth him- or herself. The old self must die so that new life can emerge.

PLUTO IN THE 2ND HOUSE

With Pluto in the 2nd house, the challenge is to identify how a connection to the collective can be expressed through personal talents and abilities. The collective energy can become a personal resource on which to draw. The Plutonian compulsion may be toward acquiring material possessions as a basis for security, or it may latch onto a person as a focus for the possessive urge. This is a highly self sufficient placement, one with enormous potential, but the energies may be entrenched in old survival strategies that have to be transformed.

With this Pluto placement, we meet our karma in the things we own and the value we place on ourselves. Since this is the house of resources, one of the challenges Pluto throws up may be of losing everything: being stripped naked and thrown out onto the street. We may also have to look deeply into just what it is we do value. Is it possessions or inner qualities? Can we find our own inner worth and value? It is in dealing with questions like these that a new energy emerges that creates inner resources which are more attuned to the collective need.

When Pluto in the 2nd is working positvely, there is an unshakeable faith in one's own abilities, founded on truly knowing the depths of one's being, and a sense of being anchored in Plutonian eternity.

Crucial transformation: To embody one's own inner Plutonian riches.

PLUTO IN THE 3RD HOUSE

When Pluto is in the 3rd house, two areas of challenge emerge—the family and communication. In either situation the intense energy of Pluto can create conflict and power struggles. Within the family, there may be a desire to dominate, or it may manifest as intense sibling rivalry. A sibling may live out a particularly Plutonian situation. The family we attract to ourselves will have karmic connections with us, and we may have to reap the karma of past domination when Pluto is in the 3rd.

As Pluto has such powerful ideals, much of the communication conflict generated with this placement arises out of deeply held, sometimes obsessive, rigid ideology. Pluto gives the ability to see beyond the surface; it adds an esoteric and occult dimension to the mind. But, once ideas have been formulated, Pluto tends to hold on to them. This is the house of self-expression and Plutonian self-expression can be compulsive and intense. The mental energy is penetrating and incisive, and does not suffer fools gladly. Pluto can be used for enlightened self-expression or self-condemnation, it all depends on how the energy is expressed.

This is also the house that shows how someone will respond to the immediate environment and Pluto here can bring an "otherworld" quality to that environment, or a perceived Underworld connection. The outside world may be seen as a threatening place. Those endings and beginnings associated with this house that are not to do with family are almost always to do with immediate surroundings, or beliefs and how they are expressed. Some life-changing event compels us into a new view of ourself and our relationship to our environment. The 3rd house can be one of the doorways into Hades.

When Pluto in the 3rd is working constructively, it opens up a different dimension, an esoteric understanding that there is far more to life than we normally perceive. Pluto can communicate with great clarity the insights received from the different worlds.

Crucial transformation: Fully expressing one's Self, remaining receptive to the new dimensions that unfold.

PLUTO IN THE 4TH HOUSE

It is in the instinctual 4th house that family karma resides. Here we meet old patterns of domination and manipulation. The person with Pluto in the 4th will encounter a mother with whom there have been long and intense power struggles in the past, a mother who carries many dark secrets in her ancestral line. This is someone with whom the ties have never been cut, the psychic umbilical cord binds mother and child tightly. She is the collective "devouring mother" made manifest in our life. Or, there may be a lives-long pattern of abandonment and rejection, a pattern that binds equally tightly to the family of origin.

So, for the 4th-house Pluto, endings often involve breaking free from the suffocating hold of a symbiotic family. Emotional dependency is stultifying, especially when heightened by Pluto. It is as though here, in this house, the dependency is heightened unbearably so that, eventually, there must be an escape from its stranglehold. The family secrets must be brought out into the light. The urge is toward finding an inner "home," somewhere safe and secure. But, the Plutonian lesson may then be that this home, in turn, becomes a trap for one's own children. Flexibility is essential wherever Pluto is found.

On the positive side, with Pluto in the 4th House, there is a certainty that, no matter what, we will survive. Roots are deep and strong, and the survival instinct powerful.

Crucial transformation: Finding emotional self-sufficiency and one's own inner roots.

PLUTO IN THE 5TH HOUSE

This is the creative house and the challenge for Pluto in the 5th is to embody creativity fully. Artistic creations tap deep into the collective energies, there is something intrinsically archetypal about the images that emerge from this Pluto placement. As always with Pluto, the expression of the creative energies is compulsive and obsessive. The person is driven to create, but sidesteps into the love affairs or children for which this house is also known. One of the karmic lessons for a 5th-house Pluto may well be that not all creation has to be on the biological level.

When the escape route is taken, all the power and intensity of Pluto goes into the relationship, which may seem especially karmic and "heavy." Relationship with children is symbiotic and emotionally incestuous. Love affairs are torrid and passionate, with all the jealousy and manipulation of Pluto operating beneath the surface. It may well be through the affairs of this house that transformation is achieved, but the cost is great in other people's broken dreams.

However, when Pluto operates positively in the 5th house, there is a deep understanding of the process of creation, a wellspring of energy that can be drawn upon to create new life in all its manifestations.

Crucial transformation: Becoming a self-created whole person who lives each moment afresh.

PLUTO IN THE 6TH HOUSE

It is through health, or the lack of it, that the 6th-house Pluto usually makes itself felt. This is the placement that has to understand disease, and to recognize, and explore, its emotional and karmic basis. The Plutonian causes of disease are devious and difficult to diagnose, based way back in the past and in the severely repressed emotional drives of childhood and other lives. Access to the Underworld through this house frequently brings one face to face with death and suffering. So often the illnesses of this house are a reflection of collective disease—Cancer, asthma, and diseases of the immune system, for example, mirroring how the polluted Earth's defenses are being broken down, how its lungs no longer work, and reflecting a collective "cancer" of unresolved rage and frustration.

However, Pluto in the 6th house also has connections to "work," and this is the work that one must do as opposed to the career one chooses. Once again, there is a compulsion about Pluto in the 6th that pushes toward a particular expression of the collective energies through work. This may be work in the sense of service or healing, or it may be the completion of a task undertaken lifetimes ago. One of the lessons of this house is that compulsive service actually serves no one. However,

290) THE HADES MOON

when Pluto is working positively, this is one placement that really does have the power to transform life for others.

Crucial transformation: To heal inner disease.

PLUTO IN THE 7TH HOUSE

When Pluto is placed in the 7th house, relationships in the widest sense of the word are the challenge—and the growing place. Pluto makes itself felt in power struggles, in manipulative and dominant relationships, and in dependency and addictive interaction. All the intensity and symbiosis of Pluto can be felt here, or isolation and alienation, depending on the sign and aspects to Pluto. This is the compulsive urge toward relationship, towards symbiosis with another person. The lesson is that, unless one is whole first, no true relationship is possible. For 7th-house Pluto, transformation comes through a relationship that takes one deep inside oneself to meet the denizens of Pluto's realm, or in a relationship that ends in a plunge into Hades icy grasp.

This is the house of karmic relationships, and Pluto's placement indicates a recurrence of old issues that must be faced and worked through. Manipulation is a common theme, as is that of conditional love, and of emotional control. So often the person with 7th-house Pluto is frightened to let go. Due to past experiences, there is a compulsive need to "pull the strings" in a relationship. The lesson is that of equal partnership. This house is a point where it is possible to become stuck on the karmic wheel, endlessly recreating the same old disasters. It takes courage to step off this wheel into the unknown, but Pluto can aid in this essential transformation.

When Pluto works positively in this house, it transforms relationships into a place for soul growth. It signifies a true meeting and sharing of being, of unconditional intimacy.

Crucial transformation: Achieving emotional equilibrium within relationship.

PLUTO IN THE 8TH HOUSE

The secretive 8th house is Pluto's natural home. This is where the collective ancestral energies run close to the surface. They can break through and "take over" an individual, or may be used to control the masses; it is one of the gateways into Hades. This is where we must recognize our immortality. An occult House of Initiation and ancient taboo, it is the place where fear of death must be confronted and new insights birthed, where forays into the unconscious and higher consciousness are demanded, where the past must be transcended. It is a place of rebirth. More than any other house, transformation is crucial, and accessible, but to reach that transformation involves a sojourn in Pluto's realm. The collective energies reach up and pull the 8th-house Pluto down into archetypal experiences through dreams, imagination, recollections, and personal initiation. One cannot live on the surface with this Pluto placement.

The 8th house represents what we inherit from our ancestors. It may well be the house of deep dark family secrets, of abuses of all kinds, polluting the lives of many generations. Family secrets are essentially Plutonian in character: addictions, death, illegitimacy and sexual abuse are common with this placement. The person with an 8th-house Pluto may well be the lineage breaker, the member of the family who breaks the hold and brings the secret out into the open so that new generations are no longer haunted by what they do not consciously know and yet act out compulsively time and time again. So, Pluto in the 8th house can bring profound healing.

This house has always been the occult house, the place where the individual seeks to master the forces of the collective for personal power. The energy is neutral; it is the use to which it is put that is constructive or destructive. The only difference between "black" and "white" magic is where that energy is focused. Black magic uses power for personal gain and domination over the collective; white magic is used for the good of others. The vehicle for that power is the personal will aligned to the collective. When Pluto fuels that will, it is a compulsive urge to power.

As this is also a sexual house, and that of resources shared with other people, sexual relationships are a great learning ground for this Pluto placement. Issues around sexuality may arise, for Pluto is the planet of secrets and hidden agendas. It may also indicate someone who takes refuge in sado-masochistic sexual fantasy. Compulsive sex is often a source of power struggles, but occasionally sexual interaction for the 8th-house Pluto becomes a tantric experience, moving into a different dimension. From the 8th house it is possible to reach out to other levels of being, to move beyond death and Earth-bound consciousness, to access the past and the future. Pluto here is naturally psychic and intuitive, but part of the lesson is to recognize just how much these abilities can be colored by our own unresolved emotional issues. Pluto shows us how involved we are in our own fate, and our perceptions of the greater whole.

Working positively, Pluto in the 8th is the doorway into a rich instinctual realm of infinite possibility, the dwelling place of immortality.

Crucial transformation: Transcending fear of death.

PLUTO IN THE 9TH HOUSE

It is in the ethical and moral dimension of life that the 9th-house Pluto most often makes itself felt. This is the position of moral certitude and enforced taboo. It is the home of the bigot and the fanatic, or the victim of such people. There may be a compulsive need to adopt a rigid belief structure to control and support a way of life. This can be a fanatical, judgmental placement, prone to an inflexible set of beliefs and standards, sometimes going along with the collective norms, but at other times seeking to impose a new view of morality. Pluto in the 9th house is fiercely ideological. Karma may arise from having imposed a rigid morality on others in the past, from fanaticism or enforced conversion, or from following too faithfully an idealism imposed from outside oneself. Reparation may be called for. A "black night of the soul," in which all faith and hope in the future are stripped away, is often experienced. A crisis of belief can be the road into the depths of oneself; the lesson of Pluto in this house is to find one's own personal belief system by which one can truly live from the heart, for then the Plutonian energies are aligned to the transformatory powers of personal depth experience. This is what brings together personal freedom and morality: we live from the heart that which we know we must be. Having this inner freedom, we are content to let others live, and believe, as they will.

Crucial transformation: Attunement to the inner morality of the open heart.

PLUTO IN THE 10TH HOUSE

Authority is the learning ground for Pluto in the 10th house, and there is an acute atunement to collective authority. This is the compulsive achiever who must get to the top at all costs. Power struggles are played out in a career, often recreating a poisonous home environment and the battles of childhood. There is frequently karma around an authoritarian attitude in the past, or an abuse of authority. The lesson is to distinguish between having authority and being authoritarian. This is an opportunity to develop inner autonomy, freed from the compulsions of adopting the collective view, or fitting into accepted norms. Endings in this house often feature loss of status and power as a way of focusing one in on who one really is. So often in the past, identity has been indissolubly linked with position in the outerworld. Now, that identity must arise out of authority on the inner levels.

Pluto in the 10th house can also indicate an extremely powerful mother figure who is compelling her child out into the world on her terms—to live out all that is thwarted and frustrated in herself. This is the autocratic mother who is obssessed with social status and being "good enough." This is the devouring mother at her most obsessive.

When Pluto is working constructively in the 10th house, it creates an autonomous being, an empowered person who can draw deeply on Plutonian resources and project them out to the world for the good of all.

Crucial transformation: Being fully autonomous.

PLUTO IN THE 11TH HOUSE

The 11th house is the house of community, and it is in group situations that this Pluto placement takes its greatest toll. Power plays, obsessive drives to control the group, and a fanatical urge toward leadership are just some of the difficulties experienced. Karma arises from all these situations, in addition to the possibility of having had a desperate need to fit into the group and therefore suppressing many facets of oneself in order to belong. Pluto's subversive activities might extend to bringing in a new world order. This house may also indicate a crusading, reforming zeal, a zeal that may be turned toward the social group to which one belongs, or to changing the world. Unfortunately, with the Plutonian tendency toward fanaticism, other people might not be appreciative of the results. Pluto in the 11th can be the natural dictator.

The endings experienced with this house may center around breaking free from an ingrained group situation, of being rejected by the group, or having been the outsider from the beginning. A natural outsider, Pluto in the 11th can have a strongly anti-social, anarchic tendency. This placement offers an opportunity to see whether one is simply going along with the collective view, or whether one is really following one's own inner direction—a direction which can lead directly into the reforming Hadean fires.

When Pluto is working positively in this house, it empowers the individual to act on behalf of the group, channeling the transforming Plutonian energies into constructive change that regenerates the whole.

Crucial transformation: Recognizing and following one's own unique path within the community.

Pluto in the 12th House

The 12th house is the karmic and ancestral house. It has one of the strongest connections to the collective unconscious and universality. This Pluto placement is plugged into the collective, so much so that there is an unconscious "reading" of other people's energies and motivation. Reactions to this psychic extrusion may vary, but it is usually experienced as an extension of oneself. There is no separation, no boundaries, in the collective unconscious, nor is there any separation from what has gone before in the family. There is a psychic umbilical cord binding the generations through the unspoken darkness of "family karma," a symbiotic dependency of covert secrets and addictions of all kinds. As a means of protection, the person with this placement may retreat into seclusion—a voluntary isolation—or the retreat may be into Plutonian fantasy and paranoia. A powerful self-destruct pattern may be running. This house's link to mental health and institutions is a deep one. Taking on other people's thoughts and feelings lessens one's sense of self, and this house is where one merges back into the whole. So, in a subtle way one becomes absorbed in the collective karma created by past generations, and part of the "universal mind" created by the present.

With Pluto in this house of concealment, right from the beginning of incarnation, there is an unconscious attunement to all that has gone before in the family, but which has been denied—the unacknowledged secrets and pervasive, unlived life imprisoned behind the facade of "the happy family." This is where the unresolved frustration festers; the clandestine, unacceptable emotions are projected "out there"; the embargoed splits in the parental marriage lurk unsuspected—and in turn have been unknowingly inherited from all the generations before. These undercurrents are the psychic food which nourish the child. No wonder, then, that the 12th-house Pluto has an unconscious identification with all that is deemed "bad" in the family. Engulfed into this boundless, all-embracing ancestral effluent, the child is unable to separate "mine" from "theirs."

Consequently, all the darkness and repressed "badness" is taken on and incorporated into "me." S/he becomes the embodiment of all that has gone before. Frequently, the child will all-unknowingly repeat the destructive patterns, such as alcoholism or chronic depression, that have been so painstakingly hidden. It is as though the 12th-house Pluto signifies a time for making manifest the family disease in order to transform it.

Pluto placed here is prone to compulsions and obsessions, to addictions and destructive behaviors, to phobias and deep aversions arising from the past, whenever that was. The karma centers around the use, misuse, and abuse of power, both as victim and perpetrator. The challenge for this placement is to overcome the compulsive patterns of the past, to find a new outlet for the transformative energies of this powerful planet.

When Pluto in the 12th is focused positively, it can help to alleviate collective karma. Pluto is the natural healer who can cut away all that is diseased in the collective psyche, who can regenerate new possibilities and kindle a rebirth of the Earth. This is where the true evolutionary potential can be manifested, the place where new life can begin. This is where power can be taken hold of and used for the good of the whole.

Crucial transformation: Stepping beyond the bounds of karma to be regenerated and renewed.

Appendix

THE PLUTO MOON DIALOGUE

Visualization is a very powerful way to utilize the energies of the Hades Moon. When you use imagery, you do not necessarily need to see anything. It is more important to allow the sensations and answers to arise in their own way, rather than trying to force or impose a specific structure. Some people receive the guidance as an inner force, compelling them toward a particular path. Others hear an inner voice or sense the way to go. But, with practice, it is possible for almost everyone to contact the planets and hear the answers they give.

It helps to set aside time, to choose a quiet place where you will not be disturbed, to turn off the phone, for instance. There are flower remedies and crystals which will help the process.[1] Burning incense can lift your consciousness, as can appropriate music. You need to be comfortable. It is impossible to relax if your clothes are too tight or your back hurts. So, wear loose clothing and sit or lie, whichever is most appropriate for you. What you are aiming for is a state of relaxed alertness, a sharply focused mind. You do not want to drift off to sleep or enter the "bliss consciousness" of meditation. There is no one right way to do this exercise. You might find it helpful to tape it, but you may prefer to have a friend read it and guide you through the different stages. If this is the case, you can ask for notes to be made of any answers you receive, otherwise have a pen and paper handy to make notes for yourself.

It can be helpful initially to do this exercise in three stages. In the first stage, you meet the Moon, in the second, you meet Pluto, and in the third stage, you meet with both of them. Or, you can do it as one long exercise as given here:

Begin by letting yourself relax. Focus your attention inward, and let the outside world drift away. If you hear any noises, let them pass by. Breathe slowly and gently, establishing a regular rhythm. Slowly open and close your eyes to the count of ten. When you reach ten, let your eyes remain closed. Your eyelids will now feel heavy and relaxed. Taking your attention to each part of your body in turn, slowly feel the relaxation travel through your body in waves, passing down through your face into your throat, then into your chest and arms, on down into your abdomen,

---

[1] See Judy Hall, *The Art of Psychic Protection* (York Beach, ME: Samuel Weiser, 1997; Findhorn: Findhorn Press, 1996), for helpful aids to visualization.

and finally flowing into your legs and feet. You should now be totally relaxed, but alert and focused.

Now, keeping your eyes closed, look up to the middle of your forehead (the third eye chakra). Focus your attention there. (You may like to imagine a white screen upon which the images will be projected.)

Picture yourself standing looking out onto a calm moonlit sea. You are at the entrance to a cave, a little way up a cliff. The full moon has just risen up out of the sea. It is bright and luminous. It throws a silver path across the sea, leading to the beach below your cave. As you watch, the moon goddess forms in the center of the moon. She gets up and walks serenely across the silver path to the beach below you. Then she climbs up the path to the cave. Watch her as she approaches. Is this a figure that you are familiar with from your dreams or meditations?

When she has greeted you, spend time with her, getting to know her. Ask her to show you how she manifests in your life. Let her tell you the history of your past, what you are reflecting from your family. Ask her to show you where you are caught up in that past and need to release. Question whether you shut her out. She may hold up her mirror so that you can look deeply into yourself. Let her show you where you can nurture yourself in a more fulfilling way. Ask her how best you can cooperate with her to manifest the lunar energies within yourself. Spend as much time as you need with her. Then ask her to wait on the beach below while you meet Pluto.

Pluto will come to you from a tunnel that goes deep into the earth from the back of the cave. Remember that Pluto usually wears his helmet of invisibility when he comes above ground, so you may need to ask him to take it off if you are to see him clearly. He may prefer to stay toward the back of the cave. If so, ask for a light to take with you when you go to meet him.

When you greet Pluto, look at him carefully. Do you know him already? Has he visited you in the depths of the night? Has he tried to make himself known to you before? If he appears in one of his more terrifying guises, remind him that you have voluntarily asked him to be with you and that you would like to see his most positive and constructive face.

Then spend time with Pluto. Ask him how he manifests in your life. Ask him where he feels you block him and your own creativity. Let him show you if there are negative aspects of his energy that you are clinging to, or facets of yourself that reflect what you would rather not know. Ask him to elucidate how you misuse your power, who you give it away to, and how you can be more empowered. Let him show you the areas of your life that need forgiveness and letting go. Ask him how you can positively express his drives within your own life.

When you have spent enough time with Pluto, ask the Moon goddess to re-join you in the cave. Talk with the two of them. Ask how they cooperate with each other, how they block each other, where they are in conflict within your life. Remind them that in combination they are a potent, creative, healing force. Ask them how to manifest more of this energy within yourself. They may have other aspects of their union to discuss with you. Take as long as you need.

When the meeting is completed, thank them both for coming to be with you. Ask them to help you to put any decisions you have made during this meeting into practice in your life. Pluto will then return down the dark passage to his underground home. The Moon goddess will make her way to the beach and follow the silver path back to the Moon.

Take a few deep breaths and take your attention down to your feet. Keep your eyes closed. If you are lying down, slowly sit up and place your feet on the floor. Feel the connection they make with Earth. Imagine that there is a long tap root going from your feet deep down into Earth. This holds you gently in incarnation. It grounds and energizes you. It also connects you to the power of Pluto's realm when this is appropriate. Then use the moonlight to surround yourself with a protective silver bubble of light. This will connect you to the lunar realm when apposite.

When you are ready, take a few more deep breaths and become aware of your surroundings, bringing your attention fully back into the room. Stand up and move around. If appropriate, write about your experience or make notes of what you learned.

Once you have become familiar with how the planets present themselves, make a list of specific questions you would like to ask, or ways in which you think the two can cooperate together, or goals you would like to achieve with their help. If you have other planets in close aspect, they can be brought into the visualization as appropriate. You might like to repeat this exercise with the quarters and dark of the Moon to see how this changes the answers you receive.

ENDNOTES

INTRODUCTION

1. Demetra George, *Mysteries of the Dark Moon* (San Francisco: HarperSanFrancisco, 1992), p. 14.

2. Judy Hall, *The Karmic Journey* (London: Arkana, 1990).

3. Clarissa Pinkola Estes, *Women Who Run with the Wolves* (New York: Ballantine, 1994; London: Rider, 1992).

CHAPTER 1

1. Stephen Arroyo, *Astrology, Karma & Transformation* (Sebastopol, CA: CRCS, 1992), p. 66.

2. Liz Greene and Howard Sasportas, *The Luminaries* (York Beach, ME: Samuel Weiser, 1992), p. 209.

3. *The Luminaries*, p. 14.

4. Joy Michaud and Karen Hilversen, *The Saturn/Pluto Phenomenon* (York Beach, ME: Samuel Weiser, 1993), p. 113.

5. D. H. Lawrence,

6. See Thomas Moore, *The Planets Within* (Hudson, NY: Lindesfarne, 1990), p. 63ff; Thomas Moore, *Dark Eros* (Dallas: Spring, 1994), especially p. 53ff; and Thomas Moore, *Care of the Soul* (New York Harpercollins, 1992; Shaftesbury, England: Element, 1991), p. 137ff.

7. Haydn Paul, *Gate of Rebirth* (York Beach, ME: Samuel Weiser, 1993), p. 251.

8. Stephen Arroyo, *Astrology, Karma & Transformation*, p. 137.

9. Thomas Moore, *Soul Mates* (New York: HarperCollins, 1994; Shaftesbury, England: Element, 1994), p. 101.

10. Sam Keen, *Hymns to an Unknown God* (New York: Bantam, 1994).

11. See Sylvia Brinton Perera, *Descent to the Goddess: A Way of Initiation for Women* (Toronto: Inner City Books, 1981).

CHAPTER 2

1. Joseph Campbell in a television interview.

2. James Hillman, *The Dream and the Underworld* (New York: Harper & Row, 1979), p. 67.

3. Robert Calasso, *The Marriage of Cadmus and Harmony* (London: Vintage, 1994).

4. Ibid.

5. Richard Idemon, *The Magic Thread* (York Beach, ME: Samuel Weiser, 1996), p. 31.

6. Haydn Paul, *Gate of Rebirth* (York Beach, ME: Samuel Weiser, 1993), p. 15.

7. M. Grieves, *A Modern Herbal*, Mrs. C. F. Leyel, ed. (London: Jonathan Cape), p. 73.

8. From *Gandhi's Letters to a Disciple*, Mohandas K. Gandhi, ed. (New York: Harper & Row, 1950), p. 87.

9. Robert Calasso, *The Marriage of Cadmus and Harmony*, p. 70.

10. *The New Larousse Encyclopedia of Mythology* (London: Hamlyn, 1959, 1958).

11. In a private conversation.

12. Robert Calasso, *The Marriage of Cadmus and Harmony*, p. 76.

13. *The Homeric Hymns*, Charles Boer, trans. (Dallas: Spring, 1970), p. 112.

14. J. E. Cirlot, *Dictionary of Symbols* (London: Routledge & Kegan Paul, 1962).

15. Jean Shinoda Bolen, *Goddesses in Everywoman* (New York: Harper Colophon, 1985), p. 197ff.

16. Roger and Jennifer Woolger, *The Goddess Within* (New York: Fawcett, 1989; London: Thorsons, 1990).

17. See Demetra George, *Mysteries of the Dark Moon* (San Francisco: HarperSanFrancisco, 1992), p. 138; also see Woolger and Bolen.

18. Jeff Green, *Pluto: The Evolutionary Journey of the Soul* (St. Paul: Llewellyn, 1995), p. 29.

19. Ibid, p. 262.

20. C. G. Jung, *Memories, Dreams, Reflections* (New York: Random, 1989; London: Fontana, 1983), p. 57.

21. C. G. Jung, *Memories, Dreams, Reflections*.

22. Jeff Green, *Pluto: The Evolutionary Journey of the Soul*, p. 264.

23. Samuel Taylor Coleridge, "Love" in *Dictionary of Quotations* (Oxford: Oxford Guild Publishing, 1985).

24. Loretta Proctor: "The Poetic Soul and the Dark Lover: Looking at the Mars-Pluto Theme in Creative Women's Lives," in *The Mountain Astrologer* Oct/Nov 1996, p. 106ff. This and other material from this article used by kind permission of the author.

25. Charlotte Bronte, *Jane Eyre* (London: Penguin, 1994), pp. 115–117.

26. Quoted in Lyndall Gordon, *Charlotte Bronte: A Passionate Life* (London: Vintage, 1995), p. 147.

27. Charlotte Bronte, *Jane Eyre*, p. 316.

28. Loretta Proctor, "The Poetic Soul and the Dark Lover: Looking at the Mars-Pluto Theme in Creative Women's Lives," p. 106ff.

29. Emily Bronte, *Wuthering Heights* (London: Penguin, 1994), p. 80.

30. Ibid., p. 80ff.

31. Lyndall Gordon, *Charlotte Bronte: A Passionate Life*, p. 30.

32. Ibid.

33. "Imagination," in Winifred Gerin, *Emily Bronte* (Oxford: Oxford University Press, 1971), p. 165.

34. Ibid., p. 19.

35. Ibid., p. 102.

36. Ibid., p. 265.

37. Ibid., p. 17.

38. Ibid., "The Philosopher," p. 194.

39. Ibid., "The Philosopher," p. 194.

40. Ibid., p. 238.

41. Charlotte Bronte, "Reason," in *Charlotte Bronte: A Passionate Life*, by Lyndall Gordon, p. 121.

42. Dr. Juliet Barker, BBC2 Bookmark program: "Charlotte Bronte Unmasked."

43. Loretta Proctor: "The Poetic Soul and the Dark Lover: Looking at the Mars-Pluto Theme in Creative Women's Lives," p. 106ff.

44. Ibid.

45. Dante was an Italian poet. He first met Beatrice when he was 9; he met her again when he was 18; she died shortly afterward. His idealized love, Beatrice was the inspiration for most of his poetic work.

46. C. G. Jung, *Memories, Dreams, Reflections* (New York: Random, 1989).

CHAPTER 3

1. Michael Gurian, *Mothers, Sons & Lovers* (Boston: Shambhala, 1994), p. 55.
2. Richard Idemon, *Through the Looking Glass* (York Beach, ME: Samuel Weiser, 1992), p. 255.
3. Ibid., p. 256.
4. Leslie Kenton, *Ludwig* (London: Mandarin, 1993), p. 294ff.
5. Untitled, unpublished poem by Lincoln (pseudonym). Used by permission.
6. BBC Horizon program, "Foetal Attraction," 1995.
7. Ibid.
8. Ibid.
9. Christine Hartley, *A Case For Reincarnation* (London: Robert Hale, 1953), p. 119ff.
10. Stanislav Grof, "Understanding the Birth Trauma," tape.
11. Michael Gurian, *Mothers, Sons & Lovers*, p. 23.
12. Loren Pederson, *Dark Hearts: The Unconscious Forces that Shape Men's Lives* (Boston: Shambhala, 1991), p. 80.
13. Michael Gurian, *Mothers, Sons & Lovers*, p. 73.
14. Dana Gerbardt, *The Mountain Astrologer* (Apr. 96), p. 66.
15. Albert Goldman, *The Lives of John Lennon* (New York: Bantam, 1993).
16. Ibid., p. 302.
17. Albert Goldman, *The Lives of John Lennon*. Also listed in other biographies and recollections of personal friends.
18. Dana Gerbardt, *The Mountain Astrologer*, p. 66.
19. Judy Hall, *Hands Across Time: The Soulmate Enigma* (Findhorn: Findhorn Press, 1997), pp. 9-10.
20. Albert Goldman, *The Lives of John Lennon*, p. 249.
21. Haydn Paul, *Queen of the Night* (Shaftesbury, England: Element, 1990), p. 26. A revised edition will be published by Weiser, Fall 1998 as *The Astrological Moon*.
22. Dr. Patricia Love with Jo Robinson, *The Chosen Child Syndrome* (London: Piatkus, 1990).
23. Thomas Moore, *Soul Mates* (New York: HarperCollins, 1994; Shaftesbury, England: Element, 1994), p. 76.
24. John Bradshaw, *Family Secrets: What You Don't Know Can Hurt You* (New York: Bantam, 1995).
25. James Hillman, *Puer Papers* (Dallas: Spring Publications, 1979), p. 119.

CHAPTER 4

1. Stan Riddle, "Moon Opposite Pluto," *Considerations* vol. viii No.1, p. 17.
2. Joan Smith, "One of the Boys?" in *The Guardian Weekend* 1.1.94, p. 2.
3. Herman Hesse, *Demian: A Novel*, W. J. Strachan, trans. (London: Panther, 1969).
4. Hans Christian Anderson, *Hans Christian Anderson's Fairy Tales* (Philadelphia: Courage Books, 1996).
5. Judy Hall, *The Zodiac Pack* (Findhorn: Findhorn Press, 1997).
6. Dr. Patricia Love with Jo Robinson, *The Chosen Child Syndrome* (London: Piatkus, 1990).
7. Melanie Reinhart, *To the Edge & Beyond* (London: CPS, 1997), p. 181ff.

CHAPTER 5

1. Sam Keen, *Hymns to an Unknown God* (New York: Bantam, 1994), p. 282.
2. C. G. Jung, *Essays on Contemporary Events: Reflections on Nazi Germany* (London: Ark, 1988), p. 10.

3. Roger Morgan, ed., *Milestones of History*, vol. 10: *Sunrise and Stormclouds* (London: George Weidenfeld & Nicolson), p. 92. Used by permission.

4. Ibid., p. 92.

5. Keith Feiling, *A History of England* (London: Book Club Associates, 1970), p. 1056. Brackets mine. Used by permission of Macmillan Ltd. © 1950. Published by Book Club Associates, 1970, by arrangement with Macmillan and Company Limited, Basingstoke, Hampshire, England.

6. Judy Hall, *Astrology of a Prophet?* (Yeovil: Mendip Press, 1993), pp. 115ff and 201ff.

7. Keith Feiling's chapter in *Sunrise and Stormclouds*, p. 76.

8. Ibid.

9. Ibid., p. 97.

10. R. A. Christoforides in a personal letter to Judy Hall, Jan. 19, 1998.

11. Ibid.

12. Wilfred Owen, "Cramped in that Funnelled Hole," in *The Poems of Wilfred Owen*, Jon Stallworthy, ed. (London: Chatto & Windus, 1985), p. 183.

13. Wilfred Owen, "Dulce et Decorum," in *The Poems of Wilfred Owen*, p. 117.

14. Dominic Hibberd, *Owen the Poet* (Basingstoke: MacMillan Press, 1986), p. 7.

15. Ibid., p. 102.

16. Robert A. Christoforides' compilation from fragments in *Wilfred Owen: The Complete Poems and Fragments*, Jon Stallworthy, ed. (London: Chatto and Windus, 1990).

17. Robert A. Christoforides, unpublished manuscript.

18. Dominic Hibberd, *Owen the Poet*, p. 51.

19. Wilfred Owen, in *Men Who March Away*, I. M. Parsons, ed. (London: Book Club Associates, 1978), p. 69; and *The Poems of Wilfred Owen*, introduced and edited by Jon Stallworthy (London: Chatto & Windus, 1985).

20. This and the quote above from Brock's article in *The Hydra*, Jan. 1918 under the psuedonym "Arcturus" (a star which is supposed to be the center of the universe). *The Hydra* was the Craiglockhart house magazine. Source: R. A. Christoforides in a letter to author.

21. Wilfred Owen, "Mental Cases," in *The Poems of Wilfred Owen*, edited and introduced by Jon Stallworthy, p. 146; and "Men Who March Away," p. 14.

22. Wilfred Owen, "Letters the 4th or 5th of October, 1918" in *Wilfred Owen: Selected Letters*, John Bell, ed. (Oxford: Oxford University Press, 1985), p. 351.

23. Wilfred Owen, "Spring Offensive," in *The Poems of Wilfred Owen*, P. 170.

24. From "The End," *The Poems of Wilfred Owen*, p. 136.

25. Performance version by R. A. Christoforides, compiled from fragments of "Strange Meeting" and "Earth's Wheels," by Wilfred Owen.

26. Heard on television program.

27. August Kubizek, quoted in Ravenscroft, *Spear of Destiny*, pp. 3, xxi, 96–97.

28. Trevor Ravenscroft, *Spear of Destiny* (York Beach: ME: Samuel Wieser, 1982; London: Sphere Books, 1990), p. 3. This and following quoted material from this title used by permission.

29. Ibid., p. 4.

30. Ibid., quoted passages from pp. 64, 65, 69.

31. Allan Bullock, *Hitler: A Study in Tyranny* (New York: HarperCollins, 1991).

32. Ravenscroft, *Spear of Destiny*, quoting Rausching, pp. 171, 176.

33. Allan Bullock, *Hitler: A Study in Tyranny*.

34. Ravenscroft, *Spear of Destiny*, p. 92.

35. Ibid., p. 93.

36. Ibid., p. 94, 95.

37. Ibid., p. 96.

38. Ibid., p. 96.

39. Thomas Gray, "Elegy Written in a Country Churchyard," line 36.

40. *Evening Echo*.

41. *Milestones of History*, vol. 11: *Decade of Crisis*, p. 104.

42. Ibid.

43. David Divine, in *Decade of Crisis*, p. 108.

44. From a radio program (BBC) many years ago.

45. This was given to me by a guide in Egypt. A slightly different translation can be found in *Awakening Osiris: The Egyptian Book of the Dead*, Normandi Ellis, trans. (Grand Rapids, MI: Phanas Press, 1988), p. 95.

46. John Anthony West, *The Traveler's Key to Ancient Egypt* (New York: Knopf, 1985).

47. Ibid.

48. Robert A. Armour, *Gods & Myths of Ancient Egypt* (Cairo: The American University in Cairo Press, 1986), p. 113.

49. Thomas Moore, *Dark Eros*, p. 8.

50. Judy Hall, *Art of Psychic Protection* (Findhorn: Findhorn Press, 1996), p. 51; and (York Beach, ME: Samuel Wieser, 1997), p. 43).

51. Judy Hall with Dr. Robert Jacobs, *The Wise Woman: A Natural Approach to Menopause* (Shaftesbury, England: Element, 1991), p. 156.

52. Clarissa Pinkola Estes, *Women Who Run with the Wolves* (New York: Ballantine, 1994; London: Rider, 1992), p. 352.

53. Demetra George, *Mysteries of the Dark Moon* (San Francisco: HarperSanFrancisco, 1992).

54. Goethe, *Faust*.

55. Clarissa Pinkola Estes, *Women Who Run with the Wolves*, p. 370.

56. John Bradshaw, *Family Secrets* (London: Piatkus, 1995; New York: Bantam, 1995), pp. 104, 109.

CHAPTER 6

1. Joy Michaud and Karen Hilversen, *The Saturn/Pluto Phemenon* (York Beach, ME: Samuel Weiser, 1993), p. 120.

2. See Judy Hall, *The Karmic Journey* (London: Arkana, 1990).

3. See Judy Hall, *Principles of Past Life Therapy* (London: Thorsens, 1996).

4. Caitlin Matthews, *In Search of Woman's Passionate Soul* (Shaftesbury, England: Element, 1997), p. 130.

5. See Judy Hall, *Deja Who? A New Look at Old Lives* (Findhorn: Findhorn Press, 1998).

6. Richard Idemon, *Through the Looking Glass* (York Beach, ME: Samuel Weiser, 1992), p. 254.

7. Jeff Green, *Pluto: The Evolutionary Journey of the Soul* (St. Paul: Llewellyn, 1995), p. 263.

8. See Judy Hall, *Principles of Past Life Therapy*.

9. See Ian White, *Australian Bush Essences* (Findhorn: Findhorn Press 1993); and Clare Harvey, *The Encyclopaedia of Flower Essences* (London: Thorsons, 1995).

CHAPTER 7

1. Demetra George, *Mysteries of the Dark Moon* (San Francisco: HarperSanFrancisco, 1992), p. 15.

2. Mark Hasselris in Jonathon Cott, *Isis and Osiris* (New York: Doubleday, 1994), p. 155.

3. Ibid.

4. Jeremy Naydler, *Temple of the Cosmos* (Rochester, VT: Inner Traditions, 1996), p. 214.

5. Jonathon Cott, *Isis and Osiris*.

6. Alison Roberts, *Hathor Rising: The Serpent Power of Ancient Egypt* (Totnes: Northgate, 1995), p. 106.

7. Ibid., p. 110.

8. In a random check on 117 murders (German AA Database), 13 had a Scorpio Moon, and about 20 percent had the Hades Moon, but what was striking was that all had heavily aspected Moons.

9. See Arthur Conan Doyle, *Hound of the Baskervilles* (New York: Ballantine, 1987).

10. Caitlin Matthews, *In Search of Woman's Passionate Soul* (Shaftesbury, England: Element, 1997), p. 96.

11. Alison Roberts, *Hathor Rising: The Serpent Power of Ancient Egypt*, pp. 8–16.

12. Richard Idemon, *Through the Looking Glass* (York Beach, ME: Samuel Weiser, 1992), pp. 35, 103.

13. Michael Gurian, *Mothers, Sons & Lovers* (Boston: Shambhala, 1994), p. 105.

14. Linda Schierse Leonard, *Witness to the Fire* (Boston: Shambhala, 1990), p. 14.

15. Clarissa Pinkola Estes, *Women Who Run with the Wolves* (New York: Bantam, 1992), p. 486.

16. Caitlin Matthews, *In Search of Woman's Passionate Soul*, p. 92.

17. Richard Ideman, *Through the Looking Glass*, p. 37.

18. Marion Woodman, *The Ravished Bridegroom* (Toronto: Inner City Books, 1990), p. 44.

19. Dr. Bruce Lloyd, "Treating the Spiritual Dimension of Addiction," *Addiction Counselling World* Nov/Dec 1991, p. 23.

20. Erich Neumann, *Art & the Creative Unconscious*, Ralph Mannheim, trans. (New York: Harper & Row, 1966), p. 133.

21. Michael Gurian, *Mothers, Sons & Lovers*, p. 21.

22. Michael Ford, in an interview presented in James Riordan and Jerry Prochnicky, *Break on Through* (London; Plexus, 1991), p. 497.

23. See John Densmore, *Riders on the Storm* (London: Arrow, 1991).

24. James Riordan and Jerry Prochnicky, *Break on Through*, p. 23.

25. Ibid., p. 510.

26. Ibid., p. 496.

27. John Densmore, *Riders on the Storm*, p. 297ff.

28. Linda Schierse Leonard, *Witness to the Fire*, p. xvi.

29. Dr. Bruce Lloyd, "Treating the Spiritual Dimension of Addiction," p. 23.

30. Sam Keen, *Hymns to an Unknown God* (New York: Bantam, 1994), p. 282.

31. Thomas Moore, *Soul Mates* (New York: HarperCollins, 1994; Shaftesbury, England: Element, 1994), p. 101.

32. Judy Hall, *The Art of Psychic Protection* (York Beach, ME: Samuel Weiser, 1997; Findhorn: Findhorn Press, 1996).

33. Sam Keen, *Hymns to an Unknown God*.

CHAPTER 8

1. Joan Hodgson, *Astrology: The Sacred Science* (Sebastopol, CA: CRCS with White Eagle Publications, 1990), p. 134.

2. See Judy Hall, *The Art of Psychic Protection* (York Beach, ME: Samuel Weiser, 1997; Findhorn: Findhorn Press, 1996).

3. Caitlin Matthews, *In Search of Woman's Passionate Soul* (Shaftesbury, England: Element, 1997), p. 122.

4. Bram Stoker, *Dracula*, World Classics (Oxford: Oxford University Press, 1996), Introduction by Maud Ellman, p. vii ff.

5. Quoted in *Dracula*, Introduction by Maud Ellman, p. xi from Bram Stoker's *Personal Reminiscences of Henry Irving*.

6. Professor Christopher Frayling on BBC TV program on Bram Stroker, 1997, "Dracula."

7. Maud Ellman, in the Introduction to *Dracula*, p. xiii; and Professor Christopher Frayling on a BBC TV program on Bram Stoker, 1997, "Dracula."

8. A supposition supported by Professor Frayling in a TV interview.

9. Maud Ellman, in the Introduction to Bram Stoker's *Dracula*, p. xv.

10. Ibid., p. xxviii.

11. David Lawson, *Eye of Horus* (New York: St. Martins, 1996), p. 42ff.

12. Ibid.

13. Rundle Clark, *Myth and Symbol in Ancient Egypt* (London: Thames and Hudson, 1959, 1978).

14. Haydn Paul, *Queen of the Night* (Shaftesbury, England: Element, 1990), p. 10. Weiser's revised edition to publish Fall 1998 as *The Astrological Moon*.

15. Clarissa Pinkola Estes, *Women Who Run with the Wolves* (New York: Ballantine, 1994; London: Rider, 1992), p. 58.

16. Ibid.

17. John Keats. From one of his letters.

18. John Keats, "Ode to a Nightingale," in *Treasury of Great Poems*, Louis Untermeyer, ed. (New York: Simon and Schuster, 1942).

19. Clarissa Pinkola Estes, *Women Who Run with the Wolves*, p. 289. The term "medial woman" was coined by Toni Wolff, a Jungian analyst, but it applies equally to men who have a Hades Moon.

CHAPTER 9

1. Haydn Paul, *Gate of Rebirth* (York Beach, ME: Samuel Weiser, 1993), p. 11.

2. Jeff Green, *Pluto: The Evolutionary Journey of the Soul* (St. Paul: Llewellyn, 1995).

3. Ibid., p. 271.

4. "The Billen Interview" in *Life* section of *The Observer*, 6.11.94, p. 14ff.

5. "The Billen Interview," p. 15.

CHAPTER 10

1. Jeff Green, *Pluto: The Evolutionary Journey of the Soul* (St. Paul: Llewellyn, 1995), p. 259.

2. Quote is from an English Astrologer Simon France, in a privately circulated paper.

BIBLIOGRAPHY

Albery, Nicholas, Gil Blist, Joseph Elliot, eds. *The Natural Death Handbook*. London: Virgin, 1993.

Amour, Robert A. *Gods and Myths of Ancient Egypt*. Cairo: American University in Cairo Press, 1986.

Anderson, Hans Christian. *Hans Christian Anderson's Fairy Tales*. Philadelphia: Courage Books, 1996.

Arroyo, Stephen. *Astrology, Karma & Transformation*. Sebastopol, CA: CRCS, 1992.

Barker, Dr. Juliet. "Charlotte Bronte Unmasked," on BBC2 Bookmark.

Billen Interview, in *Life*, Nov. 11, 1994. *The Observer*.

Blaschke, Robert P. "The Pluto in Leo Generation," in the NCGR *Memberletter*, Vol. ix, No. 1.

Bolen, Jean Shinoda. *Goddesses in Everywoman*. New York: Harper Colophon, 1985.

Bradshaw, John. *Family Secrets*. London: Piatkus, 1995; New York: Bantam, 1995.

Bronte, Charlotte. *Jane Eyre*. London: Penguin, 1994.

Bronte, Emily. *Wuthering Heights*. London: Penguin, 1994.

Brown, Peter and Stephen Gaines. *The Love You Make*. London: Pan, 1983.

Bullock, Allan. *Hitler: A Study in Tyranny*. New York: HarperCollins, 1991.

Calasso, Robert. *The Marriage of Cadmus and Harmony*. London: Vintage, 1994.

Cirlot, J. E. *Dictionary of Symbols*. London: Routledge & Kegan Paul, 1962.

Clark, Rundle. *Myth and Symbol in Ancient Egypt*. London: Thames and Hudson, 1959, 1978.

Coleman, Ray. *John Lennon*. London: Futura, 1985.

Cott, Jonathon. *Isis and Osiris*. New York: Doubleday, 1994.

Densmore, John. *Riders on the Storm*. London: Arrow, 1991.

Doyle, Arthur Conan. *Hound of the Baskervilles*. New York: Ballantine, 1987.

Eliot, George. *The George Eliot Letters*, G. S. Haight, ed. Oxford: Oxford University Press, 1954.

Ellis, Norman, trans. *Awakening Osiris: The Egyptian Book of the Dead*. Grand Rapids, MI: Phanes Press, 1988.

Estes, Clarissa Pinkola. *Women Who Run with the Wolves*. New York: Ballantine, 1994; London: Rider, 1992.

Feiling, Keith. *A History of England*. London: Book Club Associates, 1970.

Friedman, Dennis. *Inheritance: The Bitter Legacy that Threatens the Future of the Royal Family*. London: Pan, 1994.

George, Demetra. *Mysteries of the Dark Moon*. San Francisco: HarperSanFrancisco, 1992.

Gerbardt, Dana. In an article published in *The Mountain Astrologer*. Apr. 1996.

Gerin, Winifred. *Emily Bronte*. London: Oxford University Press, 1971.

Ghandi, Mohandas K., ed. *Ghandi's Letters to a Disciple*. New York: Harper & Row, 1950.

Goldman, Albert. *The Lives of John Lennon*. New York: Bantam, 1993.

Gordon, Lyndall. *Charlotte Bronte: A Passionate Life*. London: Vintage, 1995.

Green, Jeff. *Pluto: The Evolutionary Journey of the Soul*. St. Paul: Llewellyn, 1995.

Greene, Liz. *The Astrology of Fate*. London: Allen & Unwin, 1984; York Beach, ME: Samuel Weiser, 1984.

Greene, Liz and Howard Sasportas. *The Luminaries.* York Beach, ME: Samuel Weiser, 1992.

Grieves, M. *A Modern Herbal*, Mrs. C. F. Leyel, ed. London: Jonathan Cape, 1985.

Grof, Stanislav. "Understanding the Birth Trauma," tape. N.d.

Gurian, Michael. *Mothers, Sons & Lovers.* Boston: Shambhala, 1994.

Hall, Judy. *The Art of Psychic Protection.* York Beach, ME: Samuel Weiser, 1997.

———. *Astrology of a Prophet?* Yeovil: Mendip Press, 1993.

———. *Deja Who? A New Look at Old Lives.* Findhorn: Findhorn Press, 1998.

———. *The Karmic Journey.* London: Arkana, 1990.

———. *Principles of Past Life Therapy.* London: Thorsons, 1996.

———. *The Zodiac Pack.* Findhorn: Findhorn Press, 1997.

Hall, Judy and Dr. Robert Jacobs. *Menopause Matters.* Shaftesbury, England: Element, 1994.

———. *Holistic Menopause.* Findhorn: Findhorn Press, 1998.

———. *The Wise Woman: A Natural Approach to Menopause.* Shaftesbury, England: Element, 1991.

Hall, Nor. *The Moon and the Virgin.* London: Women's Press, 1980.

Hartley, Christine. *A Case for Reincarnation.* London: Robert Hale, 1953.

Harvey, Clare. *The Encyclopaedia of Flower Essences.* London: Thorsons, 1995.

Hertsgaard, Mark. *A Day in the Life: The Music and Artistry of the Beatles.* London: Macmillan, 1992.

Hesse, Hermann. *Demian: A Novel.* New York: HarperCollins, 1989; London: Panther, 1972.

Hibberd, Dominic. *Owen the Poet.* Basingstoke, England, Macmillan, 1986.

———. *Wilfred Owen: The Last Years.* London: Constable, 1992.

Hillman, James. *The Dream and the Underworld.* New York: Harper & Row, 1979.

———. *Puer Papers.* Dallas: Spring, 1979.

Hodgson, Joan. *Astrology: The Sacred Science.* Sebastopol, CA: CRCS and White Eagle Publications, 1990.

The Homeric Hymns, Charles Boer, trans. Dallas: Spring, 1970.

Idemon, Richard. *The Magic Thread.* York Beach, ME: Samuel Weiser, 1996.

———. *Through the Looking Glass.* York Beach, ME: Samuel Weiser, 1992.

Jung, C. G. *Essays on Contemporary Events: Reflections on Nazi Germany.* London: Ark, 1988.

———. *Memories, Dreams, Reflections.* New York: Vintage/Random, 1989; London: Fontana, 1983.

Keen, Sam. *Hymns to an Unknown God.* New York: Bantam, 1994.

Kenton, Leslie. *Ludwig.* London: Mandarin, 1993.

Lawson, David. *Eye of Horus.* New York: St. Martins, 1996.

Leamer, Laurence. *The Kennedy Women.* New York: Bantam, 1995.

Leonard, Linda Schierse. *Witness to the Fire.* Boston: Shambhala, 1990.

———. *Meeting the Madwoman.* New York: Bantam, 1994.

Lloyd, Dr. Bruce. "Treating the Spiritual Dimension of Addiction," in *Addiction Counselling World*, Nov/Dec, 1991.

Love, Dr. Patricia with Jo Robinson. *The Chosen Child Syndrome.* London: Piatkus, 1990.

Matthews, Caitlin. *In Search of Woman's Passionate Soul.* Shaftesbury, England: Element, 1997.

Michaud, Joy and Karen Hilversen. *The Saturn/Pluto Phenomenon.* York Beach, ME: Samuel Weiser, 1993.

Moore, Thomas. *Care of the Soul.* New York: HarperCollins, 1992; London: Piatkus, 1992.

———. *Dark Eros.* Dallas: Spring, 1990.

———. *The Planets Within.* Hudson, NY: Lindesfarne, 1990.

———. *Soul Mates.* New York: HarperCollins, 1994; Shaftesbury, England: Element, 1994.

Morgan, Roger, ed. *Milestones of History.* London: Weidenfield and Nicholson, 1975.

Nadler, Jeremy. *Temple of the Cosmos.* Rochester, VT: Inner Traditions, 1996.

Neumann, Erich. Art & the Creative Unconscious. New York: Harper & Row, 1966.

New Larousse Encyclopedia of Mythology. London: Hamlyn, 1959, 1968.

Owen, Wilfred. *Wilfred Owen: Selected Poetry and Prose,* Jennifer Breen, ed. London: Routledge, 1988.

———. *The Poems of Wilfred Owen,* Jon Stallworthy, ed. London: Chatto and Windus, 1990.

Pasons, I. M., ed. *Men Who March Away.* London: Book Club Associates, 1978.

Paul, Haydn. *Gate of Rebirth.* York Beach, ME: Samuel Weiser, 1993.

Pederson, Loren. *Dark Hearts: The Unconscious Forces that Shape Men's Lives.* Boston: Shambhala, 1991.

Perera, Sylvia Brinton. *Descent to the Goddess.* Toronto: Inner City Books, 1981.

Proctor, Loretta. "The Poetic Soul and the Dark Lover: Looking at the Mars-Pluto Theme in Creative Women's Lives," in *The Mountain Astrologer,* Oct/Nov, 1996.

Ravenscroft, Trevor. *Spear of Destiny.* York Beach, ME: Samuel Weiser, 1982; London: Sphere, 1990.

Reinhart, Melanie. *To the Edge and Beyond.* London: CPS, 1997.

———. *Pluto* (tape). Published by the author.

Riddle, Stan. "Moon Opposite Pluto," in *Considerations,* vol. VIII, No. 1.

Riordan, James and Jerry Prochnicky. *Break on Through.* London: Plexus, 1991.

Roberts, Alison. *Hathor Rising: The Serpent Power of Ancient Egypt.* Totnes: Northgate, 1995.

Sasportas, Howard. *The Gods of Change.* London: Arkana, 1989.

Smith, Joan. "One of the Boys?" in *The Guardian,* Jan. 1, 1994.

Stoker, Bram. *Dracula.* World Classics series. London: Oxford University Press, 1996.

Untermeyer, Louis, ed. *Treasury of Great Poems.* New York: Simon and Schuster, 1942.

Welldon, Estela U. *Mother, Madonna, Whore.* New York: Guilford Press, 1992.

West, John Anthony. *The Traveler's Key to Ancient Egypt.* New York: Knopf, 1985.

White, Ian. *Australian Bush Essences.* Findhorn: Findhorn Press, 1993.

Woolger, Roger and Jennifer. *The Goddess Within.* New York: Fawcett, 1989; London: Thorsons, 1990.

Woodman, Marion. *The Ravished Bridegroom.* Toronto: Inner City Books, 1990.

INDEX

A

abandonment, 115
Acheron, 35
addiction, 113, 223, 224
Admetus, 38, 39
Adonis, 43
afterlight, 258
Akashic record, 41
alchemists, 12
alcoholism, 105, 113
alienation, 115, 134
Allen, Woody, 119
Anderson, Hans Christian, 118
Angela, 203, 204
angels wings, 216
anger, 169
animus and anima, 51
Anna, 186
Anne, 215
Aornis, 35
Apep, 166
Aphrodite, 39, 43, 223
Apollo, 38, 39
archetypal expectations, 71
archetypes, 42
    creative, 48
    Demeter, 44, 145, 217
    Hades, 47
    Hades Moon, 43
    Hecate, 46
    Kore, 43
    Persephone, 42, 44, 52
    of the rapist, 48
Arroyo, Stephen, 1, 15
Artemis, 38
Asclepius, 38
aspects, 15
Asphodel, 35

astrology
    esoteric, 14
    and myth unite, 33
Athene, 37

B

Baden-Powell, Lord, 249
Barbara, 210
beast from the abyss, 157
Bennet, Dr. Phil, 76
Billy the Kid, 212
Bolen, Jean, 43
Bolshevik revolution, 143
Bradshaw, John, 106
Bronte, Anne, 60
Bronte, Branwell, 55, 56, 68
Bronte, Charlotte, 53, 58
Bronte, Emily, 53, 57
    death of, 67
Bronte, Maria, 61
Bronte, Patrick, 63
Brown, John, 18
Bullock, Alan, 159
Burning River of Desire, 36

C

Calasso, Robert, 30, 38, 39
call to the spirit, 112
Callas, Maria, 100
Campbell, Joseph, 30
Carter, Charles, 33
Case histories
    Angela, 203
    Anna, 186
    Anne, 215
    Anne Bronte, 60
    Barbara, 210
    Branwell Bronte, 55, 56, 68

311

Made in the USA
Columbia, SC
13 August 2023

21564959R00185